Unfolding Consciousness

Exploring the Living Universe and Intelligent Powers in Nature and Humans

Volume II

Peering Down the Microscope –
Man's Internal Landscapes

EDI BILIMORIA, DPhil, FIMechE, FEI, FRSA

SHEPHEARD
WALWYN
PUBLISHERS

First published in 2022 by Shepherd-Walwyn (Publishers) Ltd
107 Parkway House, Sheen Lane, London SW14 8LS
www.shepheardwalwyn.com
www.ethicaleconomics.org.uk

British Library Cataloguing in Publication Data
A catalogue record of this book is available from the British Library

ISBN: 978-08-5683-537-7

Copyedit by Elizabeth Medler
Typeset by Ian Wileman

Printed and bound through
s|s|media limited, Rickmansworth, Hertfordshire

Outline Contents for the Four Volumes

Detailed Contents for Volume II

List of Illustrations and Tables for Volume II

Abbreviations

CW-'Volume number'	*The Collected Writings* – in Fifteen Volumes by H. P. Blavatsky, compiled by Boris de Zirkoff: Volumes I to VI, The Theosophical Publishing House, Wheaton, Illinois, US, 1988 (Third Edition) to 1975 (Second Edition); Volumes VII to XV, The Theosophical Publishing House, Adyar, Madras, India, 1975 (Second Edition) to 1991.
IU-'Volume number'	*Isis Unveiled* – Two Volume Set by H. P. Blavatsky, edited by Boris de Zirkoff, The Theosophical Publishing House, First Quest Edition, 1994.
KT	*The Key to Theosophy* by H. P. Blavatsky, Theosophical Publishing House, London, 1968.
ML	*The Mahatma Letters to A. P. Sinnett* (in chronological sequence), compiled, numbered, arranged, and annotated by Virginia Hanson, The Theosophical Publishing House, Adyar, First Edition, 1998.
NPB-'Volume number'	*The Notebooks of Paul Brunton* – in Sixteen Volumes by Paul Brunton, Larson Publications, for Paul Brunton Philosophic Foundation, 1984 to 1988.
SD-'Volume number'	*The Secret Doctrine* – Three Volume Set by H. P. Blavatsky, edited by Boris de Zirkoff, The Theosophical Publishing House, First Quest Edition, 1993.
STA	*The Secret Teachings of All Ages* by Manly P. Hall, Diamond Jubilee Edition, Los Angeles, Philosophical Research Society, 1988.
TSGLOSS	Theosophical Glossary by H. P. Blavatsky, Theosophical Publishing Society, 1892.
VS	*The Voice of the Silence* by H. P. Blavatsky, introductory by Boris de Zirkoff, The Theosophical Publishing House, Second Quest Edition, 1992.

For example, *CW*-XII means *The Collected Writings*, Volume XII. Likewise, for *IU-*, *NPB-*, and *SD-*

What is Death?

Death entails the irreversible loss of those essential characteristics which are necessary to the existence of a living human person and, thus, the definition of death should be regarded as the irreversible loss of the capacity for consciousness, combined with irreversible loss of the capacity to breathe … and therefore irreversible cessation of the integrative function of the brainstem.

Academy of Medical Royal Colleges, the coordinating body for the United Kingdom and Ireland Medical Royal Colleges and Faculties, October 2008

I died as mineral and became a plant,
I died as plant and rose to animal,
I died as animal and was man.
Why should I fear? When was I less by dying?
Yet once more I shall die as man, to soar with angels blest;
But even from angelhood I must pass on …

The Mathnawi [Masnavi] of Jalaluddin Rumi (trans. Reynold A. Nicholson)

Prefatory:
'Man, Know Thyself'– but Who, or What is Man?

Reflecting admiringly and then despairingly, on the human condition, Prince Hamlet remarks:

What piece of work is a man, how noble in reason,
how infinite in faculties, in form and moving,
how express and admirable in action, how like an angel in apprehension,
how like a god!

HAMLET[1]

How divers persons witness in each man.
Three souls which make up one soul:
What Does, what Knows, what Is; three souls, one man.

ROBERT BROWNING[2]

Mahatma Gandhi (1869–1948) was well aware of what divinity would mean to a poverty-stricken man when he famously declared: 'To a hungry man, a piece of bread is the face of God.'[3] Of course, he was referring to the starving millions in his homeland, India, who see God's will either as a cause of abundance or deprivation. By contrast, the vast majority of people in affluent countries, especially in the Western world have more than enough bread, meat, and wine on their dinner tables—especially during the Christmas holidays—to render obesity a ubiquitous topic in the news.[4] Coupled with this, we see major portions of society plagued by conflict, violence, and depression. Why? Because there is also a different kind of poverty, just as oppressive and a lot more insidious. It is spiritual poverty—though the West would hardly acknowledge this as a spiritual crisis or attribute its problems to the lack of the deific countenance. Nonetheless, it seems that, like the human face, the 'face of God' also has two sides to it. The first side concerns material and physical conditions, as just stated. The second side relates to man's spiritual hunger. The latter is not appeased in the wealthy nations by resorting to atheism or an obsession with technology and wealth on the one hand; or escapism through frivolous entertainment or the usual trio of drugs, sexual indulgence, and alcohol on the other hand.

Spiritual hunger can be more insidious than material poverty

The above excerpt reinforces the importance of why Volume I of this work opened with asking that most pressing of all questions: 'Who, or What Am I?'—followed by the rejoinder: 'Man, Know *Thyself*.' But who, or what is Thyself? Does 'Self' mean just the bio-physical body or does it mean the divine light in man—soul rooted in spirit, embracing a whole spectrum of the physical and subtle bodies and associated levels of consciousness?

Mechanistic imperative of prevailing mainstream neuroscience

Volume I went to considerable lengths to show that whereas science is marvellously equipped to investigate the physical aspects of man, meaning, of course, his body and brain (never to be spurned or undervalued), yet it cannot respond adequately to questions concerning the subtler levels of man's mind and consciousness, due to its self-limiting mechanistic paradigm. It was explained in Chapters 3 to 6 that despite the burgeoning science of qualities, the breakthroughs of quantum science, the inability of neuroscience to explain the hard problem of consciousness in purely mechanistic terms, and the penetrating insights of psychologists like William James, mainstream science is still wedded to the safety and security of primary qualities characterized by the measurable and quantifiable. Given this almost exclusive focus on primary qualities, now raised to the status of an ideology, it has become a dogma in science to regard consciousness in terms of production, i.e., the mechanism that supposedly generates it, which is of course, taken to be the brain. The following example, taken from the cover flap of *The Brain*, is typical of the contemporary mainstream neuroscientific diktat on consciousness: 'The human brain contains one hundred billion nerve cells and is arguably the most complex *machine* in the known universe. Somehow it *generates* our consciousness and determines our every action and thought [emphases added].'[5] Given that the author, Michael O'Shea, is Professor of Neuroscience at the University of Sussex, and significantly, Co-Director of the Centre for Computational Neuroscience and Robotics, it is not surprising to see that he equates thought and consciousness with functional dependence on a machine—the brain. Perhaps he has not come across William James's legendary book entitled *Human Immortality: Two supposed objections to the doctrine*[6] (condensed in Chapter 6 of Volume I). However, it is comforting to see the word 'somehow', implying that science really does not know, other than, 'in common with all other manifestations of life, the brain is the result of the *haphazard* and *perilous process* of evolution by natural selection [emphases added].'[7] Assuming that it would be difficult to find that even a simple machine on the earth (say, a wheel and axle) was merely the outcome of a haphazard process, it is interesting to be informed that 'the most complex machine in the known universe' has evolved by virtue of *random* influences.

Moderate influence of quantum science on neuroscience

Be that as it may, the point is that the overall standpoint of mainstream biology and neuroscience has hardly changed during the twenty-first century, notwithstanding the enormous strides achieved in mapping cerebral processes and associated mechanisms. In essence, this science maintains that the entire gamut of human emotions, experiences, and aspirations is the result of highly transient neuron assemblies regarded as a key component of brain operations that generate what is known as consciousness. Furthermore, oscillations of some 40 Hz (cycles per second) generated by normal synaptic transmission, and up to 200 Hz mediated by gap junctions, are a perfectly adequate mechanism to explain the co-ordinated firing of a million or so neurons in a fraction of a second—notwithstanding the 'haphazard and perilous process' that, according to O'Shea, has given rise to such exquisite orchestration and co-ordination.[8]

Discriminating innate nature from outward behaviour

Admittedly, quantum science has upset the apple cart somewhat by invoking the role of the observer in the act of observation. We presented the evidence in Chapter 4 of Volume I on page 97 f. Also outlined was the quantum hybrid model developed by Roger Penrose and Stuart Hameroff, which has progressed 'beyond the brain',[i] thereby taking a

---

i The inverted commas are adopted to connote the title of the annual conference held by the Scientific and Medical Network, https://www.beyondthebrain.org/about-us/ with the overall objective of discussing and disseminating the latest ideas in science and philosophy that might suggest that consciousness need not be limited to, or generated by, the brain.

step towards esotericism by departing from the entrenched mainstream concept that consciousness is produced by the brain as an epiphenomenon.

Machines and mechanisms, however, do not run themselves. They require an operator who, by definition, stands on a level higher than what is being operated. This work accordingly argues that man in his innermost self is an immortal *spiritual* being clothed in a mortal animal body—his functioning mechanism. This means that man is emphatically not just an animal, nor just a biological mechanism operating just by the laws of physics and electro-chemistry conditioned just by time, and therefore, he is not a suitable subject of investigation for an exclusively Cartesian reductionist approach of orthodox biology. The quadruple use of the word 'just' in the previous sentence is deliberate: for it indicates that there is a fundamental distinction to be drawn between man's essential nature on the one hand and, on the other hand, his outward behaviour and mechanistic aspects, which can certainly be *like* an animal or modelled for specific purposes *like* an electro-chemical machine. It is vital to distinguish the 'as if' from the 'as IS'. *Like* an animal does not mean an animal *per se*; it means that man sometimes behaves in a manner such that he displays some characteristics that are also exhibited by animals. However, animals do not, let us be honest, display so many other characteristics uniquely betrayed by man—characteristics ranging from the sublimely spiritual to which no animal could aspire, to the most bestial, that no animal has ever degraded itself to. Equally, man shows a mechanistic aspect, but is it not absurd to regard him just as a machine that runs itself, and no more?

The profoundly significant point that emerges from this realization is the stark error of establishment science (biology and neuroscience, in particular) in viewing the whole human being as comprising just his physical counterpart—his animal body and personality. Such an attitude means that the inner spiritual being is ignored in favour of its outward mode of expression; in other words, the mechanism is not distinguished from its informing principles. This is why we went to considerable lengths in Volume I to describe the insufficiencies of the current scientific model in addressing overall issues about consciousness and non-physical realms; and then explained why the Mystery Teachings worldwide are an indispensable complement (not an alternative) to the scientific picture. These universal Teachings make it crystal clear that whereas the process of human evolution has, at times, been perilous, there is absolutely nothing haphazard about it.

Non-physical matter: its discovery and role

NASA Science Newsletter states that scientists have come up with the following composition of the universe: ~68% dark energy, ~27% dark matter, ~5% baryonic matter (i.e., all objects made of normal atomic matter).[9] Therefore, unless everything on Earth, including us humans, somehow manages to exist outside the universe, only some 5% of a human being would be 'normal matter', and the remaining 95% would be invisible to the physical senses, undetectable by physical instruments, therefore, not quantifiable or measurable to physical science and medicine. Whereas the parallel between dark energy/matter and the non-physical composition of a human being is suggested only in a general sense, and hardly to be taken literally, is it reasonable, therefore, to postulate that since the greater part of a human being (like the greater part of the universe) may not be detectable by physical science, that it cannot be detected at all? Far from it, as there is a robust case for drawing upon occult science which has studied both the physical and the non-physical aspects of nature and humans in minute detail. Could some 95% of a human being comprise his subtle bodies, namely, his non-physical vestures of consciousness?

The case for occult science

Occult science, however, leaves no stone unturned: the physical and, arguably, the approximately 95% of the non-physical composition of nature and man are all included within its sweep. Accordingly, Volume II deals with the composition of man as a complete entity comprising body, soul, and spirit. The body can, of course, be understood and investigated by the methods of physical science; however soul and spirit are informing principles that make the human being truly *human*, i.e. corporeal and spiritual, and not merely a biological machine put together by haphazard processes. They concern his inner being, his inner structure and function, his invisible anatomy and physiology, so to speak. These principles are, by definition, non-physical, hence unamenable to physical investigation by science as realized by the luminaries in science and psychology mentioned in Table I-4 in the Recapitulation to Volume I on page 325. So how have they been investigated? Man's external powers perceive outward appearances and events, whose underlying, non-physical and formative causes are recognized by his internal faculties alone. The truth of this statement will become increasingly apparent as we proceed.

NOTES

1   *Hamlet*, Act II, Scene 2 speech from 1604 Second Quarto.
2   Robert Browning, *A Death in the Desert* (London: Swan Sonnenschein, 1904).
3   'Mahatma Gandhi Quotes' <https://www.azquotes.com/author/5308-Mahatma_Gandhi> accessed 14 May 2020.
4   BBC News, 'UK Most Overweight Country in Western Europe says OECD [Organisation for Economic Co-operation and Development]', 11 November 2017 <https://www.bbc.co.uk/news/uk-41953530> accessed 14 May 2020.
5   Michael O'Shea, *The Brain: A very short introduction* (New York: Oxford University Press, 2005).
6   William James, *Human Immortality: Two supposed objections to the doctrine* (1898; 2nd edn, New York: Cosimo, 2007).
7   Michael O'Shea, *The Brain*, 42.
8   Representative examples are: Susan Greenfield, *The Private Life of the Brain* (USA and Canada: Penguin Books, 2000), 188; A. Draguhn, R. D. Traub, D. Schmitz, and J. G. Jefferys, 'Electrical Coupling Underlies High-Frequency Oscillations in the Hippocampus in Vitro', *Nature*, 394/6689 (1998), 189–92; Marcos G. Frank, 'Brain Rhythms', in *Encyclopaedia of Neuroscience*, ed. Marc D. Binder, Nobutaka Hirokawa, and Uwe Windhorst (Berlin and Heidelberg: Springer, 2009), 482–3; György Buzsáki, *Rhythms of the Brain* (New York: Oxford University Press, 2006).
9   'Dark Energy, Dark Matter', *NASA Science Newsletter* <https://science.nasa.gov/astrophysics/focus-areas/what-is-dark-energy> accessed 8 February 2020.

1 What Occult Science says about the Composition of Man – Clearing the Decks

Mind and its expression in language are thoroughly interwoven and to improve one is to improve the other.

The intellect cannot work with blurred concepts. Pitfalls wait to receive it under such conditions. This is one reason why the process of discovering and clarifying meanings leads its advance into truth. Clear concepts and lucid statements are not less needed by the metaphysical and mystical than by the scientifical.

PAUL BRUNTON[1]

The disagreement of mankind is caused by names. Peace ensues only when they advance to the reality denoted by the name.

JALĀL AD-DĪN MUHAMMAD RŪMĪ[2]

SYNOPSIS

Chapter 1 opens the first section of Volume II. It is intended to dispel the considerable confusion that abounds in the vast literature on generally esoteric, philosophical, and religious matters on the composition of man. The main causes are differences in meaning between languages, thinking in dichotomies associated with literal interpretations without discerning nuances of meaning, errors of category, misperception of levels of meaning, and obscuring the content of a subject with its form of expression. These major sources of confusion are individually discussed, and a measure of clarity injected. It is a necessary prerequisite to the following two Chapters dealing with man's constitution and nature—his occult anatomy and physiology, so to say.

KEY WORDS: confusing terminology, principles, planes, modern physics, category errors, confusing levels, constitution versus nature

A t the outset, it is as well to counsel that, despite its shortness in respect of the enormity of the subject matter, Volume II of this work will demand a fair amount of patience and force of will on the part of readers, especially so in the occult expositions on man's composition. Obfuscating mystique or needless complications are no business of ours, but that said, we make no pretence of having withheld difficulties that are germane to the subject. Whereas we have not exactly sacrificed all matters of literary elegance to the costumier, we have always erred on the side of accurateness and clarity, even at the expense of occasionally labouring the point. For example we distinguish between the term 'body' used in a general sense, and the physical body or the various subtle bodies. Likewise, we need to distinguish between the terms 'MAN', 'Man', and 'man' as clearly explained in the Definitions in Volume IV. In a subject that traditionally abounds in perplexing and ill-defined terminology, our approach to avoiding confusion will become

Meticulousness is justified for the sake of clarity

1

amply justified and our efforts at striving for clarity at all costs will be seen to be worthwhile, for we prefer the charge of being pedantic rather than vague.

Man represents a regular and progressive scale of 'principles' spanning the complete spectrum from Spirit to meta-Spirit, and to gross matter. But we must distinguish carefully between the Inner man and the outer man, or physical automaton—the mortal coil that passes for that name. From remotest antiquity, humanity has had intimations of an internal spiritual entity—a subtle body—'within' the personal physical body. The inner entity, the Spiritual soul, is known by various names such as *Christos* in the Christian world, *Kṛṣṇa* (*Krishna*) for the Hindus, or *Avalokiteshvara* for the Buddhists. This ubiquitous conviction of the *philosophia perennis* is neither superstition, nor bigotry, but an ever-present, intuition of the proximity of another invisible, spiritual world which, *though it be subjective to the physical senses of the outward man, is perfectly objective to the Inner man*. It is a belief—rather, an inner conviction based on experiment and experience—universally held by such as the ancient Hindus, Zarathuśtrians (Zoroastrians), Egyptians, and Greeks. For example, 'The Egyptians revered the "One-Only-One," as *Nut*; and it is from this word that Anaxagoras got his denomination *Nous*, or as he calls it, Νους αυτοκράτες [*Nous autokrates*], "the Mind or Spirit Self-potent," the αρχιτέκτονες Κινέιντος [*archetes kinedeos*], the leading motor, or *primum mobile* of all. With him the *Nous* was God, and the logos was man, his emanation. Our external powers perceive *phenomena*; our *Nous* alone is able to recognise their *noumena* [as also clearly stated in the penultimate sentence of the Prefatory to this Volume II].'[3]

Innate spirituality of man endemic to the wisdom philosophy

There is much debris that clouds an understanding of the occult doctrine on the composition of man. The rest of this Chapter is therefore devoted to identifying, and then sorting out, the principal sources of confusion that abound in the various esoteric and occult writings on this subject. Having thus cleared the decks, the occult doctrine is explained in detail in subsequent Chapters. It includes descriptions of man's various states of consciousness, including post-mortem states, and chief vehicles and centres of operation. It will be demonstrated that the occult doctrines thus expounded are not the ideas of any one writer, religion or philosophical system, but display a unity and self-consistency with the accumulated wisdom of all ages, from antiquity to modern times.

Main Reasons for Confusion about the Composition of Man

It can be a source of bewilderment to the student to find that the esoteric and occult literature of the Mystery Teachings around the world (e.g. Indian, Egyptian, Greek) classifies the invisible 'anatomy and physiology' of man in various ways that appear, at face value, to be inconsistent or contradictory. This confusion also exists when science grapples with subjects of a metaphysical nature. There are seven main reasons for such confusion:

1. The various Mystery traditions are replete with a plethora of terms in various languages from all over the world.
2. Classical Theosophical literature describes the composition of man in terms of principles; whereas later writings have done so using planes (the difference between the two approaches will be outlined shortly).
3. There are some minds that operate only in terms of black or white dichotomies, unable to see mental shades of grey or colour; hence unable to appreciate the common ground and the subtleties between the various systems.

4. Category errors, especially in science, in that things belonging to a particular category are presented as if they belong to a different category, or a property is ascribed to a thing that could not possibly have that property.
5. Mix-up of levels in that what is presented at one level is inapplicable or nonsensical at another level.
6. The composition of man has been described in terms of separate layers or 'bodies' constituting his vehicles of consciousness.
7. The composition of man is sometimes described in terms of man's constitution, and at other times in terms of his nature. The distinction between constitution and nature is an important one and will be fully explained.

We now expand on the above seven points in turn.

Diverse Terminology Amongst Various Esoteric Traditions

Notwithstanding the fact that the Mystery tradition is a universal one, not belonging to any particular corner of the globe, powerful centres of learning, disseminating esoteric and occult truths, have appeared since time immemorial in various locations around the world. Major centres were founded in places such as India, Egypt, Greece, the Middle East, Europe, and the Americas (refer to Volume I, Chapter 9). These centres assimilated and taught occult truths of a broadly similar nature; but such truths were formulated according to the language, idiom, symbols, and metaphors pertaining to their times to suit the temperament and mental level of the people. So it is hardly surprising that the esoteric literature, from archaic antiquity down to the present day, should be written in different languages, such as Devanagari and Sanskrit, Tibetan and Pali, Greek and Latin, Hebrew and Arabic, and English, plus many more. Helpful rules and examples to ferret out the inner meaning and deep significance of the ancient Sanskrit nomenclature are given by the Brahmin, Tallapragada Subba Row (1856–1890). Subba Row worked as a Pleader within the Indian justice system, was an outstanding member of the Theosophical Society in its early years in India and an occultist of such outstanding calibre that Blavatsky had originally planned to collaborate with him in the production of *The Secret Doctrine*, although this plan did not materialize. Four rules are given by Subba Row: (*a*) finding synonyms having other meanings; (*b*) establishing the numerical value of the letters; (*c*) examining ancient myths or allegories in connection with the word; and (*d*) examining the new combinations formed from permuting different syllables composing the word.[4]

Rules for researching diverse sources in numerous tongues

Astonishingly—perhaps, not so, according to the proverb, 'great minds think alike'—Newton formulated a not dissimilar set of rules when he was researching the vast range of alchemical literature and for interpreting the words and language in scripture and prophetic literature. His advice, stated in Chapter 8 of Volume I, is worth repeating: 'The Rule I have followed has been to compare the several mystical places of scripture where the same prophetical phrase or type is used and to fix such a signification to that phrase as agrees best with all the places: and, if more significations than one be necessary, to note the circumstances by which it may be known in what signification the phrase is taken in any place: and, when I had found the necessary significations, to reject all others as the offspring of luxuriant fancy, for no more significations are to be admitted for true ones than can be proved.'[5] In both cases, we see glorious examples of the comparative approach involving sifting through diverse literature in order to find the highest common factor of truth.

Now it was the tremendous service of Theosophical literature, both classical and later, to codify and unify these various abstruse assemblages into a single, comprehensible system for the modern student of occult science. The language used is mainly English, and Sanskrit, when unavoidable. For this reason, we shall explain the composition of man in this manner and fully define our terms. This is in accord with Blavatsky's counsel about 'definite words for definite things' regarding the problems posed by the inconstant meanings attaching to metaphysical terms.[6] She aptly remarked that, the 'Shifting of *Metaphysical terms*' applies only to their varying translated equivalents from the Eastern expressions, because in her time there never existed any such terms in English, and every Theosophist therefore had to coin his own terms to render his thought. But it was high time 'to settle on some definite nomenclature'.[7]

However, it must be pointed out that despite this valiant attempt at a constancy of terms, the enormity of the task faced by early Theosophical writers, chiefly Blavatsky, means that confusion still reigns in Theosophical literature mainly for the reasons given in points 2, 6, and 7. above. Moreover, and for quite understandable and unavoidable reasons, despite her desire for 'definite words for definite things', Blavatsky was anything but consistent in her own writings for three main reasons:

1. Whereas there was never any ambiguity associated with Eastern expressions, the translation of abstruse Oriental terms (mainly Sanskrit) into the best equivalent Western esoteric terminology (mainly into English) had not been even partially codified at the time when pioneering Theosophists, such as Blavatsky, published their works—see Endnote II-1.

Linguistic hurdles for writing arcane precepts in English

2. Blavatsky had to labour under definite constraints which obliged her to withhold certain information, some of which however, she divulged later, although in a manner that sometimes appeared to contradict her previous statements—see Endnote II-2.

3. Some information had to be given out in a veiled way so that only those who possessed the esoteric key could unlock the inner meaning of that which would be too dangerous to be revealed explicitly to the public.

The Question of Language

Every branch of study has developed its own special terminology best suited to its purpose. Esoteric and occult science are no exceptions. For example, to expect a description of a modern jet engine in ancient Sanskrit would be absurd. There are no words in that language for aero-engine components like 'compressor', 'combustion chamber', and 'turbine'. On the other hand, being a language geared more towards the subjective and experiential, rather than the objective and tangible, Sanskrit is the ideal tongue for expounding the occult composition of nature and man, and delineating the subtle realms of consciousness. By contrast, the English language is better suited to the objective realms

Sanskrit ideal, but English ill suited for esoteric literature

and can easily describe the components of a jet engine, but has difficulty in finding words for the non-physical and subjective dimensions of existence. The subtle gradations and overtones of consciousness and higher orders of existence are precisely nuanced in

Sanskrit, but there are no exact equivalent terms in English. Merely referring to such non-physical realms as 'the spirit world' and their inhabitants thereof as 'spirits' does little to advance our understanding of them. Numerous problems faced by scientists in their attempts to understand spiritual and paranormal phenomena are largely to do with the limitations and impoverishment of the English language with respect to subtle realms of existence beyond the physical. It is also worth mentioning that Sanskrit, Hebrew, and Arabic are sacred tongues, whereas Latin and Greek are ecclesiastical, or apostolic languages, which is not the same thing.

Whilst we do not expect readers to embark on a Sanskrit course, it might be helpful to acknowledge that a paucity of knowledge in this area represents something of a major drawback. Recognition of this fact will bring with it a certain helpful humility and respect for the world's oldest language. Henceforth, we shall use only the minimum of Sanskrit words out of sheer necessity and explain their derivation and meaning as fully as possible. For those who might complain that the ensuing Chapters involve needless taxonomy, we respond by pointing out that each branch of science has evolved its own system of organizing and classifying its subject areas. No serious student of botany or medicine would ever complain about excessive taxonomy and the numerous terms in Latin and Greek in those disciplines. Nor should a student of occult science therefore protest about the obligatory taxonomy required to understand the expositions on the constitution and nature of man.

Distinguishing Principles from Planes – The Contribution of Modern Physics in Bringing Clarity

Simply speaking, a *principle* is the action of some power or conscious entity, within, and up to its range of influence; put differently, a principle is a particular mode of manifesting life at any given level. A *plane* is the substance through which it acts, being both its medium (or vehicle) of expression and range of action; technically, 'the range or extent of some state of consciousness, or of the perceptive power of a particular set of senses, or the action of a particular force, or the state of matter corresponding to any of the above.'[8] The characteristic of a principle is therefore active and positive, of the same nature as the generic term 'spirit'; that of a plane is passive and negative, of the same nature as the generic term 'matter' (the term 'negative' used of course, purely in the sense of the polar opposite of positive and not in any way implying adverse or harmful). Hence, as a bare abstraction, the active potentiality of spirit is manifested through matter. In a general sense we can say that man's principles are expressed and acted out through his physical and subtle bodies, which coexist on the various planes of nature, physical and higher. These higher planes, and the subtle bodies associated with them, coexist in higher orders, or dimensions, of space and time, just as the physical body exists on the physical plane in physical, three-dimensional space and one dimension of time. (Some Theosophists use terms like 'subjective space' or 'occult space', in referring to realms that are inner and non-physical and therefore hidden to the normal senses.)

A principle is an active agent. Its plane of activity is the passive medium

Nowadays, terms such as 'field' and 'dimension of space' would be more appropriate than the classical Theosophical term 'plane of existence'—bearing in mind that the vast bulk of Theosophical writings were produced before the advent of modern physics and strongly alluded to the discoveries of the latter. The concept of 'the field' was first touched upon in Chapter 4 of Volume I in the sections on morphogenesis and the work of Gustaf Strömberg. In elaboration, modern physics defines 'field' as a region, or sphere of influence, radiated by a physical agency, the former stretching out beyond the boundaries of the entity from which it originates. For example, the agencies of mass, magnetic dipole, and charge produce their corresponding gravitational, magnetic, and electric fields. It will be seen how closely this concept of field matches the definition of plane given above. Indeed, we could provide a modern definition of a Theosophical plane thus: 'a bounding region, or field of substance-energy, existing in a dimension of space, physical or higher, under the influence of some conscious agency, physical or superphysical.' Each principle therefore acts via its associated plane. At any level, then, a principle is the noumenon, or causal influence of a phenomenon on its associated plane of action.[9]

So we may then say that man's nature is composed of various principles (spirit, soul, and body in the familiar enumeration) acting as one unit, one organic being. In this sense we may liken a principle to an *element*, not of course in the sense of modern chemical elements, but the classical elements believed to reflect the simplest ideas and essential parts of which anything can consist, or upon which the fundamental constitution and function of everything is based. Each element is active on the plane of its operation.

But as we were at pains to point out above, Theosophical pioneers were working in the nineteenth century at a time when science was ultra-materialistic, and several decades before physical field theory had been developed. They had to struggle to find ideas and metaphors then available in the English language. Resorting to Sanskrit as the rule, rather than the exception, would have made their task easier. For example, in the context of this section, the Sanskrit terms *loka* and *tala* are significant. Loka means a region, or circum-scribed place: in metaphysics, a place, or locality; a world, or sphere—all of these words signifying a particular level, or state of consciousness and not terrestrial, or celestial geographical regions. Every loka has as its twin, or counterpart, a corresponding tala, its nether pole. Lokas and talas are, so to speak, the spiritual and material aspects of the different realms of cosmos. It would be as impossible to separate a loka from its corre-sponding tala as it would be to separate an electric current (the active 'spiritual' aspect) from its conductor (the passive 'material' aspect). The Purāṇas of India speak of several graded lokas 'above', and corresponding talas 'below' our Earth: the superior worlds and the nether worlds, or the so-called heavens and hells. (A similar gradation by the North American Indians is described in Chapter 9 of Volume I). These graded states of consciousness are the key to understanding the after-death states of man, as for example: the *Kāma-loka* of occultists, the Hades of the ancient Greeks, the Amenti of the Egyptians, and purgatory of the Christians. As it is not possible to do justice to this complex subject in a few words here, fuller treatment is reserved for later Chapters.

The use of Sanskrit is sometimes unavoidable

Hence, reverting to our theme, in order to preserve consistency with Theosophical liter-ature, the term 'plane' is retained in this work, and could be understood in a modern context to mean a 'field in a dimension of space, physical or higher'. It is important to note that a principle is not separate from its plane any more than an electric charge is separate from its associated field. For they are a polarity emanating from a fundamental unity of energy–substance, hence the old idea rediscovered by modern science (the Einsteinian mass–energy equivalence) that matter is crystallized spirit and spirit is liberated matter. A celebrated remark of one of the Adept founders behind the modern Theosophical movement was 'Modern science is our best ally'.[10] In other words, the occult doctrines promulgated would slowly find their rightful justification decades later through the ongoing march of modern science. On that note, it is the writer's firm contention that further research into Superstring theory[i] and M-theory[ii] would go a long way towards explaining and deepening our understanding of the higher dimension of existence, thus casting a scientific light on the deeper reaches of esoteric philosophy.[11]

Modern physics facilitates the understanding of occult science

The above, then, implies that we can describe a system from two points of view: (*a*) the negative and passive, form-building, or material side, using planes; or (*b*) the positive and active, life-giving, or spiritual side through principles. The first concerns structure and constitution; the second deals with function and activity. (By way of a simple example, one can describe a motor car in terms of its components like spark plugs, alternator, wheels; or in terms of its energetic processes like combustion, electricity, momentum.) Both descriptions are complementary and necessary for a complete understanding and both approaches have their pros and cons, so an understanding of both in tandem is necessary for a complete understanding of how any system works. The classical Theosophical writers tended towards the latter approach, whereas later, post-Blavatsky, writers like Besant, Leadbeater, and Jinarâjadâsa have used the former. This has caused unnecessary confusion and commotion, which has stemmed largely from the fact that these disparate expositions have not clearly stated their particular standpoint.

Any system can be described in two ways

In the next two Chapters we shall describe man's composition chiefly in terms of *principles*, being better suited for explanatory purposes. The question of planes is reserved for Volume III primarily to show the indissoluble bond between nature and man.

On any plane, 'force' is the active principle and 'matter' is the passive substance, or material of the plane through which it acts. Thus, 'matter' provides the vehicle, or medium of expression for 'force', as a copper wire provides the conducting medium for an electric current.

Thinking in Dichotomies

A major source of confusion rests, unfortunately, with certain Theosophists, who think only in black-and-white dichotomies. Despite the much vaunted Second Object of the Theosophical Society (to encourage the comparative study of science, religion, and philosophy), such simplistic mentalities seem incapable of sensing the underlying overlap and unity beneath apparently diverse expositions and doctrines. As Dr Radha Burnier (1923–2013), the Seventh International President of the Theosophical Society, has repeatedly stressed in her lectures and writings, Theosophy has become just another set of concepts and beliefs.[iii] All too often members equate Theosophy with the set of doctrines given out at the end of the nineteenth century, primarily through the writings of Blavatsky and her instructors, and not with divine

---

i Superstring theory is sometimes called the Theory of Everything (TOE) because it is a theory in physics to reconcile the differences between quantum theory and the theory of relativity to explain the nature of all known forces and matter. It attempts to explain all of the particles and fundamental forces of nature in one theory by modelling them as vibrations of tiny supersymmetric strings.

ii M-theory is a theory in physics that unifies all consistent versions of superstring theory in eleven space–time dimensions.

iii Radha Burnier was born in Adyar, Madras. She was a Sanskrit scholar and a well-known exponent of Indian classical dance. Her family was Brahmin, but , as Theosphists, they did not observe the rules of segregation from other castes prevalent at the time.

wisdom. Such zealots and their followers cannot relate to other ways of formulating the same truths or other approaches, or if they do so, they have to translate the ideas into Theosophical terms. This is a dreadful crippling of the mind. They fail to realize that 'she [Blavatsky] taught us Theosophy—not as a mere form of doctrine, not as a religion, or a philosophy, or a creed, or a working hypothesis, but as a living power in our lives.'[12] Alas, human nature is ever the same: Blavatsky fundamentalists are no different, in principle, from Christian fundamentalists, or for that matter, any other kind of fundamentalists, religious or scientific; because the characteristic of a fundamentalist is a closed-mind, dead-letter, literal interpretation of his chosen book or teaching, devoid of any subtlety of understanding or plurality of approaches.

The writer earnestly hopes that this work, in particular Chapter 8 later in this Volume, will display just that plurality of approaches that point to the underlying unity and overlap between the various expositions on man's composition from antiquity to the present day, and from diverse cultures worldwide.

Errors of Category

As a simplistic example, if we tried to explain the mechanical aspects of human anatomy in terms of the mechanical principles of a motor car, the result would be nonsensical. This much is evident. However mainstream science expends a vast amount of effort in trying to understand phenomena, like the paranormal, that lie in a different category to those that legitimately fall within its model of physical realism (i.e., the materialistic paradigm). Trying to explain, or disprove astrology in terms of the laws of physical cosmology, is a case in point. Another obvious example is the current attempt to fathom consciousness in terms of purely physical science.

Arthur Ellison has described the philosophical implications of the scientific predicament succinctly:

> It is important to use our mental models correctly. To speak about psychical experiences, or about religious (transcendental) experiences in terms relating to the 'physical world' is to make what the philosophers would call 'category errors' and to talk nonsense. The realism model is inapplicable [in such cases].[13]

Mix-up of Levels

An enormous amount of confusion occurs when what is stated at one level is taken up at another level. This is such a common cause of ill-feeling and antagonism amongst people, and in groups, that it is worth explaining the reasons fully.

In general, the same object, phenomenon or precept can be described at three levels: (*a*) the physical and objective; (*b*) the abstract and scientific; and (*c*) the transcendent and subjective. For example, a fountain pen can be described as an object comprising a nib, barrel, ink feeding mechanism, and cap; as an instrument for writing along with a pencil or word processor keyboard; and as an agency for creating wars or peace—the pen is indeed mightier than the sword. Or take a candle, which is physically made of a wick embedded in a flammable solid substance like wax. It can also be used to provide heat or as a method of keeping time and, of course, a means of illumination along with a floodlight or torch. At another level, a candle can be used to evoke a romantic atmosphere. At the highest level, a candle takes on a symbolic, rather than a physical significance: just as a single candle flame can illuminate a large darkness, a glimmer of wisdom can dispel a great ignorance. All this is plain. However, a practical illustration is needed to show the misunderstanding caused by confusion of levels.

Consider the following unqualified statement: 'We are all spiritual beings'—a pious platitude often seen in popular books on self-healing and spirituality or heard amongst groups dedicated to a similar purpose. It invariably creates a warm, 'feel-good sense'; but is it true, and if so, at what level does it have meaning?

Consider first the highest level. *Tat Tvam Asi* is a legendary Sanskrit maxim in Vedānta translated as 'Thou art That', or 'That thou art', the 'That' referring to the Ultimate Reality, *Brahman*, and its spark, *Ātman*, in every creature. This means that every speck of the universe, including us, is THAT, and ultimately nothing else. Moreover, the etymology of the word 'Brahman' and also 'Ātman' are to do with 'breath', the former deriving from the root *brih*, meaning 'expansion', and the latter from the root *an*, meaning 'to breathe'. So at the highest level 'we are all spiritual beings' is an absolute truth because every particle in the universe, including us, is THAT, breathed forth from the One—the identity of individual self as a part of the whole, which is *Tat* (Brahman).

But does what pertains to our deepest and innermost core also apply to us ordinary humans on the lower terrestrial level? If it did, then Buddha and Christ, you and I, Churchill and Hitler, decent citizens and brutal child murderers are all 'spiritual beings' with no distinction between them: after all, were they not all 'breathed forth' from the One? That such an inference is so utterly nonsensical is an example of the error of investing at a lower level, the meaning of a statement meant to be taken at a higher level. Are there not levels below the highest? There are: the psychic and the physical, and therein lies the immeasurable gulf separating the saint and the tyrant, the genius and the ordinary man, the sage and the lunatic. Would that we were all just spiritual beings walking on Earth; it would make life so much easier!

Confusing meanings at different levels

Consider now the feeling of depression or soul-sickness, what Carl Jung referred to as the 'homesickness' of the soul. An advanced person administering healing to one so afflicted would consider his patient to be a spiritual being and dispense healing *at that level*. But would a dentist treating the same person for toothache regard his patient as a spiritual being, a physical being or for that matter, a mechanical object, insofar as his tooth were concerned? At this physical level, for a dentist to regard a person as a purely spiritual being would be simply idiotic.

The following metaphor should clinch the argument. There is alcohol (spirit!) in wines, beers, and hard spirits. But are these beverages therefore all the same thing? Is there no difference between vintage wines containing ethanol (alcohol) and cheap, home brewed wines that could harbour harmful, rogue alcohols?

Every human being, then, no matter whether he chooses to govern his body, or to let it govern him, has a spiritual spark, known by different names in different traditions. For instance, Agathon (Greek), Atmu (Egyptian), Fravasham (Zoroastrian), Ātma (Indian), to name but four cultures around the globe. But does that mean that every human being who walks on planet Earth is just a spiritual being and nothing else?

'Layer Cake' or 'Onion Skins' Depictions of Man's Composition

In attempting to enumerate the various aspects of man's being, these have perforce had to be described, for analytical or descriptive purposes, in a serial, sequential fashion, rather like the various layers of a cake or like geological strata, one on top of the other. This has had the unfortunate tendency (never intended by any particular writer) of conveying a static picture which loses the wholeness and inter-relationship of parts.

Another misunderstanding arises when the various subtle bodies are regarded like onion skins. As Blavatsky well cautions:

Man's various bodies are not discrete layers

Do not imagine that because man is called septenary, then *quintuple* and a triad, he is a compound of seven, five, or three *entities*; or […] of skins to be peeled off like the skins of an onion. The 'principles' [save the mortal vestures like the body], are simply *aspects* and *states of consciousness*. There is but one *real* man, enduring through the cycle of life and immortal in essence, if not in form, and this is *Manas*, the Mind-man or embodied Consciousness.[14]

The distinction made between the enduring consciousness and its transitory form, or embodiment, is crystal clear.

Difference Between the Constitution and the Nature of Man

Man is a unitary whole, but it is important to discern how his composition presents two primary aspects: his *constitution*, and his *nature*. Man's constitution is to do with man as system—his structure, how he is 'builded up', this quaint phrase used in preference to the conventional past tense 'built' in order to convey the process of building that involves definite rules of 'occult construction'. This has to do with his consciousness, what he is; hence his potentiality. Man's nature concerns man as process—how he functions, his dynamics as a natural result of what he is. This dictates his powers, how he acts and what he does; hence, his capacity.

Man is always whole

It cannot be too strongly emphasized that constitution and nature are not to be regarded as disconnected traits, but rather as a primary duality born of an intrinsic unity. Constitution and nature are completely inter-related and thus mirror one another: man can only act by virtue of what he is; and what he is determines how he acts. For example, a musical person will prefer not to run around a muddy football field; and he who revels in physical energy in sport is unlikely to be found with a vintage Stradivarius violin in his hands.

Example showing distinction between constitution and nature

For convenience, the above ideas are drawn together in Table II-1 below, which also summarizes various terms used to distinguish man's constitution from his nature.

Two examples will help to clarify the above abstruse ideas on the distinction between constitution and nature.

Consider, first, a simplistic case of a purely mechanical system such as a motor car. For a start, 'car' is a single, collective, and generalized term used to signify all the diverse interlocking and inter-related components and systems that function as a unified entity towards a specific end purpose (to transport the driver wherever he wishes to go). But no amount of detailed knowledge about how the car and its components are

Table II-1 The Constitution and Nature of Man – Their
Distinction and Inter-Dependence

Man's Composition as a whole considered in dual aspects of:	
His Constitution – *How he is Built Up*	**His Nature –** *How he Functions*
His Consciousness	His Powers
Man as system	Man as process
Potentiality of man – static quality	Capacity of man – dynamic quality
What man is, his essence	How man acts, what he does
How he is built up, his structure	His function, his dynamics

Constitution and Nature mirror each other:

- Man IS as he ACTS;
- Man can only ACT according to what he IS.

manufactured can reveal how it functions. For this we need to know the purpose for which each component was designed and its relation with the whole of which it forms the part. For example, we may know minute details about each and every component of a carburettor; but we can only conceive its function when we understand both its purpose—to adjust the fuel-air ratio to the engine—and its overall relation to the engine—downstream of the air intake.

Now let us consider a more sophisticated case of the physical body of a typical individual—'John Smith'. Again, the term 'body' is a single, collective, and generalized term used to signify all the diverse, interlocking, and inter-related biological components and systems that function as a unified entity towards a specific end purpose—to act as the vehicle and medium of expression of the soul and spirit. But no amount of detailed knowledge about how the body or its organs are built up can reveal how the body functions. For this we need to know the purpose of each organ, and its relationship with the whole of which it forms a part. For example we may know minute details about each and every muscle and bone of a finger; but we can only conceive its function when we understand its purpose—to enable the movement of the finger for a specific objective—and its overall relationship to the body—at the outer extremity of the hands. This analogy is further pursued in Endnote II-3 to show that despite the infinite variety of ways that a man can act according to his nature, the latter presents two aspects—benevolent or malevolent.

Purpose dictates function

It will be shown later that for anything to function there must be at least two principles involved: one to act, and another to provide the medium or vehicle for such action to occur. These two principles are spirit and matter, considered in the most general sense of the terms. They are inseparable. Recalling what was said earlier, spirit is the active and positive principle, and matter is the passive and negative principle, being that medium needed to nurture the spirit and provide the material (not materialistic) means of realizing its potentiality. Similar words are seed and soil—the former positive and active, the latter negative and passive. These ideas will become clear as we proceed. Meanwhile, it is worth clearing up the reason for much confusion that exists in the various descriptions of man in esoteric and occult literature.

Function depends on an active and a passive principle: spirit and matter

Reverting to our typical individual, John Smith, he generally performs a wide variety of roles and displays a virtually infinite number of moods. Depending upon the circumstances, he can adopt the role of parent, spouse, worker, and boss for example, and his moods can vary widely with infinite nuances from say, despondency to optimism. Yet when he is deeply asleep or tranquil (as when rapt in profound meditation), none of these characteristics shows overtly. It is not that they exist in discrete forms stuffed within his being, but that they are fully *subsumed*iv in his consciousness as an integrated and changeless state when asleep or calm, to manifest as particular forms of changing activity when awake or engaged in everyday duties. Let us pursue this example further using Table II-2 on the following page, which serves a dual purpose: (*a*) as an example to illustrate the essential difference and inter-dependence between the constitution and nature of an individual; and (*b*) to show that an individual, intrinsically a unified being, can nevertheless be divided in various ways for analytical purposes.

Example of how a single individual is constituted and functions in different ways

Constitution of John Smith – How He is 'Builded Up'

Let us concentrate first on how John Smith is constituted. Referring to the top half of Table II-2, of course he is in reality one, undivided individual. But for the purposes of analysis, he can be regarded as made up of two fundamental elements—head and the rest of the body. But these are general and collective terms that embody three components—head, trunk, and limbs. Furthermore, these three components comprise seven sub-components—brain, nervous system, sensory organs, circulatory system, muscular-skeletal system, internal organs, and limbs—seven in all. Further sub-divisions can be effected depending upon the prevailing circumstances.

We need not labour the point that John Smith's various anatomical components and energy systems are not discrete entities in themselves, but different parts of his unified nature. Nevertheless, for specific purposes, such as a medical examination, they can be divided, classified, and analysed in distinct ways—as two, three, seven, or whatever.

Nature of John Smith – How He Functions

Knowing how John Smith is constituted, or built up, how does he function? This is not quite as simple as it sounds. Consult now the bottom half of Table II-2 showing that constitution (or system) and function are related: a person can only do according to what he intrinsically *is*.

As previously stated, our John Smith functions as one individual during deep and dreamless sleep or when completely tranquil. During his waking hours, we can discern two fundamental areas where he lives, thinks, and acts: (*a*) within his family—his primary existence; and (*b*) in the external world—his secondary existence. So we immediately realize that the one individual can be regarded as being constituted of two 'parts', namely, the 'inner person' at home, and the 'outer person' in the world outside of home.

---

iv 'Subsumed' is an important concept. Derived from the Latin *subsumere*, 'to take under', it is not the same as dissolved, fused, mixed, embedded or combined, all of which terms imply that there is an identifiable entity that can be liberated from its surrounding containment, like a saline solution that can release salt by distillation. By contrast, the waves of the ocean are subsumed within the ocean; no single wave can be identified, or isolated, within the depths of the ocean.

Table II-2 An Example to Illustrate How an Individual Displays a Diverse Constitution and Different Functions

An individual is constituted in the following ways:			
	Dual Make-up	*Triple Make-up*	*Septenary Make-up*
One undivided individual	head	head	brain nervous system sensory organs
	body	trunk	heart, internal organs
		limbs	muscular-skeletal system internal organs arms and legs

This constitution can give rise to a variety of functions

An individual functions typically in the following ways:			
	Dual Functions	*Quintuple Functions*	*Septenary Functions*
One unified individual during deep sleep	within home	family blood relations	father husband brother
	outside home	relatives	son-in-law
		friends	worker supervisor
		associates	colleague

Within his home, he is in relationship with his own family and blood-relations; whereas outside his home he relates to his wider circle of relatives, friends, and associates. Furthermore, he has to work as a breadwinner to maintain his family.

The inner life is more important than outer circumstances

Then, by referring to him as a 'family man', we are using a single term to mean a complex combination of roles. Our family man can be all of father, husband, and brother. Also as breadwinner he can act as worker in relation to his own manager, as supervisor to his subordinates, and colleague to his peers. We see that one individual functions in three roles at home, and four roles outside his home—seven roles in all. His home life is by far the more significant than his external life. The latter, however important, is still dispensable. For he can exist at home (uncomfortably) without his job, and even after severing contact with his relatives, friends, and associates; but he can never function in the outside world and remain permanently disconnected from his home. This example illustrates the esoteric teaching that *the inner life of man is more important than his outward circumstances and activity in the world*. Observing the contrast between the smiles of the faces of the countless poor in a country like India and the dour faced demeanour of powerful billionaires will make the point.

The above example of a typical individual helps us to appreciate how any human being can be considered functioning in two, five, seven, or any number of roles depending on the prevailing need and circumstances. In all these different roles, the one human being endures through different modes of existence. So there is no contradiction between all his roles. They are different ways of looking at the single human entity functioning through his various existences, and the complex nature of each such existence; for there is but *one real human being* and all his roles are like the different octaves and overtones from one fundamental keynote. All this should help us to apprehend the various expositions on the occult constitution and nature of man. In the next two Chapters we detail the various divisions and classifications of man's constitution and nature and, as with the above analogy, show their mutual consistency and justification.

Résumé of Principal Philosophical Precepts

Distinguishing between the constitution and nature of man involves the idea of 'holons'. A holon (Greek: *holos* 'whole') is something that is simultaneously a whole and a part. The word was coined by the Hungarian-born British novelist, journalist, and critic Arthur Koestler (1905–1983) in his book *The Ghost in the Machine*[15] and the concept applies equally to organisms and mechanical systems. Stated simplistically, an entity exists within a nested hierarchy of wholes and parts: an entity is a whole in terms of its constituent parts; but in terms of the larger unit it comprises a part. Thus, reverting to the previous example of the human hand, it is a whole in terms of its specific function and constitution of five fingers, etc., but it is a part of the human arm, which is a whole in itself, but a part of the human body.

Relation of parts to the whole

Note that the idea of a holon is not quite the same as a fractal, which is a pattern that repeats itself with increasing detail and complexity, but maintains the same basic geometrical characteristic. Nor is a hologram a strictly equivalent term as this pertains to the appearance of a whole image no matter what part of the holographic plate is illuminated, though the image becomes increasingly less distinct as the illuminated area is progressively reduced.

❧ ❧ ❧

Given that the worldwide esoteric literature spans vast epochs over immense durations of time, misperceptions are bound to prevail in terminology used in a variety of ways. This Chapter has sought to expose and dispel some of the chief sources of confusion. This is an indispensable precursor to any description about the composition of man and his states of consciousness as described in the following Chapters. Meanwhile we close this Chapter with some words of advice: first from a legendary scientist, then from a world-travelled philosopher.

Everything must be made as simple as possible. But not simpler.

ALBERT EINSTEIN[16]

There are no words in human language in which Truth can find adequate expression. Words are valuable in telling us about something, but they can never take the place of that something itself.

PAUL BRUNTON[17]

NOTES

1 *NPB*-5, Part 2: *The Intellect*, 'Semantics – Clarity is Essential', ¶20, 98; ¶38, ¶36, 100.

2 Dr Massoud Homayouni, *The Origins of Persian Gnosis*, trans. F. J. Stone (London: Mawlana Centre, 1992), 3 n., quoted from Jalāl ad-Dīn Muhammad Rūmī, *Masnavi*. Rūmī, known also as Mawlânâ ('my master'), was a thirteenth-century Persian poet, Islamic scholar, theologian, and Sufi mystic originally from Greater Khorasan in Middle Persia. Note that this quote actually states: 'Peace ensures […]' but it is assumed that 'ensures' is a typographical error for 'ensues' as confirmed by searches on the Internet for the same quote.

3 *KT*, 'The Distinction Between Soul and Spirit', 94–5.

4 T. Subba Row, *Esoteric Writings* (2nd rev. and enl. edn, Adyar, Madras: Theosophical Publishing House, 1931; repr. 1980), 7.

5 Isaac Newton, 'The Language of the Prophets', in Newton, Theological MS, 119–26; quotation from pp. 119–20 (1, n.12). Quoted also in Betty Jo Teeter Dobbs, *The Foundations of Newton's Alchemy or 'The Hunting of the Greene Lyon'* (1975; repr. US: Cambridge University Press, 1984), 109.

6 *KT*, 'Definite Words for Definite Things', 171.

7 *KT*, 175 n.

8 *TSGLOSS*, 255.

9 A clear exposition on the distinction between principles and planes is in J. S. Gordon, *Self-Consistent Kosmos* (UK: Orpheus Publishing House, 1995), 23–9.

10 *ML*, Letter No. 65.

11 See Stephen Phillips: *Extra-Sensory Perception of Quarks* (Adyar, Madras, and Wheaton, Illinois: Theosophical Publishing House, 1980); *ESP of Quarks and Superstrings* (India: New Age International Pvt Ltd Publishers, 1999); *The Mathematical Connection Between Religion and Science* (Eastbourne, UK: Anthony Rowe Publishing, 2009).

12 William Kingsland, 'What H. P. Blavatsky Taught Us – The Testimony of One of Her London Students', *Lucifer* (1891) <https://www.carloscardosoaveline.com/what-h-p-blavatsky-taught-us> accessed 6 March 2020. Quoted also in *H. P. B. In Memory of Helena Petrovna Blavatsky by Some of Her Pupils* (1st edn, 1891; facs. edn, London: Theosophical Publishing House, 1991).

13 Arthur Ellison, 'Modelling, Philosophy and Limitation', *Computing & Control Engineering Journal* (August 1993).

14 *KT*, 'The Greek Teachings', 100.

15 Arthur Koestler, *The Ghost in the Machine* (UK: Hutchinson, and USA: Macmillan, 1967), 48.

16 *The Independent*, cited in *The Week*, 21 September 2019, 25.

17 *NPB*-5, *Semantics*: ¶99, 103.

2 The Occult Constitution of Man – How Man is 'Builded Up'

And the Lord God formed man of the dust of the ground, and breathed into his nostrils the breath of life; and man became a living soul.

GENESIS 2:7, KING JAMES BIBLE

The essential purpose of the Vedas is to teach you the nature of the imperishable Ātman, and to declare with authority, 'Thou art That'.

BHAGAVAN ŚRĪ RAMANA MAHARSHI[1]

SYNOPSIS

Chapter 2 concerns man's constitution: man, as structure, that is, how he is constructed. We explain the significance of the basic twofold constitution of man into Individuality (immortal Self) and personality (mortal self); then the rationale for unfoldment to the familiar threefold constitution into spirit and body, with soul as interface. This enumeration can in turn be extended to higher octaves of a fivefold and sevenfold stratification providing a much richer understanding of the inner (occult) governing principles at work, especially regarding the workings of mind. It is stressed, however, that man is an organic unity and the various subdivisions of his being are not like discrete onion skins, but aspects of his constitution at different levels. Owing to the depth of the subject, overriding considerations are presented before a detailed exposition of the sevenfold constitution ranging from the outer physical to the inner spiritual. Sanskrit terms are unavoidable, but their etymology and English meanings are carefully explained and justified. This Chapter is supported by a detailed diagram and tabular summary.

KEY WORDS: individuality, personality, spirit, soul, body, septenary constitution, Divine Self, intuition, mind, desire, life-force, etheric

At this juncture, it is necessary to point out to readers our general policy of using:

❖ lower case letters when referring to a general principle (e.g. 'spirit'); also to the mortal aspect of man's constitution (e.g. 'Animal s̲oul');
❖ upper case letters when referring to the specific application of a principle (e.g. 'Spirit'); also to the immortal aspect of man's constitution (e.g. 'Spiritual S̲oul').

This Chapter is concerned with an in-depth description of the first facet of man's composition according to divine law: his 'occult anatomy', namely, his structure and constitution at all levels necessary for life on Earth. The traditional and well-known dual and triple divisions of man's constitution are presented as a prelude to the complete occult doctrine on the septenary classification that shows how man is constituted, or builded up, so as to fit into the divine scheme of nature according to septenary law. In this sense, his component parts may be regarded as 'building blocks' (hence the quaint term 'builded up' in the title of this Chapter for reasons explained in Chapter 1), with the major proviso (as also explained earlier) that such components are not separate units placed one on top of the other (as is perforce necessary for a diagrammatic portrayal), but rather as interrelated constituents of a structure of interconnected parts.

The next Chapter describes how man acts and functions; in other words, how he performs according to his constitution.

Table II-3 on page 21 is a diagrammatic representation of the Principles of Man from the standpoint of his constitution. It is drawn so as to be compatible with the top half of Table II-2 in Chapter 1 on page 13, which was devised in order to illustrate overriding principles using an analogy drawn from everyday existence. It is important for the reader to consult Table II-3 throughout the remainder of this Chapter.

For ease of explanation, Table II-3 is presented in three sections:

1. Section 1 shows the familiar dual and triple divisions of man's constitution.
2. Section 2 concerns the complete septenary classification along with explanatory notes.
3. Section 3 shows how the principles in the septenary classification, in their various combinations, provide the basis of the twofold, threefold or fivefold classifications.

Contents of this Chapter

Before proceeding, it is important to remember that the principles are *aspects* and *states* of consciousness of the one man enduring through the cycle of his terrestrial life—see again Chapter 1, page 10 et seq.

The Dual Constitution of Man – Individuality and Personality

Referring to Section 1 of Table II-3, the first column makes the point that man is a unified entity but, as explained in the previous Chapter, he displays two fundamental aspects of his being: the inward spiritual, and the outward physical. Therefore, we can divide man into two distinct parts: the Individuality, or Higher Self; and the personality, or Lower self as seen in the second column. These dual parts are, in turn, composed of various principles that in their combinations give a triple, septenary or quintuple constitution, as explained in the simile of Table II-2 on page 13 and which will shortly be detailed below. There are good reasons why the Individuality comprising the Upper, or Spiritual being is immortal, and the personality comprising the lower, or physical being is mortal. This will all become clearer as we proceed.

Significance of dual and triple constitution of man

The Triple Constitution of Man – Spirit, Soul, and Body

The third column in Section 1 of Table II-3 shows the familiar threefold division of the constitution of man into Spirit, Soul, and Body. Equivalent terms are Spiritual Soul, Animal soul,[i] and Physical (Animal) body. This classification was adopted by Plato, Saint Paul, and many others (using different terminology, but always conveying the same essential meaning).

---

i Sometimes referred to as the 'Astral body'—the same term also used for the Etheric double, or Model body. This potential confusion alone justifies the use of Sanskrit terms.

Occult science makes use of precisely the same division but shows the complex characteristic of each of the three constituent parts as in the septenary classification now described.

The Triple and Septenary Constitution of Man – Rationale and Overriding Considerations

Table II-2 on page 13 of the previous Chapter gave an elementary example of how a unity can present as a duality, a triplicity, and a septenary. We take this consideration a stage further to show how the septenary classification of the constitution of man (and nature) is a development of the dual and triple constitutions described above. First, we need to explain the rationale for the septenary constitution, which is anything but arbitrary as is sometimes assumed by those who have not bothered to delve into such matters seem to think.

As a general rule, whenever seven *entities* are mentioned in esoteric or occult literature, in any connection whatsoever, this is because: (a) the seven entities came into existence from *three primary entities*; which in turn (b) are the product of a *basic duality*; which is (c) evolved out of a *single entity* (or monad, which term will be explained later). This is in accordance with mathematical law. From algebra, we know that the number of *combinations* of n things taken one at a time, two at a time, three at a time, and so on equals 2^n-1. Applying the formula, the number of entities born from: (a) a basic duality are $2^2-1 = 3$ primary entities; and (b) the number of entities evolved from different combinations of three primary entities are $2^3-1 = 7$ entities, comprising *three primary entities* and *four secondary entities*. Thus, taking the familiar example of the seven colours of the spectrum, these are made up of: (a) three primary colours, red, blue, and green; and (b) four secondary colours evolved from different combinations of the three primaries, namely, red-green, red-blue, green-blue, and red-green-blue.

Mathematical basis of triple and septenary constitution

Similarly, the *three primary principles*, Spirit, Soul, and Body which brought man into existence co-exist in him with the *four secondary principles* which arose from different combinations of the three primary entities. These seven principles which, in their totality constitute man, are shown in Section 2 of Table II-3 on page 21. The first column of this section gives the principles in the original Sanskrit with the nearest available English equivalent stated directly above; and the second column explains the meaning and significance of each principle. As previously stressed, there is no one way, or hard-and-fast rule about how to 'divide' man. The schemata adopted depends upon the context in question and the substance of enquiry and investigation. This point is reinforced in Section 3 of Table II-3. The three columns of this section show how combinations of the septenary principles are compatible with a twofold, threefold or fivefold division.

Concerning the twofold division seen in the first column of Section 3, the first three septenary principles (Divine Self, Intuition Principle, and Mind Principle) constitute the immortal Upper Triad; and the last four septenary principles (Desire principle, Life principle, Etheric double, or Astral body, and Physical body) constitute the perishable Lower Quaternary. The Upper Triad, or triplicate spiritual constitution, is the true Individuality which, during incarnation, becomes attached to, hence identified with, and focussed in the personality. We shall expand further on these ideas.

The threefold division is equally compatible with the septenary classification thus: (1) the Spiritual, or Upper Triad which, as before, is a trinity, (2) the Middle Duad, or Soul considered in the generic sense, comprising the Mind Principle (its lower aspect) and Desire principle; and (3) the Lower Triad made up of the Physical (Animal) body (the gross physical part), an ethereal counterpart known as the Etheric double (Model body, or Astral body), and a Vital principle, or Life principle known as *Prāṇa* and by various other names. The Soul is a complex entity that will be explored further, but, in essence, it is composed of two elements which we experience as the feeling and thinking aspects of ourselves.

Septenary division congruent with dual, triple, and quintuple divisions

The fivefold division seen in the final column of Table II-3, on page 21 comprises the Lower Triad and Animal soul (Middle Duad) of the threefold division, but subdivides the Upper Triad into the trinity of the Mind Principle (its higher aspect), the Intuition Principle, and the Divine Self, otherwise termed the Human Soul, Spiritual Soul (Monad), and Spirit, respectively.

It has been repeatedly emphasized that the reader must not conceive that because man is understood as being dual or triple or quintuple or septenary, that he is therefore a compound of two, three, five or seven discrete entities, rather like separate 'skins' that can be unpeeled like onion skins. With this proviso, the various Principles of Man can, in one sense, be regarded like bodies, or sheaths, through which the one man lives, functions and has his being.

However we 'divide' his constitution, man is always an organic unity

The various terms in Table II-3 on the constitution of man are now elucidated in descending order of refinement from their spiritual origin—the point of emanation—to the gross physical—the lowest level of descent.

Note however that there seems to be little consistency amongst various authors (including Blavatsky) regarding the numbering of the principles. Some work 'downwards' by assigning 'one' to the spiritual and 'seven' to the physical; whilst others work 'upwards' by assigning 'one' to the physical and 'seven' to the spiritual. The convention adopted here is strongly recommended because it is logical for numbering to commence *from the point of emanation*—the spiritual.

We continue with a detailed exposition of the septenary classification, being the most comprehensive account provided by occult science on the whole constitution of man.

The Principles of Man are the various aspects of the one real man. Man is therefore not an aggregate of two, three, five or seven entities, but rather all of these represent the various modes and aspects in which man can operate. The septenary constitution of man is derived from the various combinations of Spirit, Soul, and Body.

The Septenary Constitution of Man – Detailed Exposition

It will be clear by now that man is a unified, but a complex, multi-dimensional, and compound being; but for an analytical description, his implicate wholeness has, perforce, to be explicated, such that the various parts of his esoteric anatomy can be laid alongside one another and individually described. The following account of the septenary constitution of man has of necessity to be explained one principle after the other. It might be helpful too for readers to remember that this exposition is in terms of principles, and therefore any reference to planes is made quite explicit in order to avoid confusion. (The distinction between principles and planes is explained in Chapter 1, pages 5–7.)

The septenary principles of man's constitution, shown in the first column of Section 2 of Table II-3 opposite, are now described in terms of the familiar two categories of the Upper Triad and Lower Quaternary, the latter comprising the Middle Duad and Lower Triad as seen in Section 3 of the table.

UPPER IMPERISHABLE TRIAD – IMMORTAL SPIRITUAL NATURE AS INDIVIDUALITY

The Upper Imperishable Triad comprises the triplicity of the Divine Self, Intuition Principle, and Mind Principle. This is clearly seen in the septenary classification shown in the first column of Section 2 in Table II-3 and is now explained.

> *First, the Breath* [Ātma], *then Buddhi* [the Spiritual Soul] *and the Shadow-Son* [the Body] [*sic*] *were* 'CREATED'.
>
> H. P. Blavatsky[2]

1. ***Ātma*** – The Divine Self, the Sanskrit word meaning 'Pure Consciousness', believed to be derived from a verbal root *an*, meaning 'to breathe'. Thus, it is closely related to the root meaning of the word 'spirit' from the Latin *spire* 'to breathe', as in the word 'inspire'.

   Ātma: what it means

   KEY MEANING: the universal selfhood as the highest part of man, *breathed forth*, as stated in the quotation above, from the Source of ALL, the Fount of Being—Brahman.

   SIMILAR TERMS: Universal Spirit, SPIRIT, Divine Monad, Supreme Soul, Self, Universal Selfhood.

   Ātma, then, is that essential and radical faculty or power which gives to every entity its knowledge and sentient consciousness of Selfhood. In the human, it is that part of us which is universal in its aspect, rather than individualized. It is assuredly *not* the Ego, for it is not that part of us which cognizes and therefore says 'I am I', nor even that which declares 'I am', but rather, 'I am one with ALL'. Refer though to Endnote II-1 regarding the difficulty of finding English words for Sanskrit terms, Ātma being a case in point.

   But there is a subtle but important distinction, which is often overlooked, even in esoteric literature, between *Ātman*—the Divine Principle, and *Ātma*—the Divine Self as revealed by the following quote:

   > If Brahman were to utter the word 'I', that 'I' is the meaning of Ātman.
   >
   > Phiroz Mehta[3]

   Ātman and *Ātma*: nuances of meaning

   Ātman as a principle is universal; therefore belongs to nobody (or to everybody and everything).

   Ātma, however, is Brahman within the individual, so to speak. It is *the correspondence of the Divine Principle in man's constitution*, hence referred to as the 'Divine Self' being:

   > One with the Absolute, as its radiation.[4] [It] is neither your Spirit nor mine, but like sunlight shines on all. It is the universally diffused '*divine principle*', and is inseparable from its one and absolute *Meta*-Spirit, as the sunbeam is inseparable from sunlight.[5]

   So it is quite meaningless to say 'my Ātma', while entirely meaningful to say 'my body'.

   Refer now to Endnote II-4 for more insight into the different shades of meaning of Brahman—an exact term in Sanskrit, but so elusive to pin down in English.

Table II-3 The Whole Man – His *Constitution* During Earthly Life: One 'Human Territory' – Many 'Anatomical Maps'

MAN AS ONE UNIFIED ENTITY — Dual Constitution	Triple Constitution	#	Septenary (Occult) Constitution and Relationship with Two, Three, and Fivefold Groupings — Classification	Meaning and Significance	Twofold	Threefold	Fivefold
Individuality or Higher Self (Immortal)	Spirit	1	*Ātma* **the Divine Self**	Pure consciousness *per se* as universal Selfhood.	Upper Triad	Upper Duad	**Spirit**
	Soul	2	*Buddhi* **the Intuition Principle**	The 'spiritual organ' providing the faculty of discrimination and intuition that awakens man to direct understanding.	Upper Triad	Upper Duad / Upper Triad	**Spiritual Soul, or Monad**
			Buddhi-Manas the Higher Mind → **Higher**				
		3	*Manas* **the Mind Principle**	The mental faculty which makes of man an intelligent and moral being, and distinguishes him from the mere animal. It is the pivot point bridging the Individuality with the personality.	Upper Triad	Upper Triad	**Human Soul**
			Kāma-manas the Lower mind → **Lower**	A dual function in man as to whether it 'rises' to ally with *Buddhi* (creating the Higher Mind) or 'descends' to identify with *Kāma* (forming the Lower mind).			
Personality or Lower self (mortal)		4	*Kāma* **the Desire principle**	The motivating principle and impelling force; the seat of the animal desires and passions.	Lower Quaternary	Middle Duad	**Animal soul, or Psyche**
		5	*Prāṇa* **the Life principle**	The vital principle, or Life-force, that pervades and animates the Physical body.	Lower Quaternary	Lower Triad	
		6	*Liṅga-śarīra* **the Etheric double**	The Model body, or Astral body, as the causal form of the Physical body.	Lower Quaternary	Lower Triad	
	Body	7	*Sthūla-śarīra, or Rūpa* **the Physical body**	The vehicle of all the above principles during life.	Lower Quaternary	Lower Triad	

Section 1   *Section 2*   *Section 3*

It becomes obvious that such a universal principle cannot function *directly* on the lower planes, nor in the physical world. Ātma can only contact the lower planes by means of a base, or conducting medium, acting as its vehicle. Hence for human incarnation, Ātma takes on attributes, where it is linked with its vehicle, *Buddhi*; as Buddhi is linked with *Manas*; and so on down the scale to the Physical body, all the lower vehicles being imbued with the Atmic essence as seen in Table II-3, page 21. This is elaborated in the next Chapter dealing with man's nature and how he functions.

2. ***Buddhi*** – The Principle of Intuition, or Discernment, the Sanskrit word meaning 'discrimination', 'intuition', derived from the verbal root *budh*, commonly translated 'to enlighten', 'to know'; but better translated as 'to perceive', 'to cognize', 'to recover consciousness'; hence, 'to awaken'; and therefore, 'to understand', 'to judge'.

KEY MEANING: the faculty of discrimination and intuition that awakens man directly to understanding. Note carefully that by intuition we mean the faculty of direct knowing, or direct perception, therefore, quite literally, tuition from within—*in*-tuition. Intuition, although related to, is not the same as 'hunches', or 'gut feelings', which may, for all intents and purposes, be regarded as the dregs of intuition.

Buddhi: what it means

SIMILAR TERMS: intuition, discrimination, judgement, enlightenment, direct perception.

Buddhi, then, constitutes the inseparable veil, or garment, of the highest part of man—Ātma, as the quotation below affirms:

> *Bodha* means the innate possession of divine intellect or 'understanding'; 'Buddha,' the acquirement of it by personal efforts and merit; while *Buddhi* is the faculty of cognizing the channel through which divine knowledge reaches the 'Ego,' the discernment of good and evil; 'divine conscience' also; and 'Spiritual Soul,' which is the vehicle of *Ātman*.
>
> H. P. Blavatsky[6]

Being the Spiritual Soul in man, his 'spiritual organ', so to say, Buddhi bequeaths spiritual consciousness, which manifests as intuition, a direct knowing. Thus in one sense, Buddhi may be said to be both the seed and the fruit of Manas (see below)—the germ or nucleus behind the Mind Principle, as also the essence, or 'aroma', when the latter attains its fruition.

Buddhi is decidedly not the same as reason, and still less, intellect. These common mistranslations (for want of adequate expressions in English) provide a totally erroneous perception. Reason, rationality, and intellect are mental faculties and therefore aspects of the mind, whereas the Spiritual Soul, which implies divine perception and understanding, goes directly to the hidden meaning and therefore transcends rationality—in-tuition.

Buddhi in conjunction with Ātma constitutes the Human Monad—strictly speaking, the Monad manifesting in that form known as the Human kingdom. The deep significance of this is reserved for the next Chapter.

3. ***Manas*** – The Mind Principle, the Sanskrit word meaning 'mind' derived from the verbal root *man*, meaning 'to think', 'to cogitate', 'to reflect'; hence, 'the mind', or 'the thinker'.

KEY MEANING: '"the mind", the mental faculty which makes of man an intelligent and moral being, and distinguishes him from the mere animal,'[7] as the quotation below further affirms:

> Between man and the animal [...] there is the impassable abyss of Mentality and Self-consciousness.
>
> H. P. Blavatsky[8]

Manas: what it means

Manas springs forth from Buddhi as the fruit from the flower. The Mind Principle in conjunction with the Desire principle (see below) is a fundamental pivot point in the human constitution, for it is the principle which bridges, or links the higher with the lower, i.e., the Individuality with the personality. Indeed, man can be described as 'God' linked to animal *by a bridge of mind*; hence, in popular terms, spirit-soul-body.

The Mind Principle presents dual aspects when manifesting in the human constitution, as shown in Table II-3. Hence it is divided into Higher Manas and Lower manas. In other words, Manas can either 'rise' and ally itself with Buddhi and bring forth the spiritual nature, the blending referred to as *Buddhi-Manas* (the Higher Mind) shown by the upward pointing arrow in Table II-3; or Manas can 'descend' and entangle with *Kāma* (the Desire principle, next explained) and thereby inflame the animal nature, the union referred to as *Kāma-manas* (the Lower mind) shown by the downward pointing arrow. But this does not mean that man has two minds working simultaneously within him! Nor does it imply a literal association with the two hemispheres of the brain. Because consciousness is one and the same throughout man's constitution, but *limited and conditioned* by the *vehicles* through which it operates, *it means that the same mind (using both hemispheres of the brain as its vehicle) is working in different ways, and at different levels. This duality in the functioning of mind is absolutely crucial to our understanding of how man himself functions.* We discuss it fully in the next Chapter dealing with the septenary nature of man, i.e., how his sevenfold constitution functions in life.

Dual function of the Mind Principle in man

At this stage it is important to note that the Upper Triad, or Individuality, comprises Ātma, Buddhi, and Higher Manas. Lower manas is the upper part of the Middle Duad, as shown in the penultimate column of Table II-3.

Mind is a single principle; it is dual only in its function, not in its essence.

We move on to consider the mortal aspects of man's occult constitution.

LOWER PERISHABLE QUATERNARY – MORTAL PERSONALITY

The Lower Perishable Quaternary comprises the lower half of the Middle Duad and the Lower Triad, as clearly seen in the middle column of Section 3 of Table II-3, page 21.

> To understand the idea well [between the Individuality and the personality], you have to first study the dual sets of principles: the *spiritual*, or those which belong to the imperishable Ego; and the *material*, or those principles which make up the ever-changing bodies or the series of personalities of that Ego.
>
> H. P. Blavatsky[9]

Soul constitutes the interface between Spirit and Body

MIDDLE DUAD – SOUL

The Middle Duad comprises the duality of the Lower manas and *Kāma*, in other words, the personal desire-seeking mind as opposed to the spiritually aspiring mind as also seen in Section 3 of Table II-3 and now explained.

4. *Kāma* – The Desire principle, the Sanskrit word meaning 'desire' derived from the verbal root *kam* 'to desire'.

Kāma: what it means

KEY MEANING: the desire and motivating principle in life, as the quotation below affirms:

> Desire first arose in IT, which was the primal germ of mind, and which Sages, searching with their intellect, have discovered in their heart to be the bond which connects Entity with non-Entity.
>
> Ṛg-Veda quoted in *TSGloss*, 171

Generally speaking, Kāma is the driving, or impelling force. In the human constitution this force is 'the seat of animal desires and passions'.[10] It is the centre from which operates the living electrical impulses, desires, and aspirations, considered in their energetic aspect, in contrast to the structural, or form-making aspect. This fourth principle, in conjunction with Lower manas, being the middle one of the seven is, to reiterate, the turning point, being 'the centre of the animal man, where lies the line of demarcation which separates the mortal man from the immortal entity.'[11] (See also Manas above.)

Kāma as the motivating principle without Prāṇa (as the *motor* principle) would be inert. As the wind fans the flames, so as the vital breath 'Prāṇa wakes the Kāmic germs to life, and it makes all desires vital and living.'[12] (Prāṇa is next described below.)

Distinction between Kāma and Kāma-rūpa

It is important to note that the fourth principle of Kāma has been referred to as the *Kāma-rūpa* in early Theosophical literature (see Chapter 1 on page 3 regarding different terminology). This is a legacy from the early days of the Theosophical Society when there was no general agreement on the best Sanskrit term to use in regard to its closest English translation. Notwithstanding this, Kāma-rūpa means the desire body (*rūpa* means body), and therefore signifies the *vehicle or body of consciousness* for the expression of Kāma, the Desire principle. In this respect, it is helpful to remember what was said in Chapter 1 on page 5, namely: any positive, or active, principle (Kāma in this case) must work through its corresponding negative, or passive medium, or vehicle—its rūpa, in other words—for its self-expression. At this juncture, a brief mention of the after-death states is warranted.

The Post-Mortem States and Locales of Man

Strictly speaking, Kāma-rūpa does not become a distinct, subtle body until after physical death, whereupon, after the disintegration of the lowest three principles (Physical body, Etheric double, and Prāṇa) it becomes the vehicle of desire of the higher principles (the Upper Triad) of the terrestrial man that was.[ii] Thus, after physical death, Kāma-rūpa is formed from the dregs of the *Māyāvi-rūpa*, which is the vehicle of dream consciousness for the average

---

ii The Kāma-rūpa 'exists' in *Kāma-loka*, or the Desire-world—see below and in Chapter 5 for more details.

man during the life term. The role of the Māyāvi-rūpa as a vehicle of consciousness, and its significance in reports of inexplicable materializations, is given later in Chapter 4.

Since Kāma-rūpa has been referred to as a 'subtle body' (albeit the grossest of the subtle, to coin a phrase), readers may legitimately wonder where, and in what dimension, it exists. The answer is, just as the Physical body exists on the plane corresponding to physical matter, i.e., on the terrestrial plane, so the kamic body exists on the plane of appropriate 'kamic substance'. This plane is known as *Kāma-loka*, meaning the place (*loka*) of desire (Kāma)—recall the comments made in Chapter 1 about lokas and *talas*, and higher dimensions of space–time (page 6 f.). Kāma-loka is the equivalent of *Purgatorio* in the *Divina Commedia* by the Italian poet of the Late Middle Ages, Dante Alighieri (1265–1321) completed, poignantly, a year before his own death. The subject of the post-mortem states of consciousness is ever fascinating as it is complex. To delve into it in depth would not be appropriate in this work. Nonetheless, a compressed account of the principal features of man's post-mortem states of consciousness and corresponding locales is given in Chapter 5.

Kāma-rūpa: its formation and locale

Are Desires Good or Evil?

It should be apparent by now that in order to appreciate the full significance of Kāma, the Desire principle, it must be studied in connection with the Mind Principle. This is further elaborated in the next Chapter. For now, the key point to grasp is that the soul of man is a duad because during incarnation, Manas projects, so to speak, a portion of itself either into the higher planes to bring forth the spiritual nature (shown by the upward pointing arrow in Table II-3, on page 21) or into the lower planes of being (shown by the downward pointing arrow) where it becomes attached to Kāma, thus forming the duality of *Kāma-manas*, generally referred to as the 'mortal Ego' of man.[iii]

There seems to be a curious notion amongst some self-righteous people, or in sanctimonious spiritual groups, that desires are basically evil. This is nonsense. In itself, Kāma is neither 'good', nor 'evil', but like any and every force and power in nature, is completely neutral and 'colourless'. It is the manner in which such force and power is used that makes them a blessing or a curse. Just as electricity can be used to illuminate houses or to electrocute people, it entirely depends upon the motive behind, and the will directing, the desire that turns it into a benevolent or malevolent force. In association with the higher spiritual principles, Kāma is a greatly beneficent factor, since, for example, the desire to help others is obviously noble; as also the desire to advance in life and acquire knowledge—provided, in both cases, there is no motive of personal ambition or desire to hurt others in the process. The greater the degree of personal end-gaining for selfish reasons, the more the purity of Kāma is polluted. It is when selfish reasons dominate altruistic motives (i.e., the animal component of man eclipses his divine propensities) that Kāma acquires its familiar meaning of the tempting 'evil desire, lust, volition; the cleaving to existence'.[13] As the previous section on Manas has been at pains to show, this happens when the *lower* Manas increasingly identifies with Kāma resulting in the desire-driven mind—Kāma-manas. There are innumerable cases of those who use knowledge to further their own ends at the expense of others, amongst scientists,

Motive alone renders desires 'good' or 'evil'

---

iii Sometimes also referred to as the Mortal soul; but strictly speaking it is just Kāma that constitutes the Mortal, or Animal soul. This is fully explained later.

It is a cardinal error to regard Kāma as intrinsically evil. It only becomes so when perverted.

politicians, businessmen, lawyers, and many other professions; and members of spiritual societies, self-appointed Theosophists, and religious leaders are no exceptions either.

So it is the *lower* desires that must be bridled and conquered because: desires gratified result in further inflammation and intensification, rather like pouring petrol on an already raging fire. On the other hand, desires blocked create anger, like the turbulence and pressure generated behind a boulder in a roaring stream; both lead a man swiftly down the slippery slope to ruin. The point is that those desires that are nurtured are the ones that will grow. This is well illustrated by the parable of the two wolves attributed to the Cherokee Indians.iv In the tale, a grandfather tells his grandson that inside us there are two 'wolves', which are perpetually at war against each other. One of them is the good wolf, representing qualities like kindness, bravery, and love; whilst the other is the bad wolf, representing things like greed, hatred, and fear. When the grandson enquires, 'Grandfather, which one wins?' the grandfather quietly replies, 'the one you feed.'

Thoughts and desires are inextricably bound

On this theme, the American self-help author Napoleon Hill (see Volume I, Chapter 9) insisted that intense expectations are essential to improving one's life. In his own words: 'The starting point of all achievement is desire. Keep this constantly in mind. Weak desires bring weak results, just as a small fire makes a small amount of heat.'[14] This is absolutely true but it is only one half of the story as there is a price to pay for the desired outcome. The neglected half is the nature of the desired results. Evil dictators and great philanthropists have all had strong desires that resulted in 'strong results'. What distinguishes the one from the other is not the intensity but the *quality* of thought (Manas) behind the desire (Kāma). Hill might well have stressed this point in the course of his famous book *The Law of Success* (see Volume I, Chapter 9). Nonetheless, to Hill's advice we may also add this eloquent aphorism:

> Your reason and your passion are the rudder and the sails of your seafaring soul […]. For reason, ruling alone, is a force confining; and passion, unattended, is a flame that burns to its own destruction. Therefore let your soul exalt your reason to the height of passion; that it may sing […].
>
> Kahlil Gibran[15]

The central issue, therefore, is neither the satiation nor the suppression, even worse, the repression of desires, but rather their wise *control* and *management* for:

> Kama is pre-eminently the divine desire of creating happiness and love; and it is only ages later, as mankind began to materialize by anthropomorphization[v] its grandest ideals into cut and dried dogmas, that Kama became the power that gratifies desire on the animal plane.
>
> H. P. Blavatsky[16]

---

iv Apparently, there is no real confirmation of this parable, which has also been attributed to the evangelical preacher Billy Graham and the Irish Playwright George Bernard Shaw. But this uncertainty in no way diminishes the impact of its message.

v 'Anthropomorphization' meaning to reduce the whole scheme of Nature to physical mechanisms by dwarfing and force-fitting lofty spiritual principles into the strait-jacket of profane and egocentric human concepts.

LOWER TRIAD

The Lower Triad shown in the last column of Table II-3, page 21 comprises the Life principle, Etheric double, and Physical body, as seen in classifications 5, 6, and 7 in the fourth column of Table II-3 and now explained.

5. ***Prāṇa*** – The Life principle, the Sanskrit word meaning 'life-principle' derived from the prepositional prefix *pra-* 'before'; and the verb *an-* 'to live', 'to breathe', 'to blow'.

Prāṇa: what it means

   KEY MEANING: Although commonly called 'life', a better signification of Prāṇa would be the 'psycho-electrical field, or veil manifesting in the individual as vitality' as this quotation affirms:

   > Prāṇa, LIFE, the active power producing all vital phenomena.
   >
   > H. P. Blavatsky[17]

   SIMILAR TERMS: Life-force, vital breath, vital current, life-current, vital fluid, vital airs, vital winds; it is the *chi* of the Chinese, the *fu* of the Japanese (the core of the martial arts chi kung and kung fu).

   Prāṇa is universally pervasive so that the Physical body is pervaded by it as the Earth is so permeated. It should be noted that a similar term is *jiva* derived from the Sanskrit root *jiv* 'be alive'. But it is misleading to equate it with the vital breath of Life, Prāṇa, since the latter is a vital force whereas jiva is a unit of life-consciousness. When specifically pertaining to the human being, Prāṇa is the vital principle, or Life-force that pervades and animates the Physical body. It is necessary only to the mortal elements of man: to the Physical body and etheric double (see below), to the Desire principle (as explained above) and to all mental functions which operate through, and are limited to, the physical brain, namely, the Lower mind.

   But even when specifically referring to the Physical body, the term 'Prāṇa' is used in a general sense because there are, as a matter of fact, a number of life-currents, each having its own name and function. One system mentions three Prāṇas; another, five, which is the commonly accepted number; the *Anu Gītā*[vi] classifies seven; the Upaniṣads mention twelve; and even thirteen are identified elsewhere (*vide Occult Glossary*[18]). It is obvious that all these various enumerations are not discrete and separate Prāṇas, but different aspects and functional propensities, like 'overtones', of the one vital-principle in life.

Prāṇa animates man's mortal constitution

   At the moment of physical dissolution (death) the 'life-atoms' of Prāṇa (the psycho-electrical field) immediately return to their source—the pranic reservoirs of the planet—the electrical analogue being the ground or earth connection which serves as the common return path for the current from an electrical circuit to Earth. This pranic return path happens because:

   > When a body dies, it passes into the same polarity[vii] as its male energy and repels therefore the active agent, which, losing hold of the *whole*, fastens on the parts or molecules, this action being called chemical. Vishṇu, the Preserver, transforms himself into Rudra-Śiva, the Destroyer—a correlation seemingly unknown to Science.
   >
   > H. P. Blavatsky[19]

----

vi *Anu Gītā* is the Sanskrit text embedded in Book 14 (*Ashvamedhika Parva*) of the Indian epic, *Mahābhārata*.

vii This change in polarity at death is also discussed below in relation to the physical body.

6. *Liṅga-śarīra* – Etheric double, also known as the Model body, or Astral body, the Sanskrit word *Liṅga*, meaning 'model', 'pattern', 'emblem', 'template'; and *śarīra*, meaning 'form', 'body', derived from a verb-root *sri* 'to moulder', 'dissolve', 'to waste away'. The term thus signifies impermanence.

KEY MEANING: the Model body that is impermanent, as affirmed by the following quote:

> Liṅga-Śarīra; the inert vehicle or form on which the body is moulded; the vehicle of Life [Prāṇa]. It is dissipated very shortly after the disintegration of the body.
>
> H. P. Blavatsky[20]

Liṅga-śarīra: what it means

SIMILAR TERMS: double of man, astral body, etheric vehicle, phantom body; it is the *doppelgänger* of the Germans, the *eidolon* of the Greeks.

The above plethora of more or less similar terms for the Liṅga-śarīra are all suggestive of the fact that the Etheric double is (as the term 'etheric' implies) more ethereal than the Physical body. Being the mortal counterpart of the Physical body, it acts as the model, or template around which the Physical body is builded. So the Liṅga-śarīra acts as the *causative field* from which radiates the energies that enable the Physical body to be built and from which, in a sense, the Physical body extrudes and develops as growth proceeds. Just as a photographic negative is a prerequisite in order to develop a positive print from it, the Physical body needs the prior existence of the Model body, its 'negative' upon which to pattern itself. As Blavatsky affirms, 'the birth of the *astral* [the *Etheric double*], [occurs] before the *physical* body, the former being a model for the latter.'[21]

Liṅga-śarīra is confused with other terms

But here it must be said that even though Blavatsky ascribed a definite meaning to the term 'Astral body',[22] it has been interpreted variously since her time causing no end of confusion. Such difficulties encountered in the use of English words may be avoided by the judicious use of the Sanskrit terms which, as explained earlier, invariably contain a power and nuance which cannot be adequately conveyed in English. Hopefully, this work will have gone some way to inculcating this valuable truth. For example, the wide use of 'Astral body' in esoteric literature can refer to: (*a*) the *Liṅga-śarīra* (whose purpose is defined above); (*b*) the *Kāma-rūpa*, the vehicle of desire which exists after physical death (both terms are explained more fully in this and the following Chapter); or (*c*) the *Māyāvi-rūpa*, the projected thought-body, or illusory body, as explained in outline in Chapter 3 and more fully in Chapter 4.

The Liṅga-śarīra is sustained by, and has its basis in, the Astral Light, or Anima Mundi, which is the lowest aspect of *Ākāśa* (Akasha) (described in detail in Chapter 6 of Volume III). Although impermanent, it is not subject to constant change like the Physical body, but remains relatively stable during a lifetime. It is of an electro-magnetic nature and remains in close proximity to the Physical body.

The sense-organs of the Physical body are well known (ears, eyes, nose, tongue, and touch-sensitive tissue). However, the real centres for these sense perceptions are in the Liṅga-śarīra from where they are *transmitted*, so to speak, to the sense terminators in the Physical body.

The body is patterned on the Liṅga-śarīra

Inasmuch as the Liṅga-śarīra precedes the Physical body, it also outlasts the death of the latter, remaining in the astral realms and gradually fading out and dying, in its turn, as the above quote implies. The misty or grey looking wraiths that sensitive persons sometimes see hanging around graveyards are the Liṅga-śarīra of the recently departed before the former has had time to wither. These astral realms are a series of planes becoming progressively more ethereal and spiritual as they approach closer to the inner constitution and structure of Nature.

> The 'double' of man; the Liṅga Śarīra proper can never leave the body till death.
>
> H. P. Blavatsky[23]

7. **Sthūla-śarīra** – The Physical body, the Sanskrit word *sthula*, meaning 'coarse', 'gross', 'unrefined', 'heavy', 'bulky'; therefore differentiated and conditioned matter; and *śarīra*, as above, meaning 'form which disintegrates', hence the outward aspect suggesting impermanence as with the Liṅga-śarīra. It is also referred to as *Rūpa*, the Sanskrit word meaning any kind of body, or form. Here, unqualified, 'Rūpa' obviously refers to the Physical body.

KEY MEANING: 'The bulky form which wastes away', would be a good definition of the compound term, implying 'a large conveyor for innumerable tiny "lives"—which, of course, the cells of the body actually are.'[24]

Sthūla-śarīra: what it means

Man's Physical body serves as the vehicle of all his other principles and aspects during life. In another sense, 'body' is a collective and generalizing term used to denote the lowest constituent of which man is constituted and it is sometimes, loosely, classified as his seventh principle. But strictly speaking, the Physical body is not really a 'principle' since it acts like a shelter, and in another sense as a garment and carrier, to the real man. So the loss of his body (i.e., physical death) in no way implies the death of the man any more than we would physically die, should we lose our house or our clothing. Man is still a human entity without the Sthūla-śarīra, but yet this should not be taken too literally, as even the Physical body is an expression of man's constitution on the physical plane, and is needed for evolution and work on Earth. Since the body provides the vehicle for all other principles (as enumerated earlier in this Chapter) for man's terrestrial existence, it therefore forms the basis for the integration of the six principles, without which, *at our present stage of evolution*, man would be unable to function on Earth. The Physical body is formed by means of the interaction of the principles superior to it, and furthermore:

Physical body: the integrated 'end product' of all higher six principles

> The gross Matter of the body, the substance formed and moulded over the Liṅga-śarīra […] by the action of Prāṇa.
>
> H. P. Blavatsky[25]

The body, then, is built up of cosmic elements, themselves formed of living atomic entities as implied by the following quote:

> The body is as much a divine projection as the planet on which it dwells. It is not demoniacal, nor even a symbol of man's sad downfall. Every tissue cell, bone cell, nerve cell, and muscle cell of which it is constructed is itself an expression of divine intelligence and purpose. It is a miniature copy of the universe.
>
> Paul Brunton[26]

Even though it feels real enough to us (never more so than when we suffer physically), yet, the body is, in fact, the most *unreal* thing in our make-up, because it is so changeable and transitory. In esoteric philosophy, the Sthūla-śarīra is said to have a polarity opposite to that of Earth. Hence when death supervenes, the Physical body takes on the same polarity as that of the Earth, hence repelling Prāṇa from itself (refer also to Prāṇa above); the body then follows the course of natural decay, its constituent hosts of life-atoms proceeding collectively and individually to their natural place of attraction. This, it must be stressed, is the true meaning of that most sorely misunderstood word 'transmigration', which has nothing whatsoever to do with the human soul migrating over, and incarnating in, an animal body for the simple reason that the latter offers no basis or opening at all for the spiritual, intellectual, and psychical powers and faculties that make a man human (as explained in some detail in Chapter 5).

Human body: the nexus and containment of divine power/ intelligence and cosmic elements

Despite, from the higher standpoint, the unreality of the body, this is no reason for its neglect, still less its derision, or despising its normal organic functions. The above exposition has been at pains to show that the body is indeed the 'temple of the Divine' and it behoves us to maintain it in prime condition, to give it all it needs, but certainly not what it 'greeds'.

> In the human body there is at one and the same time a projection of the Overself and a channel for it. The wisdom and intelligence that have gone into and are hidden behind the whole universe have gone into the human body, too. To ignore it, as some mystics try to do—and vainly—or to deny its existence, as others even more foolishly do, is to ignore God and deny the soul. The student of philosophy cannot do that. His outlook must be an integral one, must take in what is the very basis of his earthly existence, must be a balanced one.
>
> Paul Brunton[27]

Summary

This concludes the exposition on man's constitution—his occult anatomy. The key fact to note is the emanational unfoldment of the principles, bearing in mind that Ātma interpenetrates each and every one of the six 'unrolled' principles. In other words, Ātma pervades, as well partakes of: Buddhi, Manas, Kāma, Prāṇa, Liṅga-śarīra, Sthūla-śarīra. Similarly, the six principles interpenetrate one another (*vide The Divine Plan*[28]). But without Ātma, the other six principles would be lifeless and therefore inert. The writer

All principles are needed for man's life on Earth

suggests that this is the meaning behind the graphic verse in *Genesis* 2:7 quoted in the epigraph above. This provides an explanation as to how man was 'formed' by 'the Lord God' [Ātma] [Who] 'formed man of the dust of the ground' [Sthūla-śarīra], 'and breathed into his nostrils' [Liṅga-śarīra] 'the breath of life' [Prāṇa]; 'and man became a living soul [Buddhi, Manas, Kāma].[viii]

A summary of this Chapter, in tabular form, is provided in Table II-4 on the next page. It closely follows, and amplifies, the content of Table II-3 on page 21. The next Chapter considers man's nature, namely, how man *functions* by virtue of his constitution, as just described. In order to understand this, it is necessary to 'divide' man in different ways, but

---

viii Needless to say, these analogies between *Genesis* and the Principles of Man can hardly be taken in the literal sense. We are not suggesting that the human nostrils are synonymous with the Liṅga-śarīra.

Table II-4   The Seven Principles of Man's *Constitution* – How Man is 'Builded Up': Summary Meaning and Key Doctrine
(Refer also to Table II-3 on page 21)

Classification	Sanskrit Derivation and English Similar Terms	Essential Meaning	Operation of Principle	Comment
			UPPER IMPERISHABLE TRIAD – HIGHER SELF, OR INDIVIDUALITY (IMMORTAL)	
1. *Atma* the Divine Self	Pure Consciousness, from the verbal root *an* 'to breathe'. Thus, closely related to the root meaning of the word 'spirit' from the Latin *spire* 'to breathe', as in the word 'inspire'. Similar Terms: Universal Spirit, SPIRIT, Divine Monad, Supreme Soul, Self, Universal Selfhood.	The universal selfhood as the highest part of man, *breathed forth*, from the Source of ALL, the Fount of Being—*Brahman*.	That essential and radical faculty and power which gives to every entity its knowledge and sentient consciousness of Selfhood. In the human, it is that part of us which is universal in its aspect, rather than individualized. It is assuredly *not* the Ego, for it is not that part of us which cognizes and therefore says 'I am I', nor even that which declares 'I am', but rather, 'I am one with ALL.'	It is obvious that such a universal principle cannot function *directly* on the lower planes, nor in the physical world. Atma can only contact the lesser planes by means of a *base*. Hence, for human incarnation, Atma takes on attributes, where it is linked with its vehicle, Buddhi; as Buddhi is linked with Manas; and so on down the scale to the Physical body, all the lower vehicles being imbued with the Atmic essence.
2. *Buddhi* the Intuition Principle	Discrimination, intuition, from the verbal root *budh*, commonly translated 'to enlighten', 'to know', but better translated as 'to perceive', 'to cognize', 'to recover consciousness'; hence, 'to awaken'; and therefore, 'to understand', 'to judge'. Similar Terms: intuition, discrimination, judgement, direct perception, enlightenment.	The faculty of intuition and discrimination that awakens man directly to understanding.	The 'spiritual organ' in man being the principle which gives to him spiritual consciousness, which manifests as intuition—a direct knowing without the intervention of the brain intellect. Thus, in one sense, Buddhi may be said to be both the seed and the fruit of Manas (see below)—the germ, or nucleus behind the Mind Principle, as also the essence or aroma when the latter attains its fruition.	Buddhi in conjunction with Atma constitutes the Human Monad—more strictly, the Monad manifesting in that form which we call the Human kingdom. Note that Buddhi, being direct perception, or direct knowing, is therefore not the same as intellect.
3. *Manas* the Mind Principle	Mind Principle, from the verbal root *man* 'to think', 'to cogitate', 'to reflect'; hence, 'the mind', or 'the thinker'.	The mind *per se*, the mental faculty which makes of man an intelligent and moral being, distinguishing him from the animal.	Manas springs forth from Buddhi as the fruit from the flower. The Mind Principle is a fundamental pivot point, for it is the lower aspect of this principle in conjunction with Kāma which bridges, or links the higher with the lower, i.e., the Individuality with the personality. Indeed man has been described as God linked to animal *by a bridge of mind* (see also Kāma below).	The Mind Principle displays a dual function in human nature. Hence Manas is divided into: Higher Manas and Lower Manas. So, Manas can either 'rise' and ally itself with Buddhi and bring forth the spiritual nature; or it can 'descend' and identify itself with Kāma and thereby exacerbate the animal nature.
			LOWER PERISHABLE QUATERNARY – LOWER SELF, OR PERSONALITY (MORTAL)	
4. *Kāma* the Desire principle	Desire, from the verbal root *kam* 'to desire'.	The motivating principle in life.	Generally speaking, the driving, or impelling force. In the human constitution this force is 'the seat of animal desires and passions', the centre from which operates the living electrical impulses, desires, and aspirations, considered in their energetic aspect. This fourth principle (in conjunction with the lower aspect of Manas) being the middle one of the seven is a crucial pivot point, 'the centre of the animal man, where lies the line of demarcation which separates the mortal man from the immortal entity. (See Manas above.)	Kāma, the motivating principle without Prāna (as the motor principle) would be inert. As the wind fans the flames, so the vital breath Prāna wakes the kamic germs to life; it makes all desires vital and living. Note that Kāma is intrinsically neither 'good' nor 'evil' and the manner in which desires are used makes them either a blessing or a curse.
5. *Prāna* the Life principle	Life principle, from the prepositional prefix *pra-* 'before', and a verb *an-* 'to live', 'to breathe', 'to blow'. Similar Terms: Life-force, vital breath, vital current, life-current, vital fluid, vital airs, vital winds; the *chi* of the Chinese; *fu* of the Japanese.	The psycho-electrical field, or veil manifesting in the individual as vitality.	The vital principle, or life-force that pervades and animates the Physical body. It is necessary (only) to the Physical body and Linga-sarīra (see below), to Kāma and to all mental functions which operate through, and are limited to, the physical brain, namely, the Lower manas.	At the moment of physical dissolution (death) the 'life-atoms' of the *Prāna* (the psycho-electrical field) immediately return to the pranic reservoirs of the planet—their source.
6. *Linga-sarīra* the Etheric double	Model body, from *Linga* 'model', 'pattern', 'emblem', 'template'; and *sarīra* 'form', 'body', derived from the verb-root, *srī* 'to moulder', 'dissolve', 'to waste away'. The term thus signifying impermanence. Similar Terms: double of man, astral body, astral double, etheric vehicle, phantom body; the *doppelgänger* of the Germans; the *eidolon* of the Greeks.	The Model body that is impermanent and wastes away.	The plethora of more or less similar terms for the Linga-sarīra are all suggestive of the fact that this Model body is more ethereal than the Physical body and is in fact the model, or template around which the Physical body is builded. Just as a photographic negative is a prerequisite in order to develop positive prints from it, the Physical body needs the prior existence of the Model body—its 'negative'—upon which to pattern itself.	The Model body is of an electro-magnetic nature and remains in close proximity to the Physical body. The real organs for the sense perceptions are centred in the Linga-sarīra from which they are *transmitted* to the sense terminators in the Physical body.
7. *Sthūla-sarīra*, or *Rūpa* the Physical body	Physical body, from *sthūla* 'coarse', 'gross', 'unrefined', 'heavy', 'bulky', therefore differentiated and conditioned matter; and *sarīra* 'the form which disintegrates', hence the outward aspect suggesting impermanence as with the *Linga-sarīra*.	*Sthūla* alludes to a large conveyor for innumerable tiny 'lives'—which the cells of the body actually are. Hence, 'the bulky form which wastes away' would be a good definition of Sthūla-sarīra, the physical compound.	Man's Physical body serves as the vehicle of all his other principles and aspects during life. In another sense, 'body' is a collective term used to denote the lowest constituent of which man is composed and it is sometimes, loosely, classified as his seventh principle. Since it provides the vehicle for all other principles (as enumerated above) for man's terrestrial existence, it therefore forms the basis for the integration of the six principles, without which, *at our present stage of evolution*, man would be unable to function on Earth.	The body is built up of cosmic elements, themselves formed of living atomic entities. Even though it feels real enough to us (never more so than when we suffer physically), yet, it is in fact the most *unreal* thing in our make-up, because so changeable and transitory. Note that the body is never to be despised or neglected. Depending on how it is used, it becomes either the 'temple', or the 'tomb' of the Divine—Atma.

it is important to bear in mind that during earthly life man in his innermost self is a unified spiritual being clothed in mortal vestures, as described in this Chapter and affirmed by the three quotes from the great spiritual traditions of the East and the West.

There is a natural body, and there is a spiritual body.

I CORINTHIANS[29]

The transfer of the consciousness from a lower vehicle into a higher is part of the great creative and evolutionary process.

PATANJALI[30]

Call it by any name, God, Self, the Heart, or the Seat of Consciousness, it is all the same. The point to be grasped is this, that Heart means the very core of one's being, the centre, without which there is nothing whatever.

BHAGAVAN ŚRĪ RAMANA MAHARSHI[31]

NOTES

1   *The Spiritual Teaching of Ramana Maharshi*, foreword by C. G. Jung (Boston and London: Shambhala Dragon Editions, 1988), 90.

2   *SD*-II, 'Stanza X: The History of the Fourth Race', 241.

3   P. D. Mehta, *The Heart of Religion* (UK: Compton Russell Element, 1976), 106.

4   *KT*, 'The Septenary Nature of Man', 92. Note that Blavatsky uses the terms *Ātma* and *Ātman* entirely synonymously (see *TSGLOSS*, 43). This reference correctly pertains to Ātma as quoted.

5   *KT*, 'On Individuality and Personality', 135. This reference also pertains to Ātma as quoted.

6   *SD*-I, 'Introduction', xix.

7   *TSGLOSS*, 202.

8   *SD*-II, 'Stanza III: Attempts to Create Man: Man, a God in Animal Form', 81. In this quotation, Blavatsky also states, regarding man and animal, that their 'Monads (or Jivas) are fundamentally identical'. However in absolutely no way should this be interpreted as meaning that man is fundamentally *just* an animal. Indeed, as the sub-section of Stanza III clearly states, Man is intrinsically a god, but in animal form.

9   *KT*, 'On Individuality and Personality', 135.

10 *KT*, 'The Septenary Nature of Man', 91.

11 *ibid.*

12 *CW*-XII. 'Instruction No. V', 707.

13 *TSGLOSS*, 170.

14 Napoleon Hill, *Think and Grow Rich* (1st edn, Meriden Connecticut: The Ralston Society, 1937), 97.

15 Kahlil Gibran, *The Prophet*, introd. John Baldock (London: Arcturus, 2018), 69.

16 *TSGLOSS*, 171.

17 *SD*-II, 'The Mysteries of the Hebdomad', 593.

18 G. de Purucker, *Occult Glossary* (Pasadena, California: Theosophical University Press, 1996), 131.

19 *SD*-I, 'An Attack on the Scientific Theory of Force by a Man of Science', 526 n.

20 *SD*-II, 'The Mysteries of The Hebdomad', 593.

21 *SD*-II, 'On the Archaic Stanzas, and the Four Prehistoric Continents', 1.

22 *KT*, 'The Septenary Nature of Man', 91.

23 *CW*-XIV, 'The Zohar on Creation and the Elohim', 209 n.

24 Geoffrey Barborka, *The Divine Plan* (2nd edn, rev. and enl., Adyar, Madras: Theosophical Publishing House, 1964; repr. 1980), 192.

25 *SD*-II, 'The Mysteries of the Hebdomad', 593.

26 *NPB*-1, *Perspectives*, 'The Body', ⌐ 3, 53.

27 *NPB*-4, Part 2: *The Body*, Exordium, 2.

28 Geoffrey Barborka, *The Divine Plan*, 185.

29 1 Corinthians 15:44 (King James Version).

30 Translation given in Alice A. Bailey, *The Light of the Soul: Yoga Sutras of Patanjali* (New York: Lucis Publishing, 1927), Book IV, Sutra 2.

31 *The Spiritual Teaching of Ramana Maharshi*, 91.

3 The Occult Nature of Man – How Man Functions

Man has been given not only a physical body and an ego that represents the desires of that body in the realm of the mind, but also the latent consciousness of something much greater and sublime. Such is Allah's Wisdom that these forces are caused to exist with us all, but according to our choice or will one side or the other may establish its supremacy.

AL-HAQQANI[1]

SYNOPSIS
Chapter 3 concerns man's nature: man, as process, that is, how he acts and is energized—the correlate of his constitution. *Soul* is a word that is used so loosely in everyday speech that its meaning is stretched and distorted out of all proportion. Accordingly, its meaning is precisely explained at the opening. This is indispensable for an understanding of what follows: the dual, triple, and quintuple nature of man, before the detailed exposition of the septenary nature ranging from the outer physical to the inner spiritual. As before, the question of terminology is fully addressed and the way clarity may be injected into a mass of obscure jargon, in various tongues, from diverse spiritual traditions is suggested. It is again stressed that man is an organic unity and the various subdivisions are not discrete functional layers, but aspects of his being functioning at different levels. This Chapter also has a detailed diagram and tabular summary. The next logical enquiry is about the vehicles, or subtle bodies, through which man's consciousness expresses.

KEY WORDS: individuality, personality, sheath, veil, carrier, soul, monad, mind, astral, ego, causal

Readers are requested to refer to the opening of the previous Chapter on page 16 explaining the use of upper and lower case letters for key terms pertaining to the classification of the Principles of Man.

T his Chapter comprises an in-depth description of the second facet of man's composition according to divine law: his 'occult physiology', namely, how he functions and acts as a direct outcome of his occult anatomy, as described in the previous Chapter. The need to draw a distinction between man's constitution (system/structure) and his nature (process/function) was stressed in Chapter 1 with an example to help grasp the underlying difference. It was pointed out that for anything to function there must be at least two principles involved to actuate such functioning, at any level: a superior, positive, and active principle which acts; and an inferior,[i] negative, and passive principle which provides the means by which such action can occur—its vehicle,

Action requires at least two principles: one active, the other passive

---

i 'Inferior' meant only in the sense of more material and so on a lower level than the active principle in question. This is relativity, in the occult sense.

carrier, or channel. This is intuitively obvious. A literal example would be the flow of water in a pipe (action) requiring both the water flow (active principle) and the pipe (passive principle). However, as will shortly become clear, the esoteric doctrine takes this idea much further with a finesse and attention to detail that completely overturns the popular notion that such doctrines abound in vague concepts and woolly generalities—the usual taunt levelled by those who have never bothered to grasp its underlying fundamentals.[ii]

Preliminary Considerations – The Meaning of Kośa, Upādhi, Vāhana, and Soul

It is important to throw light on the subtle differences in meaning of four closely related terms that figure strongly in our exposition on the nature of man.

Kośa – A Sheath

Kośa is a term used in the Vedānta philosophy meaning a 'sheath', the various principles regarded as sheaths, or coverings. The Vedantins accept five kośas, and they are often visualised as the layers of an onion. As the skins of an onion enwrap the core, so the five kośas 'cover' the Divine Self, *Ātma*. However, kośas as 'onion skins' is purely a metaphor standing for *aspects* and *states* of consciousness of the one man—not as separate layers that can be peeled away (as stressed in Chapter 1 on page 10).

Kośa: what it means

The first sheath is *Annamaya-kośa* which means literally, the 'sheath (kośa) built of food (*anna*), which is illusory (*maya*)'. This is of course the *Sthūla-śarīra*, or the Physical body understood as the sheath of the Self, so named from the fact that it is nourished by food, etc., and presents a temporary, hence illusory (*māyāvic*) appearance, because mortal. Living through this layer humans identify themselves with physicality.

The remaining four sheaths are elaborated in Chapter 8, together with the correspondences between the Vedānta philosophy and the septenary constitution.

Upādhi and Vāhana

A mark of the subtlety and sophistication of Indian metaphysics is the choice of words to provide the contrast between structural, or constitutional features, and active, or functional aspects. Hence, what follows is not to indulge in philological pedagogy, still less hair-splitting taxonomy, for its own sake. No one would accuse a physicist of pedantry for defining precisely words like energy, force, and power in the context of a problem in Newtonian mechanics, even though such words may be used freely and interchangeably in everyday speech. In similar vein, in presenting man's nature, we are dealing with an extremely complex subject regarding which the esoteric sciences alone can convey a subtlety and an inner depth of understanding. But this can only be gleaned by assiduous attention to the precise shades of meaning of the terminology used—terminology which, let us be clear, has been evolved by the greatest minds (from every world culture and

Meticulous terminology is indispensable

---

ii But it should not surprise us since empty vessels tend to make the most noise.

religion) who have grappled with the problem of expressing sublime precepts through the limitations of words.

Upādhi – A Base

Upādhi means a base, or deposition, derived from the Sanskrit *upa*, a prepositional prefix signifying 'direction towards', 'near', 'upon'; and *adha* 'to place on', 'to deposit upon'. It therefore signifies literally, 'standing in the place of', that which stands forth as a substitute, an appearance, a guise, a veil, a bearer of something less material than itself.

For example, light could not contact the physical plane without its upādhi—ether. Of course, it is well known that modern physics has discarded the ether as the medium of light transmission following the Michelson-Morley experiment of 1887 and Einstein's Special Relativity theory. However, in 1898, eleven years later, the great English chemist and physicist Sir William Crookes OM PRS (1832–1919) had this to say about the ether in his inaugural address as President of the British Association for the Advancement of Science: 'It is shown that ether vibrations have powers and attributes abundantly equal to any demand—even to the transmission of thought. It is supposed by some physiologists that the essential cells of nerves do not actually touch, but are separated by a narrow gap which widens in sleep while it narrows almost to extinction during mental activity. […] The structure of nerve and brain being similar, it is conceivable there may be present masses of such nerve coherers in the brain whose special function it may be to receive impulses brought from without through the connecting sequence of ether waves of appropriate order of magnitude.' Arguing along similar lines, Crookes stated, 'Confirmation of telepathic phenomena is afforded by many converging experiments […].'[2] The ether is immensely significant from the standpoint of occult science, as Crookes realized. That the famous Michelson-Morley experiment is supposed to have provided the incontrovertible evidence about the non-existence of the ether is a maxim of mainstream physics.

Ether and light as examples of upādhi

But the matter is not that simple. Appendix II-A summarizes this revolutionary period in the history of physics towards the end of the nineteenth century. With copious references to academic papers, it is argued that there is a substantial body of evidence from numerous, alternative ether-drift experiments, also cited in divers academic journals, to demonstrate the existence of ether. But these results have been suppressed by a similar sort of 'knowledge filtration', as described in Volume I, Chapter 4, page 115 et seq., to defend favoured theories upheld by politically powerful scientists.

Further 'down the scale', physical light from, say, a cinema projector could not manifest the visible pictures without another upādhi—the screen upon which the light is 'deposited'. The screen is not the cause of the pictures, nor is the ether the cause of light. The one and only reality, in this instance, is the light which, however, can only contact the physical world and manifest pictures through two upādhis. It becomes clear that at any level: (*a*) the upādhi is more material than that for which it is a bearer; (*b*) the upādhi partakes of the cause which produces it; and (*c*) no amount of changes to the upādhi can affect its cause, only the manner in which the latter presents itself (e.g. the quality of the screen affects the clarity of the pictures, but not the cause of the pictures, or stated differently, the light itself is quite unaffected by the quality of what it is deposited upon—the screen).

Blavatsky clarifies the term: 'Upādhi means that through which a force acts. The word "vehicle" is sometimes used to convey the same idea [but see below]. If [on any plane] "force" be regarded as acting, "matter" is the upādhi through which it acts. Thus the Lower Manas is the upādhi through which the Higher [Manas] can work; the Liṅga-Śarīra is the upādhi through which Prāṇa can work. The Sthūla-Śarīra is the upādhi for all principles acting on the physical plane.'[3] It therefore stands to reason that, at any level, the upādhi is the bearer, or carrier of something less material than itself.

The above quote highlights the importance of refining our vehicles of expression. For example, an imperfect body would present a hindrance to the higher impulses seeking their expression on the physical plane; a deficient brain would inadequately capture and mirror the subtleties of the intuitions playing upon it from the mind. This statement could, therefore, be understood to mean, quite literally, that brain is the upādhi of mind.

It will be shown later that man may be considered as composed of three *essential* upādhis upon which his entire nature revolves.

Vāhana – A Carrier

Vāhana means a carrier, or vehicle, derived from the Sanskrit *vah*, the verbal root meaning 'to bear', 'to carry'. It therefore signifies 'the bearer', 'the carrier', hence 'the vehicle' (as the word is generally rendered).

Insofar as an upādhi acts as a carrier, it functions as a vāhana. Vāhana refers to the way an upādhi functions. Upādhi refers to a system, vāhana to its function. Vāhana, therefore means the vehicle of something which enables it to manifest itself on a plane hierarchically lower (inferior) than its own plane. For example, an electric wire can be regarded as the vāhana of the electric current, but without a current the wire is not a vāhana, but an upādhi. In the previous example, the screen, the upādhi of light from the projector, is the vāhana or 'carrier' of the moving pictures 'deposited' upon it. Thus, generally speaking, the vāhana of man is his body, albeit man's constitution comprises a number of vehicles, or vāhanas, each one pertaining to its own plane to enable the Inner man, the manifesting spiritual being, expression and function at that level.

Vāhana is the dynamic counterpart of *upādhi*

In summary, upādhi and vāhana are, quite clearly, closely related terms. While they both convey a similar essential meaning, upādhi refers to an entity in its systemic aspect—what it *is*, and vāhana refers to the functional aspect—how it *acts*. To repeat, a system can only act according to, and by virtue of, what it *is*. Whereas upādhi implies a static quality in relation to man's constitution, vāhana conveys a dynamic meaning in relation to man's nature. Where is the place of soul in all this?

Soul – A Conveyor

'Soul' is a very broad term admitting of a wide interpretation and therefore a great deal of confusion and misunderstanding has arisen. The Recapitulation to Volume I briefly explained its rationale and role. Thus, the key meaning is that of a conveyor, or vehicle, in a general sense, whereas vāhana refers to the specific vehicle in which an entity, at any level, is working out its destiny. In reference to man, soul is regarded as the intermediary 'part'—hence vehicle, or conveyor—between the spirit, which is immortal and deathless on the one hand, and on the other hand, the body, which is entirely mortal. The soul is therefore the intermediate part of the human constitution, but intermediate at whatever level where a higher principle needs a vehicle to act as a conveyor for its expression on a lower principle. A further analogy with electricity generation would be apposite.

Soul: its generic meaning as vehicle, transformer, and reflector

Transformers are the necessary intermediaries for stepping down the high voltage electricity generated at the power station to domestic consumers. Soul is the *generic* term, in this simile, for the transformer stations that convey electricity (the divine 'current') from the generating station (Ātma) to domestic consumers (the Physical body). But just as the entire electrical distribution from the power station source to the end consumer cannot be achieved by just one transformer—several are needed for a graded 'step down' from the highest voltage to the lowest—so also, soul functions at different levels to 'step down' the 'spiritual voltage' of Ātma to the lower level required by physical man. The 'transformer stations', acting as vāhanas, are three in number: (*a*) the *Spiritual Soul*; (*b*) the *Human Soul*; and (*c*) and the *Animal soul* as we shall see as we proceed along our journey of discovery about the nature of man and his vehicles of consciousness.[iii]

In another, and equally correct sense, soul may be regarded as the reflection of the spirit. Using the simile of a fraction of sunlight caught by a mirror and beamed downwards to Earth, a portion of the spiritual nature is reflected into the Physical body. As the quality of the image on Earth will depend on the size of the mirror and how clean or dusty it is, so also—to follow our simile—physical man will display the attributes of his soul.

The Dual Nature of Man

Table II-5 on page 40 is a diagrammatic representation of the Principles of Man from the standpoint of his functioning. It is drawn so as to be compatible with the bottom half of Table II-2 in Chapter 1 (page 13) which was devised in order to illustrate overriding principles by way of a simple example. As with Table II-3 (page 21) and its amplified version in Table II-4, page 31, it is important for the reader to consult Table II-5 throughout the remainder of this Chapter.

The dual nature of man, shown in the second column of Table II-5, corresponds to the distinction in his constitution between his Individuality and his personality. Man therefore evinces a dual functioning pertaining to his spiritual nature, and his animal nature.

The Triple Nature of Man

The triple nature of man corresponds to the distinction in his constitution between his spirit, soul, and body. Man therefore evinces a triple functioning pertaining to his spiritual nature, his soul nature, and his physical nature.

Significance of dual, triple, and quintuple aspects of man

The third column of Table II-5 explains what is meant by 'psychic'—for many, an uncomfortable term, as it is invariably misunderstood and therefore tends to be associated with dark practices. Simply stated, it is the wide interface between the spiritual realm (the abode

---

iii This analogy is further developed and illustrated in the Coda.

of the spirit) and the material realm (the abode of the body). Being an interface, the psychic realms therefore partake of *both* spirit at the upper pole and body at the lower pole (see also the brief explanation given in the Recapitulation of Volume I on page 324 about this interface). The psychic realms, or psychic worlds, are therefore the abode of the soul considered in the generic sense. The level of the psychic world inhabited depends entirely on the grade of soul quality, i.e., whether gravitating 'down' to extreme materiality (*Anoia*) or aspiring 'upwards' towards sublime spirituality (*Nous*)—see again the Recapitulation of Volume I for Plato's account on the dual choice of the soul.

As we shall see, the above is crucially important for understanding the after-death states.

The Quintuple Nature of Man

The fourth column of Table II-5 overleaf shows that man, always a whole being, can yet be considered as operating in five ways: The Divine, The Spiritual, The Intellectual (or Mental), The Astral, and The Physical. Braces are utilized to indicate how these are linked together; the lower part of the superior category (at any level) overlapping with the higher part of the inferior category. For example, The Spiritual could not function without The Mental (refer to the earlier explanation of why two principles are required to actualize functioning).

The Septenary Nature of Man

The justification and rationale of the septenary classification was explained in the previous Chapter. Accordingly, the complete, sevenfold nature of man's functioning principles is shown in the fifth column of Table II-5 in a hyphenated manner in order to reinforce the idea that the principles so joined function together (for the reasons just explained). The meaning and significance of the Sanskrit terms are given in the column alongside. The functioning principles act through their respective centres of consciousness using their associated vehicles of consciousness. This is explained in the next section where the implication of the terms 'Ego' and 'Self', as used in esotericism, will become clear. What follows is a description of the paired functioning principles and their significance.

THE DIVINE

1. Ātma – the Divine Self, or Monadic Essence with its radiation –
   Hiraṇyagarbha, the Radiant Essence[4]

   Ātma is referred to as the Divine Self, otherwise known as the 'Monadic Essence'. As explained in regard to man's constitution in the previous Chapter, it is man's universal and divine principle, inseparable from its source as the sunbeam is from the sunlight. Hiraṇyagarbha is the Sanskrit word for 'golden egg', or 'golden womb'. Thus, the term best expresses the idea of a 'seed of the universe'. Esoterically it is the luminous 'fire mist', or ethereal substance from which the universe was formed. (One can discern here a faint correspondence between the esoteric teaching and modern cosmogony which also speaks of the fire mist—but obviously not in those terms—and the 'primeval atom'.) In the human being, Hiraṇyagarbha constitutes the radiant essence of Ātma.

Table II-5 The *Nature of Man* – How He Functions: Egoic Centres and Vehicles of Consciousness

Dual Nature	Triple Nature	Quintuple Nature	Septenary Nature — Functioning Principles	Septenary Nature — English Meaning of Sanskrit Terms and their Significance	Egoic Centres of Consciousness	Corresponding Vehicles of Consciousness
Individuality — The Spiritual Being	Spirit — *The Spiritual Realm*	The Divine	*Ātman* / *Hiraṇyagarbha*	the Monadic Essence with its Radiation – the Universal Self in a particular point the Radiant Essence.	*Ātma*, the Divine (Higher) Self in man	Auric Egg from pure *Ākāśa*, the source and basis of all other vehicles or 'bodies'.
		The Spiritual	*Ātma-Buddhi*	the Monad – being the Spiritual Intelligence, and the vehicle which allows Ātma to manifest on lower planes.		
	Soul — *The Psychic Realms* spanning: - the highest, bordering on the plane of spirituality, to - the lowest, touching the plane of materiality	The Intellectual, or Mental	*Buddhi-Manas*	Higher Manas, or the Higher Mind – the mental principle which is 'higher' simply because it functions in a direction faced 'upwards' to merge with Buddhi. Hence, the Intuitive Mind, or enlightened knowledge, the 'heaven-aspiring', inward-turned, contemplative mind.	Spiritual (Divine) Ego	Causal, or Karmic Body. This becomes the Devachanic Ego (*Manas-Taijasi*) after the 'second death', i.e., upon disintegration of the *Kāma-rūpa*.
			Manas-Manas	the Mind in itself, i.e., intelligence aspect as pure intellectual knowledge – the mental principle *per se*. It is either 'the Higher Mind' or 'the Lower mind' simply depending on whether it functions in a direction which is faced 'upwards' or 'downwards' (see Table II-3).	Higher, or Inner Ego	*Antahkaraṇa* – the bridge between the Personal ego and the Higher Ego, corresponding to the animal and spiritual natures
		The Astral	*Manas-kāma* or *Kāma-manas*	Lower manas, or the Lower mind – the mental principle which is 'lower' simply because it functions in a direction faced 'downwards' to merge with Kāma. Hence, desire-driven and desire-conditioned mind.		*Māyāvi-rūpa* – Kāma-rūpa after death from the dregs of the māyāvi-rūpa.
			Prāṇa-Liṅga-śarīra	the Life principle and the Etheric double, or Model body, as its vehicle.	Lower, or Personal ego	
Personality — The Animal Man		The Physical	*Kāma-Prāṇa-Sthūla-śarīra*	the Etheric double and the Life principle directly actuating the dense Physical body.	The Mortal vesture — Lower Quaternary – the 'four walls of the house' in which the Immortal man lives	Astral body, only a vehicle of consciousness under rare and abnormal circumstances.
	Physical body — *The Physical Realm*		*Prāṇa-Liṅga-śarīra-Sthūla-śarīra*	the substance of the Physical body formed over the Model body by the action of the Life principle.		Physical body, the vehicle of normal waking consciousness.

MAN AS A UNIFIED ENERGY-ENTITY, OR BEING

However, Ātma cannot function on any plane other than its own. This would be like expecting electricity from a power station to illuminate our homes without the need of any transforming stations, to use our previous analogy. So Ātma needs an upādhi in order to manifest on planes lower than Itself.

THE DIVINE–SPIRITUAL, THE MONAD

Divine and spiritual functioning principles

2. *Ātma-Buddhi* – the Monad

Ātma 'throws out of itself', or 'deposits' *Buddhi* as its upādhi in order to 'descend' and manifest ultimately on the physical plane. Put another way, in order to descend towards and manifest (act) on the physical plane, the vāhana brought about by the unrolling of Ātma is Buddhi. *Ātma-Buddhi* is referred to as the Upper Duad, or, since they really comprise a single Unit, as 'the Monad'. Ātma is also known as the Monadic Essence, the term being most suggestive of the fact that 'distillation' of the Monad would release Ātma—its essence. (The doctrine of the Monad is one of the most resplendent, but elusive in occultism. Space does not permit a full exposition in this work and a cursory account would do no justice to a sublime doctrine. Nonetheless, readers are urged to consult the various occult sources cited in this work for their own research.)

But Ātma-Buddhi cannot function alone, other than at its own level; it also needs an upādhi in order to function on the terrestrial plane.

THE SPIRITUAL–MENTAL

3. *Buddhi-Manas*

> Buddhi alone could not be called a 'Causal Body', but becomes so in conjunction with Manas, the incarnating Entity or EGO [Higher Ego—see the last column of Table II-5].
> H. P. Blavatsky[5]

The vāhana, brought about by the unrolling of Buddhi, is *Manas*. *Buddhi-Manas* is known as Higher Manas, or the Higher Mind. It represents that faculty in man of intuition, nous, or enlightened knowledge, being that quality of *direct* knowledge without the intermediary of intellection. However, even Higher Manas cannot function on the terrestrial plane without its upādhi.

THE MENTAL: HIGHER MANAS

Spiritual, mental, and astral functioning principles

4. *Manas-Manas*

The hyphenated term *Manas-Manas* is used to stress the Manas aspect of the Mind Principle of man, namely, pure mind, without the overshadowing light of Buddhi 'from above', or the conditioning influence of *Kāma* 'from below'. It represents that faculty in man which is commonly known as pure intellect, or knowledge for its own sake.

THE ASTRAL–MENTAL: LOWER MANAS

5. *Kāma-manas*

The vāhana, brought about by the unrolling of the Manas principle, is the *Kāma* principle. *Kāma-manas* is known as Lower manas, or the Lower mind. This term is used to emphasize the Desire principle in conjunction with the Mind Principle, i.e., knowledge in conjunction with, and conditioned by, desire.

For convenience the three categories of the Mind Principle are summarized in Table II-6 below.

Table II-6   The Mind Principle – its Three Categories

Mind can function in three ways

Mind Principle		Mental Quality Displayed
Sanskrit Term	*English Similar Term*	
Buddhi-Manas	the Higher Mind	Intuition, enlightened knowledge
Manas-Manas	the Mind-in-itself	Intellectual, 'book-knowledge'
Manas-kāma or Kāma-manas	the Lower mind	Knowledge commanding desire or Desire-conditioned knowledge

Manas and kāma unite the Individuality and the personality

Kāma-manas is the pivot which unites the Higher immortal and Lower mortal aspects of man's being and this is borne out in man's constitution (as explained in Chapter 2) and in his nature. Kāma-manas in conjunction with the astral and physical kośas (sheaths) fashions the personality—often termed the *false* personality because it lasts for a single lifetime on Earth, during which time it clouds the light of the Reincarnating Ego during such terrestrial life. It is for this reason that the union of Manas and Kāma is referred to as the Middle Duad, as previously noted (Table II-3, page 21). If, in the further interests of clarity, the writer were permitted to be pedantic, then he would recommend: when the mind can command and harness the desire nature, the Duad be written as 'Manas-kāma'; but when desires run amok and overwhelm the mind—as is the case with the mass of humanity—then the term 'Kāma-manas' is a better representation of the Duad. The three faculties of the Lower mind are imagination, memory, and reason. They are summarized in Chapter 4 and in detail in Chapter 8 of Volume III.

However, even Lower manas cannot function on the terrestrial plane without an appropriate sheath (kośa).

THE ASTRAL

6. (a) Prāṇa–Liṅga-śarīra

The sheath of the Kāma-manas principle is the *Prāṇa–Liṅga-śarīra* principle. However, the latter also requires a sheath in order to 'descend' and function on the terrestrial plane.

THE ASTRAL–PHYSICAL

Astral and physical functioning principles

6. (b) Kāma–Prāṇa–Sthūla-śarīra

The sheath of the Prāṇa–Liṅga-śarīra principle is *Kāma–Prāṇa–Sthūla-śarīra*, which, *inter alia*, is to do with the blood, inasmuch as the subtle Prāṇa taken in by breathing is carried by the blood.[6] However this principle also needs a sheath to function on the terrestrial plane.

THE PHYSICAL

7. *Prāṇa–Liṅga-śarīra–Sthūla-śarīra*

The sheath of Kāma–Prāṇa–Sthūla-śarīra is *Prāṇa–Liṅga-śarīra–Sthūla-śarīra*. Having now contacted the physical plane, any question of another sheath obviously does not apply—the Physical body being the final kośa.

This completes our enquiry into the principles of man from the standpoint of his functioning.

The Boundaries of Man – How He is Held Together

Our enquiry into the nature of man has of necessity, and for analytical purposes of description, had to be described in a linear sequential fashion. Despite the complexities and subtleties of all the various subdivisions of man's nature, the harmony of the whole system is maintained by two factors: (*a*) two extremities that demarcate the range of human possibilities; and (*b*) three 'platforms' that provide dynamic stability to the human system. What follows is therefore a summation of the fundamentals expounded at length in this Chapter.

Apex and Foundation – Supporting Structure Demarcating Boundaries

'Whether a man—material, ethereal, and spiritual [body, soul, and spirit]—is for the clearer comprehension of his (broadly-speaking) triple nature, divided into groups according to one or other system', states Blavatsky, 'the foundation and the apex of that division will always be the same.'[7] Accordingly, the foundation is man's Physical body; the apex is the common spiritual essence in all mankind. The human being is a divine musical instrument and these are the two 'anchor points'—the physical and the spiritual—across which the whole human being is strung.

Three Principal Upādhis – Demarcating States of Consciousness

The above exposition has placed considerable importance on the role of the upādhi— the base through which a force acts at any level or plane. As Blavatsky further elucidates:

> There being only three Upādhis (bases) in man, any number of Kośas (sheaths) and their aspects may be built on these without destroying the harmony of the whole. Thus, while the Esoteric System accepts the septenary division, the Vedāntic classification gives five Kośas, and the Tāraka Rāja Yoga simplifies them into four—the three Upādhis synthesized by the highest principle, Ātman.[8]

Notwithstanding the importance of the Physical body, these three principal upādhis are, of course, Buddhi, Manas, and Kāma—the last being the upādhi necessary to connect the first two with the terrestrial plane. (The Prāṇa–Liṅga-śarīra, Kāma–Prāṇa–Sthūla-śarīra, and Prāṇa–Liṅga-śarīra–Sthūla-śarīra are not upādhis in the strict sense, but rather, sheaths.)

Now the logical deduction of the above two quotations is this: if man can be classified in any number of ways, provided that the occult rules are obeyed—namely, the foundation

Man can be classified in different ways depending on what questions are asked

and apex of the system, and the three upādhis are maintained—then, to adopt a didactic and rigid attitude towards any one system of classifying man is nothing but obtuse. 'Let us [again] remember we are dealing with *Forces* and *States* of Consciousness, and not with water-tight compartments.'[9] There are, therefore, entirely reasonable grounds for classifying man in various ways as indeed was Blavatsky's practice, albeit, broadly speaking, in one system. Later-generation Theosophists like Besant, Leadbeater, and Jinarâjadâsa used different systems. Much time and energy has been wasted in the Theosophical Society on tedious squabbling over what is the most 'authentic' classification system. Such feuds are born of an unintelligent, bookish attitude, instead of a real understanding of the reasons and significance of the different ways of classifying man (see Chapter 1 on page 10 et seq.). Chapter 8 compares and corroborates these different classifications, along with several other systems, including those of Rudolf Steiner and the American transpersonal psychologist Ken Wilber (*b.*1949), and shows their overall congruence and consistency.

Table II-7 summarizes the importance of man's three upādhis that, so to say, actuate his spiritual, human, and animal natures.

Table II-7   The Three Upādhis – their Significance

Upādhi	Principle	functioning as a vehicle for	to enable	Correlation with
First upādhi	Buddhi	the Spiritual Soul (Spirit)*, i.e., the Atmic vehicle	Ātma, the Divine nature, to manifest on lower planes	Heart
Second upādhi	Manas	the Human (thinking) Soul, or Human Ego	Ātma-Buddhi, the Monad, to 'flow down' towards and contact the lower planes	Brain
Third upādhi	Kāma in union with Lower manas	the terrestrial, or Animal soul	Ātma-Buddhi-Manas as the Individuality working through its terrestrial personality	Generative organs

* Although 'Spirit' and 'Spiritual Soul' are both to be found in Theosophical literature, the latter term is much preferred since it conveys a more precise meaning.

Physical body and organs function by virtue of divine forces

This table also shows the all-important correlations of man's spiritual, human, and animal natures with the organs of the human body. *It cannot be stressed too strongly that the brain is only one of three principal consciousness-centres (the other two being the generative system and the heart which is primary, as explained in Chapter 3 of Volume III.)* Neurocardiology (also described in Chapter 3 of Volume III) is still in its infancy, with the vast majority of neuroscientists firmly wedded to the unwarranted assumption that the brain *generates* consciousness (notwithstanding the forthright denial of such a simplistic viewpoint by William James, as summarized in Chapter 6 of Volume I). Hence, the current drive in mainstream neuroscience to fathom the secrets of consciousness by further research into brain waves, etc., under various conditions, such as the influence of psychedelic drugs. However, to the degree that modern neuroscience chooses to ignore the heart, regarding it as no more than a biological pump—its efforts to discover the mystery of consciousness will ever be a lost cause self-doomed to the treadmill of interminable research into brain waves and associated cerebral mechanisms leading to a dead-end. This vital topic is expounded in depth in Chapter 9 of Volume III concerning the divine forces in the human body and their correlations with the bodily glands and organs in connection with the awakening of latent faculties and powers of consciousness. Meanwhile, we shall continue to explain the direct relationship between upādhis with souls and Egos; indeed, the three upādhis enable man to function as three Egos, a fact explained below.

Three Souls

As repeatedly emphasized, 'soul' is a generic term conveying the essential meaning of a conveyor, or transformer–vehicle. Man functions through three souls, strictly speaking, three *aspects* of Soul: Spiritual Soul, Human Soul, and terrestrial, or Animal soul (see the final column of Table II-3 on page 21). Of the third aspect, nothing remains after physical death; of the second, only its divine essence, *if left unsoiled* survives;[iv] while the first, in addition to being immortal, becomes *consciously* divine, by virtue of assimilating Higher Manas.[10] The direct relation of the three souls with the upādhis, the corresponding principles, and bodily centres, was summarized in Table II-7 on the previous page.

Distinguishing Ego from Self, and Individuality from Personality

The term 'Ego' is used frequently in esoteric and occult literature. What is its precise connotation? Capitalized and pronounced 'Egg-o', it does not convey the popular notion of exaggerated self-opinion. Ego is a Latin word meaning 'I', or 'Self'. So in esoteric philosophy the Ego is that consciousness in man of 'I am-ness'; or the feeling of 'I-am-ship'. But reverting to our typical man, we must distinguish carefully between (*a*) the simple fact of self-consciousness; and (*b*) the complex thought structure about being a particular person. This is none other than the difference between Individuality and personality, or Higher Ego and Lower (Personal) ego, but the two pairs of terms are not exactly synonymous.

The Individuality of man refers to the simple fact of self-consciousness, the root feeling that 'I am I'. If a man closely examines his own consciousness, he will soon know that this is the pure consciousness expressed in the words 'I am'. This 'I am' is the Self; whereas the Ego is the *cognition* of the 'I am', in other words, 'I am *I*'. It is this bare, subjective 'I am I' consciousness that a man experiences for a fleeting moment upon awakening from sleep, before all his other personal thoughts and memories supervene and later intervene. When this happens he will say 'I am "John Smith" '.

Personality refers to the accumulation of experiences of 'I am John Smith'; whereas the Lower ego is the cognition that 'I am *John Smith*'. But who is John Smith? Is he actually a permanent entity? The name really means a long series of daily experiences strung

---

iv   Divine essence *per se* cannot be soiled. What is probably meant by Blavatsky is that its expression can be soiled by the activities of the Animal soul.

together by the thread of thought as memory, and forming, collectively, what John Smith calls and identifies as 'himself'. But none of these 'experiences' is the true 'I', nor do they give John Smith the feeling that he is himself. Moreover, he forgets that the majority of his daily experiences produce in him the feeling of Egoity only while they last.

Therefore, this bundle of experiences is referred to as the 'false personality'. To reiterate, they are finite and transitory giving man his Lower, or Personal ego—being the cognition of the personality. This should be contrasted with that element in man to which the feeling of 'I am I' is due, namely, the Individuality pertaining to man's Inner, or Higher Ego.

Thus we see that Ego is intrinsically bound up with the Mind Principle, Manas. It is Manas that brings about the feeling of 'I-am-ship' or 'I am such-and-such' at any level. Table II-8 below shows how the Divine Self, Ātma, functions through three Egos: the Spiritual Ego and the two Human Egos just enumerated. To reiterate, the Higher Ego and Lower ego correspond to the Individuality and personality, respectively; whereas the three Egos correspond to the three upādhis of Buddhi, Manas, and Kāma, respectively.

Table II-8 also shows the Egoic centres of consciousness and associated vehicles of consciousness in relation to man's sevenfold functioning principles. This table should be studied alongside Table II-5 on page 40.

Mind is the basis of all experience of self and the world

Table II-8   The Three Types of Ego – their Significance

Type of Ego	Principles	Comprises	After-Death State
The Divine Self, Ātma, expresses through these three Egos:			
Divine (Spiritual) Ego 'I Am'	Buddhi and Manas	The Spiritual Soul in union with the Mind Principle. Without such union it is no Ego at all, but only the vehicle of Ātma.	Immortal and consciously divine
Human Ego — Higher, Inner, or Reincarnating Ego—Immortal 'I am I'	Manas (designated 'Manas-Manas' in Table II-6, page 42 to emphasize Mind *per se*)	The Mind Principle independent of Buddhi, (becoming the Spiritual Ego only when merged with Buddhi*).	Divine essence survives, if left unsoiled
Human Ego — Lower, or Personal ego—mortal 'I am John Smith'	Lower manas and Kāma, with Prāṇa, Liṅga-śarīra, and Sthūla-śarīra	The physical man in conjunction with his Lower self, i.e., the 'false personality', comprising the Lower mind combined with the Desire principle, and operating through the Physical body and its 'double', or Model body.	Nothing survives

*   'No materialist being supposed to have in him *such* [sic] an Ego, however great his intellectual capacities.'[11]

It will readily be appreciated why Manas, the Mind Principle, is the common factor in all three Egos. Because *without Manas there can be no Ego, properly understood*, as Ego is always associated with the feeling of 'I am-ness'. In this regard Thomas Troward's lectures on mental science are a fine, modern exposition of the Mind Principle by a leading exponent of New Thought. He writes a great deal about the significance of 'I Am', or the notion of experiencing oneself as a centre, stating, 'My mind is a centre of Divine operation.'[12] (Refer to Volume I, Chapter 9, pages 300–302 for more details.)

So to continue along these lines, the Buddhi upādhi provides man with a Spiritual Soul, i.e., a spiritual vehicle as a bare fact. But only when Buddhi is merged with Manas as the Spiritual *Ego*, can a man say, 'I AM a *Spiritual Soul*.' In other words, without Manas, or with Manas undeveloped as in an infant, man is not conscious of the fact that he is a spiritual soul—the latter being an abstract principle in him rather than an active cognition of it.

Similarly, the Mind Principle bequeaths man a consciousness of his reincarnating potential, so that he can declare, 'I will reincarnate'. Finally, with Lower manas in union with Kāma, man consciously knows about his animal tendencies and can declare: 'I can behave like an animal (my kamic proclivities), if I so choose to do so (my manasic propensities).' However, note carefully that because a man can behave *like* an animal, does not mean therefore that man *is* an animal. Otherwise an animal could also behave like a man! This vital point has already been made and is elaborated in Chapter 6 where the important difference between man and animal is further explained.

The above brings us to a consideration of man's vehicles of consciousness which fall logically into three groups outlined below and elaborated in the next Chapter.

Egoic Centres and Corresponding Vehicles of Consciousness

The previous two sections have described the functioning principles and their relation to the Mind Principle and corresponding Egoic characteristics of man. The last two columns of Table II-5 on page 40 show the Egoic centres of consciousness and the corresponding vehicles of consciousness through which the functioning principles act. As always, we see the polarity between the active principle and its vehicle, or medium of manifestation; in other words, between spirit (positive) and matter (negative) understood of course, entirely generically. Thus the three vehicles of consciousness are the:

1. Auric Envelope: the source and basis of all other vehicles and bodies as below;

2. Causal, or Karmic Body: the vehicle of consciousness of man's immortal component, the Spiritual Ego in borderless touch with the intermediate Higher Ego, realizing its true abode in higher spiritual realms whence the man is born again, i.e., after disintegration of the Kāma-rūpa (as explained fully in Chapter 5);

Three vehicles of consciousness

3. Mortal vesture: the Lower, or Personal ego being the lowest vehicle of consciousness and comprising: (*a*) the Physical body; (*b*) the Astral body (Etheric double and Prāṇa); and (*c*) the *mayāvi-rūpa*, which is explained in the next Chapter, but is essentially the illusory, subtle body of desire-thought during physical life (ultimately perishable as the *Kāma-rūpa* in the post-mortem state).

In addition to what has already been explained above, further discussion on the import of the above vehicles of consciousness is reserved for the next Chapter.

Antaḥkaraṇa: its vital role

Meanwhile, Table II-5 also mentions *Antaḥkaraṇa* (wrongly spelt as *Antaskaraṇa* by some early Theosophical writers) as a vehicle of consciousness acting as a bridge and umbilical connection between the Personal ego (personality) and the Higher Ego; namely, between the Lower and the Higher Manas. The whole fate of an incarnation and the post-mortem states of man depend on whether this connection between his animal and spiritual natures is maintained and strengthened or weakened and severed. As this is a matter of such vital significance it requires careful explanation. It is hoped that Chapter 5, which deals with death and post-mortem states of consciousness, will go some way towards providing this.

Summary

This concludes the exposition on man's nature—his occult physiology. The principal message is that the dominance of the physical over the spiritual nature (and in many cases the utter stifling of the spiritual by the physical) is the condition in which many people remain throughout the course of their lives. This is understandable in a sense, because the physical nature is more immediate and accessible than the spiritual nature, just as the natural course of water on a hill is to flow downwards. But this need not be so. For those who will to discover the inner world and consciously pursue the uphill path, that 'light upon light' shines ever more brightly so as to fulfil the real purpose of their lives. The physical aspect of man, like the physical world he inhabits, is of minor consequence in this boundless universe (and scientists take great pride in informing us about how their sophisticated astronomical observations reveal what an insignificant speck of dust we are in the grand cosmic scene); but spiritually, man has endless opportunities to attain divine knowledge and wisdom in the realm yet beyond.

The inner life and inner world are more important than outer circumstances

This, the writer suggests, is the meaning behind the extract from the Sufi saint quoted in the epigraph above, clearly elucidating that man has 'the latent consciousness of something much greater and sublime' and not merely 'a physical body and an ego that represents the desires of that body in the realm of the mind.' Crucially, 'these forces are caused to exist with us all, but according to our choice and will, one side or the other may establish its supremacy' (*vide In the Mystic Footsteps of Saints*[13])—and this is none other than the occult teaching on the double nature of Manas, the Mind Principle: Higher Manas or Lower manas.

A summary of this Chapter, in tabular form, is provided in Table II-9 on the next page. It closely follows, and amplifies, the content of Table II-5 on page 40. The next Chapter deals with the three primary vehicles of consciousness through which man lives and has his being. In order to understand this, it is always necessary to keep in mind that man is, in truth, divine consciousness embodied as underlined by our closing quote.

> *The Sun of the Soul is not that Sun in the heavens; it is the Divine Sun by whose light men and angels exist. The Divine Sun has veiled himself in Man.*
> Mawlânâ (Jalāl ad-Dīn Muhammad Rūmī)[14]

Table II-9 The Seven Principles of Man's *Nature* – How Man Functions: Summary Meaning and Key Doctrine (Refer also to Table II-5 on page 40)

Functioning Principle	Essential Function	Operation of Principle
1. *Ātma* the Divine Self, or Monadic Essence – with its radiation – *Hiraṇyagarbha*, the Radiant Essence	Ātman, the Divine Principle, with Ātma, the Divine (Higher) Self, or Monadic Essence—its correspondence in man—as its Centre of Consciousness and the Auric Envelope as its Vehicle of Consciousness; and Hiraṇyagarbha the radiant essence of Ātma.	Ātman, the Divine Principle and its correspondence in man, Ātma the Divine (Higher) Self, or the Monadic Essence. It is the Divine nature in man, (see Table II-5), his universal principle, inseparable from its source as the sunbeam is from the sunlight. But it cannot function on any plane other than its own. This would be like expecting the sunlight to contact our Earth and other celestial bodies directly, without any surrounding atmosphere. So Ātma needs an upādhi, or base, in order to manifest on planes lower than Itself.
2. *Ātma-Buddhi* the Divine-Spiritual: the Monad	The Monad, using the Divine Self as its Centre of Consciousness and the Auric Envelope as its Vehicle of Consciousness.	Ātma 'throws out of itself,' or 'deposits' Buddhi as its upādhi, or base, in order to 'descend' towards the physical plane. Stated otherwise, in order to externalize and manifest (act) on the physical plane, the vāhana brought about by the unrolling of Ātma is Buddhi. Ātma-Buddhi, the second of 'The Divine' and the first of 'The Spiritual' nature is referred to as the 'Upper Duad', or, since they really comprise a single Unit, as the Monad. However, Buddhi cannot function alone; it also needs an upādhi in order to function on Earth.
3. *Buddhi-Manas* the Spiritual–Mental	Buddhi-Manas acting through the Spiritual (Divine) Ego as its Centre of Consciousness, and for its Vehicle of Consciousness the Causal, or Karmic Body during life, which becomes the Devachanic Ego after the 'second' death (i.e., upon the disintegration of the Kāma-rūpa following upon physical death).	The vāhana, or carrier, brought about by the unrolling of Buddhi is Manas. Buddhi-Manas is thus the second of 'The Spiritual' overlapping with the first of 'The Mental, or Intellectual' of man's nature. Buddhi-Manas is known as 'Higher Manas', or the 'Higher Mind'. It represents that faculty in man of intuition, or enlightened knowledge, being that quality of direct knowledge without the intermediary of intellection. However, Higher Manas cannot function on the terrestrial plane without its upādhi.
4. *Manas-Manas* the Intellectual, or Mental: the intelligence aspect	Manas-Manas acting through the Higher, or Inner Ego as its Centre of Consciousness, and for its Vehicle of Consciousness Antahkarana, the bridge between the personal soul and the Spiritual Ego; that is, between Lower and Higher Manas, corresponding to the Animal and the Spiritual natures of man.	The second category of 'The Mental' nature is Manas-Manas. This term is used to stress the Manas aspect of the Mind Principle of man—pure Mind, without the overshadowing light of Buddhi 'from above' or the conditioning influence of Kāma 'from below'. It represents that faculty in man commonly known as 'book-knowledge'—pure knowledge for its own sake. For convenience the three categories of the Mind Principle are summarized below. | Mind Principle		*Mental Quality Displayed*
Sanskrit Term	English Equivalent	
Buddhi-Manas	the Higher Mind	Intuition, enlightened knowledge
Manas-Manas	Mind-in-itself	Intellectual, 'book-knowledge'
Manas-kāma, or Kāma-manas	the Lower mind (see Note)	Desire-conditioned, 'polluted' knowledge, or Desires under the command of the mind | Note: Presented in this fashion to stress that when the mind can command and harness the desires, the Middle Duad is more accurately written as 'Manas-kāma;' but when desires run amok and overwhelm the mind—as is the case with the mass of humanity—then the term 'Kāma-manas' is a better representation of the Duad.
5. *Kāma-manas* the Astral–Mental: the Lower manas	Kāma-manas using the Lower, or personal, part of the Human Ego as its Centre of Consciousness, and for its Vehicle of Consciousness the Māyāvi-rūpa during life, which becomes the Kāma-rūpa after physical death (formed from the dregs of the Māyāvi-rūpa).	Kāma-manas brought about by the unrolling of the Manas principle is the Kāma principle. Kāma-manas is known as the 'Lower manas', or the 'Lower mind'. This term is used to emphasize the Desire principle in conjunction with the Mind Principle, i.e., knowledge in conjunction with, and conditioned by, desire. Kāma-manas (or Manas-kāma as explained above) is the pivot which unites the Higher immortal and Lower mortal aspects of man's being. Kāma-manas in conjunction with the Astral and Physical kośas (sheaths) fashions the personality—often termed the 'false personality' because it lasts for a single lifetime on Earth during which time it clouds the light of the Reincarnating Ego. It is for this reason that the union of Manas and Kāma is referred to as the 'Middle Duad'. However even Lower manas cannot function on the terrestrial plane without an appropriate kośa, or sheath.
6a. Prāṇa–Liṅga-śarīra the Astral: the Life principle and its vehicle	Using the Lower, or Personal ego as its Centre of Consciousness, and the Astral body as its Vehicle of Consciousness (which, in fact, acts as a vehicle only under rare and abnormal circumstances).	The vāhana brought about by the unrolling of the Kāma-manas principle (above) is the Prāṇa–Liṅga-śarīra principle, which also requires a sheath to function on the terrestrial plane.
6b. Kāma–Prāṇa–Sthūla-śarīra the Astral–Physical concerning the blood	Using the Lower, or Personal ego as its Centre of Consciousness, and the Astral body as its Vehicle of Consciousness (which only acts as a vehicle under exceptional circumstances).	The sheath of the Prāṇa–Liṅga-śarīra principle (above) is Kāma–Prāṇa–Sthūla-śarīra, which also needs a sheath to function on the terrestrial plane.
7. Prāṇa–Liṅga-śarīra–Sthūla-śarīra the Physical body. The substance of the body formed over the Etheric double (Model body) by the action of the Life principle.	Using the Lower, or Personal ego as its Centre of Consciousness, and the Physical body as its Vehicle of Consciousness.	The sheath of Kāma–Prāṇa–Sthūla-śarīra (above) is Prāṇa–Liṅga-śarīra–Sthūla-śarīra. The Divine Self (Ātma) having now contacted the physical plane, any question of another sheath obviously does not apply—the Physical body being the final kośa.

NOTES

1   Shaykh Nazim Adil Al-Haqqani, *In the Mystic Footsteps of Saints*, ii (US: Naqshbandi-Haqqani Sufi Order, 2002), 66.

2   'Address by the President, Sir William Crookes, FRS, VPCS', Report of the Sixty-Eighth Meeting of the British Association for the Advancement of Science held at Bristol in September 1898 (London: John Murray, 1899), 31 [online facsimile] <https://www.biodiversitylibrary.org/item/95459#page/153/mode/1up> accessed 31 October 2020. See also: *The British Medical Journal*, 2/1967 (10 September 1898), 733; 'Inaugural Address as President of the British Association for the Advancement of Science (1898)', *Nature*, 58/1506 (8 September 1898), 438; Rebecca Northfield, 'Science of the Supernatural', *The Institution of Engineering and Technology* (October 2016), 71.

3   Henk J. Spierenburg (compiled and annotated), *The Inner Group Teachings of H. P. Blavatsky: to her personal pupils (1890–91)* (rev. and enl. 2nd edn, San Diego, California: Point Loma Publications), 168 n.

4   'Hiraṇyagarbha' is further explained in Geoffrey Barborka, *The Divine Plan* (2nd edn, rev. and enl., Adyar, Madras: Theosophical Publishing House, 1964; repr. 1980), 194.

5   *TSGLOSS*, 74.

6   Yoga International <https://yogainternational.com/article/view/understanding-prana> accessed 24 May 2020.

7   *CW*-XIV, 'The Seven Principles', 386.

8   *ibid*.

9   *CW*-XII, 'Instruction No. IV', 657.

10 Reworded from *KT*, 'On the Various Post-Mortem States', 121–2.

11 *KT*, 'Definite Words for Definite Things', 176.

12 Thomas Troward, *The Dore Lectures on Mental Science* (US: Arc Manor, 2008), 29.

13 Shaykh Nazim Adil Al-Haqqani, *In the Mystic Footsteps of Saints*, 66.

14 Dr Massoud Homayouni, *The Origins of Persian Gnosis*, trans. F. J. Stone (London: Mawlana Centre, 1992), 25.

4 The Three Selves – Man's Three Primary Vehicles of Consciousness

*The Supreme Mystery—the identity and interrelationship of the **Three Selves**—that no one to whom they did not of their own accord reveal themselves has ever secured any satisfactory information regarding either the existence or the purpose of the Order.*

MANLY P. HALL[1]

SYNOPSIS

Chapter 4 deals with the three primary vehicles of consciousness through which man lives, functions, and has his being. These vehicles are described, first the two higher vehicles pertaining to the 'aura', a loose term whose meaning and function is explained in some detail; and then the brain-consciousness of the physical man. The interrelationship between the higher and lower vehicles is outlined. We also discuss how and why the aura of a newly departed person can seemingly materialize in the form of a like appearance of the person during life; and in other cases, materializations seem to emanate from a higher source. Chapters 2 to 4 are a necessary prerequisite before detailing the process of death, and beyond, in the next Chapter.

KEY WORDS: aura, illusory body, occult powers, Higher Mind and Lower mind, Comte de St.-Germain, Peter Deunov, Shaykh Nazim

The vehicles of consciousness described at the close of the previous Chapter on page 47 were shown to fall naturally into the three (generic) spirit–soul–body groupings that were termed the 'Auric Envelope', the 'Causal (Karmic) Body', and the 'Mortal vesture'. These three vehicles of consciousness are also known in the Mystery Teachings as man's 'Three Selves'. As the epigraph implies, the subject is mysterious and profound; hence only the grace of revelation would qualify one to speak of the Selves from direct and personal experience. Nonetheless, it is of considerable profit to précis the accounts of those who have spoken from such inner understanding, which is what this Chapter attempts to do.

The Auric Egg

The Auric Egg is an envelope that is the source and basis of all other vehicles, or bodies of consciousness, that form the human septenary constitution of man from Ātma to the Physical body. It is of an oviform, or egg-shaped appearance (to the spiritual vision of a seer), from whence comes its name. It is not, however, the same as the human aura (as this term is loosely used) which is part, or rather an aspect, of the Auric Egg.

Its 'substance' is drawn from the universally diffused, primordial and pure *Ākāśa*, and for this principal reason the Auric Egg reflects all the thoughts, words, and deeds of man and endures throughout his cycles of reincarnation. As Blavatsky teaches, the Auric Egg is:

1. The preserver of every Karmic record (karma being the universal retributive Law of cause and effect, or Ethical Causation);

2. The storehouse of all the good and bad powers of man, receiving and giving out at his will—at his very thought—every potentiality, which becomes, then and there, an acting potency: this aura being the mirror in which 'sensitives' and clairvoyants sense and perceive the real man, and see him as *he is*, not as he appears;

3. That which furnishes man with his Astral Form (see the last column of Table II-5 on page 40), around which the physical entity models itself, first as a foetus, then as a child and man [adult], the astral growing apace with the human being, so it furnishes him during his life, if an Adept, with his *Māyāvi-rūpa*, or Illusion Body (which is not his *Vital* Astral body); and after death, with his Devachanic Entity and *Kāma-rūpa*, or Body of desire ('the Spook').[2]

As the Auric Egg appertains to highly recondite teachings of occultism and esoteric philosophy, no more need profitably be said in this work. Interested readers should consult the source reference from which the above exposition was taken.

The Causal, or Karmic Body and the Augoeides

> The Spiritual Ego, […]. This is the real Individuality, or the divine man. It is that Ego [acting through its Vehicle], that 'Causal Body,' which overshadows every personality Karma forces it to incarnate into; and [it is] this Ego which is held responsible for all the sins committed through, and in, every new body or personality—the evanescent masks which hide the true Individual through the long series of rebirths.
>
> H. P. Blavatsky[3]

The Causal Body is the primary vehicle of the Spiritual Ego and Higher (Reincarnating) Ego (see the penultimate and final columns of Table II-5, page 40). As the above quotation states, the Causal Body is virtually synonymous with the 'inhabiting' Spiritual Ego, being the union of *Buddhi* with *Manas*. In fact, the term 'Causal Body' is a misnomer (but the best available term in English) since it is no body as such (hence the inverted commas in the quotation by Blavatsky). More technically, in Vedānta it corresponds to both the *Vijñānamaya-kośa* (the Sheath of Intelligence) and *Ānandamaya-kośa* (the Sheath of Bliss),

the latter being the kośa (sheath) next removed from *Ātma* (see Table II-20, page 169 of Chapter 8). In the Tāraka Rāja-Yoga (also shown in Table II-20) it is called the *Kāraṇopādhi*, 'the basis of the Cause', which term is apposite as 'Buddhi', the Spiritual Soul, alone could not function as a 'Causal Body', but does so in conjunction with Manas, the incarnating Entity, or Higher Ego (see Table II-8, page 46), the cause of rebirths under karmic law. For this reason, the Causal Body is also referred to as the Karmic Body.[4] And also, why, strictly speaking, it is the primary vehicle of the Spiritual Ego and Higher Ego (see again the penultimate and final columns of Table II-5) albeit sometimes attributed by Theosophical writers only to the former (but in dealing with human states of such rarified subtlety, it is pointless to indulge in hard and fast definitions or hair-splitting taxonomy).

It is difficult to say much more about this Body since, in the main, humanity is not yet capable of appreciating the inner or higher worlds. What may be said, relative to our plane of perception, is that this vehicle of the Higher (and Divine) Ego is without form or quality; however, on its own plane, and to the perception of the Higher Ego (or a highly advanced person), it does have a form. But the form has no sensory apparatus, since the Higher Ego is not time bound by past-present-future events, so its perception to the Higher Ego is spontaneous in the ever-Present.

Related to the above, in extremely rare circumstances, the Higher Ego seems to appear to, and communicate with, the personal man. Such an appearance is not, strictly speaking, the Higher Ego itself, which is formless, but its projection—the *Augoeides*. The English politician and occult novelist Edward Bulwer Lytton (1803–1873) called this the 'Luminous Self' or 'Higher Ego'. But Occultism supplies a much profounder meaning. It is the luminous, divine *radiation* of the Higher Ego. It may appear formless as a body of light, or even as if in bodily form.[5] As we are informed, it may give warning or advice, but of an utterly impersonal nature not related to the circumstances of the physical life.[6] A modern example might arguably be the claimed visitations of the Madonna to three shepherd children in the Portuguese town of Fatima, who professed to see the Virgin Mary on the thirteenth day of the month, for six months, over one hundred years ago, and were imparted information about momentous and foreboding world events.[7] As Blavatsky relates, in the Mazdean philosophy of the ancient Persian nobles, the Augoeides denote the *Amesha Spentas* (*Amshaspends*) and *Farvashis* (*Fravashis*, or *Ferouers*). The former correspond to the Archangels of Christianity, or the *Rishis* of Hinduism; and the latter is the celestial 'double' of the former, for example, the Archangel Michael in Christianity.[8]

Augoeides: its manifestation and claimed appearance

It is significant that rare visitations of such an august nature occur in virtually all cases to self-effacing persons of humble background whose supreme quality of character is one of utmost humility, as, presumably, with the three shepherd children of Fatima.

The Mortal Vesture – Physical body, Astral body, Māyāvi-rūpa, and Lower mind

Finally, in concentrating upon the subtle bodies, we must not neglect man's most material vehicle capable of supporting his mental function—his 'temple of the Spirit', his Physical body. It is the principal vehicle of the Lower mind which feeds on the images furnished by the senses and co-ordinated by the brain. This is such an important subject that it deserves a chapter to itself. An in-depth discussion on the fashionable materialistic notion that the brain is like a 'wet computer' is therefore reserved for Chapter 7 along with the attendant question: are human beings 'lumbering robots'?

The Physical body and the Lower mind live and grow in union, the latter storing impressions as memory, the content of which is totally dependent upon the perception of the physical world accessed through its material vehicle. It must be admitted that for the vast majority of people this is their only waking reality for, despite all the talk of other worlds and higher dimensions and planes, few people can claim to have had actual and direct experience of them. However, the dream state, especially lucid dreaming, which is common to a large section of the population strongly alludes to superphysical realms.

Note that the *Liṅga-śarīra* (Etheric double, or Astral body) is not a separate vehicle of mental consciousness since it is constitutionally an aspect of the physical organism. Only in extreme circumstances (such as in the case of mediums) can it be extruded from the Physical body with which it maintains close proximity and so can move around only in a limited area.

Māyāvi-rūpa – The Illusory Vehicle

> If a man thinks intensely of another at a distance, his Māyāvī-Rūpa may appear to that person, without the projector knowing anything about it. This Māyāvī-Rūpa is formed by the unconscious use of Kriyāśakti [the creative power of thought], when the thought is at work with much intensity and concentration.
>
>   H. P. Blavatsky[9]

The word *Māyāvi-rūpa* means the 'illusive form', 'illusory body', 'illusion body', 'dream body', and 'thought body', as touched upon earlier. All these terms are significant as the Māyāvi-rūpa is a higher astral-mental form, evinced by the compound Sanskrit term *māyāvi*, an adjectival form of the term *māyā*—deriving from the verbal root *ma* 'to measure'—hence with the connotation of 'illusion', 'an appearance'; and *rūpa* 'form', 'vehicle', 'body'. Similar terms in German and French are *doppelgänger* and *perispirit*, respectively.

Māyāvi-rūpa: its role and function in life

It is important to note that the Māyāvi-rūpa pertains to the living person. It is dual in its function, being 'the vehicle both of thought and of the animal passions and desires, drawing at one and the same time from the lowest terrestrial Manas (mind) and Kāma, the element of desire.'[10]

The higher part of this body, containing the spiritual elements gathered during life, merges after death entirely into the Causal Body; while the lower part, containing the animal elements, forms the Kāma-rūpa (literally, the 'desire vehicle'), the source of 'spooks', or apparitions of the dead, as explained in the previous Chapter. However this higher teaching was not disseminated until Volume XII of Blavatsky's *Collected Writings*.[11] Her other works such as *The Secret Doctrine*, *The Key to Theosophy* and even *The Esoteric Writings* refer to *Kāma*, or *Kāma* (*rūpa*) as the fourth principle. We now touch upon a fascinating aspect of this vehicle of consciousness, namely that it is also a vehicle of projection as seen in the quote at the head of this section.

Evidence of the Māyāvi-rūpa

First-hand accounts of a sensed presence abound in legends and literature, both popular and esoteric, all over the world. A famous example is this passage by the American-born British poet and playwright T. S. Eliot (1888–1965) in his renowned 1922 poem 'The Waste Land': *Who is the third who walks always beside you? / When I count, there are only you and I together / But when I look ahead up the white road / There is always another one walking beside you.* A similar experience was narrated by Sir Ernest Shackleton (1874–1922), the Irish Antarctic explorer who led three British expeditions to the Antarctic. His book *South: The Endurance Expedition* described his belief that an incorporeal being joined him and two others during the final leg of their journey. Shackleton wrote, 'during that long and racking march of thirty-six hours over the unnamed mountains and glaciers of South Georgia, it seemed to me often that we were four, not three.'[12] His admission resulted in other survivors of extreme hardship coming forward and sharing comparable experiences.

T. S. Eliot and Ernest Shackleton admit a sensed presence

Shackleton's experience is also described fully in *The Third Man Factor: Surviving the impossible* along with accounts of other adventurers and explorers at the edge of death who experienced a benevolent presence beside them who encouraged them to make one final effort to survive.[13]

In recent years similar experiences have been reported by adventurers and mountaineers, such as the Italian, Reinhold Messner (*b.*1944), the American, Ann Bancroft (*b.*1955), and the New Zealander, Peter Hillary (*b.*1954), son of Sir Edmund Hillary (1919–2008) who, with the Sherpa Tenzing Norgay (1914–1986), first conquered Mount Everest.[14]

Opening Heaven's Door is another comparatively recent book providing examples of how survivors from life-threatening situations, such as terrorist attacks, drowning, shipwrecks, and air crashes, were guided to safety by a mysterious presence that was sometimes visible, at other times unseen; or else audible, or sensed, and at times, even bossing and prodding.[15] In all such cases, when its task is completed, the presence disappears without any trace. Another poignant case is the great Prague-born Jewish concert pianist Alice Herz-Sommer (1903–2014). When her seventy-two year old grandmother was taken to a concentration camp and she said farewell to her for the last time, she heard an inner voice clearly say, 'Practice the Chopin Études, they will save you.' She set to work in earnest and her outstanding performances of the Études in the Theresienstadt ghetto transit camp, where she gave more than a hundred concerts, indeed saved her life: she (and her son) were among the few who were not deported to Auschwitz.[16] (She is said to have spent her final days continuing to play the works of Schubert and Beethoven, from her home in central London, and died aged 110 years. She once said, 'Music saved my life and music saves me still […]. I am Jewish, but Beethoven is my religion.'[17])

Example from a pianist in a Nazi ghetto camp

Mainstream scientists, of course, look to materialistic arguments and mechanistic theories to explain away such phenomena. For example, rather than acknowledge any kind of presence or unusual experience, they contend that soldiers in the trenches suffered from sleep deprivation, polar explorers were deluded by sensory deprivation due to the white landscape, shipwreck victims hallucinated from sunstroke and dehydration, and mountaineers suffered from high altitude lack of oxygen and cold. Over the past decade, Swiss neuroscientists have attempted to replicate a sensed presence in the laboratory by using electrodes to stimulate the left temporo-parietal junction of the brain, suspecting that any dysfunction in this area—for example, from sleep deprivation, could make the victim disorientated, resulting in a blurring of the boundaries between the self and the outside world.[18] This is further related in a book, *Seeing Myself*, about a Swiss neurosurgeon who supposedly discovered the location in the brain that can apparently induce, and even control, an out-of-body-experience.[19] Moreover, virtual reality headsets can now allow convincing out-of-body illusions to be induced; furthermore, the availability of functional magnetic resonance imaging (fMRI)[i] and transcranial magnetic stimulation are supposed to be able to unravel the entire truth about the experience.

---

i fMRI measures brain activity by detecting changes associated with blood flow. This technique relies on the fact that cerebral blood flow and neuronal activation are coupled. When an area of the brain is stimulated or is in use, blood flow to that region also increases.

However, none of these theories remotely answer pressing issues such as: the veridical nature of the encounter (i.e., whether it coincides with reality); the specific instruction that guided the victim to safety; the purposeful and comforting nature of the crucial intervention; the consistent reports by survivors of the immense tranquillity felt in terrifying situations, being embraced in loving intelligence by a higher power; the utterly vivid, transcendent aspect of the experience, along with the indisputably absolute authority of the command issued; why a sensed presence can either keep reappearing or stay with the victim (sometimes for months); the sudden and total dematerialising of the entity, without trace, after the life-saving counsel is imparted.

In many cases, such appearances can be ascribed to the Māyāvi-rūpa since, to reiterate, it is a vehicle *of projection* during earthly life. The circumstances are numerous, such as the appearance to a loved one of a dying person, or even a recently deceased person (in which case the Māyāvi-rūpa becomes the Kāma-rūpa as explained in Chapter 2) or by the intervention of a higher being who intercedes to guide or rescue an individual. They cannot all be explained away under the usual labels of 'delusion' and 'hallucination'. In short, science needs to understand that the higher states of consciousness and associated spiritual experiences cannot be replicated to order at the behest of the scientist under what is fashionably known as 'laboratory conditions'. They can only happen when a person is touched by the Hand of Grace, which is drawn only to those who have managed to hold the ego (i.e., self-centredness) in complete abeyance through simplicity and holiness of living (see above regarding the Augoeides) or the state of self-forgetfulness common to scientists and artists during moments of peak inspiration. Suspension of the Personal ego can also occur in extreme survival conditions that result in sensory deprivation, thus rendering a person more receptive to higher and subtler influences. Further to the cases cited above, several hundred such instances are cited in detailed case studies in the two-volume *Phantasms of the Living* by the English psychologist and parapsychologist Edmund Gurney (1847–1888) and co-workers.[20]

The Māyāvi-rūpa can also be directed by a living person towards a relative or loved one or for the purposes of genuine scientific research. 'Lucid dreaming' and 'out-of-body experiences' are the modern terms used for this aspect of projecting the 'thought body' and this can happen spontaneously, or, for advanced persons, at will after suitable training. Recall the account, given in Volume I, Chapter 4 on page 90, as to how Arthur Ellison visited his local chemist shop, out of body, noted the labels on the medicine bottles in the shop window, then physically visited the shop the next day to verify that the bottle labels were exactly as he had 'seen', when out of the body.

From poetry and music, Schubert's sublime song *Der Doppelgänger* ('The Double') is a harrowing tale of the body of illusion projected in waking consciousness under conditions of extreme emotional turmoil. Composed, significantly, in the dark key of B minor in the year of his death, it is based on the words of the German poet and literary critic Heinrich Heine (1797–1856), telling the story of the singer looking at the house where his beloved once lived, and being aghast to see another man standing outside it in mocking torment. It transpired that the 'other man' happened to be none other than the illusory body, or double of himself, mimicking the misery of his unrequited love long ago.

At the highest stage of development, an adept can project the Māyāvi-rūpa at will, and in full consciousness as the following instances show. The adept endows the form with as much of his own mind and consciousness as is required and it is this ability which accounts for the stories we hear of adepts being seen in two places simultaneously. When the Māyāvi-rūpa is projected consciously, it is the 'thought body' as it becomes a vehicle of consciousness in the true sense of the term for the Personal ego and represents a state of activity in waking consciousness (see the last column of Table II-5, page 40). Otherwise it is the 'dream body' because, on waking, we remember the activity of the Māyāvi-rūpa as our dreams.

There are numerous authenticated cases of the projection of the Māyāvi-rūpa by the Eastern Adepts. Particularly significant are the various accounts in *The Mahatma Letters* about how the Māyāvi-rūpa is created and projected, and factual reports of the exercise of this occult faculty by the Mahātmās in such a unique manner that there could be no question of fraud. One incident, on 22 March 1882, recounts how Mahatma KH appeared to the English medium William Eglinton (1857–1933) on board the ship SS Vega.[21] Numerous authentic and recorded cases abound about the occult powers (higher siddhis) displayed by Blavatsky, such as materializing objects;[22, 23] and in one notable instance, mysteriously intervening when a close disciple in dire distress was on the verge of suicide.[24]

Occult powers exercised by Adepts behind the Theosophical movement

A fine example of such Adept-projection from the Western occult tradition is to be found in the Rosicrucian literature. Manley P. Hall relates that the English Neoplatonist occult philosopher, astrologer, and attorney John Heydon (1629 – *circa* 1667) was a prominent champion of the Rosicrucian Order who inscribed himself, appropriately, as 'A Servant of God, and a Secretary of Nature.'[25] In *The Rosie Cross Uncovered*, we find this enigmatic report:

> Now there are a kind of men, as they themselves report, named *Rosie Crucians*, a divine fraternity that inhabit the suburbs of heaven […] possessed [of] polymorphous powers [having, taking, or passing through many different forms or stages], appearing in any desired form at will […]. For it should seem *Rosie Crucians* were not only initiated into the Mosaical Theory, but have arrived also to the power of working miracles, as *Moses*, *Elias*, *Ezekiel*, and the succeeding Prophets did, as being transported where they please, as *Habakkuk* was from *Jewry* to *Babylon*, or as *Philip*, after he had baptized the *Eunuch* to *Azorus*, and one of these went from me to a friend of mine in *Devonshire*, and came and brought me an answer to *London* the same day, which is four days journey.[26]

Rosicrucian accounts of projection of the Māyāvi-rūpa at will

Another apologist of the Order was Eugenius Philalethes, pseudonym for the Welsh philosopher and alchemist Thomas Vaughan (1621–1666), who substantiates the statement of John Heydon concerning the ability of the Rosicrucian initiates to make themselves invisible at will. As reported by Arthur Edward Waite, commonly known as A. E. Waite (1857–1942), the American-born British poet, scholarly mystic, and extensive writer on occult and esoteric matters: 'The Fraternity of R.C. can move in this white mist. "Whosoever would communicate with us must be able to see in this light, or us he will never see unless by our own will".'[27] This is a pointed reminder of the difference between seeing with the eyes of flesh, or through the Eyes of Spirit, a theme that will be expanded later due to its crucial significance. Quite logically, the former makes visible the physical and sensual nature; the latter reveals the invisible secret workings of spirit. As a homely example, is it not a common experience that merely closing our eyes in order to shut out external distractions aids contemplation on any issue by internalizing our thoughts?

Comte de St.-
Germain's occult
powers

During the sixteenth, seventeenth, and eighteenth centuries a considerable number of alchemical adepts made their way from place to place throughout Europe, appearing and disappearing apparently at will. According to popular tradition, these adepts were immortal, and kept themselves alive by means of the mysterious medicine that was one of the goals of alchemical aspiration. It is asserted that some lived hundreds of years, taking no food except this elixir, a few drops of which would preserve their youth for a long period of time. That such mysterious men did exist there can be little doubt, as their presence is attested by scores of reliable witnesses. One such example is that of the illustrious German alchemist and philosopher Comte de St.-Germain (*circa* 1691/1712–1784) of whom it is recorded that he had the astonishing ability of both appearing in, and departing from, his own apartment and those of friends without using the door to enter or leave.[28]

Peter Deunov's
occult powers

Similar such powers have been attributed to the modern sage Peter Deunov. A notable incident was when he vanished from a locked room, appeared outside the door knocking on it and re-materialized inside the room—an episode that was repeated three times.[29] There are other accounts in the reference just cited where Deunov rescued disciples when in danger and asked them about this afterwards— it is as if they were in his field, or aura. The rationale behind this can be gleaned from his book *Divine Providence*.[30]

Shaykh Nazim
appears in
different places
simultaneously

Our final example from the modern West is taken from *Classical Islam*, a book of immense scholarship with a foreword by the great Iranian physicist, Islamic scholar, and philosopher of religion Seyyed Hossein Nasr (*b*.1933).[31] It concerns Nazim al-Haqqani, commonly known as Shaykh Nazim (1922–2014), a Turkish-Cypriot Sufi and leader of the Naqshbandi-Haqqani Order. A story is recounted involving the Governor of Tripoli, Lebanon, and head of the official convoy to the Hajj, the annual Islamic pilgrimage to Mecca, Saudi Arabia. The Governor pleaded with Nazim that if he were going on the pilgrimage, to accompany only him and no one else. At the Hajj, along with other witnesses, the Governor saw the shaykh walking with him around the Kabah.[ii] He then saw him in their hotel in Makkah, during the day on Mount Arafah (Arafat), and then with him in Mina (also known as the City of Tents). After the pilgrimage season the Governor rushed to the shaykh's house and in front of a hundred people asked him why he had made the pilgrimage with someone else and not with him as requested. But he was astonished when the shaykh's followers proclaimed that he did not go on the Hajj at all; he had been with them for two months in Lebanon. Small wonder that the Governor then told the shaykh that as a politician, he relied on his mind and logic; yet what he had just witnessed was the shaykh's miraculous ability and a reminder that superhuman powers are only gifted to he who is permanently divinely suffused.

Superhuman
powers cannot be
explained using
logic or scientific
rationale

This is a graphic account demonstrating how it is possible to be in two places simultaneously—the projection of the Māyavi-rūpa—powers seemingly miraculous but in fact, occult powers, displayed by a highly advanced soul, in this instance, a Sufi saint.

It cannot be stressed sufficiently that all such displays of extraordinary powers by highly advanced beings did not happen only in past centuries (hence relegated to mediæval folklore as diehard sceptics would orate) but occur also in relatively modern times, as in the case of the two events just cited. Nor have they anything to do with glamour-seeking circus acts, but are in the nature of a wake-up call to 'spiritual sleep-walkers' and rank disbelievers

---

ii The Kabah (Ka'bah) is a building central to Islam's most important mosque in Mecca, Saudi Arabia.

regarding the latent powers—truly infinite—in man when the personal self has merged with the divine Self, whereupon all action emanates from the divine reservoir of infinite power. It is not possible, and a waste of time, to attempt to explain such things in terms of physical science, for while the intellectualist flounders in an ocean of contradictory ideas, the mystic and occultist treat the problem in an entirely different manner (refer to Chapter 8 of Volume I about the contrasting methodologies of the scientist and the occultist). As Manly Hall articulates: 'These adepts were believed to have been able to teach man how to function away from his physical body at will by assisting him to remove the "rose from the cross". They taught that the spiritual nature was attached to the material form at certain points, symbolized by the [three] "nails" of the crucifixion; but by three alchemical initiations which took place in the spiritual world, in the true Temple of the Rose Cross, they were able to "draw" these nails and permit the divine nature of man to come down from its cross. They concealed the processes by which this was accomplished under three alchemical metaphoric expressions: "The Casting of the Molten Sea", "The Making of the Rose Diamond", and "The Achieving of the Philosopher's Stone".'[32]

> Occult science alone can account for the mysterious powers of adepts of both East and West

But not all apparitional appearances can be ascribed to the Māyāvi-rūpa. As stated earlier, some are due to the Kāma-rūpa[33] or in cases of recent death, the Liṅga-Śarīra or, in rare instances, from a highly advanced entity known as the Augoeides (see above). It is neither helpful, nor productive, nor what is popularly known in science as 'rigorous', to throw hard and fast dividing lines between these various unexpected appearances: to understand the essential principles is more than sufficient.

The Lower mind and its Faculties

Chapter 3 described the dual mode of functioning of the Mind Principle. It was stated that the Lower mind operates through imagination, memory, and reason, which faculties are further elaborated in Volume III, Chapter 8. But a white-hot question in neuroscience nowadays is: does the brain store information like a computer? Absolutely not.

> Is the brain a memory bank?

Memory is a faculty of the brain, not its storehouse or archive. The popular idea that 'brain equals computer' is highly misleading since the brain does not store information like the hard disk or the solid state hard drive of a computer. In terms of a simplistic analogy, the brain acts somewhat like the heads of a tape or video recorder. The heads do not store information; they record and retrieve information (from where, concerning the brain, is another matter, which will become apparent in Volume III). Obviously, then, a damaged brain would show impaired memory just as damaged or dirty video heads would produce a picture with gaps and distorted images.

The Action of the Higher Mind on the Personal Self

In a remarkable essay *Psychic and Noetic Action*, Blavatsky instructs that:

> It is the function of the physical, lower mind to act upon the physical organs and their cells; but, it is the higher mind *alone* which can influence the atoms interacting in those cells, which interaction is alone capable of exciting the brain, *via the spinal 'centre' cord*, to a mental representation of spiritual ideas far beyond any objects on this material plane. The phenomena of divine consciousness have to be regarded as activities of our mind on another and a higher plane, working through something less substantial than the moving

molecules of the brain. They cannot be explained as the simple resultant of the cerebral physiological process, as indeed the latter only condition them or give them a final form for purposes of concrete manifestation. Occultism teaches that the liver and the spleen cells are the most subservient to the action of our 'personal' mind, the heart being the organ *par excellence* through which the 'Higher' Ego acts—through the Lower Self.[34]

In this respect, the visions, or memory, of purely terrestrial events cannot be transmitted directly through the mental perceptions of the brain, *which is the direct recipient of the impressions of the heart,* because all such recollections have first to be stimulated by, and awakened in, the organs which were the originators of the various causes that led to the results, or, the direct recipients and participators of the latter. For example, a hungry stomach evokes the vision of a past banquet, because its action is reflected and repeated in the personal mind. But even before the memory of the personal self radiates the vision from the 'tablets' (Ākāśa) wherein are stored the experiences of our daily life—even to the minutest details—the memory of the stomach has already evoked the same. And so with all the organs of the body. It is these organs which originate, according to their animal needs and desires, the electro-vital sparks that illuminate the field of consciousness in the Lower (Personal) ego; and it is these sparks which in their turn awaken to energize the reminiscences in it. The whole human body is a vast sounding board, in which each cell bears a long record of impressions connected with its parent organ, and each cell has a memory and a consciousness of its kind, which is called instinct. These impressions are, according to the nature of the organ, physical, psychic, or mental, as they relate to different planes. They may be called 'states of consciousness' as there are states of instinctual, mental, and purely abstract, or spiritual consciousness.

Memory exists even at the cellular level

If we trace all such 'psychic' actions to brain-work, it is only because in that mansion called 'the human body' the brain is the *front-door*, and the only one which opens out into space, i.e., into the external and objective world. All the others are *inner doors*, openings in the private building, through which travel incessantly the transmitting agents of memory and sensation. The clearness, the vividness, and intensity of these depend on the state of health and the organic soundness of the transmitters.[35]

Substantially more details on the subtle forces in the human body, the corresponding centres of consciousness, and the nature of sensation are reserved for Chapters 7, 8, and 9 in Volume III.

❧ ❧ ❧

This Chapter has described the three main vehicles of consciousness for man's physical life on Earth. This exposition leads logically to the next Chapter dealing with man's after-death states and his post-mortem vehicles of consciousness.

> *In my Father's* **house are many mansions:** *if it were not so, I would have told you. I go to prepare a place for you.*
>
> JOHN 14:2, (KING JAMES VERSION)

NOTES

1   *STA*, 'Rosicrucian Doctrines and Tenets', CXLIV.

2   Marginally reworded from *CW*-XII, 'Instruction No. III', 608.

3   *KT*, 'On Reincarnation or Re-Birth', 136.

4   *TSGLOSS*, 74.

5   *op. cit.*, 43–4.

6   Adam Warcup, 'An Inquiry into the Nature of Mind', the Blavatsky Lecture, 1981 (London: The Theosophical Society), 11–12. See also *CW*-XII, 'E. S. Instruction No. I', 526.

7   Claudio Lavanga and Saphora Smith, 'Pope Francis Canonizes Children Behind "Three Secrets of Fatima"', *NBC News*, 13 May 2017 <http://www.nbcnews.com/news/world/pope-francis-canonizes-children-behind-three-secrets-fatima-n758531> accessed 8 February 2020.

8   See: *TSGLOSS*, 43–4, 19, 119; *SD*-I, 'Stanza VII: The Parents of Man on Earth', 478.

9   *CW*-XII, 'E. S. Instruction No. V', 706.

10 H. P. Blavatsky, *Studies in Occultism: Practical occultism* – a Collection of Articles from *Lucifer*, H. P. Blavatsky's magazine, between 1887–1891 (Montana, US: Literary Licensing, 2014).

11 H. P. Blavatsky, *Collected Writings 1889–1890*, 15 vols (Wheaton, Illinois: Theosophical Publishing House, 1987), xii, 479–713 *passim*.

12 Ernest Shackleton, *South: The endurance expedition* (London: Penguin Classics, 1914), 204.

13 John Geiger, *The Third Man Factor: Surviving the impossible* (Canada: Penguin Group, 2009), 20–43.

14 'Third Man factor', Wikipedia (last modified, 28 November 2019) <https://en.wikipedia.org/wiki/Third_Man_factor> accessed 19 January 2020.

15 Patricia Pearson, *Opening Heaven's Door: What the dying are trying to say about where they're going* (UK: Simon & Schuster, 2014).

16 'Lesson 6: The Mystical Experience', in Melissa Muller and Reinhard Piechocki, *A Garden of Eden in Hell: The life of Alice Herz-Sommer – where a mother's love triumphed over the Nazis*, foreword by Alice Herz-Sommer (unabridged edn, UK: Macmillan, 2007) <http://www.newfoundationunity.org/wp-content/uploads/2018/03/Alice-Herz.pdf> accessed 8 February 2020.

17 'Oldest Holocaust survivor dies aged 110', *Daily Telegraph*, 24 February 2014.

18 Olaf Blanke at the Mind-Brain Institute at Lausanne is a case in point. Other neuroscientists have acknowledged the weakness of such purely physical theories. One example is Martha Farah, director of the Centre for Neuroscience and Society at the University of Pennsylvania who admits that we should 'not assume we can explain everything that matters—or even what it means to matter—in terms of chemistry, biology, and physics. And certainly, we should not infer that whatever cannot be explained in those terms does not matter', quoted in Patricia Pearson, *Opening Heaven's Door: What the dying are trying to say about where they're going* (New York: Simon and Schuster, 2014), 95.

19 Susan Blackmore, *Seeing Myself: The new science of out-of-body experiences* (London: Robinson, 2017).

20 Edmund Gurney, Frederic William Henry Myers, and Frank Podmore, *Phantasms of the Living*, 2 vols (1886; New York: Cambridge University Press, 2011).

21 Joy Mills, *Reflections on an Ageless Wisdom – A Commentary on* The Mahatma Letters to A. P. Sinnett, foreword by Edward Abdill (Wheaton, Illinois: Theosophical Publishing House, 2010), 174, 216–18.

22 A. P. Sinnett, *The Occult World* (1st edn, Trübner & Co, 1881; London: Theosophical Publishing Society, repr. 1921), 37–128 *passim*.

23 Nicholas Goodrick-Clarke, *Helena Blavatsky* (Berkeley, California: North Atlantic Books, 2004), 12.

24 'Madame Blavatsky and Soobiah', *Adyar Lodge* (Adyar, Madras: The Theosophical Society, 1991), 10.

25 *STA*, 'Rosicrucian Doctrines and Tenets', CXLII.

26 *op. cit.*, CXLIII, quoted from 'Mysteries of the Rosie Cross: The history of that curious sect of the Middle Ages known as the Rosicrucians' (London, 1891; n.p., Health Research Book, 1993), 74 *passim* [online facsimile] <https://books.google.co.uk/books?id=PE3nk07PEPYC&printsec=frontcover&source=gbs_ge_summary_r&cad=0#v=onepage&q&f=false> accessed 14 May 2020. This is the sixth book in John Heydon, *English Physician's Guide Or a Holy Guide 1662* (US: Kessinger Publishing, 1997). The complete book of some nine hundred pages is subtitled, *Leading the Way to Know All Things, Past, Present and to Come, to Resolve All Manner of Questions, Viz., of Pleasure, Long Life, Health, Youth, Blessedness, Wisdom and Virtue and Teaching the Way to Change, Cure and Remedy All Diseases in Young and Old Fitted for Easy Understanding, Plain Practice, Use and Benefit.*

27 Arthur Edward Waite, *Works of Thomas Vaughan: Eugenius Philalethes* (1919; London: Forgotten Books, 2013), 354–5. Quoted also in: *STA*, 'Rosicrucian Doctrines and Tenets', CXLIII; 'Mystery Religions – Rosicrucian Doctrines and Tenets', in Marilynn Hughes (compiled), *The Voice of the Prophets: Wisdom of the ages*, 12 vols (US: CreateSpace Independent Publishing Platform, 2005), vi, 147 <https://www.academia.edu/36151498/The_Voice_of_the_Prophets_Wisdom_of_the_Ages_Mystery_Religions_2_of_2> accessed 6 March 2020.

28 See *STA*, 'The Mysteries and Their Emissaries', CXCIX.

29 David Lorimer (ed.), *Prophet for Our Times: The life and teachings of Peter Deunov*, foreword by Wayne W. Dyer (London: Hay House, 2015), 24. See also pp. 19–20, 25–6.

30 Peter Deunov, 'Divine Providence', translations from Bulgarian of Authentic Versions of the Lectures and Other Works (19 August 2008) <http://www.beinsa-douno.net/lectures/Divine-Providence.html> accessed 8 February 2020.

31 Shaykh Muhammad Hisham Kabbani, *Classical Islam and the Naqshbandi Sufi Tradition*, introd. Shaykh Nazim Adil al-Haqqani, foreword by Seyyed Hossein Nasr (Fenton, Michigan: Islamic Supreme Council of America, 2004), 480.

32 *STA*, 'The Fraternity of the Rose Cross', CXL.

33 For example the case of a World War I soldier in 1917 who was guided to safety out of his trench by the appearance and encouragement of his brother who had been reported missing in action for two years—see Patricia Pearson, *Opening Heaven's Door*, 83–4.

34 *CW*-XII, 'Psychic and Noetic Action', 369–70.

35 *loc. cit.*, reworded.

5 Death is Transition – Time at the Door of Eternity

Pythagoras taught:

And when, after having divested thyself of the mortal body, thou arrivest at the most pure Æther, Thou shalt be a God, immortal, incorruptible, and Death shall have no more Dominion over thee.

THE GOLDEN VERSES OF PYTHAGORAS[1]

Francis Bacon declared:

Death exempts not a man from being, but only presents an alteration.

AN ESSAY ON DEATH[2]

Hamlet professed:

To grunt and sweat under a weary life, But that the dread of something after death, The undiscover'd country from whose bourn No traveller returns, puzzles the will And makes us rather bear those ills we have Than fly to others that we know not of?

SHAKESPEARE (FRANCIS BACON?), *HAMLET*: ACT III, SCENE 1

SYNOPSIS

Chapter 5 presents a stepwise explanation about the three principal transitional stages involved in the cycle of reincarnation: physical death, post-mortem existence, and rebirth. It is clearly demonstrated that contrary to the scientific dictum that death equals the extinction of consciousness, since time immemorial, the *philosophia perennis* has taught that death is both transition and release from earthly bondage—not an extinguishment. The topic of apparitions is taken up again, the emphasis now placed on explaining such phenomena in terms of how it is that a strongly earthbound nature or else, unfulfilled desires and appetites during earthly life can temporarily energize the post-mortem psychic vesture. The exposition draws heavily on the core occult doctrines presented earlier on the composition of man and his vehicles of consciousness, particularly that which serves as a bridge between the mortal, or personal and the immortal, or divine elements of man. Further elucidation is provided from poetical and literary works of sublime mystical vision, primarily the Divine Comedy by Dante Alighieri. Scientific and photographic evidence is adduced in support of some of the occult tenets. Further scientific evidence from mediumship and after-death communications is cited in support of claimed memories from a past life. As indispensable elements of post-mortem existence, the concepts of 'heaven' and 'hell' are examined. It is no exaggeration to say that ideas concerning these range from the vague to the ludicrous and abound in the popular milieu and orthodox religions, as also in science. Therefore, no effort is spared in explaining, carefully, the exact meaning and significance of these admittedly inflammatory terms. A major section is devoted to explaining how the fate of an incarnation depends critically on whether the connection between the personality and Higher Self is maintained and strengthened or weakened and severed. Since this is a complex Chapter, it is fully illustrated and closes with a summary and postlude.

KEY WORDS: death, post-mortem states, transitions, purgatory, paradise, inferno, apparitions, immortality, time, rebirth, cultural intimations, scientific evidence, Dante Alighieri

This<!-- -->his Chapter presents an overview of the principal stages and associated states of consciousness of man after physical death, and the processes that impel him towards rebirth. Whereas there are myriad complex details to consider in exploring 'The undiscover'd country' (see the third epigraph), we necessarily have to confine our attention to the key features of the post-mortem and reincarnation process, drawing upon the occult teachings referenced in Endnote II-5 in order to highlight the fact that consciousness is ubiquitous: it cannot be extinguished; it never 'dies'. In other words, using the simile of ice, water, and steam being phase changes of the same H_2O, death and the post-mortem states are but changes of phase of consciousness, which is unaffected by different phase states of itself.

First and foremost, we have to ask the question: 'what exactly do we mean by death?' In occultism, the meaning is not quite as straightforward as the everyday sense of the term. And is there just one death? In fact, there are two deaths, which logically means that there have to be two births. The first death is obvious; but the second one needs explaining.

What exactly is 'death'? Who, or what dies?

Accordingly, the transition of man's consciousness after physical death and towards subsequent rebirth is described in three principal, and well-defined phase transitions: (*a*) from physical life to astral life; (*b*) from astral life to spiritual life; and (*c*) from spiritual life to a new terrestrial life. The term 'astral' is used as the best available term in English to refer to the psychic realms that encompass the broad, intermediate planes ranging from the physical to the spiritual—see Chapter 3, Table II-5, page 40. Then follows an explanation of how and why apparitions occur since such appearances are directly explicable in terms of the post-mortem states of man.

Let us start, naturally, with the transition of consciousness from physical existence. An understanding of all that death involves depends on a proper understanding of the total constitution of man during physical life. That is why it is said that the key to the secret of death is held in physical life, so poignantly expressed in *The Prophet*:

Life holds the secret of death

> You would know the secret of death.
> But how shall you find it unless you seek it in the heart of life?
> If you would indeed behold the spirit of death, open your heart wide unto the body of life.
> For life and death are one, even as the river and the sea are one.
> And when the earth shall claim your limbs, then shall you truly dance.
>
> Kahlil Gibran[3]

So it would be useful to recapitulate briefly that man, as a unit of consciousness, functions on Earth through seven principles which may be grouped in several ways, as described in Chapters 2 and 3, but for the better understanding of the death and rebirth processes, can be grouped into:

THE INDIVIDUALITY
❖ *The Upper Triad*: comprising (*a*) *Ātma* (the Divine Self) in conjunction with the Upper Duad, the latter comprising (*b*) *Buddhi* (the Spiritual Soul being the vehicle of Ātma) and (*c*) *Manas* (the Human Soul, or Mind in its higher aspect).

THE PERSONALITY
❖ *The Middle Duad*: the Animal soul (*psyche*) comprising the Kāma-manasic duality of (*a*) *Manas* in its lower aspect with (*b*) *Kāma* (Desire).

❖ *The Lower Triad*: comprising (*a*) *Prāṇa* (the Life-force), (*b*) *Liṅga-śarīra* (Etheric double) as its vehicle, and (*c*) *Sthūla-śarīra* (Physical body).

The above esoteric taxonomy is shown in the pertinent columns of Chapter 2, Table II-3, page 21. It is reproduced in this Chapter in the first two columns of Table II-10 overleaf, which portrays man during physical life and the two main stages of his post-mortem consciousness.

First Transition – From Physical Life on Earth to Astral Life in Kāma-loka

Man, who is physically born must eventually physically die. But what exactly is physical death? From the standpoint of materialism, it means the cessation of the functions of the brain, heart, and other bodily organs. This is obviously so, but there is more to consider. The popular idea that loss of brain function means the extinction of consciousness is not upheld nowadays by enlightened scientists and psychologists (see Volume I, Chapters 2, 4, and 6), and certainly not in occultism, which teaches that physical death is transition. The same H_2O existing as ice, water, and steam (or all three phases at the triple point) is an apposite simile for the transfer of consciousness to different phase states of itself. The various phases of the complex transition process are now described—in unavoidably stylised fashion, purely for simplicity.

Death represents a phase change of consciousness

Physical Death and Immediately After

In the course of dying and immediately afterwards, the lower sentient consciousness, which is of course held in subjection by the brain and physical senses, is extinguished with the death of the brain and senses. However, the higher consciousness survives forever because its root lies in Eternity. Memory is therefore dislodged from the physical brain. Furthermore, the *Māyāvi-rūpa* (the 'illusory body', fully explained in the previous Chapter) may appear to loved ones as a materialization of the newly departed person during this early transition stage (a typical example will shortly be given, but refer also to the general outline given in the previous Chapter).

Post-Mortem Consciousness in Kāma-loka

Physical death signifies the loss of the Lower Triad—see of the first column (to the right of the dotted line) of Table II-10. In the same way as the Physical body is the lowest vehicle of a man's higher (non-physical) six principles during earthly life, so the *Kāma-rūpa* now becomes the lowest vehicle of the same man's higher three principles after physical death— see the second column of Table II-10.

Soon after physical death, a review of the past life occurs in *Kāma-loka*, also known as Amenti in Egyptian mythology, Hades in Greek mythology, and purgatory in Christian theology. All these terms signify the realm of the dead, or rather, a stratified intermediate state of consciousness after physical death in which the soul must undergo purification, so as to achieve the holiness necessary to enjoy the state (consciousness) of heaven. Figure II-1 on page 67 shows a depiction of *Purgatorio* (Purgatory) based on paintings inspired by Dante's

First life review

Table II-10   The Post-Mortem Consciousness of Man – 'The Undiscover'd Country'

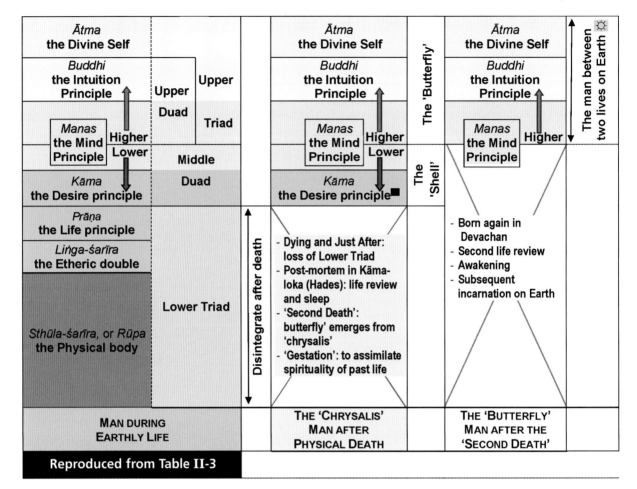

MAN DURING EARTHLY LIFE	THE 'CHRYSALIS' MAN AFTER PHYSICAL DEATH	THE 'BUTTERFLY' MAN AFTER THE 'SECOND DEATH'

Reproduced from Table II-3

■ the 'Spook', or *Eidolon*, formed after the death in Kāma-loka which can be materialized by the vitality of the medium and sitters at a seance.

☼ *Devachan*, the 'dwelling of the gods'.

NOTE: Kāma-loka and Devachan are not places that a man 'goes to' after death, but different conditions, or *states of consciousness*.

immortal poem *La Divina Commedia* by the Italian artist of the Florentine School, Sandro Botticelli (1445–1510). Needless to say, this depiction of Purgatory (and paradise and hell later) are purely allegorical referring to states of consciousness, not to material locations on Earth or elsewhere. (The numerous correspondences between Dante's epic poem and the Ancient Wisdom are shown in 'Dante – Introducing *The Divine Comedy*'.[4])

Purgatory may be likened to a school examination room: those who miss the mark are demoted to be disciplined by more hard study; and those who pass, move 'upwards' to the next higher class (and possibly also receive their prize on the annual speech day!). Botticelli's depiction shows various terraces, each corresponding to a particular characteristic (state of consciousness) of the inhabiting entity. It is always the case that the punishment fits the offence: so, fittingly, the proud are forced to bend double under the weight of heavy boulders; and the gluttons have to chase in vain around a tree laden with delicious fruit.

The grossest regions of *kāma-loka* blend insensibly into the highest regions of *Avīchi* (see below)

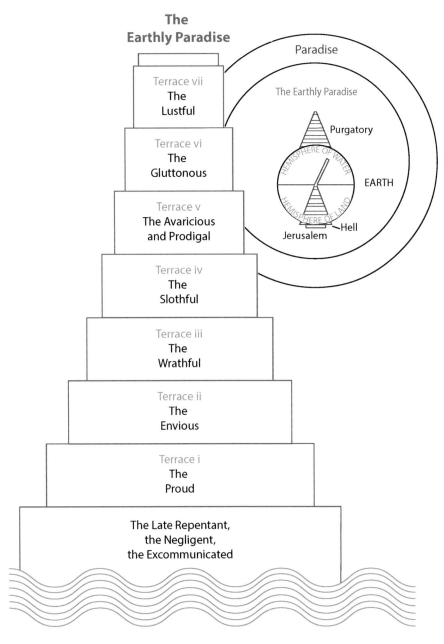

The
Earthly Paradise

Terrace vii
The
Lustful

Terrace vi
The
Gluttonous

Terrace v
The Avaricious
and Prodigal

Terrace iv
The
Slothful

Terrace iii
The
Wrathful

Terrace ii
The
Envious

Terrace i
The
Proud

The Late Repentant,
the Negligent,
the Excommunicated

Paradise

The Earthly Paradise

Purgatory

HEMISPHERE OF WATER

EARTH

HEMISPHERE OF LAND

Jerusalem   Hell

Figure II-1 *Purgatorio*

*Reproduced from the Royal Academy of London pamphlet based on N. Sapegno (ed.), 'Dante Alighieri,
La Divina Commedia' (Florence, La Nuova Italia, Scandicci, 1985). Acknowledgement clause provided on page xi
under the list of illustrations for this Volume.*

It must be stressed that the life review is not in any way concerned with the personal details of the former life, but solely with its spiritual content, in order that those spiritual elements can be distilled and assimilated into the Higher Self. Furthermore, it is important to distinguish between what may be termed *panoramic memory* and the more profound *life review* when the event is experienced from many angles, which includes, significantly, the 'inside out' experience of being on the receiving end of causes enacted during life (for example, a person who deliberately causes hurt to a loved one during life will experience the effects of that hurt upon himself). The principle of the Golden Rule of treating others as we ourselves would wish to be treated, a maxim found in practically all religions and cultures,

The highest regions of *kāma-loka* blend insensibly into the lowest realms of *devachan* (see below)

Principal role of
Kama-loka is
purification

e.g. the biblical rule of 'do as you would be done by' (Matthew 7:12, King James Version), is therefore an inexorable universal law.

With the ending of this review and its consequent striking of the keynote for the next incarnation, unconsciousness supervenes, not in the sense of an extinction of consciousness, but more like the state of deep, dreamless sleep.

The Second Death

The life review is followed by what is known in occultism as a 'death struggle' which seems to imply a conscious experience of suffering and pain but is in fact the natural separation of the Higher Ego (see Chapter 3, Table II-8, page 46) from the personal elements in the man's experience—shown in the second column of Table II-10. The two modes of functioning of the one Manasic (mind) principle, were described in Chapters 2 and 3. The struggle is between the Higher Manas and the Lower manas, the former in association with Buddhi comprising the Upper Duad; and the latter identifying with Kāma constituting the Middle Duad—see the first column of Table II-10.

Separation and
gestation

Thereafter follows a 'gestation' period in order to assimilate (digest) the 'spiritual aroma' of the past life into the Higher Egoic entity—described in the next section. Unless there are unusual circumstances in the former earthly life (such as a premature death by violence, suicide or any other reason), the gestation period for the average person may last for many years (in terms of Earth time) after which consciousness returns in the sense of an awakening from the state of deep slumber.

The enigmatic question of the time period in Devachan will be elaborated shortly. Meanwhile, we now progress to the second transition from astral (psychic) consciousness to spiritual consciousness.

Second Transition – From Astral Life in Kāma-loka to Spiritual Life in Devachan

The separation of the immortal Upper Duad from the lower portions, which remain as the Kāma-rūpa, is known as the 'second death' as just described. It is profoundly significant and well symbolized by the butterfly emerging from its chrysalis. Divested of the impediment of his last mortal remnants, man is reborn as his true immortal Self—the Upper Triad on the higher plane known as Devachan, there to remain until the hour for a new physical incarnation arrives under the divine law of harmony and adjustment—karma. This is depicted in the third column of Table II-10. ('Reborn' here does not exactly mean reincarnation, which is explained shortly.) Out of several examples that could be cited from philosophy and religion regarding the significance of the second death, the following two are striking.

Plutarch says:

Plutarch on death

> The death we die is of two kinds: the one makes man two out of three, the other makes him one out of two.[5]

By using the simple division of man into spirit, soul, and body: the first death is the loss of the body, leaving man with two out of three; and the second is the withdrawal of the spirit from Kāma-rūpa, making one out of two.

Recall now the biblical story of Nicodemus, a ruler of the Jews who visited the Christ by night hoping to find out more about his teaching since 'no man can do these miracles that thou doest, except God be with him'. In reply, Jesus pronounced:

> Verily, verily, I say unto thee, except a man be born again, he cannot see the Kingdom of God.[i]

Being one of the Pharisees, therefore fastidious in keeping to the letter of the Law, i.e., the dead-letter exoteric interpretation of the Jewish faith, the perplexed Nicodemus remarked, 'How can a man be born when he is old? Can he enter the second time into his mother's womb, and be born?' There are at least two profound inferences that can be elicited from the Christ's admittedly enigmatic comeback that 'a man be born again'.

The first one is in line with the Second Transition just outlined. But one could hardly expect the Saviour to impart esoteric truths in the Aramaic tongue to the literal-minded Nicodemus about the disintegration of the chrysalis (the Kāma-rūpa) to release the butterfly (the Immortal Triad of Ātma, Buddhi, and Manas) in Devachan! Instead, He states, 'the wind bloweth where it listeth, and thou hearest the sound thereof, but canst not tell whence it cometh, and whither it goeth: so is everyone that is born of the Spirit.' The Christ then points out that what a man sees and understands depends on his state of consciousness: 'That which is born of the flesh is flesh; and that which is born of the Spirit is spirit. Marvel not that I said unto thee, Ye must be born again.' Then to the still bewildered Nicodemus, 'If I have told you earthly things, and ye believe not, how shall ye believe, if I tell you of heavenly things?'

This is but a cursory insight into the Saviour's transcendent words about being born again after the second death—all so perplexing to Nicodemus, who could not figure out how a man could enter his mother's womb twice! Esoteric insights (from the Qabbalah) into his own religion—as the Christ admonished, 'Art thou a master of Israel, and knowest not these things?'— might have furnished the Pharisee with the insight needed to distinguish the physical uterus from the Kāma-rūpa, namely, the womb of the physical man from the chrysalis of the spiritual man.

What did the Christ mean by being 'born again'?

The second possible inference is to do with spiritual rebirth in the present lifetime. In the Mysteries it was customary to refer to initiates as *phœnixes*, or men who had been born again, for just as physical birth gives man consciousness in the physical world, so the neophyte, after the various degrees of initiation in the womb of the Mysteries, was born into a consciousness of the Spiritual world.[6] What this means, in practical terms, is that all burdensome encumbrances such as material possessions, sensual cravings, outworn intellectual concepts, and religious encrustations must be sloughed off; otherwise, 'it is easier for a camel to go through a needle's eye, than for a rich man to enter into the kingdom of God' (Luke 18:25, King James Version). Significantly, a similar proverb to the Biblical Gospel is in the Holy Qur'an: 'To those who reject Our signs and treat them with arrogance, no opening will there be of the gates of heaven, nor will they enter the garden, until the camel can pass through the eye of the needle: Such is Our reward for those in sin.'[7]

---

i All quotations in this section, unless otherwise stated, are the original from *The Holy Bible*, St. John, Chapter 3, Cambridge University Press.

Before enquiring into these 'heavenly things', what does the Christ mean by the terms 'man' and the 'Kingdom of God'? The former obviously does not refer to the physical man who has died, but to the upper middle principles, the Human Soul; strictly speaking the Human Ego (see Chapter 3, Table II-8, page 46). The latter refers to what is known in occultism as Devachan. We move on to consider the life and consciousness of man in Devachan—the state intermediate between two lives on Earth into which the Higher Ego enters after the second death (after its separation from its lower aspects, or sheaths).

Post-Mortem Consciousness in Devachan –The 'Kingdom of the Gods'

Devachan is a compound Sanskrit–Tibetan term deriving from *deva* 'a "god"' and *chan* 'land', 'region'; therefore translated as 'god-land', 'god-region', or 'the dwelling of the gods'. It is known by various other names like *Sukhavati* (Sanskrit: literally 'land of bliss') in Mahayana Buddhism, *Elysium*, or the *Elysian Fields* of the Greeks, *Sekhet-Aaru* of the Egyptians, *Valhalla* of the Scandinavians, and corresponds with *Paradiso* in Dante's Divine Comedy[8] (see the next section). Devachan bears a relation to, but is not identical with, Heaven of orthodox Christianity, which regards the heavenly state as permanent and eternal (a good example of how the exoteric adaptation of religion distorts the esoteric meaning), whereas Devachan is a temporary state intermediate between two Earth lives into which the Higher Ego enters after the second death when divested of its lower aspects, or sheaths.

Devachan is recognized in cultures worldwide

Devachanic life and consciousness can, in one sense, be seen as a counterbalance to life on Earth. In the latter, reality 'dons' a mortal vesture for a time period; in the former, reality is naked unto itself, also time bound, but in general for much longer than an earthly life (reckoned from the standpoint of Earth time).

The State of Devachan

The state of Devachan is best understood by invoking the old adage 'death is sleep', meaning that the easiest way to understand the cycles of death and rebirth is by analogy with the cycles of sleep and wakefulness in life. Just as the dream landscape during sleep is not a locality defined by co-ordinates and compass points, but a state of consciousness different from the waking state, so also Devachan (like Kāma-loka) is not a geographical place, but a phase state of consciousness (in a different order of space–time from the everyday world), a state of the beings in that spiritual condition. For this reason, time has a very different connotation in these different dimensions (discussed on page 75).

In daily life, we often find that a way to solve an intractable problem is to 'sleep on it'. The answer can sometimes appear in a dream, or just upon waking the next day. Similarly, Devachan is emphatically not a monotonous repetition of some former pleasing experience, but the 'workshop' to which an individual's 'rough diamonds'—good thoughts, words, and deeds—are taken for fashioning, after being extracted, entailing much suffering and toil, from the 'mine' of the personal life. It is a consciousness-state of complete engrossment in the bliss of all former personal earthly affections, preferences, and thoughts. All the unfulfilled spiritual and (higher) intellectual possibilities of the former life that are spontaneously presented to the devachanee (devachanic entity) are constantly reviewed and improved upon in blissful imagination. Hence, the central role

Flowering of the inner life in Devachan

of Devachan is the fulfilling of all *unfulfilled* spiritual yearnings of the past incarnation, and an efflorescence of the former which, during that incarnation, did not have sufficient opportunity for fulfilment. It goes without saying, that being a spiritual state, no frustrated earthly or material ambitions, nor any personal desires or phantasies, can have any relation to Devachan. These are all associated with the Kāma-rūpa which, like the mortal coil earlier, has been sloughed off to disintegrate over time.

Fulfillment of spiritual aspirations

Like Kāma-loka, Devachan is stratified in levels to accord with the spiritual status of the Higher Ego. Interestingly, the Eddas[ii] of the Scandinavians describe Valhalla as a majestic, enormous hall ruled over by the god Odin and containing five hundred 'doors'—each door corresponding to a different Valhallic condition, i.e., state of consciousness.[9] Valhalla, incidentally, is memorably depicted in Richard Wagner's opera cycle *Der Ring des Nibelungen* (*The Ring of the Nibelung*). Put simplistically, just as a hot-air balloon will rise in the air to a level of neutral buoyancy, so the devachanee will 'rise' to that level corresponding to his spiritual status. Archimedes' principle has its metaphysical equivalent! This is well illustrated in Botticelli's depiction of *Paradiso* (Paradise) shown in Figure II-2 on page 72. Just as the punishment fits the crime in Purgatory, so the reward fits the meritorious deed in Paradise: the artist, scientist, poet or philosopher will rise to their appropriate 'grade', there to reap the fruits of good deeds sown on Earth and fulfil yet higher aspirations.

Devachanic levels

It is a total enigma to mainstream psychology how some artists and scientists display genius 'out of the blue'; they seem to know what they have never been taught. In music for example, Frédéric Chopin (1810–1849) had no teachers of especial merit, yet he was one of the greatest pianists of his day and his compositions still move us to tears well over a century later. From the start, Franz Liszt (1811–1886) revealed a prodigious musical talent: no sooner was he told anything than he seemed to know it already.[10] Mozart was never taught psychology or psychiatry at a university; yet his operas display an unerring insight into human character—of both sexes. Who then taught him to read the Book of Life? And how many six year old children do we know who can compose a difficult harpsichord concerto as Mozart did?[11] In mathematics, Newton seemed to derive his knowledge by something more like direct contact with the unknown sources that surround us, with the world of mystery, than has been vouchsafed to any other man of science. Asking how Newton could be both a mathematician and a mystic, Sir Robert Robinson (1886–1975), the English Nobel laureate and past President of the Royal Society, answered that it was because Newton 'perceived a mystery beyond and did his best to penetrate it.'[12] A modern case would be the Indian mathematician and autodidact Srinivasa Iyengar Ramanujan FRS (1887–1920), the subject of the drama film, *The Man Who Knew Infinity*. He had virtually no formal training in pure mathematics; yet he made substantial contributions to mathematical theory. Deeply religious, Ramanujan credited his mathematical capacities to divinity, declaring that an equation meant nothing to him unless it expressed a Thought of God. (Chapter 9 of Volume III gives more referenced details about this.) Would it not be true to say that crediting mathematical attributes or any other capacities to divinity is just another way of

The question of genius

---

ii 'Eddas' is a term used to describe two thirteenth century AD Icelandic manuscripts that are the main sources of Norse mythology and skáldic (old Norse) poetry that expound the religion, cosmogony, and history of Scandinavians and Proto-Germanic tribes.

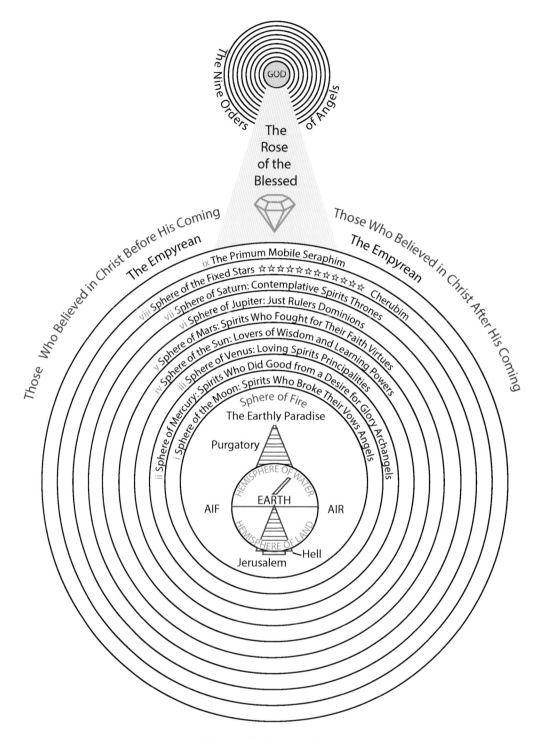

Figure II-2 *Paradiso*

*Reproduced from the Royal Academy of London pamphlet based on N. Sapegno (ed.), 'Dante Alighieri,
La Divina Commedia' (Florence, La Nuova Italia, Scandicci, 1985). Acknowledgement clause provided on page xi
under the list of illustrations for this Volume.*

acknowledging, in everyday language, the devachanic experience on spiritual planes?
Such genius can, arguably, be explained (in part) by innumerable incarnations, and their
associated devachanic experiences, ever improving upon and refining the faculties, and
renewing the aspirations of former lives, the ultimate flowering of which materializes
as seeming miracles on Earth. Another example is the polymath Walter Russell, whose

highly intuitive and visionary cosmogony united spiritual cause and scientifically observable effect (see Volume I, Chapter 9, pages 305–307). But his formal education ended at the age of around ten.

However, to whatever level the devachanee may 'rise', there is an absolute oblivion of all that gave pain or sorrow in the past incarnation, and even oblivion of the fact that such things as pain or sorrow exist at all. The devachanee lives his intermediate cycle between two incarnations surrounded by everything noble that he had aspired to, but in vain, and in the companionship of everyone he loved whilst on Earth. He has reached the fulfilment of all his soul-yearnings. And thus he may live for long centuries an existence of unalloyed happiness, which is the reward for his sufferings during Earth-life, whilst gathering in the fruit of worthy actions.

What is Conscious in Devachan?

The personality, or Lower self being the mortal part of man, and the Animal soul, or psyche pertaining to it are neither divine, nor immortal, nor eternal (see the first and second columns of Table II-10, page 66). This is confirmed in the Zohar, a foundational text for the Qabbalah comprising the esoteric methods and disciplines of the school of Jewish mystical thought. Volume II of the Zohar contains esoteric commentaries on the Book of Genesis. In it, we find this key passage: 'The soul, when sent to this earth, puts on an earthly garment, to preserve herself here, so she receives above a shining garment, in order to be able to look without injury into the mirror, whose light proceeds from the Lord of Light.'13 Furthermore, the Zohar teaches that the soul cannot reach the abode of bliss, unless she has received the 'holy kiss', or the reunion of the soul *with the substance from which she emanated*—Spirit. Here again is further confirmation of the esoteric doctrine: that alone which is indissolubly joined by Ātma-Buddhi is immortal.

In view of this, that which is conscious in Devachan is the spark of consciousness that preserves in the Spiritual Ego (Buddhi and Higher Manas) the idea of the personal 'I' of the last incarnation, which lasts as a separate distinct recollection, only throughout the Devachanic period, after which time it is added to the pool of innumerable incarnations of the Reincarnating Ego (the Higher Manas—see Chapter 3, Table II-8, page 46). Immortality is one unbroken stream of consciousness; hence the personal consciousness can hardly be expected to last longer than the personality itself; and such consciousness survives only throughout Devachan, after which it is reabsorbed, first, in the individual, and then in the universal Consciousness.

For terrestrial existence, man comprises a trinity of the Upper Triad, Middle Duad, and Lower Triad (i.e., Spirit, Soul, and Body) as seen in Table II-10, page 66, unless his degeneration is such as to have caused his divorce from Spirit (as explained shortly). 'Woe to the soul which prefers to her divine husband (spirit) the earthly wedlock with her terrestrial body,' records a text of the *Book of the Keys*, a Hermetic work on the destiny of the soul.14 When this fateful condition happens, nothing will remain of that personality to be recorded on the imperishable tablets of the Higher Ego's memory. However, as repeatedly stressed, soul, in the generic sense of the term, displays a dual characteristic and while the soul is feminine, the spirit is masculine, which has nothing to do with gender. Soul can be seen as feminine in the sense that she is the Life principle proceeding from the One, filling all creation with the animating breath of Spirit. Spirit, again in the generic sense, can be

Only Spirit, the Upper Triad, is conscious

seen as masculine in the sense of being a stable principle from which all else proceeds. It may therefore be helpful to readers to regard these less as 'feminine' and 'masculine', with their inevitable connotations of gender, and more as the two contrary and *complementary* principles, or forces of 'yin' and 'yang'.

The objection could legitimately be raised that since Devachan has been likened to the dream state, albeit magnified a hundredfold, what intrinsic value is there in a dream? After all, in daily life objective reality is given far more credence over subjective states like dreaming. In fact, it is quite the reverse. The waking state which is so valued in our predominantly materialistic culture is also a dream of sorts—a māyā, or illusory appearance. This fact was acutely presented to the mind of the great Nobel physicist Werner Heisenberg, who enunciated the principle of indeterminacy. First mentioned and referenced in Chapter 6 of Volume I, Heisenberg's dying words to his student von Weizsäcker bear repeating in the context of this Chapter because of their tremendous import:

Werner Heisenberg's near-death insight

> It is very easy: I did not know this before. I see now that physics is of no importance, that the world is illusion.

When the shadow of death became his tutor, Heisenberg was able to see real facts for what they truly *are*, and not as they *appear to be*. This does *not* mean that the exterior world that physics studies is non-existent and merely a subjective presentation to the mind, but that it stands out to the human mind that tries to understand and interpret it as a mirage, hence an illusory aspect of man's thoughts—a waking dream. The point to be made is that māyā plays a central role in man's evolution[15] and the 'stuff of dreams' is as important to the physical life as it is to the devachanee.

A similar experience of the illusory nature of matter is reported in *The Near Death Experience* regarding the British philosopher, mathematician, historian, writer, and Nobel laureate Bertrand Russell FRS who allegedly communicated after his death through the English medium Rosemary Brown (1916–2001) thus:

Bertrand Russell's reported post-mortem clarity

> Now here I was, still the same I, with capacities to think and observe sharpened to an incredible degree. I felt earth-life suddenly seemed very unreal almost as if it had never happened […] that matter is certainly illusory although it does exist in actuality; the material world seemed now nothing more than a seething, changing, restless sea of indeterminable density and volume. How could I have thought that that was reality […]? Yet it is completely understandable that the state in which a man exists, however temporary, constitutes the passing reality which is no longer reality when it has passed.[16]

Two chief points emerge. First, the last sentence from the above quotation about the relativity of reality is easily illustrated by the fact that a dream, a 'passing reality', is very real to the dreamer—until he wakes up. Second, the heightened perceptions of Russell and Heisenberg make a complete nonsense of the materialistic dogma that a dying brain could only result in progressively jumbled perceptions leading to the eventual extinction of consciousness, as stated in no unceratin terms by the Oxford chemistry professor Peter Atkins, who opines: 'Science, especially through psychology, shines its brilliant light on the afterlife and instead of illuminating it causes it to shrink and die, revealing its core: anxiety.'[17] A truthful statement suggested by the writer in keeping with the latest science would have been: 'quantum science shines its brilliant light on scientism and instead of illuminating the primacy of matter causes it to shrink and transmute into light, mind, and consciousness.'

Does consciousness 'die' with the brain?

Clarifying Some Common Misapprehensions

At this juncture it might be helpful to clear up a few commonly asked questions.

Who Enters Devachan?

Having just outlined what is conscious in Devachan, the next logical question is, who enters and then inhabits Devachan? It is best answered by asking who does not enter Devachan. Occultism teaches that not all who physically die enter Devachan. For example, children who die young (usually before the age of seven), get reincarnated quickly as they have not yet gathered the experiences that will reap a blissful condition in Devachan. So also heinous criminals who, obviously, have reaped practically no spiritual harvest in life and are therefore reborn swiftly (see later for further insights). Other exceptions are some of those who die prematurely and who may be reborn immediately, those who commit suicide, and victims of murder or accident as described by Ian Stevenson in his several books detailing his investigations of cases of children who claim to remember their previous incarnation(s), as well as in articles written by some of his associates (refer to Volume I, Chapter 4 and the associated Endnote I-5).

The more spiritual seeds are sown during life, the greater the spiritual harvest

Other exceptions are advanced souls who defer Devachan and choose to be reincarnated quickly in order to serve humanity in physical life. At the highest level of advancement are initiates and adepts who have transcended the illusory veils of the mind and therefore have no need of Devachan.

From the above, it may correctly be inferred that death is indeed a promotion in the classroom of life! Other than the few cases just cited, the vast majority of mankind are indeed 'promoted' to the higher and purer life of Devachan until such time as each soul is prompted by karmic law to commence a fresh chapter and thus incarnates to a new classroom in the stern school of life.

The Question of Time

It is natural to enquire about the length of time spent in Devachan. But as previously stressed, time measured on Earth (clock time) is very different from the subjective sense of time. It is commonly known that what seemed to last for a long time in a dream, in fact took only a few seconds, as shown by measurements of the rapid eye movement (REM) of the dreamer, indicating the onset and interval of the dream state. That said, the following general points can be made.

The overriding principle is that the period in Devachan is *proportionate to the unexhausted spiritual impulses* originating during Earth life. However, the time in Devachan is enormously greater than time according to Earth life. Moreover, such time varies widely with different human beings. Since the devachanic experience is meant to be an elaboration of what the human being has learnt during his physical existence, to unfold it freely, to make it suitable to a new life, it is obvious that the time spent in Devachan is proportional to the 'devachanic store' of the individual. A man who has immersed himself in little more than the life of the five senses, would dwell only a short time in this abode to 'process' the spiritual content of his earthly experiences. Conversely, a man who has collected rich experiences obviously has to process a lot more; hence, has a longer stay in Devachan.

Devachanic time is proportional to spiritual processing time

Depending, therefore, on the degree of spirituality and the merit or demerit of the last incarnation, that interval can last a few minutes, one year or a million years. The average time (from the standpoint of Earth-time and not to be taken literally), as we are informed, would be around fifteen hundred years for the majority of those who wish for a release and for an enjoyment of bliss. But note in this connection, the exceptional cases mentioned earlier (for reasons shortly to be explained) regarding child mortality, criminals, premature (violent) deaths, and adepts.

But on the question of time, does it mean that the idle periods in our life would be experienced in Devachan as protracted boredom? That we surely will find out for ourselves! Nevertheless, for all mortals who yearn for immortality, the following witticism by the British novelist Susan Ertz (1887–1985) may not go amiss:

> Millions long for immortality who do not know what to do with themselves on a rainy Sunday afternoon.[18]

The Question of Immortality

Death and immortality are the two opposing polarities of time: the former approaching the infinitely small, the latter the infinitely large, but both in the realm of time. Therefore, immortality is not exactly the same as eternity, which is out of time, or the timeless state. Stated otherwise, immortality has a beginning but no ending; however, eternity has no beginning and no end.

Taken at face value, and in the popular sense, immortality means a continuous and unending existence or being. But there is nothing in nature that remains static and does not evolve over time. What varies is the periodicity, or time periods of change, not the fact of change. For example, compared to the mayflies (also called 'one-day insects') who live for twenty-four hours and some species that die within a few hours, the average life span of the modern American of seventy-nine years (World Health Ranking, Data Source: WHO Publish Date 2018) would seem 'quasi-static' or 'immortal'. But human life would seem like the 'twinkling of an eye' to the 2,307 year-old (in 2019) sacred fig tree *Ficus religiosa*, which is a species of the banyan tree, called the *Jaya Sri Maha Bodhi*, in Anuradhapura, Sri Lanka. It was planted in 288 BC and reputed to be the oldest tree in the world.[19]

Hence, there is only 'relative immortality', or 'quasi-immortality', phrases that are confessedly clumsy and misnomers, but the best available to communicate that just as complete death, that is, the entire annihilation of consciousness, is an impossibility in nature, just so, continuous and unending immutability of any condition or state is a philosophical absurdity and also an impossibility in nature, because movement and progress are subsumed in eternity.

Time is relative: one stream of consciousness runs throughout all time

What is indeed immortal is the uninterrupted stream of consciousness, albeit undergoing continuous and unceasing changes of phase states in its realizations of itself throughout endless duration.

In occult science, the endless cycles of duration correspond with the waking and sleeping cycles in the life of man: 'As above, so below' according to the Hermetic Axiom (see Volume I, Chapter 8). Thus, the Sanskrit words *manvantara* and *pralaya* mean, respectively: a period of manifestation pertaining to the various life-cycles, terrestrial, planetary, solar, and beyond; and the converse period of rest and dissolution. They may be thought of in the most general sense as 'world periods', but readers should refrain from making direct comparisons with the postulated age of the universe according to physical cosmology. (For interest, the length of a Planetary manvantara, also known as the Day of Brahmā, is 4,320,000,000 years. However, the lengths of other cyclic time-periods are not relevant to this Chapter.) From the standpoint of man, then, immortality refers to the immense period of time spanning a world period, after which the divine entities thus passing out enter into still higher realms to reappear at the end of pralaya at the dawn of the succeeding manvantara. But this need not concern us as there is more than enough on the plate of humanity to digest in our present manvantara, let alone a future one!

There is arguably no finer example of the subtle and exquisite distinctions of meaning between 'infinite' and 'infinity', 'duration' and 'to endure', 'eternal' and 'eternity' than this succinct extract from the 'General Scholium'—Sir Isaac Newton's inspired essay appended to his *Principia*:

> He [the Supreme God] is eternal and infinite, omnipotent and omniscient; that is, his duration reaches from eternity to eternity; his presence from infinity to infinity; [...]. He is not eternity and infinity, but eternal and infinite; he is not duration or space, but he endures and is present. He endures for ever, and is everywhere present; and, by existing always and everywhere, he constitutes duration and space. Since every particle of space is *always*, and every indivisible moment of duration is *everywhere*, certainly the Maker and Lord of all things cannot be *never* and *nowhere*.[20]

The clarity of Newton's thought on time and the Divine

This legendary passage has been put on the rack of scholastic debate and endlessly subjected to the dreadful instruments of left-brained, intellectual torture by those scholars and academics for whom the idea of metaphysical thought, or any notion of divinity, would be anathema (many examples of such types were cited in Volume I). To the writer, it speaks volumes as embedded within it are innumerable hidden and increasingly subtle layers of meaning, with no need of any assistance from academic debate. Apropos, does not the phrase in the last sentence 'the Maker and Lord of all things cannot be *never* and *nowhere*' clearly imply that 'the Maker and Lord of all things', or, the spark of Ātma/Spirit/Divine Consciousness, by whatever name, is ubiquitous, undying and eternal—a central theme of this work? As eloquently put by Blavatsky:

> That which in the mind of the great mathematician assumed the shadowy, but firmly rooted image of God, as the *noumenon* of all, was called more philosophically by the ancient (and modern) philosophers and Occultists— 'Gods,' or the *creative* fashioning Powers.[21]

Therefore, in further explanation by the Theosophist Gottfried de Purucker (1874–1942):

> What men call 'unconsciousness' is merely a form of consciousness which is too subtle for our gross brain-minds to perceive or to sense or to grasp; and, secondly, strictly speaking, what men call death, whether of a universe or of their own physical bodies, is but the breaking up of worn-out vehicles and the transference of consciousness to a higher plane. It is important to seize the spirit of this marvel[l]ous teaching [of occult science], and not allow the imperfect brain-mind to quibble over words, or to pause or hesitate at difficult terms.[22]

The need to transcend literalism

The Question of Reward and Punishment

The Higher Ego in the devachanic state is not omniscient and is not aware of what is happening in the physical world that it has left behind. The karma of evil deeds is temporarily suspended, and only the karma of benevolent thoughts and deeds are carried into Devachan. Suffering is reserved for the subsequent Earth life, not in the post-mortem states, because the causes generated on any plane have to meet with their consequences on the same plane. What is sown in the physical world must be reaped in the physical world. In other words, causes generated on Earth can exhaust in no other state but on Earth. There are exceptions, however. For example, a case of suicide where an individual retains a degree of consciousness and remains for a while in an unhappy limbo state for having been deliberately responsible for taking their own life. However, such a person's post-mortem state would depend entirely on their motive for ending their physical life. There is an absolute world of difference in motive between a person who takes their life because of, say, unbearable physical pain or to avoid terrorist–interrogation under torture in prison, and another who decides to do so to escape the course of justice for some criminal act. Suffering may also be the lot of a person who dies in the clutches of some abnormally strong unsatisfied ambition or an uncontrollable passion for the physical satisfactions of food, drink, sex or material possessions. Extreme sorrow also inhibits a departed soul from going ahead towards greater peace and freedom. Other than such exceptional cases where an individual brings suffering upon himself by excessive attachment to gross physical appetites or excessive grief, there is no post-mortem punishment for evil or misguided conduct when in the body, nor is there any experience corresponding to *eternal* damnation or the traditional hell. But, as always, there is a major exception to the common rule: it is the state known as *Avītchi* and this is touched upon later.

Meanwhile, the very fact of Devachan shows the preponderance of good over evil in the former personality of the vast majority of people. So while the karma (of evil doing) is held in abeyance for the time being to follow a man in his future incarnation on Earth, he brings along with him only the karma of his good deeds, words, and thoughts into Devachan. That said, words like 'evil' and 'good' are entirely relative terms. The absolute constant is the unerring *Law of Retribution—the only law that never errs*. Retribution must not be equated solely with reprimand. It applies equally to rewards justly earned. In summary, whereas man will have to pay for his wrongdoings, both voluntary and involuntary during incarnation, temporarily he receives in Devachan the *effects* of the benevolent *causes* produced by him during life.

Third Transition – From Spiritual Life to a New Life on Earth

Reincarnation is the cyclical process whereby the Reincarnating Ego in Devachan takes on entirely fresh mortal vestures (the Lower Triad as shown in Table II-10, page 66) for a new life on Earth. Strictly speaking, then, rebirth refers to the physical event as a final outcome of the cyclic process of reincarnation. However, only a fraction of the spiritual nature 'descends into', and clothes itself in, material existence for an individual life on Earth. Chapter 7 of Volume III delves into these matters in more detail.

The devachanic experience goes through stages analogous to Earth life, being the post-mortem analogue of physical growth and death: the first flutter of sentient life, the

Is there punishment after death?

The Law of Retribution

attainment of 'prime', the progressive exhaustion of force passing into semi-consciousness, gradual oblivion and lethargy, total oblivion and then—not death, but rebirth: birth into another personality on Earth. Why does it occur?

> Forget not that I shall come back to you. A little while, and my longing shall gather dust and foam for another body.
>
> Kahlil Gibran[23]

In daily life we are naturally drawn to revisiting familiar experiences or scenes, say a favourite restaurant or the place of a memorable holiday. Just so, what draws the devachanee back into rebirth is the force of *Taṇhā*, a Pāli word,[iii] familiar in Buddhism, meaning the 'thirst' for material life, the desire to live and cling to earthly life. But what is this thirst based on? *Tṛṣṇā* (*Trishna*) is a Sanskrit word, which also means 'thirst', but with the added qualification of thirst for things and familiar scenes which the human ego formerly knew from past experience, and which it wills and desires to know again. Attracted to the old and familiar experiences and scenes, it thirsts for the manifested (embodied) life comprising them. Obvious attractors are desires unfulfilled, love unrequited, duties left incomplete, yearnings unfulfilled, and all thoughts and actions sown that must of necessity reap their fruits on the plane where they were sown—Earth. This thirst for the familiar, material life which brings the Reincarnating Ego along the downward arc back to Earth-life is the strongest individual cause for reincarnation than all else.

Longing for sentient life and familiarity

Generally speaking, the process of incarnation from Devachan to rebirth on Earth is the reverse of that constituting the upward arc. The Reincarnating Ego takes on subtle bodies on the different planes of nature, finally acquiring its mortal coil. However, the actual details are not a literal mirroring of the upward cycle of post-mortem states. For example, there is no question of a Kāma-rūpa when 'returning' to Earth. (The reincarnation process is depicted in the final column of Table II-11 shown on page 98 of this Chapter.)

Reincarnation is a highly complex subject with numerous interfaces: pre-existence, re-embodiment, metempsychosis, and transmigration are all related to, but not the same as, it. Moreover, no comprehensive account of reincarnation can be given without a full treatment of the Law of Karma. It is not possible to do adequate justice to this important Law in such a short exposition, as candidly stated in the opening to this Chapter. Full details can be found in the occult sources provided in Endnote II-5. However, there are a few vital points to stress.

As at the solemn moment of death when each man sees in a flash the whole of his life marshalled before him and is shown the whole chain of causes that have been at work during his life, similarly at the moment of rebirth, the Higher Ego has a prospective vision of the life which awaits him and realizes all the causes that have led to it. All the vices, desires, and especially the passions of the preceding incarnation become, through definite Laws of Affinity and Transference, the germs of the future potentialities in the Animal soul (Kāma) with its dependence on the astral double (the Etheric double, or Liṅga-Śarīra). The Higher Ego—the *Christos* principle in each man—as Parent, remains always the same; its unruly child, the personality, alone changes from one incarnation to the next. And it is the Parent's karma that guides and dictates the moral traits of its former child (the old personality) that

Reincarnation and karma are inextricably linked

---

iii The Buddhist scriptures are all written in Pāli, the language of Magadha (an ancient country in India under Buddhist Kings) that preceded the more refined Sanskrit.

the Parent knew not how to control, that will reappear as the child in the new man that will be. Therefore it is said that the 'new man is but the son and progeny of the old man that was'—unless the Parent managed, to some degree to conquer and control the irresponsibility of its former child (the role of Antaḥkaraṇa being crucial here, as explained below).

This deeply occult teaching finds its crassest distortion in orthodox Christianity in statements such as, 'Jesus died for our sins', the argument being that Jesus came into our world and lived a perfect life, so death had no hold on Him, but yet in His grace and out of His compassion for us poor sinners, He chose to die *on our behalf*—so He took our punishment for us and for our sins, *as our substitute*. And so all who put their trust (or blind faith) in Jesus will be forgiven by God.

If orthodox Christianity knew anything about the sublime esotericism concealed in the scriptures the last sentence above would read: 'Every man who actively seeks to unite his personal life with his Higher Self will call upon himself the radiance of spiritual light.'

It must not be imagined that the parents provide a soul to the incoming reincarnating entity. Human parents bequeath only the appropriate physical vehicle and psychic vesture to the Reincarnating Ego (soul, in popular terms), which must then work out its own karma through its new, karmically conditioned psycho-physical body. For example, an advanced 'musical soul' would naturally be drawn to parents that can provide a highly sensitive nervous system.

Finally, the popular idea about the human soul reincarnating as, say, an animal, or even a stone, as a punitive measure for evils committed in an earlier existence and then having to work its way up through the kingdoms of nature by way of moral rectitude is to misunderstand both the nature of the human soul and reincarnation. Deeply rooted in *orthodox* Brahmanical eschatology, this idea is another gross distortion of the original meanings of metempsychosis and transmigration of souls. Even the great Schrödinger, for whom the writer has boundless regard, is not free from committing the error of confusing the popular exoteric theology of the Brahmins with its esoteric import. In his book *My View of the World* he remarks on 'the question of how a poor toad can work its way up, by moral conduct, to being a hare, and then become at least a Sudra [an untouchable in the Hindu caste system], is a problem in itself.'[24] Of course there are many humans who are toad-*like*, displaying, for example, the nocturnal characteristics of a toad, but that does not mean that their souls have transmigrated from a human existence into an amphibian one. *Once a human, always a human* is the law, and other than in the rarest of abnormal circumstances, which need not be entered into here, it is virtually inviolable.

The Phenomena of Apparitions

Having just sketched the transcendent aspect of death, what do we now make of the stories that abound in the legends and fables of all cultures and religions about what are generally known in the Occident under a variety of names like 'spooks', or 'ghosts'? How do such apparitions occur, and do they have any consciousness to speak of?

After the second death, whereupon man is 'born again', or in other words, the Spirit in man, that is, the Higher Ego (Higher Triad) has 'ascended' to Devachan, there can obviously be no return to Earth, since there is then no connecting link. Released of its divine inhabitant the Higher Ego, the Kāma-rūpa becomes a psychic corpse known in occult literature as a 'shell', in the same way that the body becomes a corpse upon physical death. Just as a cast-off overcoat may retain the shape and the odour of its former wearer for a time, so the discarded vesture (shell) of the Higher Ego retains some of the characteristics of the deceased personality. Stated otherwise, being the residue of the mortal personality that was, the shell retains some residual consciousness for a while. For this reason, the shell is temporarily an exact astral duplicate in appearance and mannerism of the man who died; quite literally his *eidolon*, or 'image'.

How, and when, do apparitions occur?

Left to its semi-senseless self, the discarded Kāma-rūpa of the late personality—the shell—subsequently disintegrates when its residual psychic energies are dissipated, where-upon its constituents are then recycled back to the psychic planes of the universe in the same way as the physical body dies when the physical energies are spent and the detritus of the physical corpse reverts to the physical plane (Earth). However, when the discarnate man is still strongly earthbound, i.e., unable to loosen his earthly ties to persons, places, and possessions, the shell can hover in the terrestrial atmosphere and sometimes appear as an apparition. Séance room phenomena are due to the artificial activation of the shell by the vitality of the medium or sitters before the former has had time to disintegrate. The overriding principle is that the duration of the Kāma-rūpa, and subsequently the shell, depends entirely on the sensual energies of the man during life; in other words, the extent to which his thoughts have energized and fuelled his desire nature, which, if not fully sati-ated or exhausted during physical life will have to expend its pent up energies after death.

If the man has turned his thoughts towards the higher life and loosened his grip on sati-ating his desire nature, then the shell may exist for a short time before disintegrating and releasing the immortal triad. But, if forcibly drawn back into the terrestrial sphere the 'spook', so named, may prevail for a period greatly exceeding its natural existence in Kāma-loka. There are essentially two ways in which this can happen.

If during earthly life the man harboured strong passions or died with unfulfilled lustful appetites or with thoughts of murder, violence or revenge, then the spook, comprising those pent up psychic energies could be attracted earthwards by the atmosphere of debauched places and the aura of dissolute persons or, worst of all, by abominable necro-mantic practices. Once the Kāma-rūpa has 'learnt' the way back to living human bodies (i.e., established a magnetic affinity with a person), it becomes a vampire, feeding on the vitality of those who invited its company. (In a sense, one could regard this as the psychic equivalent of the law of conservation of energy in physics. On any plane, pent up energies cannot just disappear—they must find an appropriate outlet and release.) In India these eidolons are called *Pisachas* and are much dreaded, as also in other cultures. It is precisely for this reason that capital punishment, considered from the occult standpoint, is not to be recommended. A murderer in his body serving his life sentence in prison is a lesser threat to humanity than one forcibly thrown out of his body by execution with all his criminal propensities in full flood—such only serve to poison the psychic atmosphere.

Malevolent apparitions: their circumstances

The other case is that of a perfectly good and upright man who has suffered a sudden, invariably violent, death in the prime of life. One can instinctively feel that because such a man has not lived his allotted life span, the Kāma-rūpa will be charged with unspent psychic energies and affinities to matters left undone or to family ties left behind. The Kāma-rūpa may then be drawn into the terrestrial atmosphere by the excessive grief of friends or loved ones. Such a spook, although startling to the beholder, is harmless and benign. There have been many reports of soldiers killed in World War II, whose apparitions later appeared in their homes. Their surviving colleagues have reported that when mortally wounded, many a young soldier cried out to his mother at the moment of death, for example, at the Battle of Normandy on 6 June 1944 (D-Day). It is not difficult to envisage that a strong emotionally-charged final thought of a dying youth towards his home and mother, reinforced by his mother's own constant loving thoughts towards her son on the battlefield, would result in a materialization subsequently appearing, unsurprisingly, in the family bedroom of his former home.

Benign
apparitions: their
circumstances

Such cases are substantiated in *In Times of War – Messages of Wisdom from Soldiers in the Afterlife*, which documents conversations with soldiers who purport to have been near death or killed as a result of war.[25] There are classic extracts from Lord Dowding (1882–1970), the British commander of RAF Fighter Command during the Battle of Britain, and from Wellesley Tudor Pole (1884–1968), the spiritualist and early British Bahá'í. Many individual cases are cited which bear witness to the fact that soldiers who died suddenly sometimes appeared to loved ones with comforting messages to the effect that they were well. *In Times of War* also contains noteworthy extracts from the case histories assembled by Carl Wickland (1861–1945) the Swedish–American psychiatrist and psychical researcher and the chief psychiatrist at the National Psychopathic Institute of Chicago.[26] Known as the Wickland scripts, they include ostensible communications from the American businessman, real estate developer, and investor John Jacob 'Jack' Astor IV (1864–1912), and the wealthy American businessman Alfred Gwynne Vanderbilt Sr. (1877–1915) who were drowned in the RMS Titanic and RMS Lusitania disasters, respectively. Both reflect on what they then realized, namely, that their lives had been self-serving instead of devoted to serving others.

It seems that knowing nothing about the possibility of post-mortem states of consciousness results in unnecessary difficulties during the transition to afterlife. This view is supported by the British psychologist, parapsychologist, and author David G. J. Fontana FBPsS (1934–2010) who possessed evidence to suggest that those who experience sudden death or have no belief in an afterlife may remain 'earthbound', that is, still attached to the material world, unaware in some cases that death has occurred and resentful at the prospect of others enjoying their old homes and possessions. It is said that such earthbound individuals may be responsible for poltergeist and perhaps other hauntings, and possibly for influencing the thoughts and behaviour of susceptible individuals.[27]

When the afterlife
becomes
'earthbound'

For this reason, however hard and difficult it may seem, occult science counsels that overwhelming and extended grief, beyond the natural course of bereavement, is selfish because it holds back the departed from their onward journey towards empyrean realms. The real tragedy is for those left behind in their personal bereavement, not for the newly departed who has been (except under exceptional and rare circumstances) freed of all sorrow and pain, albeit temporarily.

The effect of grief

> Of course, we would not be human if we did not miss loved ones; but in feeling lonesome for them we don't want selfish attachment to be the cause of keeping them earthbound. Extreme sorrow prevents a departed soul from going ahead toward greater peace and freedom.
>
> Paramahansa Yogananda[28]

However, it should be noted, carefully, that not all materializations are the handiwork of the Kāma-rūpa. There are many other factors and phenomena at play, like the Liṅga-śarīra and Māyāvi-rūpa, previously explained, and these account in large measure for deathbed apparitions, especially during crisis.

Photographic Pictures in Support of Apparitional Phenomena

Given that throughout the ages there have been innumerable cases of apparitions seen not just by sensitives but also by otherwise perfectly normal persons, it should be possible in our current age of modern science to obtain photographic evidence of such occurrences soon after death during the borderline between death and afterlife. There is indeed evidence to support this contention.

Harry Oldfield (1953–2019) was a British inventor, scientist, and explorer of undiscovered realms. The visual presentation of energy fields was his especial area of interest and to that end he invented the Polycontrast Interference Photography (PIP) imaging system pioneered in the 1980s (now superseded by the New Energy Vision Camera). Using microchip technology, Oldfield developed a scanner which could provide a real time, moving image of the energy field of the human body and other objects. He then devised a computer program to analyse the different light intensities being reflected from the person or object being scanned. In simple terms, what is shown is an energy interaction with light, providing insight into the energy counter-part, i.e., the etheric template, or Etheric double on which the Physical body is moulded (see Table II-3 Chapter 2, page 21). In 2006, the International Society for the Study of Subtle Energies and Energy Medicine awarded Oldfield the Alyce and Elmer Green Award for Innovation in respect of his photo-imaging work. The Society noted that it, 'allows us to experience our multi-dimensional existence through his extraordinary images.'[29]

Modern technology employed to verify subtle energies on the physical plane

Oldfield used the PIP instrument to conduct experiments, as ethically as possible, under the direction of a professor of pathology in a mortuary. His objective was to photograph spectral energies and 'presences' to demonstrate that the psychic manifestations of the newly deceased have a basis in science. Four corpses were brought into the mortuary within the previous twelve hours of the experiment and the coroner was requested that none of the bodies be kept in the fridge so as to be maintained in their 'natural' state. One body was that of a young man who had died a few hours earlier in a road traffic accident. Another body was of an elderly man who had suddenly expired whilst chatting with friends twelve hours previously. The third and fourth bodies were of a man and a woman who had died approximately twenty-four hours before from deliberate drug overdoses. All films were confidential, and out of respect for the deceased and their families, names were withheld and under no circumstances were faces shown to outside parties.

Circumstances of death determine quality of post-mortem energies

In the case of the young man and the elderly man, there appeared to be residual energy around both bodies and, looking above the bodies, there were configurations of energy, approximately the same length and width of the physical body and reaching up to about four feet above it. Regarding the suicide cases, the post-mortem changes were the most advanced and the PIP images showed a very low-grade energetic pattern which appeared as dark red and black, denoting that the life-force was absent. Moreover, energy configurations did not seem to be present above the bodies as in the case of the young man and the elderly man. This finding bears out what we have stated earlier in this Chapter (which is none other than the unequivocal verdict of the perennial wisdom) regarding the post-mortem state of suicide victims, namely, that their degree of unhappiness is dependent on the motive behind the act.

In evaluating the worth of these discoveries, it must be stated that Oldfield was not the archetypical international scientist with high academic qualifications, accolades, learned books, and scholarly, peer-reviewed papers to his name. However, this work has made the point, more than once, that the 'famous' are not necessarily the 'great', and the 'great' invariably do not become 'famous'. There are many scientists whose quest after truth involves a journey outside that of mainstream science (see the opening of Volume I, Chapter 5). Such researchers tend to work in virtual solitude in their homes, or garage workshops, and are known only to their immediate colleagues. Their output, however, should be appraised on its own merits being no less worthy for not originating from Oxbridge or an Ivy League university. Just so, the writer has attended Oldfield's workshops, lectures, and investigative demonstrations on numerous occasions over many years and can personally bear witness to the genuineness of the scanned images of the human energy field and associated photographs. On these grounds, there are no reasons to doubt, a priori, the testimony from the images scanned in the mortuary as described in *Harry Oldfield's Invisible Universe*.[30]

We continue with a subject, necessarily unpleasant, but of grave importance if we are to gain any understanding about the darker regions of consciousness that mainstream science is singularly unable to comprehend. Our whole purpose, as with all else in this work, is not to revel in details for their own sake but only to mention as much of the latter as is needed to recognize the underlying principles in order to surmount the more sombre aspects of existence with intelligence and understanding. This applies to what is popularly known as 'hell'.

The State of Avītchi and the Eighth Sphere

Avītchi (*Avīchi*) is a Sanskrit word, the general meaning of which is 'waveless', 'without happiness', 'without repose', which all imply complete immobility and total stagnation of life, therefore no happiness and continuous agony. According to Blavatsky, the literal meaning is 'uninterrupted hell', so this state may be likened to the Inferno of Dante's *Divine Comedy*[31] at the entrance to which are inscribed the words 'Abandon hope, all ye who enter here'.[iv] It is symbolized, debatably, by the rough-hewn underground crypt of the Great Pyramid of Giza. At one end of the crypt is a passage of polished stone—leading to an absolute dead end. Avītchi may, in this sense, be regarded as the counterpart, or 'shadow', of Devachan. It afflicts all those who have slipped down into the mire of unredeemable sin and bestiality. When that happens, the stream of personalities eventually comes to an end because the immortal Ego—the Higher Ego (the 'Parent')—will have lost all influence over its lower selves—the Personal ego (personality, its 'child')—and the connection between the two, becoming ever more tenuous, will have become severed

Truth is not the special prerogative of those with 'Ivy League' credentials

Circumstances leading to *Avītchi*

---

iv Some translations from the Italian give, 'Have faith, all ye who enter here'; however the correct version is as stated above.

forever. (Why this happens is summarized in the section on the Antaḥkaraṇa.) The fate of the Personal ego, bereft of its parent Ego then becomes dismal beyond compare. It is drawn out of the terrestrial atmosphere and exists for ages without repose—Avītchi—where, 'abandon[ing] hope', it relives all the calamitous steps which led it thence before finally withering and dying out altogether. (The Higher Ego is also affected by such a breakdown. Having failed to gain the experience of earthly life that its personalities were supposed to supply, it too becomes a failure in its own realm and falls into a dreamless sleep awaiting the next planetary cycle to re-evolve its humanity, this time in full consciousness, through all the forms of the lower kingdoms of nature.[32])

Where do such dire traits of consciousness exist? Does this imply that there are states even lower than the physical; lower in the sense of being yet more suffused in selfishness and materiality? The occult doctrines do not shirk from pointing out that this is indeed so, but carry a heavy warning that humanity must have no truck with such states which belong to a distant past. That being the case, there can be, and have been, not infrequent breakouts from such subterranean vaults of consciousness whereby individuals or groups have inflicted unspeakable brutality upon humanity in ways that the conventional mental sciences (psychiatry and psychology) are at a complete loss to explain.[33] We need not labour the point that there are many examples of such derelicts during the long period of human history. The crimes perpetrated by the Nazis upon humanity, intensified in their horror by the mental element of strong premeditation, meticulous planning, and ruthless organization, are just one of many recent examples. It would not be unreasoning to suggest that this phenomena of breakouts of lone individuals or groups from the so called, 'nether regions' is symbolized in the popular phantasy novel, and related film, *Harry Potter and the Prisoner of Azkaban*,[34] where the prisoner Sirius Black has escaped from the Azkaban prison and wants to murder Harry.[v]

Subhuman states of consciousness

But Avītchi is not necessarily a post-mortem state only, or between two births: it can also exist on Earth. This writer personally knows two individuals who recently went on a conducted tour of the sites of the former Auschwitz and Birkenau extermination camps. Their abiding impression was the eerie stillness of the atmosphere with no signs of life—no birds flying overhead. This is not the stillness of tranquillity, but indeed the 'waveless state' of utter stagnation of life. However, Avītchi is not a place of eternal damnation or 'punishment' in the orthodox Christian sense (another example of how an exoteric religion distorts the esoteric meaning), but a generalized term for places, namely, *states of consciousness* of extreme evil realization, where the will for evil and the unsatisfied evil longings for utter brutality, bestiality, and selfishness find their opportunity for expansion—*and the final extinction of the evil entity itself, ground over in Nature's laboratory*, which is known as the Eighth Sphere, or Planet of Death.

Avītchi is an extremely evil state of consciousness

Occult science is even more guarded about divulging details about what is, in effect, a state of psycho-mental degeneration (consciousness) more advanced even than Avītchi, being the habitat of what is called in the esoteric philosophy 'lost souls'. Where there is

---

v The staggering popularity of the Harry Potter series and films, full of tales of magic, makes it plain that however much mainstream science may attempt to indoctrinate society with the concept of materialism, the public in general are irresistibly drawn to novels that embody occult truths about life and existence. It was J. K. Rowling's brilliance to transmit such truths in strongly characterized story form, hence bypassing cold scientific scepticism.

the glimmer of re-ensoulment in Avītchi by way of the umbilical connection with the Monad (Ātma-Buddhi), such a possibility vanishes in the Eighth Sphere. We are informed that whereas Avītchi is exclusively a state or condition, the Planet of Death, besides being a state or condition, is an actual globe. (It may be tempting to think of Black Holes in this regard but there is no justification or evidence for such an assumption.)

The point to grasp is that Nature has all things in her, including her facilities for waste recycling at all levels. For just as there are grades of 'heavens' where good men elevate according to their spiritual status, so also Avītchi has many grades and degrees where those who must find an outlet for their burning evil passions sink to the appropriate level. This is illustrated in Botticelli's depiction of *Inferno* (hell) shown in Figure II-3. Here, the punishment fits the offence as in *Purgatorio*, but much more severely because of the greater severity of the crimes: so, for example, the punishment might entail being imprisoned in an icy lake in perpetuity, or wandering forever lost in a dark wood confronted by savage beasts (the beasts being the effects received in the afterlife of the savage thoughts and deeds put out as causes during life). Given that esoteric truths were utterly distorted by the malign influence of the material hell superstition then prevailing (during the Middle Ages), it bears repeating that the sufferings depicted in *Inferno* and *Purgatorio* (and the delights in *Paradiso*) all refer to states of consciousness. Nonetheless, it is quite possible, as Blavatsky points out, that the modern West has still to understand that the souls of some evil men might have already passed away (though not to the fabled *Inferno*, taken literally), whilst such men themselves still lived (see more later).[35] Contemporary examples are not difficult to cite.

A possible reason as to how and why such an unfortunate state of affairs can occur is now outlined regarding the role of *Antahkarana*. Other than this, there is no value in pursuing this unsavoury topic any further, the sole reason for mentioning it here is, as said earlier, 'forewarned is forearmed'; the most sensible way to avoid danger is to become aware of it through understanding and by reading the signs, without getting involved or caught up with it in any way.

Antaḥkaraṇa – The Connection Between the Personal and the Divine: Man's Spiritual Life-Support

> *Antaskaraṇa* is the lower *Manas*, the Path of communication or communion between the personality and the higher *Manas* or human Soul.
>
> H. P. Blavatsky[36]

The Sanskrit word *Antaḥkaraṇa* (also spelt *Antaskaraṇa*) literally means 'internal instrument'; hence, 'path', or 'bridge' derived from the compound *antar*, meaning 'interior', 'between'; and *karana*, sense-organ derived from the verbal root *kri* 'to act', 'to do'—hence 'action', 'cause'.

So the essential meaning behind Antaḥkarana (in the technical sense used by Blavatsky) is the intermediate instrument, or vehicle of consciousness, functioning as a narrow *bridge* between the Lower and the Higher Manas. In this sense, therefore, it is a vehicle of consciousness, as shown in the last column of Table II-5 of Chapter 3 on page 40.

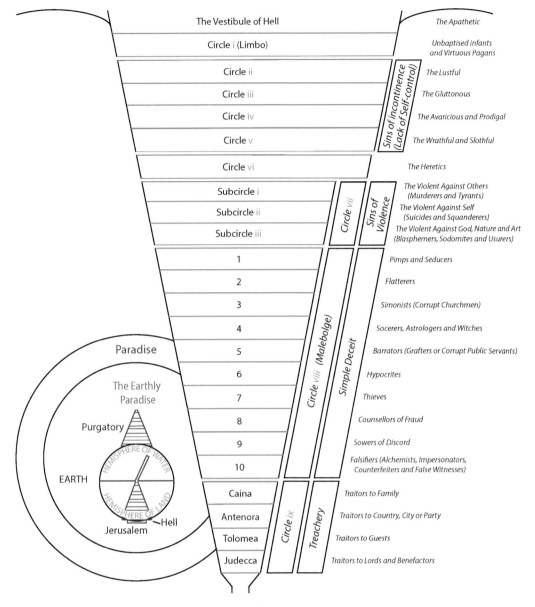

Figure II-3 *Inferno*

Reproduced from the Royal Academy of London pamphlet based on N. Sapegno (ed.), 'Dante Alighieri,
La Divina Commedia' (Florence, La Nuova Italia, Scandicci, 1985). Acknowledgement clause provided on page xi
under the list of illustrations for this Volume.

(For simplicity, the primary function of Antaḥkaraṇa has been described in the foregoing as the path, or bridge, linking the Lower and Higher Manas, i.e., the Lower, or Personal ego (self) with the Higher, or Inner Ego (Self). (In fact, as Purucker explains, the human septenary constitution has several Antaḥkaraṇas, one for every interface between any two of the several monadic centres in man. As microcosm of the macrocosm, man is therefore a unity in diversity, a unified composite; and Antaḥkaraṇas are the links of vibrating 'consciousness-substance' uniting these various centres.[37])

Antaḥkaraṇa provides spiritual life-support

Interestingly, however, some Australian Aboriginal tribes speak of a similar 'bridge' between the Lower self and the spirit (in popular terms) which they call 'the Rainbow Snake'.[38]

Another helpful metaphor is an umbilical connection. During a space walk, astronauts require an umbilical cord from their spacecraft to their spacesuits to supply oxygen and an environmental control system; an umbilical cord from a mother to a baby supplies the foetus with oxygenated, nutrient-rich blood. Invoking the Hermetic axiom 'As above, so below', Antaḥkaraṇa thus serves as the umbilical connection between the Higher Ego as 'Parent' with its 'child' the personality. In the first two examples it is a matter of physical life-support: with Antaḥkaraṇa it is psycho-spiritual life-support. But the principle is always one and the same. It is obvious that, at any level, severing an umbilical connection prematurely would have dire consequences. How this pertains to Antaḥkaraṇa will soon become obvious.

Purpose and Function

Antaḥkarāṇa serves as the medium of communication between the Lower ego and Higher Ego, conveying to the latter all those personal thoughts and impressions which, by their nature, can qualify to be assimilated by the undying higher entity and thus be made immortal with it. Therefore, whatever is so conveyed are only those elements of the ephemeral personality that survive death and time. It thus stands to reason that only those thoughts and aspirations that are noble, altruistic, and of a spiritual nature can be so absorbed by the Higher Ego into Eternity.

Besides providing solace to bereaved family and friends, the main purpose of the funeral ceremonies and prayers of practically all religions, in whatever form, is to assist the newly departed person cross the antahkaranic bridge by severing former earthly ties and moving towards higher realms of consciousness. This is especially significant if the person has suffered a violent or sudden death (as in the war time cases cited above) and therefore been denied the grace of a life review during the natural dying process.

Antaḥkaraṇa enables the transfer of consciousness

How Formed

How is this link between the lower and the Higher Mind formed? It is not possible to identify it objectively as a substantial entity. Nevertheless, it is entirely real for the conscious experiencer of it. Technically speaking, Antaḥkaraṇa is a projection of the Lower mind, being that part of the latter which retains its purity by virtue of not becoming identified with, and thus defiled by, lower desires and emotions. But as previously explained, the Lower mind itself is an emanation of the Higher Mind and so there is always the possibility of a reunion with its parent source.

Accountability for Human Traits

Human traits span the virtually limitless range from utter criminality, to common humanity, to supernal genius. How Antaḥkaraṇa features in these three broad categories is now outlined.

For the average person, Antaḥkaraṇa disintegrates at death and its remains survive for a while as the Kāma-rūpa, or later as the 'shell'. Ultimately however, the antahkaranic bridge has to be destroyed, or rather transcended, during life by the merging of the personal nature with the divine Self. But a serious warning is given in occult literature that any premature attempt at such destruction 'before the personal [Personal ego] is absolutely under the control of the impersonal Ego [Higher Ego], we risk to lose the latter and be severed forever from it, unless indeed we hasten to re-establish the communication by a supreme and final effort.'[39] The reasons are as follows.

Blavatsky mentions the example of the Scottish novelist, poet, and musician Robert Louis Stevenson (1850–1894) who glimpsed a true vision in his novel *Strange Case of Dr Jekyll and Mr Hyde*[40] about the struggle between good and evil that Dr Jekyll faced and how, in the end, his own good nature was overpowered by the evil in himself—a perfect allegorical account about the dreadful catastrophe resulting from the premature destruction of Antaḥkaraṇa, when the psycho-animal Lower self detaches from its divine parent source.[41] This archetypal tale of a man taken over by his dark side has become an entrenched metaphor of the shadow. Presumably, however, in order to show her students that the Jekyll and Hyde phenomenon is not just the stuff of novels, Blavatsky also cites an actual example of criminality that has become imprinted on the public mind for sadistic brutality—the serial killer Jack the Ripper of Victorian London.[42] There is no shortage of modern instances of lone, brutal serial killers, especially of young women or innocent children. We prefer not to mention any names.

Accounting for the Jeyll & Hyde and Jack the Ripper phenomena

Real life societal examples during any epoch of human history are also, unfortunately, not hard to find. In modern times, for example, it is the writer's persuasion that the monstrous crimes perpetrated against humanity by totalitarian dictators and their henchmen (their names, again, need not be mentioned), who commit crimes in full awareness of their actions but without any subsequent trace of penitence, may be due to the premature destruction of Antaḥkaraṇa (happening for all sorts of reasons too complex to enter into here), thus freeing the animal nature to run amok without the conscience-bestowing connection to its (former) spiritual source. These are what is known in occultism as 'soul-less beings on earth'.

Let Blavatsky explain:

Consequences when Antaḥkaraṇa is prematurely severed

> Thus we find two kinds of *soulless* beings on earth: those who have lost their higher Ego in the present incarnation, and those who are born soulless, having been severed from their Spiritual Soul in the preceding birth. The former are candidates for Avichi; the latter are 'Mr. Hydes,' whether *in* or *out* of their human bodies, whether incarnated or hanging about as invisible but potent *ghouls*. In such men, cunning develops to an enormous degree, and no one except those who are familiar with the doctrine would suspect them of being soulless, for neither Religion nor Science has the least suspicion that such facts actually exist in Nature.[43]

It is important to appreciate that extreme criminality has nothing whatsoever to do with the intellectual stature of the offender. The above passage supplies more than a mere hint at why some of the worst criminals in history have been men of great persuasion and high intellect—in the service of animal cunning.

Distinguish between intelligence, intellect, and cunning

Animal cunning, as the Blavatsky intimates, is not so easily discerned, since such persons can be possessed of much charm and influence. It is the writer's contention that the extent to which a person displays cunning and manipulative characteristics (never to be confused with intelligence and disciplined authority), is a measure of the extent to which such a person is an agent, or instrument for the workings of dark forces. Such persons can be found in all walks of life, including spiritual societies. This extremely important point is taken up in the final summation (Chapter 11) and Epilogue to this work in Volume III.

Thus it is that even nowadays, 'neither Religion nor Science has the least suspicion that such facts actually exist in Nature'. It is occult science, *par excellence* that supplies the missing pieces of the psychological jigsaw puzzle. But to continue this subject, as complex as it is highly dangerous if taken perfunctorily, would not be helpful. Serious readers can consult the source references cited.

Note that the above is in no way suggesting that all offenders and 'ordinary criminals' (if the phrase be permitted) have lost the antahkaranic connection—only those who, it bears repeating, whilst fully aware of their criminal actions, revel in their brutality and display absolutely no remorse, thus indicating the complete severance of the umbilical connection between the child-personality and its divine parent-source. As the chronicles of the Law Courts amply testify, the majority of offenders experience much shame and repentance for their behaviour. For such (and many other) reasons, it is suggested, the Christ taught, 'I tell you, there will be more joy in heaven over one sinner who repents [thus re-establishing, or strengthening, the antahkaranic connection with the divine source, 'heaven'] than over ninety-nine righteous persons who need no repentance.'[44]

Related to the above, it will be apparent that strengthening the Antahkaraṇa is of paramount importance to the awakening of genius. Because each step across the bridge is won by personal effort in disciplining and purifying the lower nature, which concomitantly increases the power and influence of the higher nature—the wellspring of genius, which whole subject is further explored in Chapter 9 of Volume III.

Finally, and in rare circumstances, when the personal self is indissolubly linked with, and merged into Divine Mind, Antahkaraṇa has fulfilled its role and is no longer needed. After all, why maintain a bridge after crossing it from A to B: why maintain the umbilical cord between mother and child when the latter is born and breathing normally? It seems evident that this may be the case in Mahātmās such as the Buddha, the Christ, and Ramana Maharshi, to name but a few.

The conventional nature versus nurture—genes or environment—argument has value regarding the relative contribution of both influences towards human behaviour, such as personality, cognitive traits, temperament, and psychopathology— as regards common humanity. Taken in isolation, such debates and arguments are sterile in exceptional cases of criminality on the one hand or genius on the other hand. Talking, here, of genetic predisposition and aberrant neural pathways in the brain and/or of environmental influences and early childhood experiences explains nothing whatsoever. It is therefore high time that criminologists, psychologists, psychiatrists, neurophysiologists, and ministers, as a body, come to the stark realization that Occult Science *alone* can explain such extremes of aberrant behaviour or genius that these mainstream disciplines, by their own admission, singularly fail to comprehend.

Appendix II-B on page 215 provides further elaboration on the role and function of the Antahkaraṇa.

Telltale signs of premature severance

When Antahkaraṇa has served its purpose

Mounting Scientific Corroboration of the Occult Doctrine on Near-Death and Post-Mortem States

Having presented the occult doctrines on the post-mortem stages, conditions, and associated states of consciousness of man in the foregoing sections of this Chapter, readers are justified to ask whether there is any robust scientific evidence on a subject where there is no shortage of opinions—few of which are well-informed or based on thorough research and evidence. What is more, it is the duty of those who promulgate eternal verities to support it by such evidence as can lawfully be divulged 'with direct inferences deduced from and corroborated by the evidence furnished by modern exact science.'[45]

Chapter 4 in Volume I described phenomena unaccountable in terms of the physical sciences (physics and chemistry) and theories of mind based exclusively on the latter, for example, near-death and out-of-body experiences, telepathy, and *psi* phenomena in general. The life-transforming experiences of NDE subjects, scientific confirmation of the survival of consciousness apart from the brain, and the reality of the paranormal, as espoused by individuals such as Eben Alexander, Rajiv Parti, Jill Bolte Taylor, and Arthur Ellison eminent in their respective fields of neurosurgery, cardiac anesthesiology, neuroanatomy, and electrical and electronic engineering, were summarized. Their individual experiences and investigative reports were clearly not the tales of gullible soothsayers.

Science must corroborate occult doctrines whenever possible

The painstaking research over decades on reincarnation by Ian Stevenson, summarized in Chapter 4 and Endnote I-5 of Volume I, are especially noteworthy. The following sections take this subject a step further, focussing on the evidence from scientific investigations into death as transition entailing the sequence of near-death and afterlife stages and associated states of consciousness. But if we are to show how science has validated some of the occult tenets on death as transition, described in this Chapter, then such evidence had better come from scientists exceptionally qualified to scrutinize and evaluate masses of data impartially. As with the scientists mentioned above, such is also the case with those physicians and scientists who have investigated the transitional state between life and afterlife.

The Transitional State between Life and Afterlife – The Evidence

The case of Dr Wiltse, the physician of Skiddy, Kansas, suffering from acute typhoid fever, is well documented[vi] and a summarized account appears below in the form of an excerpt from *Human Personality and Its Survival of Bodily Death* by the English-born Frederick W. H. Myers (1843–1901). Myers was a poet, philologist, and classical scholar who taught at Trinity College, Cambridge and from there turned to the scientific investigation of spiritualism and related phenomena. In 1882 he became a principal founder of the Society for Psychical Research.

> Although I was pulseless about four hours, this state of apparent death lasted only about half-an-hour. I lost, I believe, all power of thought or knowledge of existence in absolute unconsciousness. Of course, I need not guess at the time so lost, as in such a state a minute or a

---

vi The case was first published in the *St. Louis Medical and Surgical Journal* (November 1889) and subsequently appeared in the *Mid-Continental Review* (February 1890) and in the article by F. W. H. Myers, 'On Indications of Continued Terrene Knowledge, &c.', *Proceedings of the Society for Psychical Research*, viii, (1892), 180–93.

A physician,
recounting his
own near-death
experience,
affirms man's
immortality

thousand years would appear the same. I came again into a state of conscious existence and discovered that I was still in the body, but the body and I had no longer any interest in common. I looked in astonishment and joy for the first time upon myself—the me, the real Ego, while the not me closed it upon all sides like a sepulchre of clay. […] I am about to get out of the body. I watched the interesting process of the separation of soul and body. By some power, apparently not my own, the Ego was rocked to and fro, laterally, as a cradle is rocked, by which process its connection with the tissues of the body was broken up. […] I began slowly to retreat from the feet, towards the head, as a rubber cord shortens. […] As I emerged from the head I floated up and down and laterally like a soap-bubble attached to the bowl of a pipe until I at last broke loose from the body and fell lightly to the floor, where I rose slowly and expanded into the full stature of a man. I seemed to be translucent, of a bluish cast and perfectly naked.[46]

Dr Wiltse's experience would seem to corroborate many of the details, expounded in the earlier section of this Chapter, addressing the intermediate state between physical death and immediately after. Moreover, his experience of the relative nature of time is in accord with our earlier remarks on this matter. In conclusion, the overriding message of this qualified physician is:

I learned that the epidermis was the outside boundary of the ultimate tissues, so to speak, of the soul. I realised my condition and reasoned calmly thus. *I have died, as men term death, and yet I am as much a man as ever* [writer's emphasis].[47]

Psychic Communications – The Evidence

The British scientist Robert Crookall (1890–1981) qualified in chemistry, botany, and psychology, and lectured at Aberdeen University. He then joined the staff of the Geological Survey of Great Britain rising to the rank of Principal Geologist, H. M. Geological Survey, London (Department of Scientific and Industrial Research). He was awarded a Doctorate in Science. Crookall then resigned from his geological work in order to devote the rest of his life to psychological studies and psychic investigations. In that capacity he was a Member of the Society for Psychical Research, Honorary Member of the American Society for Psychical Research, and of related bodies.

In his meticulously compiled volume *The Supreme Adventure: Analyses of Psychic Communications*[48] Crookall has sifted the vast literature of the subject with exceptional thoroughness and brought together, from a great many different sources, what appear to be personal testimonies of experiences of death and survival. Taken together, they form an impressive body of evidence on a topic in which, to reiterate, strong opinions are frequently expressed but objective evidence is seldom considered—particularly by those scientists who denigrate such evidence out-and-out on a priori grounds. Crookall maintained that by analysing the reports of numerous psychic communications from mediums (many examples of which are cited in *The Supreme Adventure*), it is possible to penetrate the veil that obscures death and the immediate hereafter. Such analyses not only indicate survival but also provide the means by which it is possible to envisage the general conditions under which survival is possible, namely, the various stages and states of consciousness, thus enabling an understanding of why certain experiences are undergone at certain stages in the process of disembodiment.

Accordingly, the evidence in Crookall's book is structured in three parts, followed by conclusions and six supporting appendices. The first part concerns death as transition described as a succession of seven experiences, each one assigned a chapter title, and each described from the standpoint of natural death and enforced death. The names assigned to these experiences are revealing: 1. 'The Call'; 2. A Review of the Past Life; 3. Shedding the Body; 4. The 'Sleep'; 5. The 'Awakening'; 6. The 'Judgement'; 7. The Assignment.

The second part in two major sections comprises itemized statements as to the total death-experience: natural death and enforced death; and the correlation between bodily constitution, consciousness, and environment. In the third part, also in two sections, the statements from the reports in the first part are scrutinised and tested; and the correlation scrutinised and tested.

The conclusions to Crookall's book discuss: the internal consistency and inherent probability of communications; a basic conception in communications; the harmony of the several lines of approach; and the nature of communicators. Finally, the appendices deal with: the admissibility of the evidence; 'pointers' to survival; two sources of genuine communications; the role and efficacy of prayer; and the place of psychic studies in religion.

The stages in the total natural death-experience are conveniently enumerated in http://www.afterlife101.com/Supreme_Adventure.html (accessed on 1st February 2020). In summary, taken collectively, the results:

1. demonstrate an afterlife description with a high degree of credibility because so many sources contributed the same information even though they were independently produced—see the explanation on proof by consilience in Volume I, Recapitulation, page 319–320;
2. provide strong evidence for the existence of an afterlife for the same reason—a rationally consistent set of statements derived from many independent sources;
3. contain a high degree of correlation with the descriptions –
   (i)   on the near-death experience described in Volume I, Chapter 4 of this work, and particularly
   (ii)   the after-death states summarized in the foregoing sections of this Chapter especially, the First Stage pertaining to the dying process and post-mortem consciousness.

The correlations between the seven experiences enumerated in *The Supreme Adventure* and similar descriptive sections from this Chapter, are as follows:

Experiences enumerated as Chapter Titles in *The Supreme Adventure*	Similar Sections from this Chapter Summarized in Table II-11 on page 98
1. 'The Call'	First stage
2. A Review of the Past Life	First transition: First stage to Second stage
3. Shedding the body	Second stage
4. The 'Sleep'	
5. The 'Awakening'	Second transition: Second stage to Third stage
6. The 'Judgement'	Third stage
7. The Assignment	

Robert Crookall's meticulous scientific investigation provides exceptional evidence on the afterlife

Needless to say, the above correlations must be viewed in a broad sense: there is no place for pedantry.

When considered as a whole, then, this impressive body of evidence from a scientist eminently multi-qualified in both the physical and life sciences would strain to breaking point the prejudices of other than the most diehard materialist sceptics who would maintain that the numerous reports of the post-mortem survival of consciousness are the delusions of naïve simpletons, which attitude is underlined by the words of materialists like the Oxford professor Peter Atkins who pronounces unequivocally: 'Without exception, all spiritualists are sharks feeding on the gullibility of the weak, distressed, and hopeful who inhabit the oceans of the world.'[49]

Would Atkins also opine that numerous people in England, France, and Spain who have reported after-death communications have also joined the ranks of 'the weak, distressed, and hopeful who [also] inhabit the oceans of the world'; and that the world-renowned scientists who have meticulously investigated their reports are displaying 'gullibility'?

Do the 'weak' and 'hopeful' fear darkness and extinction; or do the materialists and atheists dread light and an expansion of consciousness?

After-Death Communications – The Evidence

An ambitious multilingual project entitled *Investigation of the phenomenology and impact of perceived spontaneous and direct After-Death Communications (ADCs)* was conducted from February 2018 to January 2020.[50] The three objectives of this two-year research programme to gain a better understanding of the phenomenology and the impact of perceived spontaneous and direct After-Death Communications were: to describe the *phenomenology* of perceived ADCs; to analyse the *impact* of perceived ADCs on those who experienced them (referred to in the study as 'experients'); and then to *disseminate the research results as widely as possible* to the scientific community and the general public.

The methodology comprised a specially designed online questionnaire, the data from which were expected to provide insights into the nature of ADCs, specifically: the profile of the experients; the profile of the deceased person supposedly initiating the contact; the circumstances surrounding the occurrence; the type, content, and period of time over which messages were communicated; and their composite impact on experients. It was intended that the details and results of the project would be disclosed to the scientific community and the public by means of publications, conferences, and media events.

To achieve the various objectives of the research project, the team developed an on-line questionnaire of 194 questions (including follow-up questions after affirmative responses), which was accessible online for six months. A total of 1,004 questionnaires were completed: 416 in English; 440 in French; and 148 in Spanish. This comprised more than 2 million words for the full ADC accounts alone, effectively constituting the largest multilingual collection of spontaneous modern-day ADCs worldwide.

Modern scientific evidence on after-death communications

The seven types of ADCs investigated were:

1. sensing a presence—feeling the familiar presence of a deceased family member or friend, without seeing or hearing them, or feeling a physical contact, or smelling a fragrance characteristic of the deceased;

2. hearing a voice—either from an outside source, in the same way that they would hear a living person; or perceiving the communication without an external sound;

3. feeling a physical contact—on a part of their body, for example a touch, a pressure, a caress, a kiss, a hand placed on the shoulder or a real embrace;

4. sensing the deceased—as apparitions that can occur indoors, for example at night in the bedroom; or outside, even in a car, on an aeroplane, etc;

5. smelling a fragrance characteristic of the deceased—as an olfactory contact during which fragrances associated with a deceased person are perceived, like perfume, after-shave lotion, soap, tobacco, a characteristic body scent, etc;

6. during sleep—when falling asleep or waking up; or just falling asleep or just waking up;

7. crisis—within a 24 hour window before and after death.

Crisis ADCs are particularly significant, and even evidential, since experients claim that they were informed of the death of a family member or friend *by the deceased themselves.* In a waking state or waking up at night, experients hear or see the deceased who announce their death with serenity, sometimes even with joy ('I came to say good-bye, I am leaving now'). Significantly, they often seem to use the verb 'to leave', as if they were preparing to embark on a journey. Not without good reason have we headed this Chapter 'Death is Transition'.

Furthermore, a large majority of participants had multiple ADCs with one or several deceased persons. This surprised the researchers since the literature does not report such a high number of multiple ADCs.

Sceptical scientists would find it hard to fault the pre-eminence of the following seven members of the international project team and consultant scientific committee members:

1. Evelyn Elsaesser, specialist of experiences related to death, Switzerland

2. Professor Chris A. Roe, Centre Lead for the Psychology and Social Sciences Research Centre, University of Northampton, UK

3. Dr Callum E. Cooper, Lecturer in Psychology, University of Northampton, UK

4. David Lorimer, Programme Director of the Scientific & Medical Network, UK

5. Professor Kim Penberthy, Professor of Psychiatry & Neurobehavioral Sciences, Division of Perceptual Studies, University of Virginia, School of Medicine, USA

6. Professor Peter Fenwick, President Emeritus of the Scientific & Medical Network; Consultant Neuropsychologist at the Maudsley and John Radcliffe hospitals; consultant at the Institute of Psychiatry, Kings College, London; worked with the Mental Health Group at the University of Southampton, UK

7. Professor Kenneth Ring, founding editor of the Journal of *Near-Death Studies* and Professor Emeritus of psychology at the University of Connecticut, USA.

International scientists on ADC investigative committee

The team published their findings in two booklets, including a literature review:

1. A presentation of research findings[51] by anchoring those to previous literature in the form of an ADC literature review.[52]

2. Documentation of individual cases, and thoroughly describing the phenomenology of ADC experiences.[53]

The results presented in the booklets refer to the totality of the collected data, namely the combination of the replies of the 1,004 questionnaires completed in English, French, and Spanish. Whereas the thematic analyses of the collected data will be the subject of future individual papers, the purpose of the two publications was to present some of the *quantitative results* of the survey. This is shown in Figure II-4, a comparative graph showing the number of occurrences by type of ADC of the sample.[54]

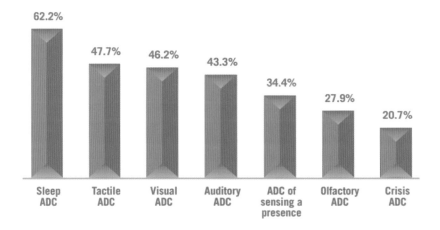

Figure II-4   Comparative Graph of Number of Occurrences by Type of
After-Death Communication

Image Credit from Evelyn Elsaesser: https://www.evelyn-elsaesser.com/research

It is hoped that the above research findings will influence the views of psychotherapists on post-mortem consciousness. This, in turn, should have a bearing on their work with clients. The latest doctoral research suggests that this is indeed the case. Furthermore, it indicates that the current scientific paradigm on which counselling and psychotherapy is based represses the presentation of more open and speculative views about what it means to be human, thereby limiting issues that clients might otherwise bring to therapy, including belief in post-mortem consciousness.[55]

Summary of the Cycle of Reincarnation and Post-Mortem States – Death as Transition and Release

> The destination of the physical body is the grave, but the spiritual body is a heavenly being, and its life is the real life. This body is like a cage and our soul like a bird. The bird comes from heaven and enters the cage. There it remains confined, awaiting the time for the guardian to come and open the door saying: 'You are free.'
>
> Al-Haqqani[56]

The writer is hesitant about providing a summary on a subject that is so subtle and interconnected with innumerable nuances of meaning. Nevertheless, in the interests of providing a framework for understanding, what follows is a schematic outline of the principal phases and transitions in the *cyclic journey of consciousness* that propel man from physical death through the post-mortem states towards reincarnation and final rebirth in a new body. The presentation is necessarily sequential and several details have necessarily been withheld.

The post-mortem and reincarnation processes, so nostalgically expressed in the above quote, can however, for analytical purposes be categorized in the following four broadly defined stages, phases, and transitions, all corresponding with different states of consciousness as summarized in Table II-11 overleaf:

❖ *First stage*: life and consciousness in the previous physical body;
  First transition to Second stage: from physical consciousness to astral consciousness.

❖ *Second stage*: consciousness and existence in the early, lower post-mortem astral, or psychic planes;
  Second transition to Third stage: from astral consciousness to spiritual consciousness—emergence of the 'butterfly' from the 'chrysalis'.

❖ *Third stage*: consciousness and existence in the later, higher post-mortem spiritual planes;
  Third transition to Fourth stage: from spiritual consciousness to life and consciousness in a new physical body.

❖ *Fourth stage*: rebirth in a new physical body.

Reincarnation is a cyclical process

The first, second, and third transitions closely correspond to the narrative in *The Tibetan Book of the Dead*. In describing its contents, Carl Jung, in his commentary on the book, mentions that 'it falls into 3 parts': the first 'describes the psychic happenings at the moment of death', the second, 'the dream-state which supervenes immediately after death', and the third, 'concerns the onset of the birth-instinct and of prenatal events'.[57] To reiterate, the parents provide just the karmically conditioned psycho-physical vehicle to the incoming Soul-entity.

In essence, within mortal man, resides an immortal entity, 'divine Mind', or Nous, whose pale reflection we call mind and intellect in ordinary man. The rational, but earthly or physical intellect of man is encased in a vesture of matter and that encasement is all that science can uncover, wonderful as its discoveries are. The Higher Manas in man, i.e., the Higher Ego is that which reincarnates periodically according to karmic law, while its reflected 'double', or shadow, the Lower manas in man, i.e., the Personal ego, changing with every new incarnation or personality, is therefore self-conscious, but for a life-period.[58] Therefore, it makes eminent sense to strengthen the Antahkaranic connection between the Personal ego and the Higher Ego to ensure that a future incarnation would embody even more of the *spiritual guidance* of the latter.

From all this (excepting the extreme cases of criminality cited), death as transition is equivalent to death as release from earthly bondage. In physical life it is only sensible not to allow oneself to become overweight so as not to impose unnecessary strain on the heart, limbs, and other bodily organs. This is also the case when it comes to the discarding of material possessions that have become encumbrances. Most of all, though, it makes sense to shed psychological baggage so that the inner self is encumbered as little as possible by

Table II-11 Stages and Transitions: Death → Post-Mortem → Reincarnation

One Consciousness in different phase states of Itself … like H₂O as ice, water, steam

FIRST STAGE — Previous Physical Life and Consciousness	SECOND STAGE — Post-Mortem Existence and Consciousness Between two Earth Lives	THIRD STAGE	FOURTH STAGE — New Physical Life and Consciousness
Physical Plane – Earth	Kāma-loka – Astral (Psychic) Planes	Devachan – Spiritual Planes	Physical Plane – Earth
	FIRST TRANSITION: PHYSICAL DEATH PHYSICAL → ASTRAL	*SECOND TRANSITION: 'SECOND DEATH'* ASTRAL → SPIRITUAL	*THIRD TRANSITION: PHYSICAL RE-BIRTH* SPIRITUAL → PHYSICAL
Ātma the Divine Self	Ātma the Divine Self	Ātma the Divine Self	Ātma the Divine Self
Buddhi the Intuition Principle	Buddhi the Intuition Principle	Buddhi the Intuition Principle	Buddhi the Intuition Principle
Manas the Mind Principle — Higher / Lower	Manas the Mind Principle — Higher / Lower	Manas the Mind Principle — Higher	Manas the Mind Principle — Higher / Lower
Kāma the Desire principle	Kāma the Desire principle		Kāma the Desire principle
Prāṇa the Life principle			Prāṇa the Life principle
Liṅga-śarīra the Etheric double			Liṅga-śarīra the Etheric double
Sthūla-śarīra, or Rūpa the Physical body			Sthūla-śarīra, or Rūpa the Physical body
Man In Earthly Life	Man After the Physical Death The 'Chrysalis'	Man After the Second Death The 'Butterfly'	Man In the Next Incarnation on Earth

FIRST STAGE: Disintegrate after death

SECOND STAGE: The Kāma-rūpa, later the 'Shell' — The 'Butterfly'

- *Dying and Just After:* Memory dislodged from physical brain. Māyāvi-rūpa (Doppelgänger) may appear to loved ones. Lower Triad disintegrates. Kāma-rūpa becomes lowest vehicle of consciousness.
- *Later After Death in Kāma-loka (Hades):* past life reviewed in terms of spiritual content. Deep sleep supervenes.
- *'Second Death':* to separate Higher Egoic Triad from lower personal elements.
- *'Gestation' period:* to assimilate spiritual aroma of past life into Higher Egoic entity.

THIRD STAGE: The man between two Earth lives

- *Born again in Devachan* ('dwelling of the gods').
- *Second life review:* Psychic residue of late personality discarded as shell (of séance room phenomena).
- *Ego awakens in Devachan.* A purely subjective 'dream state' of no sorrow or punishment and unalloyed bliss. Unfulfilled aspirations, affections, and yearning for former Earth life revisited and worked upon.
- *Gradual exhaustion and oblivion* prior to re-birth in a new body under karmic law.

FOURTH STAGE: New personality conditioned by *skandhas*, i.e., the residual tendencies and characteristics of previous lives dictated by karma the past. *Obesity—whether physically, or psychologically is never to be recommended!* And death is the ending of all three types of bondage: first, the obvious 'shuffl[ing] off this mortal coil' which brings all joys and sufferings of the world and 'the thousand natural shocks that flesh is heir to' to an end; [59] second, the loss of all personal possessions; and third, the divesting of the chrysalis, or psychic vesture, constituting the final, mortal residue.

Death as release and renewal

Thus, when viewed from the higher vantage point of occult science, far from being a morbid or fearful affair, death is actually a sublime process in the continuity of consciousness and life. Death most certainly signifies an ending, but what exactly is it that ends? Only the past, meaning the ending of the known. But does not the old, the past, the time-bound and time-worn have to end completely in order to make space for the new? Do we wear the same three-piece suit all our earthly lives? Does it not make sense to discard and renew our three-piece mortal vesture—the Lower Triad—when it becomes threadbare? Too many mainstream scientists these days have allowed science to get in the way and blind their sensibilities to the subtler facts of consciousness. This happens when the Lower manas blocks the light from the Higher Manas, resulting in wisdom becoming suffocated by excessive intellect. Such a statement needs no proof: the evidence speaks amply for itself.

> It is life in quest of life in bodies that fear the grave. 'A little while, a moment of rest upon the wind, and another woman shall bear me.'
>
> Kahlil Gibran[60]

Postlude – The Silent Door of Eternity

> The magic sounds of Mozart's music show us in the darkness of this life a bright and beautifully remote world to which we confidently look forward. O Mozart, immortal Mozart, how many, infinitely many, beneficent images of a brighter, better life have you engraved in our souls.
>
> Franz Schubert[61]

Death, then, is the ending of the past caught in time. Truly great men have ever seen death in its rightful context—as transition and release and not extinction of consciousness—a portal to eternity. In an elegiac song written for the husband of a young woman who died in childbirth, a certain composer wrote the words: 'No eyes shall weep for the Divine Spirit hath returned Home'—a statement, not of poetical fancy, but literal fact. The composer of that song was—Beethoven, who kept this deeply personal work to himself for over a decade before handing *Elegischer Gesang* (Elegiac Song) over to his publisher. Indeed, the Austrian composer Anselm Hüttenbrenner (1794–1868), who was a witness of Beethoven's death in March 1827 wrote: 'there came a flash of lightning accompanied by a violent clap of thunder, which garishly illuminated the death-chamber. After this unexpected phenomenon of nature [...]. The genius of the great master of tones fled from this world of delusion into the realm of truth!'[62]

Beethoven on death as transition

The 'unexpected phenomenon of nature' is of deepest significance. We find its resounding echo in this passage from the *Voice of the Silence*:

> ALL NATURE'S wordless voice in thousand tones ariseth to proclaim:
> JOY UNTO YE, O MEN OF MYALBA
> A PILGRIM HATH RETURNED BACK 'FROM THE OTHER SHORE'.[63]

Moreover, what is genius in this context? None other than the immortal Upper Triad. 'Myalba' is this world of delusion which is, of course, our Earth, the region of māyā—recall Heisenberg's dying insights on the illusory characteristic of the material world quoted earlier.[vii] And the realm of truth?—The higher, spiritual planes of post-mortem existence.

Thus, it is the writer's persuasion that, more often than not, the composer, the public performer or the artist who travels the world, experiences diverse cultures, speaks several languages, and converses with poets, philosophers, and scientists is far closer to an understanding of consciousness and the pulse of life than a scientist or doctor with a one track approach trying to fathom the mystery of life and unravel the secrets of time and eternity by peering into his telescope or microscope at what he regards as inertless matter, all alone in his laboratory—unless in rare circumstances (like the neurosurgeon Eben Alexander, see Volume I, Chapter 4), he has been blessed with a life-transforming experience such as a near-death experience. The term 'artist' is conventionally associated with the musician, painter, sculptor, dancer, etc. but there is also a deeper meaning: the *application* of anything is its Art, so the right application of science or medicine makes the scientist and doctor an Artist automatically. Does an NDE or other profound spiritual experience transmogrify a scientist or doctor into an Artist? Who knows. But let us never forget that the whole richness of human life, with all its grandeur and foibles, its unrequited love and pain, its joys and sufferings, was poured into the compositions of sublime composers like Mozart and Beethoven, Schubert and Chopin, who were able to infuse their entire *soul experience* into their music in full self-conscious knowledge of what they were doing. Hence, the enduring power of their output that unfailingly touches our souls centuries later.

Afterlife illumined through Art

Mozart probably knew nothing at all about the anatomy of the human brain and body; but he knew more about the human *condition* than a thousand dry, academic books on psychology, all put together—witness the human drama in his operas. And along with an understanding of life was a profound insight into life's counterpart—death, as seen in his letter to his father reproduced in the Epilogue in Volume III of this work.

So also was the foresight of Franz Schubert (1797–1828) who revered Mozart as the above epigram makes quite plain. His String Quartet No. 14 in D minor, known as *Death and the Maiden*, is one of the pillars of the chamber music repertoire. It was composed in 1824, after the composer suffered a serious illness and realized that he was close to death. It is named for the theme of the second movement, which Schubert took from a song he wrote in 1817 of the same title. The theme is a dialogue between The Maiden and Death. In terror, The Maiden pleads with Death not to touch her and leave her alone. But Death responds by asking for her hand, saying that he comes to her as a friend and not to punish: 'Within mine arms shalt softly rest thee!'[64]

The power of music

It is perhaps timely here to recall the life review process in the transition from physical death to the early post-mortem state of consciousness as described earlier. The writer believes that it is possible to see this process reflected in the two great song-cycles by the

---

vii 'Myalba' is the enigmatic Northern Buddhist name for our Earth, which they considered a 'hell' in the sense of a man-bearing planet, or place of punishment for those whose karma it is to reincarnate on it in order to gain valuable life experience and to learn through suffering as a remedial process. But that does not mean that Earth is a hell-realm in itself; only when one is in a state of delusion. For those gifted with pure vision it is a beautiful and multi-layered projection of what is Above—the Empyrean.

German composer Robert Schumann (1810–1856). In the first, the piano postlude at the close of *Frauenliebe und -leben* (Woman's Love and Life), evokes a mood of nostalgic recollection of the joy, fulfilment, and sorrows during the course of a woman's life through love, marriage, and widowhood.[viii] In the second, *Dichterliebe* (A Poet's Love), the piano postlude is one of poignant reminiscence on amorous disappointments in the life of a young poet.[ix]

Nobody has expressed death as transition more eloquently than one who, as a twelve-year-old boy, was anointed with a kiss on his forehead by Beethoven—Franz Liszt—legendary pianist and composer of course, but also a tremendous philanthropist and philosopher.[65] In his biography on his great companion Frédéric Chopin, Liszt describes the dying composer's supreme moments in these words:

> **The musician invariably has more insight into the human *state and condition* than the scientist despite the latter having such detailed technical knowledge about the *mechanics and mechanisms* of the human body and brain. The landscapes of the mind embracing the whole spectrum of human experience from the devastating to the ecstatic are sometimes best painted by, and experienced through, music.[x]**

> However violent or frivolous are the passions that stir the heart, the spectacle of a lingering and beautiful death […] the slow and gradual departure of one among us for the unknown shores, the mysterious solemnity of his dreams, his recollection of thoughts and actions while still breathing upon that narrow threshold that separates the past from the future, affects us more deeply than anything else in this world. Catastrophes, abysses that gape beneath our feet, conflagrations that engulf whole cities, bloodshed in battles, the fate of storm-tossed ships, even the horrors of the plague, none hold our attention like the sight of a soul *contemplating the nature of time at the silent door of eternity* [emphasis added].[66]

Liszt depicts Chopin's transition

This Chapter has drawn upon science, philosophy, religion, and art in order to illuminate the transitional stages following death and to obtain a truly integral view of it. The following Chapter deals with the main topics that cause much confusion and misperception about death and esotericism in general. Meanwhile, we close with four quotes that draw upon different disciplines to capture the essential message of this Chapter, namely that death is simply a transition from one state of consciousness to another and that our destiny is to undergo the second birth, or spiritual awakening, prior to a new physical incarnation on Earth.

> *Every soul that has perception is, though in different times and in different organs of sense and motion, still the same indivisible person.*
>
> Isaac Newton[67]

---

viii The cycle of eight poems are from Adelbert von Chamisso (1781–1838), the German poet and botanist.

ix The texts for the sixteen songs are from the *Lyrisches Intermezzo* (Lyrical interlude) of the German poet and writer Heinrich Heine (1797–1856).

x Examples of the 'lowlands' and the 'highlands' that immediately spring to mind are Schubert's song cycle *Die Winterreise* (Winter Journey), a setting of twenty-four poems by Wilhelm Müller, and the Choral finale of Beethoven's Ninth Symphony based largely on the text of Friedrich Schiller's 'Ode to Joy', with a few additional introductory words written by Beethoven himself.

The body is only a garment. How many times you have changed your clothing in this life, yet because of this you would not say that you have changed. Similarly, when you give up this bodily dress at death you do not change. You are just the same, an immortal soul, a child of God.

PARAMAHANSA YOGANANDA[68]

'Personality is suspended upon a thread from the nature of Being', declares the secret work [the universal, esoteric teachings—theosophy]. Man is essentially a permanent and immortal principle; only his bodies pass through the cycle of birth and death. The immortal is the reality; the mortal is the unreality. During each period of earth life, reality thus dwells in unreality, to be liberated from it temporarily by death and permanently by illumination.

MANLY P. HALL[69]

Can death be sleep, when life is but a dream,
And scenes of bliss pass as a phantom by?
The transient pleasures as a vision seem,
And yet we think the greatest pain's to die.

How strange it is that man on earth should roam,
And lead a life of woe, but not forsake
His rugged path; nor dare he view alone
His future doom which is but to awake.

JOHN KEATS[70]

NOTES

1   *The Golden Verses of Pythagoras and other Fragments*, selected and arranged by Florence M. Firth, introd. Annie Besant (1904), Verses 70, 71 < https://www.sacred-texts.com/cla/gvp/gvp03.htm> accessed 31 October 2020.

2   'An Essay on Death', in *The Works of Francis Bacon, Baron of* Verulam*, Viscount St* Alban*, and Lord High Chancellor of England* (London: Impensis R. Gosling, 1730), iv, 462 §7 [online facsimile digitized 7 December 2010] <https://books.google.co.uk/books?id=kmlUAAAAYAAJ&pg=PA462&lpg=PA462&dq=Death+exempts+not+a+man+from+being,+but+only+presents+an+alteration.&source=bl&ots=UOTyqsDN4T&sig=ACfU3U03dfOws8vUiGqR9rlDGM0T6_ETEA&hl=en&sa=X&ved=2ahUKEwiq4f3myrDpAhUzShUIHYx8CiIQ6AEwAHoECAcQAQ#v=onepage&q=Death%20exempts%20not%20a%20man%20from%20being%2C%20but%20only%20presents%20an%20alteration.&f=false> accessed 13 May 2020.

3   Kahlil Gibran, *The Prophet*, introd. John Baldock (London: Arcturus, 2018), 111, 112.

4   Edi D. Bilimoria, 'Dante – Introducing *The Divine Comedy*', *The Theosophist*, 131/11 (August 2010), 16–21.

5   *Plutarch, On the Face in the Moon* (London and Harvard University: Loeb Classical Library edition, 1957). Quoted also in I. Abrahams, *Studies in Pharisaism and the Gospels* (Cambridge: Cambridge University Press, 1924), 42.

6   See *STA*, 'Fishes, Insects, Animals, Reptiles, and Birds: Part Two', XC.

7   Yacub, 'Eye of the Needle', *Islamic Form* (4 January 2012) <https://www.gawaher.com/topic/737699-eye-of-the-needle> accessed 8 February 2020.

8   See Edi D. Bilimoria, 'Dante – Introducing *The Divine Comedy*'.

9   Geoffrey Barborka, *The Divine Plan* (2nd edn, rev. and enl., Adyar, Madras: Theosophical Publishing House, 1964; repr. 1980), 406 n.

10 Alan Walker, *Liszt* (London: Faber and Faber, 1971), 16.

11 H. C. Robbins Landon, *Mozart: The golden years 1781–1791* (London: Thames and Hudson, 1989; quotation from rev. and repr. edn, 1990), 14.

12 *NPB*-5, Part 2: *The Intellect*, 'Science and Metaphysics', ¶ 101, 128. See also *Newton Tercentenary Celebrations at the Anniversary Meeting of the Royal Society 30 November 1942* (London: Royal Society, 1942).

13 *The Zohar*, trans. Daniel C. Matt, iii (Pritzker edn, Stanford, California: Stanford University Press, 2005), 616.

14 *KT*, 'The Physical and the Spiritual Man', 108.

15 Seymour Ballard, 'The Role of Māyā in Man's Evolution', the Blavatsky Lecture, 1986 (London: The Theosophical Society).

16 Lee W. Bailey and Jenny Yates (eds), *The Near Death Experience: A reader* (New York: Routledge, 1996), 361.

17 Peter Atkins, *On Being: A scientist's exploration of the great questions of existence* (New York: Oxford University Press, 2011), 104.

18 Susan Ertz, *Anger in the Sky* (New York and London: Harper & Brothers, 1943), 134.

19 'The Coming of the Bodhi-Tree', in Thera Mahanama-sthavira, *The Mahavamsa: The great chronicle of Sri Lanka* (Asian Humanities Press, 1999).

20 Isaac Newton, *Philosophiæ Naturalis Principia Mathematica* [Mathematical Principles of Natural Philosophy], trans. Andrew Motte, rev. Florian Cajori, 2 vols (Berkeley, Los Angeles: University of California Press, 1962), ii, 'The System of the World – General Scholium', 545.

21 *SD*-I, 'Is Gravitation a Law?', 492.

22 G. de Purucker, *Occult Glossary* (Pasadena, California: Theosophical University Press, 1996), 64.

23 Kahlil Gibran, *The Prophet*, 126.

24 Erwin Schrödinger, *My View of the World*, trans. Cecily Hastings (New York: Cambridge University Press, 1964), 100; see also 98–104 passim.

25 Jonathan Beecher (ed.), *In Times of War – Messages of Wisdom from Soldiers in the Afterlife* (UK: White Crow Books), 2019.

26 C. A. Wickland, *Thirty Years Among the Dead: Historic Studies in Spiritualism; A psychiatrist's investigation of spirit mediums and psychic possession in his patients* (1924; London: Spiritualist Press, 1978; UK: White Crow Books, 2011).

27 Professor David Fontana, 'The Nature of a Possible Afterlife' <http://whitecrowbooks.com/features/page/the_nature_of_a_possible_afterlife_professor_david_fontana> accessed 12 December 2019.

28 'Understanding Death and Loss', *Yogoda Satsanga Society of India* <https://yssofindia.org/spiritual/Understanding-Death-and-Loss> accessed 1 February 2019.

29 Evy King, 'Harry Oldfield's Amazing Imaging Technologies', *NEXUS* (April–May 2007), 33–7, 78 <https://nextexx.files.wordpress.com/2016/08/harry-oldfield-s-amazing-imaging-technologies1.pdf> accessed 23 September 2020.

30 Jane and Grant Solomon, *Harry Oldfield's Invisible Universe* (UK: Campion Books, 1998), 28–34.

31 See Edi D. Bilimoria, 'Dante – Introducing *The Divine Comedy*'.

32 See Adam Warcup, 'An Inquiry into the Nature of Mind', the Blavatsky Lecture, 1981 (London: The Theosophical Society), 18.

33 An entirely safe and meaningful account in terms of the oscillation of consciousness between two focal extremes is in James Perkins, *A Geometry of Space–Consciousness* (1964; rev. and enl. 3rd edn, Adyar, Chennai: Theosophical Publishing House, 1977, repr. 2004).

34 J. K. Rowling, *Harry Potter and the Prisoner of Azkaban* (London: Bloomsbury, 2010).

35 'Fragments of Occult Truth, No. 1', *Theosophist* (October 1881), endnote <http://www.blavatskyarchives.com/humefrags1.htm> accessed 7 March 2020.

36 *VS*, 'Glossary to Part III', 88–9.

37 G. de Purucker, *Occult Glossary*, 5.

38 *Theosophical Encyclopedia*, ed. Philip S. Harris, Vincente R. Hao Chin, Jr., and Richard W. Brooks (Philippines: Theosophical Publishing House, 2006), 38.

39 *CW*-XII, 'Instruction No. III: The Philosophical Rationale of the Tenet', 634. Appendix II-B provides more details on the role of *Antaḥkaraṇa* extracted from the full account in *CW*-XII, 629–41 *passim*.

40 Robert Louis Stevenson, *Strange Case of Dr. Jekyll and Mr. Hyde* (London: Longman, 1886).

41 *CW*-XII, 'Instruction No. III: The Philosophical Rationale of the Tenet', 632.

42 *ibid.*

43 *CW*-XII, 'Instruction No. III', 638.

44 Luke 15:7 English Standard Version.

45 'Letter No. 1 – The Theosophical Society and Its Work', in *Letters From the Masters of the Wisdom: First Series*, ed. C. Jinarâjadâsa, foreword by Annie Besant (US: Quest Books, 1988), 1.

46 Frederic W. H. Myers, *Human Personality and Its Survival of Bodily Death*, 2 vols (London, New York, Bombay: Longman, Green, and Co., 1903), ii, 316.

47 *ibid.*

48 Robert Crookall, *The Supreme Adventure: Analyses of psychic communications* (UK: James Clarke & Co, 1961; 2nd edn, 1974; rev. and enl. edn, 1987). For a summary of the statements relating to the total natural death-experience see 'The Supreme Adventure, *Analyses of Psychic Communications*, Robert Crookall, 1961, James.[,] Clarke & Co., Ltd.' <http://www.afterlife101.com/Supreme_Adventure.html> accessed 7 March 2020.

49 Peter Atkins, *On Being*, 90.

50 Evelyn Elsaesser <https://www.evelyn-elsaesser.com/research> accessed 12 April 2020.

51 Evelyn Elsaesser, Chris A. Roe, Callum E. Cooper, and David Lorimer, 'Investigation of the Phenomenology and Impact of Spontaneous and Direct After-Death Communications (ADCs): Research findings' <https://www.cvelyn-elsaesser.com/wp-content/uploads/2020/02/Booklet_Web_English_Research.pdf> accessed 12 April 2020.

52 After-Death Communication – Key References <https://www.evelyn-elsaesser.com/wp-content/uploads/2019/02/ADC-Research%E2%80%93Key_References.pdf> accessed 12 April 2020.

53 Evelyn Elsaesser, Chris A. Roe, Callum E. Cooper, and David Lorimer, 'Investigation of the Phenomenology and Impact of Spontaneous and Direct After-Death Communications (ADCs): Cases' <https://www.evelyn-elsaesser.com/wp-content/uploads/2020/02/Booklet_Web_English_Cases.pdf> accessed 12 April 2020.

54 Evelyn Elsaesser, et al., *op. cit.*, 'Research Findings', 10.

55 Claudia Nielsen, 'Post-mortem Consciousness: Views of psychotherapists and their influence in the work with clients', PhD thesis, University of Chester, 2019.

56 Shaykh Nazim Adil Al-Haqqani, *In the Mystic Footsteps of Saints*, ii (US: Naqshbandi-Haqqani Sufi Order, 2002), 9.

57 W. Y. Evans-Wentz (compiled and ed.), *The Tibetan Book of the Dead*, psychological commentary by C. G. Jung, foreword by Lama Govinda and John Woodroffe (3rd edn, US: Oxford University Press, 1975).

58 Paraphrased from *CW*-XII, 'Psychic and Noetic Action', 366.

59 In the soliloquy, 'To be, or not to be' by Prince Hamlet in Shakespeare's (Francis Bacon's?) *Hamlet*, Act 3, Scene 1.

60 Kahlil Gibran, *The Prophet*, 119, 127.

61 'Naxos' <https://www.naxos.com/lifeandworks/schubert> accessed 8 February 2020.

62 *Thayer's Life of Beethoven*, rev. and ed. Elliot Forbes (Princeton: Princeton University Press, 1970), 1050–1.

63 *VS*, 'Fragment III: The Seven Portals', 72.

64 P. Jurgenson (trans.), *Book of Songs in Repertoire of Feodor Chaliapin, the World's Greatest Singer* (New York: Botwen Printing Co., *circa* 1920), 40.

65 Alan Walker, *Franz Liszt: The Virtuoso Years, 1811–1847* (US: Cornell University Press, 1988), 83–4.

66 Meirion Hughes (trans., ed., and introd.), *Liszt's Chopin* (Manchester and New York: Manchester University Press, 2010), 135–6.

67 Isaac Newton, 'The System of the World – General Scholium', 545.

68 'Understanding Death and Loss', *Self-Realization Fellowship* <https://yogananda.org/de/understanding-death-and-loss> accessed 1 February 2020.

69 *STA*, 'The Human Body in Symbolism'. LXXV.

70 John Keats, 'On Death', in *The Complete Poems of John Keats* (New York: Modern Library,1994).

6 Clarifying Some Common Misconceptions

Aristotle maintained that women have fewer teeth than men; although he was twice married, it never occurred to him to verify this statement by examining his wives' mouths.

BERTRAND RUSSELL[1]

SYNOPSIS

Chapter 6 opens the second section of Volume II. It is concerned with clarifying numerous misconceptions that abound on topics such as the meaning of soul and the associated distinction between soul and spirit, the dual nature of mind and whether man is just an animal, only more sophisticated, or, crucially, whether he has some characteristics of mind unique to himself. The last topic is of such importance that the whole of the next Chapter is devoted to it.

KEY WORDS: individuality vs personality, soul vs spirit, spiritualist vs occultist, man vs animal, mind principle, Allan Octavian Hume

Several misunderstandings abound about man's composition. The purpose of this Chapter is therefore to inject a measure of clarity by providing further insights and elaborating the meaning of words in common use.

The Distinction Between Individuality and Personality

The previous expositions have emphasized the importance of drawing a clear distinction between man's Individuality and his personality—a distinction not of essence, but of quality—in order to understand why man is a complex being having several 'selves', or bodies, as his vehicles of consciousness for a terrestrial existence. Having just seen how man functions in his sevenfold nature we can draw upon the foregoing expositions further to justify the need for making such a distinction.

The term 'individuality' derives from the Latin *individuus*, which means 'indivisible', from *in-* 'not', 'opposite of' and *dividuus* 'divisible', from *dividere* 'divide'. The essential meaning, therefore, is that which cannot be divided; thus, it is not heterogeneous, nor composite, nor compounded of other elements. It is the thing in itself—indivisible, uncompounded, original, pure and simple in the philosophical sense. This abundance of terms is useful because it helps us to appreciate the wide context in which this term is used, but always conveying the essential meaning just outlined.

Individuality denotes wholeness

As stated in Chapters 2 and 3, Individuality refers to the 'Upper Imperishable Triad' (*Ātma-Buddhi-Manas*). However the term 'permanent *Individuality*' is used by Blavatsky

105

to refer to just the Manas principle (independently of Buddhi) also known as the Inner Ego, Higher Ego, or 'Reincarnating Ego'.[2]

In another sense Individuality and Monad are identical terms, insofar as the Individuality comprises the expression of the Monad (Ātma-Buddhi) through Manas. However, the former word is used in a general sense, whereas the latter is used more in a specific and technical context. Thus both words are convenient because of the distinctions in their usage.

In contradistinction to the Individuality, the personality, comprising the intermediate and lower natures, is a composite. Therefore it is mortal and subject to decay and death.[i] The term 'personality' is also highly suggestive of its essential meaning. It comes from the Latin word *personare* 'to sound through', i.e., the 'mask' or 'false face', as something spoken through, such as worn by actors for an assumed character for their part in a drama as, for example, in later Roman theatre.

Personality is
subject to change

So the personality is the mask which the actor, the spiritual Individuality, 'speaks', or 'sounds through'. The personality, then, is the Lower Quaternary, or four lower principles of man—his Lower self. It comprises therefore, the whole bundle of psychical, astral, emotional, (lower) mental, and physical proclivities. All the karmic attributes of a physical life—its characteristics, memories, impulses, etc. are contained within the range of the personality.

What we call 'man', or a 'human being' is the combination of the Higher Triad (Individuality) and Lower Quaternary (personality) into a unity during the span of a life on Earth (see Table II-3, page 21). But it is a mistake to regard the personality as separate from the Individuality. On the contrary, it is a projection, and thus a reflection, of the Individuality (as an actor's mask matches the shape of his face). Being a material manifestation however, the personality can lead man astray. Therefore to free oneself from the domination of the Lower self enables the true Individuality to shine forth unhindered by the veil of personality.

Another common error is to think of the personality as intrinsically evil or at best just an encumbrance. It is decidedly neither of these. For a little deliberation will show that no useful work on Earth can be accomplished without a suitable terrestrial vehicle in which, and through which, to work. We can only act on Earth using tools from materials that are of the earth. What is evil, then, is the domination or excessive burden of the personality over the Individuality. Therefore, to free oneself from the personality does not mean to annihilate one's lower nature, but rather to align and attune it to become the obedient and faithful servant of one's higher nature—its master.

An example is given in the Coda of this Volume II to highlight the absolute necessity of the personality traits of Desire and Lower Mind conjointly *for a terrestrial existence*.

The Distinction Between Soul and Spirit

A detailed clarification of what is meant by soul was given in Chapter 3 where it was explained that soul is a generic term having the core meaning of a carrier, or vehicle, of any principle to its expression at a lower level.

---

i The Buddha taught that anything compounded is subject to decay and death—see N. G. Heap, 'Buddhism: Beliefs – Teachings – Practices', Eton College, EDUQAS GCSE, 59 < http://www.q3tipton.org.uk/wp content/uploads/2018/12/Complete-GCSE-EDUQAS-Buddhism-Beliefs-Teachings-Practices.pdf> accessed 28 February 2021.

Towards the latter half of the nineteenth century, spiritualistic phenomena were common occurrences. Most spiritualist writers distinguished only between body and spirit. But a few spiritualists, like Allan Kardec, pen name of the French educator and author Hippolyte Léon Denizard Rivail (1804–1869) also mentioned a layer of abstract, ethereal material serving as the connection and covering between the spirit and physical body of a person. They named this layer *perispirit*, the term used by way of direct analogy with *perisperm*, which is the layer of nutritive tissue that surrounds the embryo of a seed in some flowering, fruit-bearing plants having seeds within an enclosed ovary.3 In any case, séance room manifestations were ascribed to the activities of spirit. Blavatsky wrote *Isis Unveiled* during that period of heightened interest in spiritualistic phenomena, one of the purposes of her enormous work being to explain the distinction between soul and spirit. Blavatsky pointed out that the majority of the trivial séance room manifestations were not the operation of the (immortal) spirit, rather the near automatic actions of the discarded terrestrial soul elements of previously living men, i.e., the *Kāma-rūpa*.

Insights from mediumistic phenomena

Table II-12 overleaf shows a comparison between the divisions of the spiritualists with the subdivisions according to occultism by Allan Octavian Hume (1829–1912), a member of the Imperial Civil Service and founder of the Indian National Congress, also an ornithologist and botanist.4 Along with his fellow Englishman Alfred Percy Sinnett (1840–1921), the esoteric author, scholar, and Editor of *The Pioneer*, the leading English Daily of India, Hume was privileged to be in contact with, and receive letters from, Blavatsky's Adept teachers. The divisions from Hume's article are based on teachings he received from H.P. Blavatsky and Mahatma Koot Hoomi.

The Dual Nature of Manas and the Function of Antaḥkaraṇa

Tremendous significance is attached in occult literature to the fact that Manas, the Mind Principle, is a single principle in terms of man's constitution, yet displays a dual function. How does this come about? Let a man carefully examine his own thoughts. Despite the fact that he may have (and invariably does have) countless millions of thoughts, he can generally assort them into two groups: those thoughts that are impersonal, ennobling, philanthropic, and helpful towards others; and those that are personal, demeaning, self-serving, and harmful towards his fellows. These two groups display the qualities of the Higher Mind and the Lower mind; the former striving to ascend 'upwards' towards its spiritual origin; the latter gravitating 'downwards' towards the desire-ridden animal nature.

Composite nature of man's thoughts

This does not imply that the thought life of man can be apportioned at all times into two watertight compartments: Higher Mind and Lower mind, the former uncontaminated by the personal nature and the latter tainted with self-seeking motives. Other than the saint or irredeemable criminal, in the average man there will naturally be an intermingling of the 'pure' and 'impure' elements; however, in any one situation one or another mind quality will *predominate*. Hence the importance of *Antaḥkaraṇa* serving as a bridge of consciousness enabling the noblest elements of the personality and the Lower mind to be assimilated and absorbed into the Higher Mind and Spiritual Ego. (see pages 86–90).

Mind as system is unitary; Mind as function is dual.

This brings us to a point where we can clarify the important difference between a human being and an animal.

Table II-12   The Classification of Man's Nature by the Spiritualists
Contrasted with the Occultists

Divisions of the Spiritualists	Subdivisions of the Occultists
1. The Spiritual Soul, or Spirit.	1. The Spirit—an emanation from the ABSOLUTE; uncreated; eternal; a state rather than a being.
	2. The Higher or Spiritual intelligence or consciousness, or spiritual Ego, in which mainly resides the sense of consciousness in the *perfect* man, though the lower dimmer animal consciousness co-exists in No. 3.
2. The Animal Soul, or *Perisp[i]rit.*	3. The animal or physical intelligence or consciousness or Ego, analogous to, though proportionally higher in degree than, the reason, instinct, memory, imagination, &c., existing in the higher animals.
	4. The Astral shape (*Kāma-rūpa*) or body of desire, a principle defining the configuration of—[No. 3. below].
3. The Body.	5. The Astral body (*Liṅga-śarīra*) composed of highly etherealized matter; in its habitual passive state, the perfect but very shadowy duplicate of the body; its activity, consolidation and form depending entirely on the *Kāma-rūpa.*
	6. The Vital principle—(or *Jiv-ātma*)—, a form of force, indestructible and when disconnected with one set of atoms, becoming attracted immediately by others.
	7. The Physical body, composed wholly of matter in its grossest and most tangible form.

Note: the classification and orthography of Sanskrit terms in this Table are re-ordered so as to be consistent with Table II-3, page 21.

Is Man Just an Animal?

> The difference between animals and men is this: the former are ensouled by the 'principles' *potentially*, the latter *actually*. Do you understand now the difference?
>
> H. P. Blavatsky[5]

This is further elaborated by Hume in an endnote clarification to the subdivisions outlined in subdivision No. 3. in Table II-12, regarding the physical intelligence in man, 'analogous to, though proportionally higher in degree than [...] existing in the higher animals':

> Western Science, of course, as a rule, holds that animals have no conscious Ego, but this we know to be erroneous; they possess no spiritual, but they *do* possess an animal, consciousness. Could men communicate with them, they would discover not only this, but also that many of the anthropoid apes possess an intelligence, consciousness &c., little inferior to that of lunatics and madmen, and some desperately wicked and depraved men who have, in fact, become animals, through the loss, temporary or permanent, of their sixth and seventh principles [second and first principles in Table II-12 above], even while the combination of the other five principles is still intact, *i.e.*, even during life.[6]

Mainstream science and evolutionary biology regard a human being as intrinsically no different from an animal, at best as a biped beast modified—and both are regarded as just biological machines. Does this ring true?

It was mentioned earlier that humans can choose whether or not to behave like an animal. This does not need complicated proof since any person can discover this for himself. It is the Manasic principle that enables humans to know about their animal-like nature—for no true animal, we suggest, actually knows that it is an animal. Moreover, the animal has no such choice about whether or not it wishes to behave as an animal—it instinctually plays out its innate animal nature. This is because the Mind principle in animals is only potential and so animals, unlike humans, are not endowed with *self*-consciousness—they certainly have consciousness, but are not aware of the fact.

Distinguishing conscious behaviour from innate nature

Now it is a fact of common experience that there exists in man a vast range in his animal propensities, from utter bestiality to highly refined sensibilities. Which quality man displays depends entirely on the extent to which either *Manas* or *Kāma* dominates in the *Kāma-manas* union. The more the light of Manasic reason dominates the desire-nature of Kāma, the more mindful will such an individual be about his animal-like behaviour, and consciously choose to bridle and overpower it—and the more remorseful will he be when, out of momentary weakness, he lapses into behaviour (like drunkenness or vulgar speech) that his higher nature would be ashamed of. But except in extremely rare circumstances, when there is a complete severance of the higher nature (see Chapter 5) from the lower, even the coarsest and most sensual type of person will still possess some moral sense (however dimmed) of his actions. This is commonly known as the silent voice of conscience. Interestingly, the etymology of the word 'conscience' derives from Latin *conscīre*, 'knowledge within oneself', from *con-* 'with' and *scīre* '(to) know' (source of the English 'science'). This implies that conscience, the moral awareness and ability to differentiate between right and wrong, is not a static personality trait but grows with knowledge and understanding.

Endowed with Manas, a human being can be animal-like; eliminate Manas and a human would always be *an* animal, pure and simple.

It is again stressed that there is no principle or quality in man that is *intrinsically* evil. The same applies to Kāma. For it is Kāma that gives man his passion and urgency to act. But like a horse-drawn chariot, the horses (Kāma) must pull in the direction of the reins (Manas) held by the charioteer (*Buddhi*), and not be allowed to run amok. The importance of a wise blending and usage of both Kāma and Manas is beautifully illustrated in this sublime passage (quoted in part in Chapter 2) from *The Prophet*:

The more Kāma dominates over Manas, the stronger a person's animal-like nature.

> Your reason [Manas] and your passion [Kāma] are the rudder and the sails of your seafaring soul. If either your sails or your rudder be broken, you can but toss and drift, or else be held at a standstill in mid-seas.

> For reason, ruling alone, is a force confining; and passion, unattended, is a flame that burns to its own destruction. Therefore let your soul [Buddhi-Manas] exalt your reason to the height of passion; that it may sing; And let it direct your passion with reason, that your passion may live through its own daily resurrection, and like the phœnix rise above its own ashes.

> Kahlil Gibran[7]

Did Human Beings Evolve from Apes?

The physical body of man has not evolved from the physical bodies of animals, or the apes, as in Darwin's theory, which is now taken to the level of a pseudo-religious cult of scientism by the modern neo-Darwinists. The evolution of animal bodies took place, so we are told, not to provide, in the final stage, a physical vehicle for the Monad, but only to prepare a mental vehicle in which individualization could take place. The evolution of animal bodies therefore takes place to bring the 'group soul' to a particular level of development and it is in this highest form of the group soul (belonging to the higher animal species), which is mental in nature, that makes it possible for individualization to occur. And this individualized soul, then, incarnates in a human body derived from human parents. More technically, referring to the last column of Table II-3 on page 21, the Monad, or Spiritual Soul, cannot directly contact and take root in an earthly body without the intermediate mental vehicle of the Human Soul one step 'below', so to say. So it is the evolutionary purpose and role of the Animal kingdom, existing as a group on the emotional plane (the Animal group soul), to 'pierce through' to the next higher step and touch the mental plane that provides, co-operatively, the physical-emotional-mental vehicles, or Animal soul and Human Soul, for the Spiritual Soul, or Monad in which to incarnate.

Animal kingdom: its evolutionary purpose

The process of human evolution is described in detail in Chapter 10 of Volume III with robust scientific and esoteric evidence in support of the contentions that have fractured the backbone of neo-Darwinism and genetic determinism hitherto regarded as the sole explanatory mechanisms.

This Chapter has provided clarity on common mistaken beliefs in the general esoteric field. The next Chapter deals, at length, with major confusions in science and philosophy about minds, brains, and computers.

> *Simplicity is the ultimate sophistication.*
>
> LEONARDO DA VINCI[8]

> *The art of being wise is the art of knowing what to overlook.*
>
> WILLIAM JAMES[9]

> *Change will come slowly, across generations, because old beliefs die hard even when demonstrably false.*
>
> E. O. WILSON[10]

NOTES

1   Bertrand Russell, *The Impact of Science on Society* (1st edn, UK: Simon & Schuster,1953), 6.
2   *KT*, 'Definite Words for Definite Things', 176.
3   Allan Kardec, *Le Livre des Esprits* [The Spirits' Book], trans. Anna Blackwell (São Paulo, Brasil: Federação Espírita Brasileira, 1996) <https://www.awakening-intuition.com/ The_Spirits_Book_-_Allan_Kardec.pdf> accessed 7 March 2020.
4   Allan O. Hume, 'Fragments of Occult Truth, No. 1', *The Theosophist* (October 1881), 17–22; see also Blavatsky Study Centre, 2004 [online edn] <http://blavatskyarchives.com/humefrags1.htm> accessed 17 May 2020.
5   *KT*, 'The Physical and the Spiritual Man', 104.

6 Endnote (1) to subdivision No. 5 [subdivision No. 3 in Table II-12, p. 108], in Allan O. Hume, 'Fragments of Occult Truth, No. 1', 17–22.

7 Kahlil Gibran, *The Prophet*, introd. John Baldock (London: Arcturus, 2018), 68, 69–70.

8 *goodreads* <https://www.goodreads.com/quotes/9010638-simplicity-is-the-ultimate-sophistication-when-once-you-have-tasted> accessed 20 November 2020.

9 *BrainyQuote* <https://www.brainyquote.com/quotes/william_james_108497> accessed 20 November 2020.

10 Edward O. Wilson, *Consilience: The Unity of Knowledge* (New York: Alfred A. Knopf, 1998), 280.

7 Is the Brain a 'Wet Computer' – Are Humans 'Lumbering Robots'?
The Closing of the Scientific Mind

Unless we learn how to prepare for, and avoid, the potential risks, AI [artificial intelligence] could be the worst event in the history of our civilisation.

STEPHEN HAWKING[1]

Man is the measure of all things, *Protagoras said.* **Today we add,** **and computers are the measure of all men.**

DAVID GELERNTER[2]

SYNOPSIS

Chapter 7 is intended to disperse the fog of mistaken ideas by shining a floodlight on the chief subject of our enquiry— 'Who, or What Am I?' and relatedly, 'Does my Mind have Unique Characteristics that Distinguish it from an Animal or a Computer?' This is a substantial Chapter where we explore, in stepwise fashion, whether the brain is just a 'wet computer' or a 'biological computer made of meat'—two commonly used crude phrases to convey the mainstream neuroscientific idea that there is fundamentally no difference between the way the brain and the computer operate. We approach this subject by describing what the 'brain-equals-computer' analogy purports to show, and then unravel the philosophical weaknesses and several flaws in this simile. Concrete cases are given to demonstrate the breakdown of the computationalist argumentation. Specific examples are cited of how scientists of impeccable standing are treated by their colleagues when the former dare to question the inviolability of materialistic theories about mind and consciousness, human life and evolution. We suggest a possible way forward to resolve the brain-versus-mind conundrum and close with the question of whether robots will eventually overtake humanity, as confidently predicted by several international computer scientists associated with prestigious universities or who work for Google.

KEY WORDS: brain, mind, computer, computationalist analogies, roboticism (zombieism), functionalism, materialism, brain hemispheres, David Gelernter, Helen Keller, Iain McGilchrist, Francis Walshe

Having reached the midpoint of this work it should be apparent that although the brain does display some of the mechanical functions and characteristics of a computer, this is no reason to declare, as the majority of mainstream neuroscientists do, that the brain is nothing other than a 'wet computer'.[i] In the light of the research outlined in this work, this is clearly a gross over simplification (somewhat like saying that because a concert pianist displays some characteristics of an office typist—using ten

---

i Referred to as 'wet', because the hardware is biological rather than constituted of silicon and other physical chemicals.

fingers on a keyboard—that a pianist and a typist, are one and the same thing, or a piano and a typewriter are the same instrument because they both have a keyboard). For a start, it is minds and brains that created and produced computers, not the other way round. The product stands hierarchically on a lower plane than the producer of the product. Brains therefore must stand hierarchically at a higher level of sophistication and subtlety than the computers created by them. The fallacy of likening the brain to 'just a computer' has been pointed out in no uncertain terms by some of the world's greatest philosophers and psychologists, as well as scientists like the American David Gelernter (*b.*1955), professor of computer science at Yale University. In his article, appropriately entitled *The Closing of the Scientific Mind* (used as the subtitle of this Chapter), he demolishes what he aptly calls the 'master analogy' unquestioningly accepted by the vast majority of mainstream scientists, namely, that minds are to brains as software is to computers; to put it another way, the mind is the software of the brain.[3]

Delusions of simplistic analogies

This is the foremost view about the mind amongst mainstream scientists—never mind (excuse the pun) that science (by its own admission) has, to date, barely understood the subtleties of human consciousness. However, this idea is now so ingrained that it would be instructive first to review in some depth the arguments behind it, also known as 'computationalism', or 'cognitivism', before exposing the fatal weaknesses in the analogy. Accordingly, this Chapter is written in two major parts: first, an elucidation and substantial development of the core theme of Gelernter's article about the dangers of unquestioning, and exclusive, acceptance by science of computationalism, in turn, associated with artificial intelligence, posited as the sole means of understanding consciousness, mind, and human experience; then, a suggested way out of the bleak prospects for society and humanity that such acceptance would imply—see the epigraph.

The Master Analogy – 'The Brain is Just a Computer'

The Russian chess grandmaster and former World Chess Champion Garry Kasparov (*b.*1963) was beaten by the IBM supercomputer Deep Blue in 1977.[4] So the obvious conclusion would be that artificial intelligence (computers) are smarter than even the finest of human brains. Or is it so obvious?

What is a computer? It may be rather surprising to ask what appears to be an obvious question. But the word 'computer' is now so commonly used that the meaning of the term has become lost in the mass of popular connotations attaching to it. Here is a comprehensive list of definitions of a computer from authentic literary and scientific sources:

❖ 'A usually electronic device for storing and processing data, (usually in binary form[ii]), according to instructions given to it in a variable program' – *Concise Oxford English Dictionary*: Ninth edition, 1995.

❖ 'An electronic computer in which the input is discrete rather than continuous, consisting of combinations of numbers, letters, and other characters written

---

ii The binary code in a computer is a coding system using the binary digits 0 and 1 to represent a digit, letter, or other character.

in an appropriate programming language and represented internally in binary notation' – *Collins English Dictionary*: https://www.collinsdictionary.com/dictionary/english/computer/related, accessed 12 March 2021.

❖ 'A machine that stores programs and information in electronic form and can be used for a variety of processes' – *MacMillan Dictionary*: New (second) edition, 2007.

❖ 'A device, usually electronic, that processes data according to a set of instructions' – *Collins English Dictionary*: Complete & unabridged, Sixth edition, 2018.

❖ 'A programmable usually electronic device that can store, retrieve, and process data' – *Merriam-Webster*: https://www.merriam-webster.com/dictionary/computer, accessed, 12th March 2021.

❖ 'A machine capable of following instructions to alter data in a desirable way and to perform at least some of these operations without human intervention' – *Que's Computer User's Dictionary*: Second edition, Lloyd J. Short, 1991.

Numerous definitions of 'computer' with a common theme

All of these definitions have certain terminology in common: words and phrases like 'programmable', 'according to instructions given to it', 'written in an appropriate programming language', 'that stores programs and information', 'storing and processing data', 'that processes data according to a set of instructions', 'capable of following instructions'. All these terms make it patently obvious that a human programmer is involved. A computer cannot program itself; neither can it store programs and information by itself; nor can it alter data 'in a desirable way' unless such 'desires' are input by a human programmer. Computers (and machines in general) do only what humans program them to do. This was clearly foreseen as early as 1936 by 'the English mathematician Alan Turing [who] showed that a single machine (the future computer) could process any problem given rules for the solution.'[5] Did the supercomputer that beat Gary Kasparov program itself, or did human programmers input the necessary rules of the game—'rules for the solution' in Turing's terms—which the computer then followed, mechanically? More recently, IBM's Project Debater, a 6ft-tall black panel robot with an animated blue 'mouth', participated with human prize-winning debaters in two debates, one on the merits of subsidised space travel and the other on telemedicine[iii]—and performed so well that the audience voted the contest a draw. The robot's delivery was reckoned 'not as effective as the humans', but it was deemed to have more substance to its arguments. Why did the robot have more substance to its arguments? Quite simply because, as stated by Indian born American Arvind Krishna (*b*.1963), Senior Vice President IBM Hybrid Cloud,[iv] it had access to a vast data bank containing 'hundreds of millions' of research papers and articles. These were drawn upon to build an argument, and a narrative to support it, using speech recognition to analyse its opponents' arguments and respond to specific points raised.[6]

But despite what may seem to be obvious, one of the arch-champions of the idea that the brain is no different in principle to a computer—and *is* in fact a computer—is the American philosopher Daniel Dennett (*b*.1942). In his highly influential book *Consciousness Explained* (a better title would be *Consciousness Explained Away*) he asks us

---

iii Telemedicine is the remote diagnosis and treatment of patients by means of telecommunications technology.

iv Arvind Krishna is also Director of IBM Research at International Business Machines Corporation.

to 'think of the brain as a computer'.[7] For Dennett, 'human consciousness is *itself* a huge complex of memes[v] (or more exactly, meme-effects in brains) that can best be understood as the operation of a *"von Neumannesque"* virtual machine *implemented* in the *parallel architecture* of a brain that was not designed [by whom?] for any such activities;' which means that human consciousness is a software program, or application, designed to run on any ordinary 'computer' such as the brain—hence the reference, and a debasing reference at that, to John von Neumann (1903–1957), the great Hungarian mathematician accredited with pioneering the digital computer. Von Neumann never maintained that minds are to brains as software is to computers. In fact, he once said 'there probably is a God. Many things are easier to explain if there is than if there isn't.'[8] A pity that Dennett does not seem to have appreciated this.

<aside>Daniel Dennett equates brain with computer</aside>

The analogy, though, is alluring and in a limited sense it seems fitting. The reason being that software comprises coded instructions given to hardware. We can dismantle and dissect the hardware with a scalpel and view it under a microscope if we feel like it, but we cannot dissect software to find out the mathematical code or the program, or the software programmer. The structure of software and hardware are wholly different, albeit the former is embodied by the latter (without hardware, software would have no significance, and vice versa—the one depends upon the other).

So far so good, but this idea of embodiment of an entirely different structure is extrapolated to the notion of mind embodied by brain and is a good example of errors of category. It is argued (reasonably upon first appearance) that the brain has its own structure and so does the mind, which exhibits reason, memory, imagination, emotions, and happens to be 'conscious', whatever the latter term may mean to materialists. (However, the Scottish philosopher and educationalist Alexander Bain (1818–1903), Regius Professor and Lord Rector of the University of Aberdeen, has written a paper on the resemblances between the life-principles of plants, animals, and human beings—see more in Endnote II-9.) Nonetheless, the content of the mind cannot be dissected with scalpels, seen through a microscope, or revealed by magnetic resonance imaging ('MRI') scans, but the structure of the brain can indeed be so dissected and seen because the brain is a dense mass of physical matter comprising neurons and other cells. Yet the mind cannot exist apart from the brain which wholly embodies it. Therefore minds are to brains as software is to computers; and minds cannot exist without brains just as software cannot exist without hardware. Put another way, without the associated hardware in each case, minds and software are mere abstractions.

<aside>Confusion caused by category errors</aside>

Some computationalists take this notion to extremes. For example, the American computer scientist, inventor, and futurist Ray Kurzweil (*b.*1948) who works, unsurprisingly, for Google, predicts that by 2029 computers will outsmart us and that the behaviour of computers will be indistinguishable from that of humans. (In fact computers do outsmart us even today—in speed of number crunching, if nothing else—but that is because human beings have designed and programmed them to do so.) And after the year 2045, Kurzweil maintains, machine intelligence will dominate human intelligence to such an extent that humans will no longer be capable of understanding machines.

<aside>Google scientist predicts when machines will outrun human intelligence</aside>

---

v Memes are the cultural analogues to genes, acting as units for carrying ideas, symbols or practices, by transmission from one mind to another through writing, speech, gestures, rituals, or other imitable phenomena, with a mimicked theme.

By then humans will have begun a process of machinization, or what he refers to as 'transhumanism', which is the merging of humans and machines by cramming both human bodies and their brains with semiconductor chip implants, along with the fine tuning of their genetic material.[9] (This theme is revisited in the Epilogue to this work in Volume III.) In passing, the Editor-in-chief of *The Week* sums up the whole thing very neatly. He points out that such predictions are a geek's pipe dream. Being *like* a human is not *to be* human. Sophisticated machine codes and algorithms may provide the former, but never the latter.[10] But to continue in the computationalist line of argument, the American computer scientist and authority on artificial intelligence Drew McDermott (*b.*1949) at Yale University believes that biological computers (meaning human brains) differ only superficially from modern digital computers. He goes on to assert that according to science, humans are just a strange animal that arrived pretty late on the evolutionary scene, that 'computers can have minds' and that his avowed purpose is 'to increase the plausibility of the hypothesis that we are machines and to elaborate some of its consequences.'[11] (A strict syllogism would also mean that animal brains also equal computers.)

Yale University scientist believes computers have minds

And Kurzweil and McDermott are by no means alone. But it is reassuring to learn that a galaxy of scientists and entrepreneurs on the world stage have taken the step of pointing out their grave concerns about the threat posed by artificial intelligence and the ethical dilemma of bestowing moral responsibilities on robots. For example, Niklas Boström (*b.*1973), the Swedish philosopher, Oxford University don, and Director of the Strategic Artificial Intelligence Research Centre, warns that supercomputers will outsmart us. Readers are referred to his paper outlining the case for believing that we will have *super-human* artificial intelligence within the first third of the next century, and how fast we can expect superintelligence to be developed, once there is human-level artificial intelligence.[12] Then, according to the American entrepreneur, investor, engineer, and inventor, Elon Musk FRS (*b.*1971), artificial intelligence (AI) poses a greater threat to humanity than nuclear war. In his address to students at the Massachusetts Institute of Technology he stated, 'if I had to guess at what our biggest existential threat is, it's probably that.'[13]

Elon Musk and Stephen Hawking warn that AI poses a threat to humanity

Stephen Hawking joined Elon Musk, and hundreds of others, in issuing a letter unveiled at an International Joint Conference in Buenos Aires, Argentina. The letter warns (as does Musk) that artificial intelligence can potentially be more dangerous than nuclear weapons. Refer also to Hawking's further warning in the epigraph, Microsoft co-founder Bill Gates has also expressed concerns about artificial intelligence. During a question and answer session in January 2015 on Reddit (a platform for internet communities), he said, 'I am in the camp that is concerned about super intelligence. First the machines will do a lot of jobs for us and not be super intelligent. That should be positive if we manage it well. A few decades after that though the intelligence is strong enough to be a concern.'[14]

Can such serious warnings be ignored?

On the basis of the warning notes sounded by the likes of Hawking and Gates, can all this hype from the aficionados of artificial intelligence and computationalism then be dismissed as the phantasies of nerds? We cannot do so because the latter have gained such prominence; moreover, their ideas are highly pertinent to the whole question of the nature of consciousness and mind. We need to uncover, and recover, our humanness at all costs and the impending war against man-equals-computer, and then, computer-surpasses-man has to be fought in earnest. (Hopefully this will be a bloodless war, at least regarding the computers, as they do not, as yet, have a blood supply.) Therefore, we need to unearth the fallacies in the predictions by computationalists. But first, out of fairness to them, we need to understand more of what they are contending, and their reasons for doing so.

The Computationalist Strategy and Argumentation

Regarding the human being, the overriding strategy is to eliminate all subjectivity (which includes, of course, consciousness and feelings), to the merely physically observable and measurable (strong echoes of the metaphysical basis of materialism pertaining to the Vienna Circle of Logical Empiricism—see Volume I, Chapter 3, page 23). Precisely because feelings and subjectivity are incompatible with the machine paradigm of man-equals-computer, once subjectivity is eliminated, the case for the computer-mind is strengthened. And once the mind is reduced to a computer, all sense of personal responsibility, our pangs of conscience, our feelings for divinity and higher aspiration—all to do with being truly human—are eradicated or explained away at one stroke. The adopted strategy for doing so can be enumerated in three stages.

Stage 1: Argue the case that man is just a computer and nothing more, by ignoring everything that distinguishes man from a computer.

Stage 2: Eliminate feelings and subjective states, in which case man is no different from a computer. Can a computer feel anything? Obviously not. In fact, Daniel Dennett has written a lengthy scholarly paper on why computers cannot feel pain.[15] Surely, being such a distinguished and award-winning scholar, cognitive scientist, philosopher of science, and philosopher of biology, particularly in those fields that relate to evolutionary biology and cognitive science, he of all people must know.

Computationalist strategy is to reduce mind to a physical machine (computer)

Stage 3: If it can't be measured, it obviously doesn't exist, because science only recognizes: accuracy which can be repeatably quantified over so-called truth which is a matter of subjective opinion; precision over meaning; quantity over quality; theory over experience; and establishment respectability over validity and evidence.

This strategy is implemented by way of a three-pronged attack against subjectivity using the interrelated arguments of:

1. roboticism, or zombieism;
2. functionalism;
3. brain states.

We now describe each of the above three arguments in turn, and then expose the overall weaknesses in their line of reasoning, taken as a whole.

Roboticism, or Zombieism

The term 'roboticism' is apt, since Richard Dawkins, of world renowned fame in biological science and evolutionary theory, has described human beings as 'lumbering robots'—which necessarily also includes himself in the epithet. He goes on to assert what he finds a truth, which still fills him with astonishment, namely: 'We are survival machines—robot vehicles blindly programmed to preserve the selfish molecules known as genes.'[16] Such a 'truth' may fill us with sheer incredulity, even more so because he goes on to affirm that 'we animals are the most complicated things in the known universe.'[17] But we may not take issue with it. Nor are we allowed to ask who the blind programmer happens to be or what 'software' he used. Why?

Because, in essence, the arguments go like this. With the current increase in technology, it is not difficult to imagine a time when a robot could be constructed with all the needed software to display all the characteristics of someone we know, say our best friend. We may ask that friend about his/her feelings, or whether (s)he has consciousness or indeed whether (s)he is human, and (s)he would answer 'yes' to all of these. But the answer is merely due to the clever software programming (never mind by whom) that has been built into the robot. There is no way of telling whether the robot is actually feeling or experiencing anything at all. (S)he is, in short, indistinguishable from the human one takes oneself to be. But why assume that one is human? Why isn't one just like our lumbering robotic friend? After all, what is the point of consciousness? Has not Darwinian theory fully explained that nature selects the fittest creatures based on entirely practical grounds like survivability in 'survival machines—robot vehicles'? If we and our robotic friend behave in the same way, what survivability purpose does consciousness serve?

Functionalism

The important point to note here is that subjectivity has been reduced to the physical, therefore to the observable and measurable. An example: let us take something that has made generations of music lovers (including the writer) tearful, such as Schubert's song *Ave Maria*. What does 'being tearful' mean according to functionalism? It means that a certain set of physical events (like a compact disc playing music, sound waves in the air from the speakers, the action of the salty glands in the eyes), but not actually crying, is the cause of the state of mind known as 'tearful'. This state of mind (along with others) makes one want to do certain things, like shedding tears. So 'I want to cry' means that the mental state (i.e., being tearful) has not been eliminated but reduced to just certain physical circumstances, to what one has been doing and what actions one plans to do, like putting on a record of the *Ave Maria* in anticipation of becoming tearful. (Schrödinger would have trouble with this line of reasoning—see later.)

Argument
employed is to
reduce
subjectivity to
physical
mechanism

It is no good arguing that one can be reduced to tears without any physical events—like a live performance or a recording—simply by imagining the song. After all, MRI scans can show localised changes in brain states when we experience so-called feelings even without external stimulus. It is simply a matter of biochemical activity like neurons and neurotransmitters that make us tearful. To reiterate, the thorny problem of the relationship (and crossing over) between physical brain states and subjective experience is neatly solved (that is, conveniently explained away) not by eliminating the latter, but by reducing it to the physically observable and measurable. Once subjective states are so dispensed with, one can indeed ask: 'What then is the difference between a man's brain and a computer? Can computers have feelings?' One sees a colour (say, red) on one's computer screen, but how foolish it would be to think that our computer actually *experiences* red! Colour on the screen of our computer liquid crystal display is produced by careful control and variation of the voltage applied over the subpixels. It takes an enormous number of semiconductor transistors to produce the whole palette of colours on our computer.

Analogously, colour in one's head involves an enormous number of neurons firing under precise electro-chemical conditions. So what's the difference, in principle? None at all, it would appear, as the translation of physical brain states to mental states and subjective experience is neatly solved—by eliminating consciousness and feeling or regarding them as being superfluous or illusory or an epiphenomenon, the technical term conveying the mask of scientific respectability but in point of fact camouflaging the *underlying sterility* of the ideology, shortly to be exposed.

Brain States

This argument is really a variant of functionalism. It posits that changes in our emotions and feelings are caused solely by changes in brain states. Our mind is simply the product of our genes and brain, so to destroy or damage a part of the brain is to affect the personality trait corresponding to the damaged region. This contention is based on the grounds of considerable data and research showing how persons who have suffered brain damage through injury or stroke display marked changes in emotional behaviour and personality after their injury. Indeed there are numerous learned books and peer reviewed scholarly articles in international journals in support of this contention.[18] An arbitrary review of such journals like *Neuropsychological Rehabilitation*, *Journal of Consulting and Clinical Psychology*, and *Annals of Neurology* reveal some common features. The most frequently quoted example is that injury, or damage through stroke to the brain, especially the part that controls emotion and behaviour—the frontal lobe and limbic system—can alter the way the victim expresses or feels emotion and can confer a variety of emotional problems or motivational disturbances. The victim can have difficulty in controlling his/her emotions or 'mood swings'. Whereas some may experience emotions (such as anger) intensely and quickly but with minimal lasting effect, others display what is known as emotional lability, i.e., being on an 'emotional rollercoaster', whereby they can be sad, happy, and angry in quick succession. There can also be sudden episodes of crying or laughing sometimes without any apparent connection between the emotional expression and the situation in question (such as crying without feeling sad, laughing without feeling happy, or laughing at a sad story).

Argument posits that all subjective feelings can fully be explained solely by brain states

As before, we may not take issue with all this. We are not permitted to question what appears to be an unwarranted inference, namely, that there is no subjective state and that changes in brain states (i.e., physical mechanisms and processes in the brain) are the sole determining factor affecting our emotions and feelings. Because, to use a simplistic analogy, a motor car moves solely because of its steering mechanism and wheels. Damage the steering mechanism or the wheels, and the car would turn corners awkwardly; analogously, damage the brain, and emotions are affected because specific personality traits and emotions are governed by specific centres in the brain. So, it is argued, there can be no subjective individual to experience the emotion any more than there is an inner 'car soul' to 'feel' any change in its steering mechanism. We are, quite simply, the way we behave corresponding to how our brain states respond to external physical stimuli, just as our car behaves on the road according to the way its mechanisms respond to the driver (who, in any case, is just another kind of machine). Here it is interesting to note that every machine, even the most primitive kind, has a purpose for which it was designed; but the most complex machine on Earth—the human being—is supposed to have no purpose, let alone free will.

Applying this logic, then, any deprivation or non-functioning of the human sensory apparatus would not register any feelings or emotion associated with the corresponding sensory input. So persons both blind and deaf could not possibly feel any emotion that a normally sighted and hearing person would experience from, say, the view of a city from a tall building or a sublime piece of music. Or could they?

The Computationalist Master Analogy – Its Fatal Flaws

Taking our cue directly from the above paragraph, we first cite a famous example that challenges the computationalist argument that it would be impossible to feel or experience anything if the physical sensory organs of a person were inoperative or atrophied. This then forms the basis for drawing out the neurological and philosophical issues that expose the flaws in the master analogy. Thereafter, the main arguments that repudiate the master analogy are summarized and followed by a list of numerous phenomena in life that it cannot explain.

Seeing Without Eyes – Hearing Without Ears

Helen Keller (1880–1968), the great American author, political activist, and lecturer was rendered blind and deaf from the age of nineteen months through contracting scarlet fever or meningitis. According to the concepts of functionalism and brain states described above, she could not possibly experience any *emotion* associated with a complete lack of eyesight and hearing. However, in 1932 she wrote an evocative letter describing the view from the top of the Empire State Building seeing 'New York spread out like a marvellous tapestry beneath us. There was the Hudson—more like the flash of a sword-blade than a noble river. The little island of Manhattan, set like a jewel in its nest of rainbow waters, stared up into my face, and the solar system circled about my head!'[19] Note her depiction of specific colours, shapes, and forms that are not merely the products of her imagination or hearsay.

Helen Keller 'sees' details of New York City

Even more moving than this was her letter, eight years previously, to the New York Symphony Orchestra after 'hearing' the radio broadcast of their performance of Beethoven's Choral Symphony at Carnegie Hall in New York, conducted by Walter Damrosch on 1st February 1924. Here she described 'the joy of being able to tell you that, though deaf and blind, I spent a glorious hour last night listening over the radio to Beethoven's "Ninth Symphony". I put my hand on the receiver [to] see if I could get any of the vibrations. What was my amazement to discover that I could feel, not only the vibrations, but also the impassioned rhythm, the throb and the urge of the music! The intertwined and intermingling vibrations from different instruments enchanted me. I could actually distinguish the cornets, the roll of the drums, deep-toned violas and violins singing in exquisite unison. When the human voice leaped up trilling from the surge of harmony, I recognized them instantly as voices. I felt the chorus grow more exultant, more ecstatic, upcurving swift and flame-like, until my heart almost stood still. As I listened, with darkness and melody, shadow and sound filling all the room, I could not help remembering that the great composer who poured forth such a flood of sweetness into the world was deaf like myself. I marvelled at the power of his quenchless spirit by which out of his pain he wrought such joy for others.'[20]

Helen Keller 'hears' details of Beethoven's Choral Symphony

Figure II-5   Helen Keller 'Listening' to
Beethoven's Choral Symphony on the Radio
Copyright © American Foundation for the Blind, Helen Keller Archive

Notice, in this instance, how she was able to discern pitch, different instruments, the human voice, melody, and rhythm—and convey her emotions. A full version of this letter is shown in Endnote II-7. To peruse it is a deeply humbling and illuminating experience.[21]

Helen Keller was able, apparently, to 'hear' by touch. The photograph shown in Figure II-5 above shows her right hand touching the loudspeaker of the radio. Human beings have a subtle, non-physical counterpart to their senses: for hearing it is known in popular terms as 'listening with the inner ear'. But robot-human is not allowed subtle bodies or senses as (s)he is supposed to be just physical, so presumably (s)he could not compose when deafened, assuming that (s)he could compose anything at all beforehand—mindless electronic muzak, termed 'aural pornography' by the writer, not deemed as music. Would a robot be moved to his/her physical tears by such a cacophony? Perhaps (s)he would if (s)he were programmed to do so. Programmed to do so? Enter the human programmer!

And in passing, speaking of the great Beethoven, the fact of his stone-deafness is legendary, but how many people bother to enquire how this can be, or whether there is a subtle sense associated with a subtle body that makes inner hearing possible? Chapters 7 and 8 in Volume III supply a possible clue.

Deeper Neurological and Philosophical Issues at Stake

At this juncture one is entitled to ask two deeper questions. Firstly, human beings vary enormously in the subtlety of their emotional responses and in their capacity for such responses. Some people may be largely unaffected by music, but would be reduced to tears by great poetry; others by lofty literature, or by witnessing acts of great compassion, or, as in the case of Helen Keller, by a majestic scene and great music. Even within a particular art form, emotional responses vary widely; for example, some musicians are highly moved by Bach, but less so by Chopin; with others it is very much the converse. So how would the tear-and emotion-producing software in robot-man be programmed so as to cater for the infinite variety of robotic-responses to various art forms; furthermore, to the equally infinite shades of response within a single art form itself, as in the human examples just cited? In other words, how would the software decide, for a particular robot-man amongst millions of other robot-men, whether to produce tears upon hearing, say, Schubert's music, but not William Blake's poetry for this specific robot-man in question; and even for this particular robot-man, whether Schubert's songs would be more moving than, say, his *Death and Maiden String Quartet*?

Can robots emulate infinite nuances of human subjectivity?

Secondly, one presumes that the 'hearing' of robot-man is produced by the appropriate acoustic software linked to his/her robot-brain. If this specific piece of software were removed, would our robot-man—now rendered completely 'deaf'—be able to compose music like the great Beethoven who composed the titanic *Hammerklavier Sonata* and the *Choral Symphony* when completely deaf?

The answers to such questions lie above and beyond mainstream physical theory. *My Stroke of Insight*[22] by Jill Bolte Taylor, is an excellent, and all too rare example of a neuro-scientist capable of not only seeing the limitations of mainstream theory but also able to explore the wonderful unknown. Her book describes the way in which stroke survivors might develop new skills and sensory subtleties, and most importantly, the role of awakening the right hemisphere, which Bolte calls the 'divine brain' (see Volume I, Chapter 6, page 162 for more details about her extraordinary experience). There is, arguably, no finer explanation of the scientific, physiological, psychological, and philosophical problems resulting from the domination of the right hemisphere by the left hemisphere of the divided brain, as now summarized.

The Divided Brain

Iain McGilchrist rose to prominence after the publication of his seminal book *The Master and His Emissary*, subtitled *The Divided Brain and the Making of the Western World*.[23] Thrice elected a Fellow of All Souls College, Oxford, McGilchrist is a literary scholar and taught English literature whilst pursuing interests in philosophy and psychology. He then trained in medicine, to become a Consultant Psychiatrist at the Bethlem Royal and Maudsley Hospital in London, where he was Clinical Director of their southern sector Acute Mental Health Services. He is a Fellow of the Royal College of Psychiatrists and is specially approved by the Secretary of State under Section 12(2) of the Mental Health Act, 1983. He also worked as a Research Fellow in neuroimaging at the Johns Hopkins Hospital in Baltimore, USA. In addition to neuropsychiatry, his wide ranging clinical experience includes epilepsy, eating disorders, depression, psychosis, personality disorders (especially borderline cases), anxiety disorders, chronic low self-esteem, phobias, and alcohol and drug abuse.

With his eminent qualifications in the literary, philosophical, medical, and psychiatric fields, he is uniquely qualified to inform about the wider, cultural issues about mind and brain, as well as provide detailed information about mental functions and brain processes. His work has attracted international acclaim (often in hyperboles); a list of over seventy-five tributes to his work is given in http://www.iainmcgilchrist.com/comments.asp #content, accessed 6 February 2020. They come from world authorities in clinical psychology, brain and cognition, medicine, psychiatry, cognitive science, neurology, neuroscience, neuropsychiatry, sociology, and philosophy. They include professors at Cambridge, Oxford, Harvard, and California, a Fellow of the Royal Society, and editors of leading newspapers and academic journals. Why such worldwide acclaim?

McGilchrist's book argues that the division of the brain into two hemispheres, whilst being essential to human existence, gives possibly incompatible versions of the world, with quite different priorities and values. There are significant differences between the structure and function of the two hemispheres. However, to apportion specific brain functions exclusively to one hemisphere or another is an erroneous concept, as we now know that every type of function—including reason, emotion, language, and imagery—is subserved not by one hemisphere alone, but by both. In other words, the brain acts as a whole and not in a compartmentalised fashion. Notwithstanding this, the differences in hemisphere function lie not, as has hitherto been supposed, in the 'what', but in the 'how', i.e., not which skills each hemisphere possesses, but the way in which each uses them, and to *what end*. His book examines the relation between the two brain hemispheres, not just in terms of neurology and structure, which has already been done in several erudite medical books, but most importantly, in the light of the complexity of the connection between the two hemispheres leading to the divided nature of thought that has been a decisive factor in moulding our culture. This horizontal division of the brain into two hemispheres leading to the divided nature of thought corresponds, arguably, on the physical plane, to the occult teaching on the 'vertically divided' double nature of the Mind Principle (the Higher Mind and the Lower mind 'below' it) as explained previously in Chapters 2 and 3.

Divided nature of thought parallels occult teaching on the Mind Principle

Reverting to the brain, McGilchrist shows that the relationship between the hemispheres is not symmetrical (the reason for this is suggested below). In simple terms, it is as if the left hemisphere, though unaware of its dependence, could be thought of as an 'emissary' of the right hemisphere, valuable for taking on a role that the right hemisphere—the 'Master'—cannot itself afford to undertake. However, it transpires that the emissary has its own will, as it were, and secretly believes itself to be superior to its Master. And it has the means to betray him. *What the emissary does not realize is that in doing so, it will also betray itself.* Crucially important as McGilchrist shows, *the hemispheres are more than mere machines with functions like computers; instead they are shown as underwriting whole, self-consistent, versions of the world.* Through an examination of Western philosophy, art, and literature, his book reveals the uneasy relationship of the hemispheres being played out in the history of ideas, from ancient times until the present. Here we again find a close parallel with the occult teaching on the dual nature of *Manas*, the Mind Principle; moreover, the outcome to be anticipated when *Kāma* usurps Manas resulting in *Kāma-manas*, or desire-driven thought (though it is not in any way suggested that Kāma and Manas can literally be correlated with, or correspond to, the left and right hemisphere, respectively.)

McGilchrist's suggestion is that the encouragement of precise, categorical thinking at the expense of background vision and experience—an encouragement which, since Plato, has flourished to such impressive effect in European thought—has now reached a point where it is seriously distorting both our lives and our thoughts. As noted by the British philosopher and 'foremost scourge of "scientific pretension"'[24] Dr Mary Midgley (1919–2018) in her excellent review of McGilchrist's book, the drive towards precision (which, incidentally, is often confused with rigour and accuracy) encourages a continuous narrowing of perspective towards the microcosm of details at the expense of looking outwards to appreciate the wider picture, the macrocosm; or not even bothering about its presence or relevance.[25] So a weakness of specialization is not knowing when to consult the generalist possessing a higher viewpoint. However, we do have some control over this shift between detailed and general thinking, a tendency that can be helped or hindered by the ethic that prevails in the culture around it.

Heavy price of left brain dominance in science and society

Our whole idea of what counts as scientific or professional has shifted towards literalism and precision—towards elevating quantity over quality, theory over experience, precision over truth—in a way that would have astonished even the seventeenth century founders of modern science, although they were already far advanced on that path. And the ideal of objectivity has developed in a way that would have surprised those early founders still more. In this wise, as Midgley recounts in her review, a shocked nurse lately told her that it is proposed that all nurses must have university degrees. 'Who', she asked, 'will actually do the nursing?'[vi] (But see Volume I, Chapter 3, pages 43–45 about the increasing need in mainstream science to invoke such ideas as a science of qualities and syntropy as a counterbalance to prevailing scientific materialism based predominantly on primary qualities.)

Aptly, and with unerring insight, McGilchrist's conclusion to his book is entitled 'The Master Betrayed'. He suggests 'that we may be about to witness the final triumph of the left hemisphere—at the expense of us all.' In a 10,000-word essay, *The Divided Brain and the Search for Meaning*,[26] written to complement *The Master and His Emissary*, Iain McGilchrist asks why—despite the vast increase in material well-being—people are less happy today than they were around half a century ago.[vii] He suggests that the division between the two hemispheres of the brain has a critical effect on how we see and understand the world around us. The current left-brain-driven frenzy to convince us that we, thinking-feeling human beings are just computing machines and nothing more ('lumbering robots', to use Richard Dawkins's egregiously rhetorical epithet about humanity), is fitting proof of McGilchrist's prediction. No surprise, then, as Mary Midgley points out, that some reviewers of McGilchrist's remarkable work see no more in it than just another glorification of feeling at the expense of thought. Such a work, the writer emphasizes, cannot be apprehended by a reviewer using just his/her left-brain hemisphere! Unlike the computationalists who regard mind and brain in terms of just software and hardware, McGilchrist shows that the mind and brain can be understood only by seeing them in the broadest possible context of our whole existence, and of the wider human culture in which they arise—the cyclical process of the culture which helps to mould, and in turn is moulded by, our minds and brains. Note, carefully, that the whole of our existence includes our spiritual and, naturally, our physical existence; however, the

Humanity's fate when in the thraldom of left brain thought

---

vi The Royal College of Nursing stipulates: 'To work as a nurse, you need a degree in nursing and you must be registered with the Nursing and Midwifery Council (NMC)'. See <https://www.rcn.org.uk/professional-development/become-a-nurse> accessed 3 October 2020.

vii This trend is also borne out by the statistics adduced by the writer in the Introductory, page lix and Chapter 1, page 4 in Volume I of this work.

former cannot be explained away by reduction to a mere subset of the latter, although the latter is subsumed in the former as this and other Chapters in our work argue.

On a philosophical note, if we are 'about to witness the final triumph of the left [brain] hemisphere' perhaps that is good news in a way, maybe indicating the apotheosis and subsequent decline of the Kali Yuga ('the fourth, the *black* or iron age, our present period'[27]) signalling the beginning of the Path of Return.

The Computationalist Argumentation – Its Philosophical Background

The philosophical origin of this situation is the dualist notion of a complete separation between spirit and matter, or soul and body. It is a tragedy, both for science and for humanity, that the science of polymaths, such as Leonardo da Vinci (1452–1519), has not managed to influence the ideas of later generations of thinkers or to stem the tide of the mechanistic science that emerged some two hundred years later. *Learning from Leonardo*[28] is a recent book by Fritjof Capra (*b.*1939), the Austrian born American physicist, systems theorist, and deep ecologist, whose first book *The Tao of Physics*[29] was a classic. From Leonardo we learn that nature was always vital and alive, so his science was one of living forms. (This was of course Goethe's teaching and that of other great sages and philosophers of the East and the West.) Naturally, the mechanisms of nature could be scrutinized and studied empirically as Leonardo did in his drawings of the anatomy of the human body or the structure of the wings of birds, but he never reduced nature just to mechanisms or machines. Do we understand flight by observing the living bird in flight, or by viewing its lifeless wings under a microscope? Both aspects are necessary for a complete understanding: the first to perceive the living form; the second to study the physical mechanisms it uses for flight.

Leonardo and Goethe both adopt a holistic, systems approach

Capra shows that, besides inventing the empirical scientific method over a century before Galileo and Francis Bacon, Leonardo was what we would call nowadays a systemic thinker, believing that a true understanding of the world lay in perceiving the connections between phenomena and the larger patterns formed by those connecting relationships. And in the tradition of the great sages he worked on the principle of the Hermetic philosophy, so whenever exploring the forms of nature in the macrocosm he looked for similar principles, patterns, and processes in the human body—the microcosm. But then came the radically different mechanistic science of the followers of Descartes, Galileo, and also Newton (however see below). As a necessary diversion, we insist in saying 'followers of' because such great thinkers as Descartes and Galileo were absolutely right in pioneering the age of rationalism to counter the superstitions and dogmas rife in institutionalised religion. But their followers have taken their ideas to extremes, formed their own cult of rationalism (now scientism), and arbitrarily excised the spiritual components, however imperfectly these may have been have expressed in their times.

Scientism is no fault of Galileo, Newton or other pioneers of science

A case in point is Newton, to whom the idea of the clockwork universe is attributed. But this just shows the ignorance and prejudice of those scientists and scholars who have, until recently, chosen to ignore Newton's colossal writings on alchemy and theology. With unmistakable clarity and force Newton proclaimed that nature is a living being and his writings glow with a love and reverence for deity, nature, and man, considered as an organic unity. Newton's is one of the finest translations of the Hermetic philosophy (see Volume I, Chapter 8, page 249), where again, in the tradition of the sages and occultists, he saw the law of analogy operating on all planes of nature: that which operates in the microcosm is a reflection of correspondingly higher principles in the macrocosm.[30]

Reverting to Descartes, in his *Passions of the Soul* and *The Description of the Human Body*, he suggested that the body works like a machine, that it has material properties. But the mind (or soul), on the other hand, was described as non-material and not following the (mechanical) laws of nature, which alludes to an occult truth. This idea of matter being dead or inert and the body, a machine, has persisted even to this day, especially in the context of the ever increasing supremacy of scientific technology, whereas the spirit and soul aspects (which Descartes also considered at length) have either been conveniently ignored, or explained away in terms of matter. So the root cause of the current malaise in thinking epitomised by the computationalist cult is this notion, which now involves seeing everything natural as an object—inert, senseless, and detached from us. And such thinking might well explain the attitude that has led to the present ecological crisis whereby our planet is regarded as an inert object to plunder at our will for technological advance and commercial expansion. Whereas quantum physics has repeatedly shown with such impressive theory, backed by sophisticated experimental evidence, the interconnectedness of things in the world, the non-materiality of so-called physical matter, and the role of consciousness in any consideration of quantum behaviour, yet the collective psyche of the vast majority of mainstream scientists, especially biologists, has hardly progressed beyond the outworn paradigm of the 'billiard ball' notion of dead matter behaving according to mechanical laws. Consequentially, life is reduced to the mechanical laws of classical (meaning, pre-quantum) physics without any higher informing principle, by whatever name. Indeed, it is the avowed aim of mainstream biology (especially molecular biology) to reduce all things to physics and chemistry, which amounts to attempting to explain everything and all life as the action and product of inert matter in motion (see Volume I, Chapter 3).

Side note (left margin): Science has ignored the non-material soul and spirit in Descartes' philosophy

The magnificent discoveries of quantum physics have not penetrated the thinking and outlook of other than a handful of scientists and doctors. The machine paradigm largely prevails.

The Computationalist Master Analogy – Why it Breaks Down

This final section of the first part of this Chapter draws together the preceding insights into the deficiencies in the arguments of computationalists. As ever, the flaw is one of philosophy, not methodology—a rigorous methodology can be built upon philosophical quicksand. Accordingly, we deal first with the philosophical weaknesses in the master analogy, move on to list numerous facts of life and experience that cannot be explained by it, and then round off with the overriding and overwhelming reasons for the obstruction of progress in science and philosophy of mind: what Gelernter aptly refers to as 'the closing of the scientific mind' as per the subtitle of this Chapter.

The Philosophical Weaknesses in the Computationalist Argumentation

The whole essence of the problem is the failure to perceive the distinction between the machine and the mechanic, between the instrument and the performer—or whatever similar such metaphor we may ascribe to the confusion caused by a blurring of categories. Reminding ourselves of this terse quote by Peter Leggett stated in Volume I, Chapter 2:

A pianist needs a piano to make music

> By analogy with a pianist and a piano, the mind corresponds to the pianist and the brain to the piano. If either pianist or piano is inadequate, so will be the music. If either mind or brain is inadequate, so will be the person.[31]

No one could have expressed the barrenness of materialistic theories about mind and consciousness better than the great British neurologist Sir Francis Walshe FRS (1885–1973). Exposing the naiveté of identifying the mechanism with its informing principle he writes:

Every instrument demands a performer. So does the brain

> From sheer psychological and philosophical necessity ... [there is the] existence in man of an essential immaterial element […] psyche, entelechy, anima or soul […] setting him above the merely animal. It has also to be recognized that for the soul's functioning as an essential element in the hylomorphic human person,[viii] it needs some data, of which the brain is the collecting, integrating and distributing mechanism. Yet it would be quite childish to identify the instrument with its user, even though the user be dependent upon the instrument for operating. [32]

Then in the same article he identifies the root cause of the problem, stating that:

> We shall have to accept the ancient concept of the soul again: as an immaterial, incorporeal part of the human person, and yet an integral part of his nature, not just some concomitant aspect of man, but something without which he is not a human person […]. There is a sense in which the present is an age of which characteristic is its failure to understand the status of its own abstractions, and this, perhaps, is the inevitable fruit of the divorce of natural science from metaphysics [and from religion and mysticism we might add], to have achieved which was the empty triumph of the nineteenth century.

Neurologist Francis Walshe argues for the need of a soul and the dignity of Man

Walshe then comments on the immaturity of reducing the human being to a machine and the mind to a virtual machine, saying:

> For me, the chill physico-mathematical concept of the human mind is a muddy vesture of decay in which I am not willing to be enfolded. It is unworthy of the dignity of Man.

Not for Francis Walshe, then, is the mind merely a von Neumannesque machine as it is for Dennett. Indeed, Walshe eventually demolishes the charge that such an attitude is unscientific by stating:

> And if any say that this is not a scientific attitude I am unmoved by the irrelevance, for, outside its proper field of discourse, the word 'science' does not intimidate me. Man was not made for science, but science by man, who remains more and greater than his creations.

Like Francis Walshe, wise Schrödinger also saw deeper. These quotations, first encountered as epigraphs to Chapters 3 and 4 in Volume I are highly apposite and again worthy of deep reflection:

> We do not belong to this material word that science constructs for us. We are not in it, we are outside. We are only spectators. The reason why we believe that we are in it, that we belong to the picture, is that our bodies are in the picture. Our bodies belong to it. Not

---

viii 'Hylomorphism' is the philosophical theory developed by Aristotle, which conceives Being as a compound of matter and form.

only my own body, but those of my friends, also of my dog and cat and horse, and of all the other people and animals. And this is my only means of communicating with them.

Science cannot tell us a word about why music delights us, of why and how an old song can move us to tears. Science, we believe, can, in principle, describe in full detail all that happens in our sensorium and 'motorium' from the moment the waves of compression and dilation reach our ear[s] to the moment when certain glands secrete a salty fluid that emerges from our eyes. But of the feelings of delight and sorrow that accompany the process[,] science is completely ignorant—and therefore reticent.[33]

The above is a condensed account of a fuller excerpt from Schrödinger's major philosophical works provided in Endnote II-6 along with all references.

In fact the true test of a scientist is his ability and humility to see the limits and limitations of his theories and to work within them, rather than forcing them into areas where they are patently incapable of operation or explanation of the phenomena in question, as in the numerous examples cited in Volume I, Chapter 4 and in this Chapter. How many scientists these days are able to say, 'I don't know, but I'll try and find out'? Unfortunately, significant numbers of scientists seem unwilling to recognize (or to acknowledge) the limits of science and their own limitations and are extremely fearful of not being able to explain away literally everything from divinity to the whole universe in materialistic terms.

A Summary of What the Computationalist Master Analogy Cannot Explain

Shown below is a comprehensive, but by no means exhaustive, list of the fatal flaws in the master analogy theory, which, to recapitulate, states that brain and mind are analogous to a (wet) computer and software, respectively:

1. Minds cannot be totally erased, as computer software can.
2. Minds cannot be made to operate precisely as we choose (to 'program' them), the way that computers can.
3. Minds are ordinarily impenetrable (but see below), but software is transparent in that the entire state of the program can be read at any time.
4. Telepathy between minds (as between humans and animals) has been well demonstrated (see Volume I, Chapter 4) but computers cannot read each other's software unless interconnected and programmed to do so.
5. Only one 'program' operates, or can ever operate, on any one human brain, whereas any number of different programs can be run on a computer at will.
6. Mind cannot be transferred from one brain to another (even if brain transplants were ever feasible), whereas software programs can easily be transferred from one computer to another.
7. Near-death experiences have shown that consciousness seems to operate apart from the physical brain, and also when the latter is declared to be clinically 'brain-dead'; a software program can never run with the accompanying computer hardware removed or virtually inoperative.
8. The latest developments in brain research involving stroke victims have shown what is known as brain plasticity in that the brain displays a holistic, or plastic function, such that if one part of the brain is damaged, other parts of the brain take over the function of the damaged portion (this is in contrast to the previously held

compartmentalised notion that specific portions of the brain perform specific tasks). Moreover, damage to one part of the brain can lead to increased activity (and skill) in another. However, the same cannot be said about different parts of a computer. So if part of the computer hardware were damaged, or the software corrupted, there is no way that other parts of the computer hardware or software could, automatically, of their own accord, compensate for the damaged components or corrupted sectors. The software system tool in DOS, OS/2, and Windows known as CHKDSK (short for 'check disk') can check the surface and repair damaged or corrupted sectors of a computer hard drive; at best the functioning of the disc will be restored, but this will not automatically result in increased speed or performance of the hard disc as a whole. But, in any case, CHKDSK was written by human programmers for specific functions and has to be initiated by a human operator.

9.   Human minds want to know all about such things as consciousness, and to understand the mindset of computationalists who seem frantic to try and convince the world that human brains are basically just computers; but real computers are never concerned about knowing about themselves or convincing other computers about what they are.

10.   The human brain has evolved intrinsically over aeons caused by both the stimulus from the external environment and the innate propensities of the organism (nature and nurture); computers only evolve, or develop extrinsically, as a result of human intervention.

11.   The human brain grows in size and capacity over a lifetime. Computers do not grow automatically of themselves unless another component is added to them by a human.

12.   The human mind matures and increases in power and capacity over a lifetime. Software does not improve itself without human programmer intervention.

13.   The common term 'body language' indicates that both brain *and body* are intimately involved in expressing the human state of mind and inner, subjective feelings and experience. Mind is embodied by both brain and body, not just brain. By contrast, computers do not, of their own accord, change their physical appearance or alter their machine language to reflect their performance speed and efficiency. (Machine language is the numeric codes, written by a programmer, for the operations that a particular computer executes.)

14.   Computers are, in essence, data processing machines transferring one batch of data into another (see the various definitions of a computer at the beginning of this Chapter). That data becomes information when something meaningful is ascribed to it by a human. But the mind is neither a data processor nor an information processor. States of mind or feelings are states of being, not information—for example, there is no data or informational content in feeling delighted. The whole subjective realm of experience, feelings, and consciousness is incompatible with the ideology that humans are 'just machines'. Experience is a state of being, not of doing, such as information processing. Humans can do both—computers only the latter, according to the coded instructions by human programmers.

15.   Thinking is necessarily metaphorical—what few people seem to recognize. This is argued in a seminal paper, 'Mapping the Brain's Metaphor Circuitry', by George Lakoff (*b.*1941), the American cognitive linguist, philosopher, and Professor of Cognitive Science and Linguistics at the University of California, Berkeley.[34]

Lakoff shows how metaphorical ideas affect how we act; and how metaphorical thought and the metaphorical understanding of situations arise independently of language. The paper presents the basics of metaphorical thought and language from the perspective of neurocognition (the integrated interdisciplinary study of how conceptual thought and language work in the brain). Crucially, it outlines a theory of *metaphor circuitry* and discusses how everyday reason makes use of embodied metaphor circuitry. Computers, however, are driven by electrical circuitry, not by metaphor circuitry.

One might therefore ask: given the turbulent world we live in, would computers—unless human-programmed to do so—inform their robotic bodies to fight over territory and slaughter one another (whatever slaughter might mean to a computer-informed robot)? It is no good arguing that, in point of fact, robots do regularly kill humans; for example, in Japan which has the highest proportion of robots used in industry for repetitive tasks, assembly line robots are known to turn on their human operators. But that is solely because of malfunctioning of the software, sensing mechanisms or hardware that was human designed and installed in them, or indeed because of error on the part of the human operator who programmed them.[35]

What do wars, slaughter, and death mean to computers?

What then, does death mean to a computer? Obviously, a loss of power to its components or the natural degrading and ultimate failure of the latter over time, as indeed may be said to be the case with humans organs. But as humans approach death, they often mature and become wiser. At this stage of life, great artists are known to produce their finest works or achieve an understanding of life not known to them in earlier years. Would a computer know when it was about to 'die'? In fact, this is quite easily done using algorithms to check, periodically, the physical condition of its components, hence predict the computer life ahead. But such algorithms would have to be input by human programmers. However, would a computer's performance improve by itself with the ageing of its components, as with the maturing wisdom of so many of us when we have time for reflection during the inevitable physical decline of the final years of our lives? Would a computer of its own volition write, say, sublime music like Schubert did in the last months and weeks of his short life, or a deeply spiritual work like the monumental B minor Mass that Bach wrote a year before his death when he was virtually blind; or would that faculty also have to be programmed into it? It could not be pre-programmed because the final works of a genius are a summation of their entire, rich, inner life experience, a commentary on humanity and divinity, and intimations of the immortality of the Soul. The South African educator, humanitarian, philosopher, explorer, and conservationist Sir Laurens van der Post (1906–1996) put his finger on the scientism pulse when he observed that:

> Human beings [and we might add computionalists] are perhaps never more frightening than when they are convinced beyond doubt that they are right.[36]

The Closing of the Scientific Mind – The Inviolability of Materialistic Theories

In the final section of the first part of this Chapter, we make our case about the impregnability of materialistic theories by way of an actual example. *Mind and Cosmos* is a book by Thomas Nagel[37] (whom we first mentioned briefly in Volume I, Chapter 5). The subtitle to his book, *Why the Materialist Neo-Darwinian Conception of Nature Is Almost Certainly False* would be guaranteed to produce howls of protest, which is precisely what happened. It is irrelevant that Nagel is a distinguished professor of philosophy at New York University, or that he presents his case meticulously, without any reference to religion or, for that matter, attacking religion, or indeed that he proposes some of his own ideas on consciousness tentatively in the tradition of good science. As his subtitle suggests, Darwinian evolution is insufficient to explain the emergence of consciousness; and that there are significant inadequacies in the mainstream dictum rooted in the Darwinian paradigm on the workings of the mind. But even to question Darwinism politely is seen by the *cognoscenti* of science as an attack upon the omniscient 'God' of evolutionary theory. To risk doing so provokes the same hysterical outburst as to attack the 'God' of religious fundamentalists—the very 'God' that these materialists heartily decry. Here we have to draw a clear distinction between Darwin's ideas that he presented by way of scientific propositions and those same ideas that the neo-Darwinians have elevated to 'biblical' status. For the latter, to question molecular mechanisms, or Darwinism, is tantamount to questioning their 'God' and 'His' creation, and the resulting excommunication by the scientific fraternity (the 'church of scientism') is swift and severe. Sober scientists are not physically burnt at the stake, but the personal abuse and the backlash against their careers is no different in principle.

Thomas Nagel attacked for highlighting deficiencies in neo-Darwinism

Alfred Russell Wallace clearly saw the painful process involved in proclaiming new scientific discoveries since any revolutionary ideas will always first be met with resistance from the establishment.[38] But it is deeply ironical that such insight should come from none other than an independent co-discoverer of the theory of natural selection who also co-authored a paper with Charles Darwin. And this opposition to new truths prevails even in the teeth of evidence, as for example, when the Victorian medical profession refused to acknowledge the methods used by the British surgeon and President of the Royal Society, Sir Joseph Lister (1827–1912). Lister was the first doctor to use antiseptics in surgery, yet despite his breakthrough evidence that washing hands, surgical instruments, and the site of an operation with carbolic acid mixed with linseed oil dramatically cut post-operative death rates, the authorities of the Glasgow Royal Infirmary roundly condemned him.[39]

Evidence of new truths rarely overturns outworn preconceptions

Another fine example of the inviolability of the materialistic paradigm, especially concerning molecular science is the editorial that appeared on the front page of *Nature* under the title 'A book for burning?' The book in question, unsurprisingly, was the first edition of *A New Science of Life* by Rupert Sheldrake,[ix] which the editor Sir John Maddox denounced in a savage attack saying that 'even bad books should not be burned; works such as [Hitler's] *Mein Kampf* have become historical documents […]. His [i.e., Sheldrake's] book is the best candidate for burning there has been for many years.'[40] Moreover, in a later BBC interview, Maddox said, 'Sheldrake is putting forward magic instead of science, and that can be condemned in exactly the language that the Pope used to condemn Galileo, and for the same reason. It is heresy.'[41] It is worth pausing at this juncture and fully taking in the import of all this. A powerful and prestigious man of science upon whom a knighthood was conferred, a Fellow of the Royal Society, and editor

---

ix   This book proposed the hypothesis of morphic resonance to explain the characteristic form and organization of nature.

Sheldrake castigated as a heretic for proposing a new scientifically testable hypothesis of life

of one of the leading international science journals is recommending, and in all serious-ness, that a book by the Nazi dictator should be retained owing to its historical value 'for those concerned with the pathology of politics', as he put it, but that Sheldrake's book, written by an eminent Cambridge Fellow, should be eradicated. Rupert Sheldrake was a Scholar of Clare College, Cambridge and was awarded the University Botany Prize. He then studied philosophy and history of science at Harvard University, where he was a Frank Knox Fellow, before returning to Cambridge, and becoming a Fellow of Clare College where he was Director of Studies in biochemistry and cell biology. As the Rosenheim Research Fellow of the Royal Society he carried out research on the develop-ment of plants and the ageing of cells at Cambridge. (See Profiles in Volume IV for more details on Sheldrake.) However much Maddox chose to revile its content, should not Sheldrake's book (and others along similar lines of pioneering research) also be of value to those interested in the history and evolution of biological science? (See, for example, Endnote II-9 for brief mention of the correlations and resemblances between the life-principles of plants, animals, and human beings.)

Enough has been said to demonstrate the power of prejudice; and that those deemed as heretics, whether in religion *or in medicine and science*, are dealt with by the orthodox church of scientism in essentially the same way as the religious heretics in Galileo's day. Burning and ostracising the religious heretic now takes the form of condemning the work and crushing the career of the heretic scientist concerned. But a few legendary scientists have found the courage to sound a warning note, such as the Nobel physicist Brian Josephson, who wrote a riposte in *Nature* stating that the editor 'show[ed] a concern not for scientific validity but for respectability.' Josephson further censured that:

> The rapid advances in molecular biology to which you [i.e., the editor, John Maddox] refer do not mean very much. If one is on a journey, rapid progress on the way implies neither that one is close to one's destination, nor that the destination will be reached at all by continuing to follow the same road […]. The fundamental weakness is a failure to admit even the possibility that genuine physical facts may exist which lie outside the scope of current scientific descriptions. Indeed a new kind of understanding of nature is now emerging, with concepts like implicate order and subject-dependent reality (and now, perhaps formative causation). These developments have not yet penetrated to the leading journals. One can only hope that the editors will soon cease to obstruct this avenue of progress.[42]

Brian Josephson derided for suggesting that quantum theory can help to understand telepathy

Alas, even Josephson has been belittled wholesale by the science community at large for his interest in, and exploration of, topics such as meditation, mysticism, and the whole field of parapsychology, including phenomena like telepathy, deemed to lie outside mainstream physics. A good case in point is the facetious headline *Royal Mail's Nobel guru in telepathy row* that appeared in a leading UK national newspaper.[43] This is in connection with an issue of six special stamps to honour the hundredth anniversary of the Nobel Prize. However, a bitter row emerged because scientists were furious that a booklet, published as part of the stamps' presentation package, contained claims that modern physics would one day lead to an understanding of telepathy and the paranormal. This statement, deeply offensive to mainstream scientists, had been written by Josephson, who subsequently commented to *The Observer*, 'Yes, I think telepathy exists, and I think quantum physics will help us understand its basic properties.' The point Josephson was making was simply that there is a good case that quantum theories may lead to an explanation of processes still not understood within conventional science, telepathy being one example. However, the emotionally charged and insulting retorts such as 'utter rubbish' and 'complete nonsense' by fellow scientists,[44] reveal that their violent opposition to the idea was based not on the grounds of scientific evidence, of which there is plenty (see again Volume I, Chapter 4), but prejudice. Apropos, is it the case that a Nobel scientist of Josephson's eminence has not been awarded a knighthood because his long-standing interests in paranormal phenomena have riled the powerful scientific orthodoxy?

This clearly makes the point that nothing is more effective at exposing the weakness of fundamentalists of the neo-Darwinian camp, or for that matter the materialist camp (including, sadly, Fellows of the Royal Society and Nobel laureates like Steven Weinberg and Philip Anderson—see the Recapitulation to Volume I), than when they themselves resort to mass attacks and expletives[45] or use terms like 'witchcraft' and 'snake-oil' or resort to cheap language, as in the example cited above, against a serious scientist who proposes sensible, scientific counter arguments, or anomalous findings that shatter their ideological stronghold and dent their egos, along with their reputations and associated massive research grants.

Aggresive language reveals weakness of the counter-argument

From an esoteric perspective, however, these emotional counterattacks by the orthodox fraternity, can be viewed as part of the backlash which is said to occur when one aspect of a universal Principle[x] is withdrawing and another is coming forward. When a new order is emerging, those from the earlier order cling on to habitual patterns and ways of doing things to maintain status quo. Unable to move forward, invariably through fear, any new insights or discoveries are forcibly quashed, rather than carefully cherished. Moreover, the fact that things have reached such a 'pitch' is a good indicator of an incipient new paradigm for a new epoch. The current period of transition may well be seen by history as a crisis time.

Concluding Remarks

Unsurprisingly, the most vociferous attacks, either upon religion or upon scientific theories with even a whiff of a hypothesis beyond pure materialism, come from the materialist camp—those who maintain that scientific materialism is the sole arbiter of truth. (It is immaterial here, whether or not we substitute 'physicalism' for 'materialism'—see Volume I, Chapter 3 for the hair-splitting differences in meaning.) The pre-eminence of the scientist under attack is of no consequence, as in the examples cited above. The need to attack, rather than resort to reasoned arguments and dignified language, demonstrates two facts. Firstly, it shows the weakness of the attacker's position: otherwise why attack someone unless what he says is a threat to your own presuppositions and preconceptions, and the power, position, and fame that go along with upholding the former at all costs. But it also shows that the head and the heart are at loggerheads, so to speak, in the attacker's psyche; that something deeper inside the person, something that transcends his left brain hemisphere is declaring that all is not well, hence the need to attack in order to fortify and police the paradigm. The instances of Nagel, Sheldrake, and Josephson (amongst several others)

———

x In the Theosophical tradition this is referred to as the Seven Rays, typifying seven types of universal energy that manifest in distinct values, characteristics, and behaviour. The Seven Rays are a single Septenary Principle. All manifestation is seen as being 'shot through' with this Septenary Principle, each Principle being a distinct Ray, identified with a particular 'colour'.

are fine examples of this. Their detractors, being of the materialistic camp, have resorted to emotionally-laden tirades. But Sheldrake and Josephson, to mention but two, have always responded with calm dignity. They can well afford to do so as they are responding from a position of strength where they know and acknowledge the value of materialism and reductionism in their proper context, but are also fully aware of, and have extensively researched phenomena (such as telepathy), that cannot be explained away by the indiscriminate remarks of disparagers. (Refer to the final section of Chapter 4 of Volume I on page 115 et seq. describing the process of knowledge filtration in establishment science.)

Similar calumny and insult, but far more virulent, was heaped upon Blavatsky who also showed, with painstaking detail, that materialistic theories and Darwinian evolution were not wrong, as such, but wholly incomplete and therefore inadequate to account for consciousness, life, and evolution—without invoking the grand occult doctrines that she transmitted through her magnificent works.

A highly topical example displaying the need to attack when reason falters is the raging tirade against Greta Thunburg, the Swedish environmental activist nominated for the Nobel Peace Prize. What was her 'offence'? Simply to point out, unequivocally, to world leaders in September 2019, at the UN Climate Action Summit in New York, that the dream of unsustainable and eternal economic growth at the expense of the environment would spell imminent disaster for ecosystems, the natural world, and life on the planet. Some may argue that she was somewhat blunt in her approach, but perhaps this was necessary. For this, Thunburg has been likened by one commentator to a figure in a Nazi propaganda poster,[46] and by another as being 'mentally ill', and the 'deeply disturbed messiah of the global warming movement' in an Australian newspaper column.[47] (The 'mentally ill' are in fact those who have hijacked the environmental cause, using it as a bandwagon to vent their own suppressed violence and hatred of society.) And to those who would wag a condescending finger at Thunberg's lack of scientific facts and training, we point out that it does not need a college degree in economics to state what is blatantly obvious to all and sundry (other than to those who are blinkered by the idea of unlimited economic growth at the expense of permanent environmental degradation); nor is she pontificating about what specific economic measures world leaders should adopt, but pleading that they listen to, and act on, what the scientists are saying. But what of her supposed childlike naïveté? We politely respond from Psalm 8:2, King James Version:

> Out of the mouths of babes and sucklings hast thou ordained strength.

As with all these examples, and numerous others, the principle is exactly the same: *it is far easier for uninformed critics and cowards to attack a person's character and mental stability than to discredit reasoned arguments put forward*. Those who are brave enough to challenge the reigning orthodoxy will always have to summon the added courage to endure the wrath of the rabidly orthodox.

What, then, is the remedy? We explore this now in the scond part of this chapter.

A Suggested Way Forward

Longing to find beauty in what was for him an ugly and terrible world (during the First Industrial Revolution), the doctor and legendary English Romantic poet John Keats

Emotionally charged language used by attackers reveals their weakness

When reason fails, character gets attacked

(1795–1821) talks about what he calls 'negative capability'—the capacity to sit with the unknown, but with an inner conviction that something truly precious will come out of the unknown. In other words, to trust the process and have faith that there is a greater Consciousness that we can tune into, as explained in his letter to his brother: 'At once it struck me, what quality went to form a Man of Achievement especially in Literature & which Shakespeare possessed so enormously—I mean *Negative Capability*, that is when man is capable of being in uncertainties, Mysteries, doubts, without any irritable reaching after fact & reason […].'[48] But living with uncertainties, and being with the unknown, is something that the mainstream scientific and medical community find very intimidating and irritating. It underscores the deterministic characteristic of left brain orientation towards precision, certainty, and objectivization, whilst eschewing uncertainty, the unknown, and the unknowable. But the right brain hemisphere, preferring to deal with wholes rather than parts, and with qualities over quantities, has no problem with subjective experience or waiting patiently in silence attuning to a higher power. So this is the kind of holistic approach used by luminaries of science, such as Leonardo and Newton—an approach that would help us greatly in facing the complex problems we face today. It is highly significant that Leonardo was as much a genius of science as of art. Moreover, Newton's alchemical writings and drawings reveal great sensitivity and poetry.

Doubt and uncertainty are anathema to 'left-brained scientism'

Perhaps the deepest insights into the inner, human condition and state (as opposed to the human body) come from sublime art, literature, poetry, and music. Luminaries like Shakespeare (Francis Bacon?), Keats, Mozart, Beethoven, Schubert, and Liszt knew, and expressed through their art, infinitely more about our minds and what it means to be truly human, than establishment scientists and neurobiologists can ever hope to do—see, for example, the close of Chapter 5 on page 99. That is why their works have elevated the moral and ethical status of humankind.

Meanwhile, we round off this Chapter with the words of three luminaries—a scientist, an occultist, and a philosopher—which, taken as a whole, elucidate the problems we face, and the way out of the impasse. We would be well advised to heed their counsel.

Firstly, the problems for society arising largely from excessive emphasis upon left hemisphere thinking of the divided brain, so comprehensively expounded by McGilchrist (see earlier), were, in fact, foretold well over half a century ago in this quote attributed to Einstein:

> The intuitive mind is a sacred gift and the rational mind is a faithful servant. We have created a society that honours the servant and has forgotten the gift.[49]

Perhaps it was a profound understanding of the difference between rationalisation and intuition, plus an acute awareness of the dangers for science of excessive quantification, that lay behind this message, again attributed to Einstein, written on a blackboard hanging in his office at Princeton University:

Einstein understood the limitations of quantification

> Not everything that counts can be counted, and not everything that can be counted counts.[50]

Next, we turn to the question of why, despite the massive amount of money and energy expended on research, the corpus of mainstream scientists, neuroscientists, and neurobiologists have barely approached—by their own admission—a true understanding of the origin and nature of consciousness (with the exception, of course, of the ilk of 'all-knowing'

Dennett, who maintains that consciousness is an illusion or an unessential epiphenomenon). As rightly diagnosed by Sir Francis Walshe (see earlier), this is because they are looking at purely physical means to discover that which is beyond the physical. The following quotation from the great seer and occultist, H. P. Blavatsky makes this contention very clear:

> The minority [of scientists] strive very sensibly to enlarge the domain of physical science by trespassing on the forbidden grounds of metaphysics, so distasteful to some material- ists. These scientists are wise in their generation. For all their wonderful discoveries would go for nothing, and remain for ever *headless* bodies, unless they lift the veil of matter and strain their eyes to see *beyond*. Now that they have studied nature in the length, breadth, and thickness of her physical frame, it is time to remove the skeleton to the second plane and search within the unknown depths for the living and real entity, for its SUB-*stance*—the noumenon of evanescent matter.[51]

The need to look beyond physical matter

Allied to the above, we can say that physical science on its own, embedded in the materialistic paradigm, will never understand the nature of consciousness, because as Blavatsky further says, much in line with Keat's intimations on negative caability:

> 'Mystery is the fatality of science.' Official science is surrounded on every side and hedged in by unapproachable, forever impenetrable mysteries. And why? Simply because physical science is self-doomed to a squirrel-like progress around a wheel of matter limited by our five senses.[52]

Limitations of the five physical senses

And applying this reasoning to the enquiry into the nature of mind, Blavatsky says:

> Scalpels and microscopes may solve the mystery of the material parts of *the shell of man* [the Physical body and brain]: they can never cut a window into his soul to open the smallest vista on any of the wider horizons of being.[53]

The inability by science to supply a satisfactory answer to the nature of mind, after several decades of painstaking research and experimentation, vindicates Blavatsky's assertion of well over one hundred years ago.

Following on from the above, we highlight the essential difference, yet intimate relationship, between the inner subjective state of man and his outward, physical expression through brain and body. As Blavatsky states, whereas the former represents the quintessentially subjective quality of the human being, the latter is no less important for objective physical expression and existence:

> That which makes one mortal a great man and another a vulgar, silly person is [...] the quality and makeup of the physical shell or casing, and the adequacy or inadequacy of brain and body to transmit and give expression to the light of the real, *Inner* man; and this aptness or inaptness is, in its turn, the result of Karma. Or, to use another simile, physical man is the musical instrument, and the Ego, the performing artist. The potentiality of perfect melody of sound, is in the former—the instrument—and no skill of the latter can awaken a faultless harmony out of a broken or badly made instrument. This harmony depends on the fidelity of transmission, by word or act, to the objective plane, of the unspoken divine thought in the very depths of man's subjective or inner nature. Physical man may—to follow our simile—be a priceless Stradivarius, or a cheap and cracked fiddle, or again a mediocrity between the two, in the hands of the Paganini who ensouls him.[54]

Concerning our essential nature—Mind—the following three quotes, in the words of that illimitable modern sage and philosopher Paul Brunton, elucidate the common error of identifying the instrument (brain) with its user (mind, or the thought producer), even though, as Walshe said, the user be dependent upon the instrument for its operation.

> It is a mistake to believe that the body, via the brain, makes its own thoughts. To correct it, reverse the assumption and perceive that thoughts are projections from Thought, that Consciousness comes first.[55]

> The materialist who regards thought as solely an activity in the brain, and consequently as a physiological product in its entirety, has overlooked the thinker of the thought.[56]

> If the blood, bone, and flesh of the human brain secrete thought then the wood and string of a violin secrete music.[57]

Discerning the Inner man from the physical brain and body

The third Brunton quote above is charmingly illustrated by the story of a fan of the Russian–American violinist Jascha Heifetz (1901–1987) exclaiming to the legendary virtuoso, 'Mr Heifetz, your violin produces such beautiful sounds.' Whereupon Heifetz tapped the wooden belly of his priceless instrument remarking, 'does it really?'[xi]

This makes it plain that any manifestation, whether it be music, literature, or thought, involves the interaction of a duality to produce a triplicity. In other words: (*a*) an active, (positive, masculine) principle interacting with (*b*) a passive (negative, feminine) principle and (*c*) their product. So by way of some arbitrary examples to illustrate this general principle in any sphere of manifestation, the three elements are:

active principle
- violin maker
- violinist
- seed
- sperm
- consciousness

interacting with a passive principle
- wood
- violin
- soil
- egg
- brain

produces
- violin
- music
- plant
- embryo
- thought

The next quote, again from Paul Brunton, is in line with the 'filter model' in neuroscience. It is the latest theory about the role of the brain, acting as a sort of filter and transducer of consciousness, but not a generator or originator of the latter.

> The materialist asserts that consciousness has no existence apart from the body, is indeed a product of the brain. A blow on the head may deprive a man of consciousness; an operation on the brain may change its mode of functioning. The mentalist says that these only provide the conditions which normally *limit consciousness* [emphasis added], thus making it seem as if the brain created it. But under abnormal states (like anaesthesia, hypnotism, drugs, or deep meditation) consciousness shows its own separate being.[58]

Great sages have always known this. So did William James, as we saw in Chapter 6 of Volume I. Nonetheless, even though the filter model of the brain is upheld by only a minority of metaphysically inclined scientists and psychologists,[xii] yet it is heartening to note the slow harmonising of science with occult science as predicted

The need to look beyond physical matter

---

xi This story is attributed to the taxi driver who fetched Heifetz on his arrival at Tel Aviv airport to embark on a concert tour. The details may be inaccurate, but the message is unmistakable.

xii Rupert Sheldrake and Eben Alexander for example.

well over one hundred years ago in the famous maxim 'modern science is our best ally.'[59]

The following quote, also from Brunton, shows the reason for the common error of identifying the instrument with its user.

> The notion that consciousness is a sort of 'gas' generated in the fleshy brain is the modern Western error, although an easy one into which to fall. There is, of course, a very close interrelation between body and mind, but it is one wherein the latter is expressed through the former, although narrowed and confined by the brain's limitations.[60]

This is indeed the position adopted by computationalists who regard the brain as nothing more than a mechanism for thinking or problem-solving. When asked how it creates consciousness, David Gelernter remarks:

> Most computationalists default to the Origins of Gravy theory set forth by Walter Matthau in the film of Neil Simon's *The Odd Couple*.[xiii] Challenged to account for the emergence of gravy, Matthau explains that when you cook a roast, '*it comes*'. That is basically how consciousness arises too, according to computationalists. It just comes.[61]

Whether we use the metaphor of 'emergence of gravy' or '"gas" generated in the fleshy brain' the point is made: consciousness is merely an epiphenomenon of brain mechanisms.

The final Brunton quote is an extended one that synthesises the thoughts and counsel of Walshe and Blavatsky above, thus serving as a summary of the principal arguments of this Chapter:

> The materialist argument is essentially that mental function varies with bodily condition, that alcohol can convert the coward for a time into a brave man, that the increase in size and weight of the brain as man passes from infancy to maturity runs parallel with the increase of mental capacity, and that therefore mind is nothing else than a product of body [and brain].
>
> Mentalism says these facts are mostly but not always true but that even granting their truth, the materialistic conclusion does not necessarily follow. It is just as logical to say that mind uses brain as a writer uses a pen, that the body is merely instrumental and the limitations or changes in the instrument naturally modify or alter the mentality expressed. The thoughts and feelings, the ideas and memories, the fancies and reasonings which constitute most of our mental stock can be detected nowhere in the brain, can be seen by nothing physical, and can only be observed by the mind itself as acts of consciousness.[62]

So Are Human Beings 'Lumbering Robots' After All?

Are we then in reality nothing but lumbering, robotic machines or are we beings of flesh and blood, mind and consciousness? If the latter, then, as said earlier, humans will have to wage a war against computers. The film *Space Odyssey* presaged just this by installing HAL 9000, a sentient computer (i.e., with 'emotional software') that was every bit humankind's equal, and had full control over the spacecraft. When things went wrong and HAL endangered the crew's lives, then for the sake of the mission, the astronauts had to overpower the computer by dismantling its memory banks. One can envisage a similar situation arising in the not too distant future when humans and computers will be in

Consciousness emerges from brain as an epiphenomenon

Impossible for robots to outpace mankind

---

xiii 'The Odd Couple', Wikipedia (last modified 2 October 2020)
<https://en.wikipedia.org/wiki/The_Odd_Couple_(film)> accessed 3 October 2020.

mortal combat, not by way of robotic soldiers or drones destroying what is left of humans, but human beings themselves fighting against the dehumanization and depersonalization of life produced by excessive reliance and takeover of their lives by computers. It will be a struggle but the victor is too obvious to mention. Enough is enough—it is high time we reclaim our spirituality and our humanity right now.

But lingering doubts may still prevail. Certainly, the computationalists would side with the Hungarian–American psychologist Mihaly Csikszentmihalyi (*b*.1934) that 'it is easier for us to imagine ourselves living among better appliances than any better human beings'.[63]

Postlude – Will Robots Overtake Humanity?

In view of all that we have said above, is it remotely possible that given the current exponential advances in technology, robots and androids will eventually outpace humanity? It is not an unreasonable qualm. After all, Ray Kurzweil, the world renowned pundit of artificial intelligence, has confidently predicted that this will happen by 2029—see earlier. At first glance it seems that this might actually happen. The South Korean firm Samsung are due to open an artificial intelligence research laboratory in Cambridge to teach computers to recognize human emotions and improve the way they interact with us.[64] Would teaching computers to recognize human emotions be a step along the path to building a sentient computer like HAL 9000 as in the *Space Odyssey* film? What is more, in April 2018, the UK government announced investment of nearly £1bn in artificial intelligence. The American multinational business magazine *Fortune* states that the companies involved 'include Microsoft, Hewlett Packard Enterprise, IBM, McKinsey and Pfizer.'[65] Certainly, it would appear that the human–machine boundaries are becoming increasingly blurred.

So, for example, if you were jogging through the woods close to Waltham, Massachusetts in the US, the chances are that you might be joined by a fellow runner who appeared to traverse the forest path and negotiate rocky terrain as nimbly as yourself. Only after a few minutes it may dawn on you that your companion was in fact a humanoid robot—see Figure II-6 below. Weighing 320 lbs at 6ft 2in tall and named Atlas, it was created by Google-owned Boston Dynamics.[66]

A robotic 'runner'

Figure II-6   Atlas, the Humanoid Jogger in the Woods
near Waltham, Massachusetts

Photo Credit: https://commons.wikimedia.org, montage by Artefact Design

Figure II-7   Nadine, the Android Receptionist at Nanyang
Technological University

Image Credit: Nanyang Technological University

Or were you to visit Nanyang Technological University in Singapore you would initially be impressed by Nadine, the receptionist dressed in a smart black suit as seen in Figure II-7 above. She parts her long, dark hair neatly, smiles politely and would greet you with a friendly 'hello', even remembering your name and previous conversations if you had met her before. She appears to be proficient at her job and exhibits personality, moods, and emotions. So if you were to tell her that you had a hospital appointment, she would naturally respond in a different tone to the one she would use if you said you were getting married. You would be excused, however, for harbouring a nagging feeling that Nadine appeared to be only slightly less than human, which is not surprising, since 'she' is one of a new generation of androids.[67]

A robotic 'receptionist'

Researchers at the Royal Society, writes Philip Collins in *The Times*, claimed that a computer 'had passed the Turing test and thereby achieved human intelligence.' Collins goes on to state that, 'scientists are so far from comprehending the mystery of human consciousness that they are in no way equipped to create it.'[68] Coming from an esteemed institution, like the Royal Society, the fallacy of such a statement is deplorable. As the article pointedly questions, on what grounds is the Turing test[xiv] a measure of human intelligence?[69] As Collins observes, 'The fact a computer can fool a third of a panel of people into believing that its responses to a set of questions put to it are human ones merely shows the ingenuity of [human] programmers.' Moreover, what exactly is meant by 'human intelligence'—something that ranges from below the imbecile to the genius and beyond? Again, from Collins:

Can we 'teach' an android about human emotions and responses?

> The computer is just a big calculator: it can no more be said to be thinking than a clock can be said to be telling the time.[70]

Alan Turing would surely have said much the same thing—see his earlier observation on page 114 that a computer could process any problem—provided that it were given rules by human programmers for the solution.

---

xiv The 'Turing test' is a test which determines the ability of a machine to exhibit intelligent behaviour equivalent to, or indistinguishable from, that of a human.

Let us make our final case for the overall supremacy of human over artificial intelligence by citing a highly revealing throwaway remark by the American technology entrepreneur Mark Zuckerberg (*b*.1984), Chairman and Chief Executive Officer of Facebook. Inspired by the fictional superhero appearing in American comic books, Iron Man, who has his own robot assistant, Zuckerberg has decided to install the latest home automaton in his house. He wants it to be able to let his friends in by 'looking at their faces when they ring the doorbell'. But here comes the rub. 'I'll start teaching it to understand my voice to control everything in our home—music, lights, temperature', he wrote on his Facebook page. Note the words: 'I'll start *teaching it* [emphasis added]'. This is the giveaway: a perfect attestation that however much robots may become a part of human lives and society, they will never surpass human beings because the one thing they singularly lack—creative freedom—comes from the human heart, mind, and brain—not from computers, 'wet' or 'dry'.

Robots may well excel in any mechanically repetitive, rule-based activity, but for anything involving human qualities of sensibility, judgement, creativity, and imagination, robots can only mimic or impersonate the human behaviour that has been pre-programmed into them—even by other robots perhaps, but in the final analysis, always by humans as the first link in the chain. For example, in the case of Nadine, the receptionist described above, it does not take much (human) intelligence to see how emotive words like 'hospital' or 'married' can be pre-programmed into the android software to produce appropriately different response tones.

Humanoid performance is always programmed by humans

Would the zealous protagonists of artificial intelligence who like to tell the world that we humans known as 'lumbering robots', will be outstripped by androids in a matter of a few decades, find the courage of their own convictions by being content with an android mate for an intimate and loving physical relationship, as an alternative, or in preference to a human being of flesh and blood? Nonetheless, it is incumbent upon us humans not to become robot-*like* as a result of rampant technology mechanizing and de-humanizing our lives. The real danger is not that robots will become more human-like but that *humans will become increasingly robot-like* as a result of over-reliance on technology, excessive artificial intelligence, mechanization and the machine characteristic of existence—the tasteless fruits of a predominantly materialistic philosophy—slowly eating into the spiritual core of our human life.

It is easy, then, to become intimidated by such scary stuff, especially so nowadays, given the burgeoning transhumanist movement in science—see the Epilogue in Volume III. However, the resolution rests in a simple appeal to common sense—common amongst so-called ordinary folk, but a rare quality amongst the boffins of super-science because of the complete subjugation of wisdom by excessive intellect, by the mind usurped by its emissary, or in occult parlance, by the light of Buddhi-Manas clouded by Kāma-manas.

Grounds for long term optimism

As there are no grounds for concern *in the long term*, we may remain calm and revert to our overriding theme about the unfolding of consciousness and the composition of man at all levels of his being.

The real menace to mankind is not so much from robots becoming more like humans but humans behaving more like robots.

❧　❧　❧

This Chapter has provided evidence from a variety of sources to show that there is no question of human beings, constituted of spirit and soul, flesh and blood, being overtaken by robots. The next Chapter demonstrates the essential oneness of teaching about man from diverse cultures worldwide. Meanwhile, reflecting on whether human intelligence can be equated to that of a computer, and whether sight and hearing are solely dependent on physical eyes and ears, we close with the thoughts of one of the most celebrated Nobel physicists of our age, followed by the insights of a pioneer of the 'medical revolution' of the Renaissance.

Human mathematicians are not using a knowably sound algorithm [like a computer] in order to ascertain mathematical truth.[71] *Intelligence cannot be present without understanding. No computer has any awareness of what it does.*[72]

ROGER PENROSE

The power of sight does not come from the eye, the power to hear does not come from the ear, nor the power to feel from the nerves; but it is the spirit of man that sees through the eye, and hears with the ear, and feels by means of the nerves. Wisdom and reason and thought are not contained in the brain, but they belong to the invisible and universal spirit which feels through the heart and thinks by means of the brain. All these powers are contained in the invisible universe, and become manifest through material organs, and the material organs are their representatives, and modify their mode of manifestation according to their material construction, because a perfect manifestation of power can only take place in a perfectly constructed organ, and if the organ is faulty, the manifestation will be imperfect, but not the original power defective.

PARACELSUS[73]

NOTES

1   Address by Stephen Hawking to the Web Summit technology conference in Lisbon, Portugal, one of the biggest tech events in the world. See Sean Martin, 'Stephen Hawking: AI will be the WORST ever invention and could DESTROY us all', *Express*, 7 November 2017 <https://www.express.co.uk/news/science/876550/stephen-hawking-end-of-the-world-artificial-intelligence-ai-university-of-cambridge> accessed 2 March 2020.
2   David Gelernter, 'The Closing of the Scientific Mind: Reflections on the zombie-scientist problem', *Commentary* (January 2014) <http://www.commentarymagazine.com/article/the-closing-of-the-scientific-mind> accessed 8 February 2020.
3   *ibid.*
4   Garry Kasparov and Mig Greengard, *Deep Thinking: Where machine intelligence ends and human creativity begins* (UK: John Murray, 2017).
5   *The Oxford Reference Dictionary* (Flexicover edn, 1989), 178.
6   *The Week*, 30 June 2018, 19.
7   Daniel Dennett, *Consciousness Explained* (UK: Penguin, 1993).
8   Norman MacRae, *John Von Neumann: The scientific genius who pioneered the modern computer, game theory, nuclear deterrence and much more* (New York: Pantheon, 1992), 379.
9   David Gelernter, 'The Closing of the Scientific Mind'.
10 *The Week*, 1 March 2014.
11 David Gelernter, 'The Closing of the Scientific Mind'.
12 Nick Bostrom, 'How Long Before Superintelligence?' *International Journal of Future Studies*, 2 (1998); rev. and postscript (25 October 1998); second postscript (28 August 2000); third postscript (30 October 2005); fourth postscript (12 March 2008). Repr. *Linguistic and Philosophical Investigations*, 5/1 (2006), 11–30.

13　*The Guardian*, 27 October, 2014.

14　*Observer* [US], 19 August 2015.

15　Daniel C. Dennett, 'Why You Can't Make a Computer That Feels Pain', *Synthese*, 38/3, 'Automaton–Theoretical Foundations of Psychology and Biology, Part I' (*Springer*, July 1978), 415–456; Stable URL: http://www.jstor.org/stable/20115302 <https://web.ics.purdue.edu/~drkelly/DCDWhyCantMakeComputerFeelPain1978.pdf> accessed 2 March 2020.

16　Richard Dawkins, *The Selfish Gene* (Oxford: Oxford University Press, 2006), xx.

17　Richard Dawkins, *The Blind Watchmaker* (New York: W. W. Norton & Company, 1986), 1.

18　Learned publications on the impact of brain injury on emotion are given in 'Google Scholar' <http://scholar.google.co.uk/scholar?q=impact+of+brain+injury+on+emotion&hl=en&as_sdt=0&as_vis=1&oi=scholart&sa=X&ei=XbsBVPKnKayw7Abip4GACQ&ved=0CC0QgQMwAA> accessed 8 February 2020.

19　'Letters of Note' <http://www.lettersofnote.com/2012/03/empire-state-building.html> accessed 8 February 2020.

20　The Auricle, II/6, American Foundation for the Blind – Helen Keller Archives (March 1924).

21　'Helen Keller Letter on Beethoven's Ninth Symphony Goes Viral', *AFBblog* (2 April 2014) <https://www.afb.org/blog/entry/helen-keller-letter-beethovens-ninth-symphony-goes-viral> accessed 8 February 2020.

22　Jill Bolte Taylor, *My Stroke of Insight* (UK: Hodder Paperbacks, 2009).

23　Iain McGilchrist, *The Master and His Emissary: The divided brain and the making of the Western world* (2010; rev. and enl. 2nd edn, New Haven and London: Yale University Press, 2019).

24　Andrew Brown, 'Mary, Mary, quite contrary', *The Guardian*, 13 January 2001.

25　'The Master and His Emissary: The Divided Brain and the Making of the Western World by Iain McGilchrist – Mary Midgley enjoys an exploration of the left-brain/right-brain divide', *The Guardian*, 2 January 2010 <http://www.theguardian.com/books/2010/jan/02/1> accessed 8 February 2020.

26　Iain McGilchrist, *The Divided Brain and the Search for Meaning* (New Haven and London: Yale University Press, 2012).

27　*TSGLOSS*, 170.

28　Fritjof Capra, *Learning from Leonardo: Decoding the notebooks of a genius* (San Francisco: Berrett-Koehler Publishers, 2013).

29　Fritjof Capra, *The Tao of Physics: An exploration of the parallels between modern physics and Eastern mysticism* (London: Flamingo, 1992).

30　See Edi Bilimoria: 'Newton: "The Last Wonder-Child to Whom the Magi Could do Sincere and Appropriate Homage"', in Ana-Maria Pascal (ed.), *Multiculturalism and the Convergence of Faith and Practical Wisdom in Modern Society* (Hershey, Pennsylvania: IGI Global, 2017), 39–47; '"Newton – The Last Wonder-Child to Whom the Magi Could do Sincere and Appropriate Homage": How religion underpinned science and technology', *Journal of the Scientific and Medical Network*, 125 (2017), 3–7; book review of Rob Iliffe, *Priest of Nature: The religious worlds of Isaac Newton* (New York: Oxford University Press, 2017), in *Journal of the Scientific and Medical Network*, 125 (2017), 37–40.

31　D. M. A. Leggett, *The Implications of the Paranormal* (First 'Leggett' lecture, University of Surrey, April 1977), in D. M. A. Leggett, *The Sacred Quest: By Experiment and Experience: The next step* (Norwich, UK: Pilgrim Books, 1987), 51.

32　Sir Francis Walshe, 'Thoughts Upon the Equation of Mind with Brain', *Brain – A Journal of Neurology*, 76/1 (March 1953), 1–18.

33　Erwin Schrödinger, 'Nature and the Greeks' from the Shearman Lectures delivered at University College, London, 1948, in *Nature and the Greeks* and *Science and Humanism*, foreword by Roger Penrose (Cambridge: Cambridge University Press, 1961), 95–6, 97. See also Ken Wilber (ed.) *Quantum Questions: Mystical Writings of the World's Great Physicists* (Boston and London: Shambhala, 1985), 75–97.

34　George Lakoff, 'Mapping the Brain's Metaphor Circuitry: Metaphorical thought in everyday reason', *Frontiers in Human Neuroscience* (16 December 2014).

35　Y. Shimon (ed.), *Handbook of Industrial Robotics* (USA and Canada: John Wiley & Sons, 1999).

36　Laurens van der Post, *The Lost World of the Kalahari* (London: Vintage Classics, 2002), 57.

37　Thomas Nagel, *Mind and Cosmos* (Oxford: Oxford University Press), 2012.

38 '"Alfred Russel Wallace", An interview by W. B. Northrop', *The Outlook*, 105 (New York, 22 November 1913), 622. See also Charles H. Smith (ed.), 'Obituary Interview W. B. Northrop on Alfred Wallace', *phpBB* (5 January 2010) <https://www.spiritualismlink.com/t728-obiturary-interview-w-b-northrop-on-alfred-wallace#3310> accessed 2 March 2020.

39 Lindsey Fitzharris, *The Butchering Arts: Joseph Lister's quest to transform the grisly world of Victorian medicine* (UK: Penguin, 2017).

40 J. Maddox, 'A Book for Burning?' *Nature*, 293 (1981), 245–6.

41 Tony Edwards, *Heretic: Rupert Sheldrake*, BBC 2 (19 July 1994) <https://genome.ch.bbc.co.uk/f2ff3746e43e472fb35c4a7ceb68e2e8> accessed 19 May 2020.

42 Brian Josephson, 'Incendiary Subjects', *Nature*, 294 (1981), 594.

43 Robin McKie (science ed.), 'Royal Mail's Nobel Guru in Telepathy Row', *The Guardian*, 30 September 2001 <https://www.theguardian.com/uk/2001/sep/30/robinmckie.theobserver> accessed 8 February 2020.

44 *ibid.*

45 An obvious example of such reactions being Richard Dawkins. Unable to understand the symbolism and inner meaning of religious doctrine his only resort is to revile it in sentences such as 'I have described atonement, the central doctrine of Christianity, as vicious, sadomasochistic, and repellent. We should also dismiss it as barking mad'—see Richard Dawkins, *The God Delusion* (Sydney: Transworld Publishers, 2006), 287.

46 'Greta Thunburg: Why all the hate?' *The Week*, 5 October 2019, 21.

47 Michael Collett, 'Greta Thunberg, the Teen behind Climate Strikes, Hits Back at Andrew Bolt Column', *ABC News*, 2nd August 2019.

48 John Keats, 'Selection from Keats's Letters (1817)', Poetry Foundation <https://www.poetryfoundation.org/resources/learning/essays/detail/69384> accessed 8 February 2020.

49 Quoted in Gary Klein, *The Power of Intuition: How to use your gut feelings to make better decisions at work* (US: Currency, 2004).

50 Quote Investigator <http://quoteinvestigator.com/2010/05/26/everything-counts-einstein> accessed 8 February 2020.

51 *SD*-I, 'Gods, Monads, and Atoms', 610.

52 *CW*-XII, 'Kosmic Mind', 135.

53 *CW*-VIII, 'The Science of Life', 241.

54 *CW*-XII, 'Genius', 15.

55 *NPB*-13, Part 3: *Mentalism*, 'The Sensed World', ¶ 82, 15.

56 *NPB*-13, *op. cit.*, ¶ 87, 15.

57 *NPB*-13, *op. cit.*, ¶ 89, 16.

58 *NPB*-13, *op. cit.*, ¶ 91, 16.

59 *ML*, Letter No. 65. Note however the cautionary note struck in the next sentence: 'Yet it is generally that same science which is made the weapon to break our heads with.'

60 *NPB*-13, *op. cit.*, ¶ 73, 14.

61 David Gelernter, 'The Closing of the Scientific Mind'. The citation is in the section appropriately headed, 'Besmirching consciousness'.

62 *NPB*-13, *op. cit.*, ¶ 67, 13.

63 Mihaly Csikszentmihalyi, *The Evolving Self: A psychology for the third millennium* (New York: HarperCollins Publishers,1993), 279.

64 Jeremy Kahn, 'Samsung Will Open AI Research Center in Cambridge, England', *Bloomberg Technology* (22 May 2018) <https://www.bloomberg.com/news/articles/2018-05-22/samsung-will-open-ai-research-center-in-cambridge-england> accessed 8 February 2020.

65 'Good News for Business', *The Week*, 30 June 2018, facing p. 43.

66 'Boston Dynamics Unveils Humanoid Atlas Robot that Can Run Outdoors and Handle Rocky Terrain', *International Business Times* (18 August 2015) <http://www.ibtimes.co.uk/boston-dynamics-unveils-humanoid-atlas-robot-that-can-run-outdoors-handle-rocky-terrain-1515921> accessed 8 February 2020; [video] <https://interestingengineering.com/video/impressive-new-video-shows-humanoid-atlas-robot-go-for-a-run-outdoors> accessed 8 March 2020.

67 Avianne Tan, 'Human-Like Robot "Nadine" Who Has a "Personality, Mood and Emotions" Unveiled in Singapore', *abcNEWS* (31 December 2015) <http://abcnews.go.com/Technology/human-robot-

nadine-personality-mood-emotions-unveiled-singapore/story?id=36032196> accessed 8 March 2020; [video] <https://uk.video.search.yahoo.com/yhs/search?fr=yhs-itm-001&hsimp=yhs-001&hspart=itm&p=video+oof+Nadine+receptionist#id=6&vid=e72ca514db6277293f4892df22e 8b38f&action=click> accessed 8 March 2020.

68　Philip Collins, 'Stay Calm: The robots are not taking over', *The Times*, 8 August 2014.

69　A. M. Turing, 'Computing Machinery and Intelligence', *Mind*, 59 (1950), 433–460.

70　Philip Collins, *art. cit.*

71　Reinstating the Leibniz–Mill argument concerned with the relationship between mentality and machines, in Roger Penrose, *Shadows of the Mind: A search for the missing science of consciousness* (Oxford: Oxford University Press, 1994), 76.

72　Quoted in John Swanson, *God, Science and the Universe: The integration of religion and science* (Durham, Connecticut: Eloquent Books, 2010), 260.

73　Paracelsus, *De Viribus Membrorum* [Of Organic Powers] (1572; repr. Generic, ASIN : B07R2MHYLK, 2019).

8 Diverse Classifications of the Composition of Man – Harmony with Different World Teachings

The commonest failing is the sectarian spirit in which people diminish themselves by rejecting others.

GOTTFRIED LEIBNIZ[1]

Since truth can be looked at from different standpoints, since it has different aspects, it is desirable that there should exist a variety of doctrines and views. Where the attempt is made to congeal it into a fixed creed, for all time, a sect is created and sectarian prejudices are introduced.

PAUL BRUNTON[2]

SYNOPSIS

Chapter 8, which opens the third section of Volume II, has a primary objective in mind. On the question of man's 'internal landscapes', we have consistently maintained that the *philosophia perennis*—whether from the West or the East, either ancient or modern—is essentially one in essence. This is now demonstrated by summarizing major teachings from diverse sources that both complement and corroborate the detailed exposition in Chapters 2 and 3 on man's composition based on the core occult doctrines disseminated through classical Theosophy. These supplementary teachings are: (*a*) the diverse expositions during the period of classical Theosophy, the post-classical era, and subsequent teachings based on the Theosophical tradition; then (*b*) from the East: the Buddhist, Vedānta, and Tāraka Rāja-Yoga systems of India; and the Egyptian, Indian (generic), and Zarathuśtrian (Zoroastrian) teachings; and (*c*) from the West: the Greek and Pauline traditions; the Fourth Way School; the twentieth century Anthroposophy of Rudolf Steiner; and modern transpersonal psychology from Ken Wilber, et al.

The self-consistency and unity amongst these various doctrines from far flung regions of the globe during eras, ancient and modern, should forcefully demonstrate that the Principles of Man are the distilled wisdom of the ages and no fanciful conjecture of any one individual, religion or cult. (The Proem in Volume I of this work explains exactly what is meant by unity. It also addressed the criticisms of academics like Jorge Ferrer and R. C. Zaehner about the postulated unity of the perennial wisdom tradition.) For this reason, the Chapter closes with some practical steps, based on the recommendations of Gottfried Leibniz, for establishing a framework to act as a reconciling system of harmony which would incorporate what is true in different, contrasting, philosophical systems, while rejecting what is false.

KEY WORDS: classical Theosophy, post-classical Theosophy, Indian systems, Egyptian system, Zarathuśtrian systems, Greek systems, Fourth Way system, Anthroposophical systems, transpersonal system, sectarianism, harmony, H. P. Blavatsky, Annie Besant, I. K. Taimni, T. Subba Row, Rudolf Steiner, Ken Wilber, Gottfried Leibniz

The objective of this Chapter is to reinforce a recurrent theme of this work: that since time immemorial, the diverse esoteric and occult teachings the world over have regarded man in a manner broadly consonant with the fundamental doctrines of occult science bequeathed to humanity through the instrumentality of modern Theosophy.[i] Chapters 2 and 3 summarize this core occult doctrine regarding man's constitution and nature, respectively. This objective is realized by comparing and corroborating the core occult doctrines with these various worldwide teachings in order to support the contention that the former are no figment of 'Theosophical imagination', but are backed up by numerous bona fide sources, all of which have been referenced.

An added benefit of such a comparative approach is to provide further insights into man's composition drawn from the different shades of meaning pertaining to the various occult systems in the East and the West.

Field of Enquiry

The various ways of classifying the composition of man from diverse, worldwide sources are categorized, for explanatory purposes, in the three major groups shown in Table II-13 below.

Table II-13   Major World Traditions on the Composition of Man

Theosophical tradition	Eastern traditions	Western traditions

• the period of classical Theosophy
 	
• the post-classical Theosophical era
 	
• subsequent teachings based on the Theosophical tradition
 	
Note: the above embraces both the Eastern and the Western traditions.
	• Indian
	  – Buddhist
	  – Vedānta
	  – Tāraka Rāja-Yoga
	
	• Egyptian
	
	• Zarathuśtrian (Zoroastrian).
		• Greek and Pauline
		
		• Fourth Way School of Gurdjieff and Ouspensky
		
		• Anthroposophy of Rudolf Steiner
		
		• Modern transpersonal psychology of Ken Wilber, et al.

Method of Comparing the Various Occult Teachings on the Composition of Man

In order to provide meaningful comparisons and corroboration of these occult systems worldwide there has to be a constant baseline serving as a point of reference. In all cases, this baseline is Table II-3 on page 21 in Chapter 2 and Table II-5 on page 40 in Chapter 3, as appropriate, as both are regarded as representing the most definitive and complete versions to date on the occult teachings on the constitution and nature of man that were disseminated through the instrumentality of modern Theosophy. All the comparative tables in this Chapter follow the same format and layout. The

A common baseline for comparison

---

i 'Theosophy' capitalized here and elsewhere to distinguish between theosophy—*theosophia*, or the *philosophia perennis*—and its modern expression through the Theosophical Society—refer to Figure I-8 in Chapter 7 of Volume I on page 185.

first four columns on the left of the table in question are reproduced from the same four columns to the left of Table II-3 or Table II-5. This is our benchmark for comparison with the system in question, which is set out in the remaining columns of the comparative table.

Comparisons During the Era of the Theosophical Movement

As seen in Table II-13 above, the Theosophical tradition can broadly be divided into three eras. First, the period of classical Theosophy when the stupendous literature was written and disseminated. This occurred soon after the formation of the Theosophical Society in 1875 and consisted mainly of the output of H. P. Blavatsky and her instructors (the Mahātmās, or Adepts).

Three eras of modern Theosophy

Next, the post-classical tradition after Blavatsky's death in 1891, when outstanding Theosophists, notably Annie Besant, continued broadly in the vein of the foundational literature and teaching, but added their own insights and clarifications to the mass of complex and occasionally indigestible classical literature. The contribution of these writers is indispensable and there is no reason to devalue their worth on the basis of upholding the so-called purity of the original teachings.

The third era comprised several teachings in the Theosophical tradition, notably those of Alice Bailey of the Arcane School and several other writers who concerned themselves mainly with the human aura and subtle bodies. Initially, in this third era, Rudolf Steiner was one of these individuals but he subsequently split from the classical Theosophical tradition and founded the Anthroposophical Society based on the Western approach to spirituality. For this reason, his system is outlined in the section on Western traditions as seen in the third column of Table II-13.

The Evolution of Classical Theosophical Literature

Classical, or First Generation, literature pertains to *The Mahatma Letters to A. P. Sinnett*, *Esoteric Buddhism*, and the works of H. P. Blavatsky comprising *Isis Unveiled*, *The Secret Doctrine*, *The Key to Theosophy*, *The Esoteric School*, *The Inner Group Teachings*, *The Voice of the Silence*, and *Collected Writings*.[ii] The contribution of post-classical, or Second Generation, literature is summarized subsequently.

Problems due to changing English terminology

The reader is asked to recall what was said earlier, namely, that despite the endeavours of Theosophical writers to recast the disparate esoteric teachings the world over, since time immemorial, into an intelligible, scientifically based system for the modern student of occult science, confusion stills prevails over the use of terms. The original Theosophical teachings on the composition of man were presented gradually over some five years; and later versions were given out by post-Blavatsky writers covering a period of several decades. In fact, the subject has never been cast in stone and continues to be one of lively debate and further enquiry. All this implies that the meaning of certain terms has evolved and changed over a period of time of well over a century since 1877 when Blavatsky's first work *Isis Unveiled*

---

ii The above works are referenced as and when appropriate in this Chapter as also in other Chapters in this work.

was published. Hence, if he is not to be misled by the subtle nuances of the words used, when attempting to study a particular passage in Theosophical literature, readers are strongly urged to bear in mind two key factors: (*a*) the period in which it was written; and (*b*) for whom it was written.

Always relate the meaning of words to their context, both historical and contextual.

Table II-14 on page 152 attempts to rationalize the parallels between the terms used to describe the Principles of Man, from the standpoint of his constitution, during the evolution of the early (classical) Theosophical literature.[3] In accordance with the method just described for comparison, the core occult teachings in the first four columns of Table II-3 (on page 21) have been reproduced in the equivalent position in Table II-14, alongside the five systems shown to the right of the dividing column. However in attempting to draw parallels with early literature, it would be needlessly pedantic to make hard-and-fast distinctions between the various systems. The subject can, nevertheless, conveniently be regarded in five major periods as explained below.

'Isis Unveiled': Year 1877

The first column to the right of the dividing column of Table II-14 shows the original classification used in 1877 by Blavatsky in *Isis Unveiled*. This is the classical division of man's constitution in harmony with the well-known Pauline teaching. The significance of the threefold division of man was explained in Chapter 2 on pages 17–18.

'The Mahatma Letters' and 'Esoteric Buddhism': Period 1880–1883

By 1880 the familiar sevenfold classification had been introduced, but only in a preliminary and rudimentary form. It was used throughout *The Mahatma Letters to A. P. Sinnett* and therefore used by Sinnett himself in his book *Esoteric Buddhism*,[4] and also by Blavatsky in her articles for *The Theosophist* during that period. The second column to the right of the dividing column of Table II-14 shows this classification. Note that this description does not distinguish the duality of the Mind Principle, *Manas*. At this stage, the word 'Manas' was equated with the brain mind, or physical intelligence—later described as the Lower mind, or *Kāma-manas*. In this description, the word '*Buddhi*' included Higher Manas, and could be equated with *Buddhi-Manas* as used in later writings. The fourth principle (counting upwards from the body) was called *Kāma-rūpa*, but strictly speaking this applies only after death—during life there is no *rūpa*, or form, associated with this principle (as explained in Chapters 2 and 5). The second and third principles, i.e., *Prāṇa* and *Linga-śarīra*, were reversed in later expositions. Furthermore, Blavatsky fairly consistently used the term 'Astral body' to refer to the Linga-śarīra only, and not to the overall psychic vehicles of consciousness, as some other writers have done.[iii]

'The Secret Doctrine' and 'The Key to Theosophy': Period 1888 – 1889

As a preamble, we point out that Blavatsky's exposition of Theosophy represents the convergence of Western occultism, Eastern philosophy and occultism, religion, science,

---

iii Refer to the remark in Chapter 1 regarding the term 'astral body', and our preference for using precise technical Sanskrit terms to avoid confusion.

and mysticism. *The Secret Doctrine* and *The Key to Theosophy* combined the Vedantic concept of five *kośas* with Western esoteric traditions (particularly Neoplatonism). Blavatsky refers to three subtle bodies. Counting from the lowest, they are:

1. Liṅga-śarīra, the Double, or Astral body
2. Māyāvi-rūpa, the Illusion body
3. Causal Body, the vehicle of the Higher Ego (refer also to Table II-5 on page 40).

Expanding on earlier explanations of these terms, the Liṅga-śarīra (see Chapter 2, page 28) is the invisible double of the human body, elsewhere referred to as the 'etheric body', 'doppelgänger', or 'bioplasmic body' and serves as a model, or matrix, of the Physical body which conforms to the shape, appearance, and condition of its 'double'. With suitable (occult) training, the Liṅga-śarīra can be separated, or projected, a limited distance from the body. When thus separated it can, apparently, be wounded by sharp objects so that when it reverts to the physical frame, the wound will be reflected in the physical counter-part, a phenomenon known as 'repercussion' well known to mediums. At death, together with the Physical body, it is discarded and eventually decomposes and disintegrates.

The *Māyāvi-rūpa* (see Chapter 4, page 54) is dual in its functions, being 'the vehicle both of thought and of the animal passions and desires, drawing at one and the same time from the lowest terrestrial *Manas* (mind) and *Kāma*, the element of desire.'[5] The higher part of this body, containing the spiritual elements gathered during life, merges after death entirely into the Causal Body; while the lower part, containing the animal elements, forms the Kāma-rūpa, the source of 'spooks', or apparitions of the dead.

The Causal Body, called 'the basis of the cause' in the Tāraka Rāja-Yoga system (see later in this Chapter) is Buddhi in conjunction with Manas, the incarnating Entity or Ego and is so called because it is the direct cause leading to the highest state of *Samādhi*: the eighth and final state of Yoga, the attainment of which enables the practitioner to enter a state of ecstasy and to exercise absolute control over all his faculties, physical and mental.[6]

From 1888 and 1889 onwards when *The Secret Doctrine* and *The Key to Theosophy*, respec-tively, were published, the classification of the Principles of Man was revised according to the typical version shown in the third column to the right of the dividing column of Table II-14 on page 152. Although the same terminology is used, the associated meaning has changed. The most important fact to note is that Manas is now shown to be dual in its function (see also Chapter 3, Table II-3, page 21) with the Higher Manas being iden-tified with the Reincarnating Ego. This means that Buddhi is now shown above Higher Manas in a position beyond anything that ordinary man may expect to contact in full consciousness. Furthermore, the Liṅga-śarīra is now shown to be the vehicle of Prāṇa and so is listed below it. There are also allusions in the literature to Prāṇa being not just a human principle, but a universal principle.

Progressive
sophistication of
Blavatsky's
teachings

'Collected Writings Volume X – A Dialogue Between the Two Editors': Year 1888

'A Dialogue Between the Two Editors' refers to an article, so titled, between Blavatsky and the British Theosophist and prolific author Mabel Collins (1851–1927), joint editors of the magazine *Lucifer* at that time. The salient features of their dialogue, shown in the penultimate column of Table II-14, concerned the various vehicles of consciousness through which man may operate. The most significant feature here is that whereas previous classifications have shown man's Desire principle as being the Kāma-rūpa, it is referred to in the later teachings as the Māyāvi-rūpa. The distinction is apposite, since the Māyāvi-rūpa is the vehicle of dream consciousness for the average man during life (but a vehicle of waking consciousness for an adept); whereas the Kāma-rūpa is formed from the dregs of the Māyāvi-rūpa after physical death. Refer again to Chapter 4 on pages 54–59 regarding the creation, function, and projection of the Māyāvi-rūpa and the examples cited of such phenomena.

'The Esoteric Writings' also 'The Secret Doctrine Volume III': Period 1889–1891

In 1889 a major development was inaugurated when Blavatsky presented her Esoteric Section with a series of study Papers in which much hitherto guarded material was revealed.[iv] It should be borne in mind that some of these teachings were given orally, and although Blavatsky did see some of them in written form, it is possible that she might have made alterations had she lived longer.

These Papers showed the Hermetic relationship between the macrocosm and the microcosm, which will be considered in depth in Volume III of this work, particularly in Chapter 5. A modified classification of the Principles of Man was provided, as shown in the final column of Table II-14 overleaf. Interestingly, *Ātma* was excluded altogether from this classification, because 'ĀTMAN, although exoterically reckoned as the seventh principle [that is, in counting from the bottom], is no individual principle at all, and belongs to the Universal Soul.'[7] Refer to Chapter 2 about the distinction between Ātma and Ātman; but for overall consistency it is shown within square brackets in its relevant position in Table II-14.

Abstruse oral teachings progressively divulged in print

The classification clearly shows the dual functioning of the Mind Principle. Moreover, the Physical body is entirely ignored on the grounds that it 'is no principle'[8] (nor ever was one), but rather the ultimate vehicle of all the other principles (refer again to Chapter 2). Again, for consistency, it is shown within square brackets in its relevant position in Table II-14. The seventh *individual* principle (again counting from the bottom and ignoring the body) 'is the AURIC EGG [ENVELOPE], the Magnetic Sphere round every human and animal being.'[9] The only place where explicit reference is made to this sacred and most important principle is in these esoteric Papers. The reasons for such a cautious disclosure are not difficult to fathom.

Finally, the esoteric Papers also provide a wealth of information on the correspondences of the human principles with numbers, metals, planets, days of the week, colours, and sounds as exemplified by the musical scale of both the Sanskrit and Italian gamuts. Relevant sections from the esoteric Papers of Blavatsky are shown in Chapter 7 of Volume III.

Post-Classical Theosophy

The era of classical Theosophy ended with Blavatsky's death in 1891. Subsequently, the (overly) abstruse, technical, and complicated classical doctrines were further systematized and simplified by later generations of renowned Theosophists, like

---

iv These Papers were subsequently published as part of the Third Volume of *The Secret Doctrine* which also appeared as the fifth volume of the six volume Adyar Edition of *The Secret Doctrine*.

Table II-14 Parallels at Various Stages in the Development of Classical Theosophical Literature

Dual Constitution	Triple Constitution	#	Septenary Constitution	Isis Unveiled (1877)	The Mahatma Letters and Esoteric Buddhism (1880–1883)	The Secret Doctrine and The Key to Theosophy* (1888–1889)	The Collected Writings Vol. X – A Dialogue Between the Two Editors (1888)	The Esoteric Writings also The Secret Doctrine Vol. III (1889–1891)
Individuality or Higher Self (Immortal)	Spirit	1	Ātma the Divine Self	Spirit	Ātma the Divine Self	Ātma the Divine Self		[Ātma the Divine Self]
		2	Buddhi the Intuition Principle		Buddhi the Intuition Principle	Buddhi the Intuition Principle	the Causal, or Karmic Body (the Devachanic Ego after death)	the Auric Egg
	Soul	3	Manas the Mind Principle — Higher / Lower	Soul	Manas the Mind Principle	Higher Manas the Higher Mind		Buddhi the Intuition Principle — the Higher Mind (Higher Manas)
Personality or Lower self (mortal)						Lower manas the Lower mind	the Body of Illusion Māyāvi-rūpa	the Lower mind (Lower manas)
		4	Kāma the Desire principle		Kāma-rūpa the seat of Desires	Kāma-rūpa the seat of Desires	(the Kāma-rūpa after death)	Kāma (rūpa) the Desire principle
		5	Prāṇa the Life principle	Body	Liṅga-śarīra the Etheric double	Prāṇa the Life principle	the Protean, or Plastic Double, the Astral body	Prāṇa the Life principle
		6	Liṅga-śarīra the Etheric double		Prāṇa the Life principle	Liṅga-śarīra the Etheric double		Liṅga-śarīra the Etheric double
	Body	7	Sthūla-śarīra, or Rūpa the Physical body		Sthūla-śarīra the Physical body	Sthūla-śarīra, or Rūpa the Physical body	the Physical body	[Sthūla-śarīra the Physical body]

MAN AS ONE UNIFIED ENTITY

Reproduced from **Table II-3**

* Enumeration taken from the description on pages 175–6 of *The Key to Theosophy*; but note that Blavatsky reverses the order of *Prāṇa* and *Liṅga-śarīra* in the table on page 91 of her book.

Annie Besant (Blavatsky's great pupil), C. W. Leadbeater (a co-worker with Annie Besant), C. Jinarâjadâsa, I. K. Taimni, and P. T. Pavri, amongst several others. In fact, before her passing, Blavatsky urged her pupils to reform the terminology, which she felt had been too carelessly put together, and the attempts of Besant and others are, in the writer's opinion, a reasonably successful attempt to fulfil this wish. In general, then, these later writers and researchers divided Blavatsky's dual Māyāvi-rūpa into two different bodies: the emotional and the mental bodies. They also redefined some terms. The Liṅga-śarīra (sometimes called the Astral body by Blavatsky) was denominated the Etheric double by Besant; C. W. Leadbeater regarded the emotional body as the seat of the kamic (desire) principle of Blavatsky's enumeration, and named it the Astral body. Therefore, the subtle bodies in the enumeration of the post-classical writers are, in general, counting from the lowest:

<aside>Blavatsky encourages her pupils to refine terminology</aside>

1. Etheric body (Etheric double) – the vehicle of Prāṇa
2. Emotional, or Astral body – the vehicle of desires and emotions
3. Mental Body – the vehicle of the concrete, or the Lower mind
4. Causal Body – the vehicle of the abstract, or the Higher Mind.

<aside>Generally more emphasis on subtle bodies than principles</aside>

Each subtle body has its own aura and set of *cākras*, and corresponds to a particular plane of existence (i.e., level of consciousness).

The Besant and Vedānta Systems

In 1889, the prominent British socialist, women's rights activist and one time secularist, educationist, philanthropist, and orator Annie Besant (1847–1933) was invited by *The Pall Mall Gazette* (London) to review Blavatsky's monumental tome *The Secret Doctrine*.[10] After reading it Besant experienced what can only be described as an epiphany and sought an interview with its author, meeting Blavatsky in Paris. Being intensely drawn to the universality and spirituality of the doctrines espoused by Theosophy, Besant later became the Second International President of the Theosophical Society and, to this day, may be counted as one of the most prolific writers and powerful orators the Society has ever known. Along with her Theosophical activities, Besant continued to participate actively in political matters, having joined the Indian National Congress as an ardent campaigner for the Indian Home Rule Movement.[11] Mahatma Gandhi (1869–1948) said of her: 'I would have been more than satisfied if I could have touched the hem of her garment.'[12]

<aside>Mahatma Gandhi's veneration for Annie Besant</aside>

The whole point of mentioning this is that the message of Theosophy of universal brotherhood, and the obligation of service, resonated forcefully with her own humanitarian and socialist ideals. Add to this the fact that she remained a lifelong pupil of the principal Founder of the Theosophical Society (Blavatsky), and we can appreciate the practical import and direct simplicity of Besant's tremendous writings. For they were based not on dry theory, but upon the experience of a lifetime in service to humanity, allied to a deep understanding of the underlying philosophical and esoteric precepts of life.

What follows is taken from Besant's voluminous writings, principally *The Seven Principles of Man*[13] and *The Ancient Wisdom*.[14] Table II-15 on page 157 shows the Besant system alongside a useful comparison with that of the Vedantic classification (using the precise notation for English and Sanskrit terms, as shown on page 194 of *The Ancient Wisdom*). As before, this table is flanked on the left by the four columns showing the core occult doctrine on the constitution of man reproduced from Table II-3 on page 21.

The most interesting feature of Besant's classification is the three columns showing: life (the middle column) flanked by the principles to the left and forms to the right. This, it is suggested, is a fine way of both drawing the distinction, and showing the interconnection between the one permanent life, its various active modes of manifestation and associated passive forms, as its materials and vehicles of expression. Regarding the latter, the Besant system aligns with the ancient Vedānta classification, which also describes man's constitution on the form-side, as seen in the last two columns of Table II-15. (The Vedantic classification and Sanskrit terms used are fully explained later in the exposition on the Indian systems.)

Besant informs us that the various subtle bodies form, *in their aggregate*, what is usually called the aura of the human being. This aura, detectable under genuine clairvoyant vision, has the appearance of an ovoid luminous cloud, with the dense Physical body in the 'midst' (inverted commas used as explained below). Note, however, that what is called the aura is merely such parts of the subtle bodies as 'extend' beyond the periphery of the dense Physical body; each body is complete in itself, and 'interpenetrates' those that are coarser (i.e., on a lower plane) than itself. The aura is thus composed of the 'overlapping portions' of the Etheric double, the Desire body, the Mental Body, the Causal Body and, in rare cases, the Buddhic Body, all illumined by the Atmic radiance. The stage of evolution attained by the man—especially his moral and mental character—determines the size and radiance of the aura, dependent on the development of his different bodies. Endnote II-8 provides a list of books on the human aura by scientists, healers, and genuine clairvoyants who have described how the aura reflects a man's state of mind, i.e., his thoughts and feelings, his state of health, and interaction with others.

Observe that the words in inverted commas in the above paragraph are to be understood in the metaphysical sense as they pertain to higher dimensions of space–time than the ordinary four-dimensional physical world of three space dimensions and one time dimension with which we are familiar. As explained early in Chapter 1, the Theosophical pioneers were working in the nineteenth century at a time when science was ultra-materialistic, and several decades before physical field theory and string theory had been developed, along with associated concepts of higher dimensions of space and time. They had to find concepts and metaphors (such as 'interpenetrate' and 'overlap') then available in the English language.

The next striking feature in the classification, conspicuous by its absence in the Principles, is the Life principle, or Life-force, *Prāṇa*. Besant explains this omission on the grounds that Prāṇa in general is not exactly regarded as being a 'principle'. The reason she advocates this is that the life-force of our planetary system is universal and Prāṇa is but a name for this universal life while it is absorbed by an entity and is supporting its separated and individual life. In other words, when thus appropriated, the Life-force is called Prāṇa and it becomes the life-breath of every creature. In the human, Prāṇa is the life specialised for the support of the physical organism. Furthermore, Blavatsky's later classifications removed both Prāṇa and the dense Physical body from the rank of Principles, on the grounds of the body being the mere counterpart of the Etheric double, and constituted of constantly changing materials built into the etheric matrix, and Prāṇa the associated life-support to its changing existence.[15]

So with the Besant classification, there are two essential changes, or rather re-orderings of the principles. The sixth principle, the Liṅga-śarīra, is now the conglomerate of the fifth and sixth principles, Prāṇa and Liṅga-śarīra, respectively, of the core occult classification. The Desire principle occupies the same position in both classifications but whereas the core classification shows the dual aspect of the Mind Principle with the lower aspect gravitating towards Desire, hence forming the compound unit known as *Kāma-manas*, Besant highlights this lower mental aspect by showing it as an explicit principle, Lower manas, constituting the lower 'half' of the Human Soul.

These small, but not insignificant, changes made for specific and carefully considered reasons have caused no end of consternation and division in the Theosophical Society for many decades. Opposing camps have taken up the side of either Blavatsky or Besant and denounced the 'opposition'. Furthermore, the Blavatskyites—meaning those of a purist (we desist from saying fundamentalist) mindset who take her teachings in the literal, dead-letter sense—have spared no effort in trying to prove how Besant corrupted the purity of the original teachings given out via the Adepts through Blavatsky, whilst conveniently ignoring how dramatically the nomenclature and terminology changed during Blavatsky's own era—much of this change effected by Blavatsky herself, as we have just demonstrated.

However let Besant speak for herself in defence:

> This sudden change in the method of naming is apt to cause confusion in the mind of the student, and as H.P. Blavatsky, our revered teacher, expressed much dissatisfaction with the then current nomenclature as confused and misleading, and desired others and myself to try and improve it, the above names, as descriptive, simple, and representing the facts, are here adopted.[16]

So the Besant system is perfectly compatible with the core classification evolved by Blavatsky: it is just another 'slice through the esoteric cake' at a different angle, namely, another way of cross sectioning the constitution of man from a changed esoteric perspective on the Mind Principle. We need to stress, vehemently, that in matters of such highly abstruse and esoteric nature, there is no rigid, hard-and-fast rule. Please refer back to the section in Chapter 1 explaining the reasons for the confusion amongst the various systems that have evolved to describe the composition of man.

Besant aimed to clarify and simplify Blavatsky's classifications

It is the writer's earnest wish, therefore, that the above exposition may help to dispel the mindless prejudice and uncharitable attitude of many Theosophists[v] against the Besant system and, indeed, in some cases the rank antipathy towards Besant herself. Indeed, like Leadbeater, her unfortunate errors of judgement in her declining years were the result of gullibility, especially during the events surrounding the Krishnamurti episode. But we need, constantly, to bear in mind Blavatsky's deepest admiration and affection for her pupil and friend. It would not therefore be labouring the point to show a few relevant extracts from letters that Blavatsky wrote in her last years to Besant.

Sublime doctrines are not ideologies to be cast in stone and set in concrete. There is always an in-built elasticity of meaning dependent on the context and the era.

From Jersey, Blavatsky writes: 'My dearest alter Ego, […] behold me in the astral light standing on my knees before you, if such a feat could be accomplished even in the astral light [the invisible region surrounding our globe corresponding to the Etheric double in

---

v Or rather, as we prefer to say, the uncharitable attitude of those professing to be Theosophists.

Blavatsky's love
for Besant
man].'[17] Then from Holland Park in London she writes: 'Annie […] I believe in but one person in England and this is *YOU*.'[18] In her last year we find Blavatsky writing from Regent's Park in London on New Year's Eve, 1891: 'I *am* your true friend till the blessed day of my deliverance.'[19] Perhaps the most fitting tribute is contained in her letter, dated 27th March 1891, to the Irish–American mystic, esotericist, and occultist William Quan Judge (1851–1896), a co-founder of the Theosophical Society and later head of the Society's American Section. In this letter Blavatsky speaks of Annie Besant as '*the soul of honour and uncompromisingly truthful*,' and describes her heart as 'one single unbroken diamond, … transparent so that anyone can see how filled to the brim it is *with pure, unadulterated theosophy and enthusiasm*.'[20] Continues Blavatsky, 'UNSELFISHNESS AND ALTRUISM is Annie Besant's name […].'[21]

The Leadbeater System

The English Theosophist C. W. Leadbeater (1854–1934) attracted worldwide prominence and notoriety in equal measure, regarding his writings and also his personal life. About the latter, this Chapter is not the place to delve into the complexities of the numerous scurrilous attacks against him—the staple diet of low-level journalists and mean mentalities (even amongst those who fancy themselves as 'Theosophists') that thrive on gossip and slander. But suffice it to say, in his defence, that these accusations have never been proven conclusively.[22] More to the point, together with his co-worker Annie Besant, he was a lifelong occult researcher and clairvoyant investigator. Most significantly, it was Leadbeater who clairvoyantly discerned the aura of a young bedraggled boy playing on the beach at Adyar, Madras and then, with Besant, cared for him. That Indian boy, who was later to become a world renowned modern speaker, writer, and educator on philosophy and spirituality was—Jiddu Krishnamurti (1895–1986).[23]

But turning to his writings, Leadbeater, like Besant, was to suffer from the 'back to Blavatsky' authenticity cult within the Theosophical Society—'Blavatsky Theosophy' being regarded by them as the 'pure' Theosophy untainted by Leadbeater's psychism. The writer wishes to make it plain that there is no question of withholding facts behind a smokescreen of wanting to preserve appearances. Leadbeater's later writings, based on his occult investigations, did indeed 'run off the rails' in part because of the phenomenon known as unconscious *kriyāśakti*. This is the image-making of the (unconscious) mind, whereby what a psychic claims to see clairvoyantly is in fact his own mental imagery, the phantasizing and dramatizing power of his own mind. It is a common hazard of clairvoyance (and most certainly of psychedelic-drug-induced visions) that only the most rigorous training, under true adept guidance, can surmount. Indeed it was a danger that Blavatsky herself, so trained, warned him about.[24]

C. W. Leadbeater's
valuable
contribution to
Theosophy and
the scientific
study of
clairvoyance
However, Leadbeater's earlier works are inspiring and lucid. Chief among these, and proof of his genuine clairvoyance, is *Occult Chemistry* written in collaboration with Besant; but this is outside the scope of this work, other than the brief mention in Volume I, Chapter 4. What now follows is taken from his other earlier works, chiefly, *The Inner Life*[25] and *A Textbook of Theosophy*.[26]

The fifth and sixth columns of Table II-16 on page 158 show the Leadbeater classification set against the benchmark of the core occult doctrine shown in the first four columns of

Table II-15 Parallels with the Besant Classification and Comparison with the Vedantic Classification

Dual Constitution	Triple Constitution	Septenary Constitution	Besant Classification — Principles	Besant Classification — Life	Besant Classification — Forms	Vedantic Classification — Forms	Vedantic Classification — Form
Individuality or Higher Self (Immortal)	Spirit	*Ātma* the Divine Self	*Ātma* Spirit	*Ātma*	Bliss-Body	Buddhic Body	*Ānandamaya-kośa* [the 'sheath of Bliss']
	Soul	*Buddhi* the Intuition Principle	*Buddhi* Spiritual Soul		Causal Body	Causal Body	*Vijñānamaya-kośa* [the 'sheath of Intelligence']
		Manas the Mind Principle (Higher / Lower)	Higher *Manas* / Lower *manas* — Human Soul		Mental Body	Mental Body	*Manomaya-kośa* [the 'sheath of the lower Mind']
Personality or Lower self (mortal)		*Kāma* the Desire principle	*Kāma* Animal soul		Astral body	Astral body	
	Body	*Prāna* the Life principle			Etheric double	Physical body	etheric — *Prānamaya-kośa* [the 'sheath of life']
		Linga-śarīra the Etheric double	*Linga-śarīra*				
		Sthūla-śarīra, or *Rūpa* the Physical body	*Sthūla-śarīra*		Dense body		dense — *Annamaya-kośa* [the 'sheath built of food']

MAN AS ONE UNIFIED ENTITY

Reproduced from **Table II-3**

Table II-16   Parallels with the Leadbeater Classification

Dual Constitution	Triple Constitution	Septenary Constitution	Leadbeater Classification	
			Old Names given in Vol. II of *The Inner Life* [*]	New Names as in *A Textbook of Theosophy*
Individuality or Higher Self (Immortal)	Spirit	*Ātma* the Divine Self	Adi Plane	Divine World
		Buddhi the Intuition Principle	Anupādaka Plane	Monadic World
	Soul	*Manas* the Mind Principle — Higher	Atmic, or Nirvanic Plane	Spiritual World
		Manas the Mind Principle — Lower	Buddhic Plane	Intuitional World
Personality or Lower self (mortal)		*Kāma* the Desire principle	Mental Plane	Mental World
		Prāna the Life principle	Astral Plane	Emotional, or Astral World
		Linga-śarīra the Etheric double		
	Body	*Sthūla-śarīra, or Rūpa* the Physical body	Physical Plane	Physical World

MAN AS ONE UNIFIED ENTITY

Reproduced from Table II-3

* An extensive search of Vol. II of *The Inner Life* as referenced above revealed no such classification. What is therefore shown is the reference to it which appears in *A Texbook of Theosophy* in the adjacent column.[27]

the table. At first sight, this is apt to cause some confusion because Leadbeater describes man's constitution in terms of the several 'worlds' or 'planes' that man inhabits, that is to say, in which his consciousness functions and has its being. Put another way, Leadbeater's description is from the aspect of form rather than principles, or matter rather than spirit, using such terms in the generic sense, of course. (Please refer again to the section in Chapter 1 on pages 5–7, regarding the distinction between planes and principles.)

As said before, there is no 'black or white' way of expounding the subtleties of man's complex constitution. Based on an unbiased evaluation of what we have just stated, the reader should therefore make up his own mind (and be prepared to change his mind when necessary) about the value of the Leadbeater system. That Leadbeater changed the old names in *The Inner Life* to the new names in *A Textbook of Theosophy* shows the challenges facing an author struggling to keep abreast of the shifting comprehension of his readers regarding the translation of exact Sanskrit words into the best available English equivalents.

The Jinarâjadâsa System

The Sri Lankan Theosophist Curuppumullage Jinarâjadâsa (1875–1953), a graduate from St John's College, Cambridge, was a linguist, author, and occultist who became the Fourth International President of the Theosophical Society. He was closely associated with Besant, Leadbeater, Krishnamurti, and several other prominent members of the movement. His wide range of interests and writings included religion, philosophy, literature,

Table II-17 Parallels with the Jinarâjadâsa Classification

MAN AS ONE UNIFIED ENTITY			Jinarâjadâsa Classification				
Dual Constitution	**Triple Constitution**	**Septenary Constitution**	*Functioning Principles*	*Forms*	*Plane of Action*	*Purpose*	*Outcome*
Individuality or Higher Self (Immortal)	Spirit	*Ātma* the Divine Self	The Spirit				
	Soul	*Buddhi* the Intuition Principle	Intuitions			*Vehicles of the Soul*	
		Manas the Mind Principle — Higher	Ideations	Causal Body	Higher Mental	To evolve with	Ideals — Abstract thoughts
		Manas the Mind Principle — Lower	Concrete Thoughts	Mind Body	Lower mental	To think with	Ideas — Concrete thoughts
Personality or Lower self (mortal)		*Kāma* the Desire principle	Personal Emotions, Impulses	Astral body	Astral	To feel with	Emotions — Desires
	Body	*Prāna* the Life principle	Bodily Activities	Etheric Physical body	Physical	To act with	Sensorial reactions — Actions
		Linga-śarīra the Etheric double					
		Sthūla-śarīra, or Rūpa the Physical body		Gross Physical body			

art, science, and occult chemistry. His book *First Principles of Theosophy*[28] is a classic and a model of lucid and clear exposition of occult fundamentals.

C. Jinarâjadâsa shows relations between principles, forms, and planes

The Jinarâjadâsa classification is shown in Table II-17 on the previous page, taken from his above mentioned book, and set against the core classification shown in the first four columns of the Table.[29] Like Besant, he successfully attempts to promote clarity by classifying man's constitution in terms of active functioning principles, and the forms through which they function on the various planes of existence. The three lowest principles of Life principle, Etheric double, and Physical body are subsumed under the designation of Bodily Activities, which is quite correct. So it will be observed that his system is entirely compatible with the core classification and a simple, clear way of expressing the latter.

The three columns to the right of the table provide a useful summary of the four vehicles of the soul, or in other words, the conveyors of consciousness at four levels as regards, at each level, the plane of action, purpose, and outcome. Consciousness (Spirit) is the active, masculine principle and Soul, the negative, feminine principle that provides the material, or vehicle, for its manifestation and expression on any plane. Accordingly, the vehicles of the soul shown in Table II-17 are entirely in accord with the description of the vehicles of consciousness contained in Chapter 4.

The Pavri System

Pestanji Temulji Pavri was an Indian Professor of mathematics and engineering by profession. He was a profound student of Theosophy, having joined the Theosophical Society in 1905. His classic primer *Theosophy Explained in Questions and Answers*[30] is, as the title suggests, a systematic exposition of Theosophical doctrine in the form of questions and answers. Being highly readable, it is also a valuable reference book aided by a comprehensive index, and has been popular and continuously in print. The material is drawn from over seventy books and pamphlets, mainly the writings of Besant and Leadbeater, and also Ernest Wood (1883–1965), who was a leading English Theosophist, professor of physics, Indologist, yoga exponent, author, and Sanskrit scholar.

P. T. Pavri highlights connection between the immortal and mortal aspects of man

The Pavri classification is shown in Table II-18 on the next page set against the core classification shown in the first four columns of the table.[31] As one would expect from a mathematician and a practical engineer, Pavri's classification is simple and direct. Entirely in line with the core classification, his system highlights the connection between the Upper Triad and the Lower Quaternary, each with their respective principles, through the Thinking, or Intelligence principle as the interface and fulcrum between the immortal, spiritual and the mortal, personal aspects of man's constitution. Notice however, that he reinstates Prāṇa as an independent principle.

The Taimni System

Iqbal Kishen Taimni (1898–1978) was an Indian professor of chemistry, an occultist, and an influential scholar in the fields of yoga and Indian Philosophy. Being both a scientist and an occultist, his writings display the ideal combination of authenticity expressed with great clarity and lucidity. Taimni was also a leader of the Theosophical Society and authored numerous books on Eastern Philosophy, including a modern interpretation of

Table II-18   Parallels with the Pavri Classification

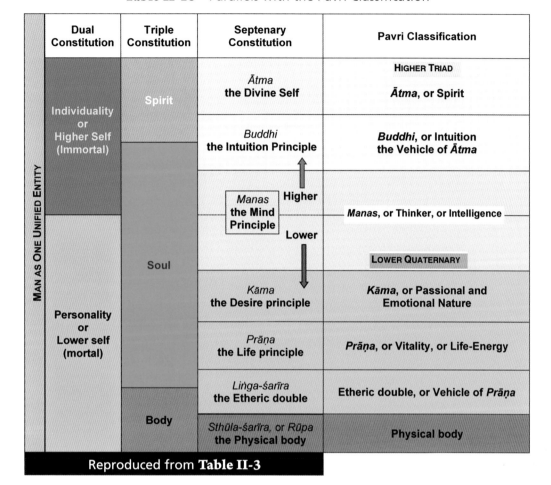

Reproduced from **Table II-3**

Patanjali's Yoga Sutras. For his contribution to Theosophical literature he was awarded the prestigious Subba Row Medal.[vi]

Taimni takes a somewhat different, and much broader, approach than several other writers in the Theosophical Society of his period. He deals with man's constitution in terms of planes rather than principles (see the explanation in Chapter 1 on page 5 about the difference between these two approaches). His focus is rather less on the taxonomic details of the constitution of man and more on showing man's overall relation to deity and the universe, as per the title of his classic book *Man, God and the Universe*,[32] from which the following features have been extracted.

Taimni stresses three key points:

1. Despite the multiplicity of man's vehicles, or subtle bodies, and the great differences in the manifestations through them, the consciousness functioning through the vehicles is one and the same, but in different expressions of itself conditioned by the nature of the vehicles.

---

vi The Subba Row Medal is awarded to exceptional writers in theosophy. It was established in 1883 in honour of T. Subba Row, an outstandingly learned member of the Society. Awardees included: H. P. Blavatsky, Annie Besant, C. W. Leadbeater, Rudolf Steiner, J. Krishnamurti, and E. Lester-Smith FRS.

2. As we move from the periphery to the centre, i.e., from the material to the spiritual, these vehicles become progressively less complex and material, and consciousness becomes increasingly predominant and all-inclusive.

3. Although the various vehicles are on different planes of nature, the consciousness working in each is a unity, although this unity is subordinate to, and contained, or subsumed, within the larger unity of the next higher plane of manifestation.

I. K. Taimni situates man's constitution in a universal context

Taimni's classification is shown in Table II-19 on the next page. The first four columns show, as always, the core occult classification and Taimni's classification is in the remaining columns. For ease of reference, the latter has been adapted from the adjacent figure, which provides a better pictorial appreciation of man's constitution, within the overall scheme of the universe, than the familiar tabular setting which is obviously easier to read.[33]

The lowest component of man's constitution, the mortal personality, is that realm of human consciousness which is limited and constrained to work through the Animal soul, namely, the lower mental, astral, and physical bodies (vehicles); therefore changing completely with every new incarnation. The higher component is the Individuality, or Higher Self (the union of the Divine Self with the Higher Mind), which works through the Higher Mental, Buddhic, and Atmic vehicles. These vehicles, *collectively*, represent the Human Soul whereby the spiritual element in man, that is, the immortal Self that endures from life to life, gradually unfolds all the mental and spiritual attributes and powers from within itself over the long course of human evolution.

But even this spiritual element in man is not the highest aspect of man's nature, which is the eternal Monad, or in terms of the Sāṁkhya philosophy, *Puruṣa* (*Purusha*)—that mysterious Being at the very core of our own being (elucidated in Volume III, Chapters 7 and 8). Whereas the Reincarnating Ego (Higher Ego) is immortal in the sense of having an existence for an immeasurably long time, as compared with the personality, it is true to say that it too must at some time or other cease to be. This is because it came into existence at a particular moment during a world period. However the Monad is above time and exists in the eternal, being one with the Logos and having its roots on the *Ādi* plane and its Centre of consciousness on the *Anupādaka* plane, as seen in Table II-19 and the adjoining figure.

These higher planes above the Atmic are extremely abstruse matters of occult metaphysics and any discussion about them must lie outside the scope of this work. It is enough to know that such exalted states of consciousness exist, and can be studied, if only theoretically, as in Taimni's book, and also in Besant's splendidly concise book *A Study in Consciousness*.[34] For now, the Taimni system can be seen to be entirely in accord with the core occult classification as shown in Table II-19.

Later Teachings in the Theosophical Tradition

The Theosophical teachings were taken up with many twists and turns by several others who were inspired by Blavatsky, like Alice Bailey, and then found their way into the world-view of the New Age. A necessarily arbitrary selection of a few of these later exponents is outlined below. It is not comprehensive, the intention being to show how the eternal stream of the *philosophia perennis*, strongly fortified by Theosophy, has

Table II-19 Parallels with the Taimni Classification

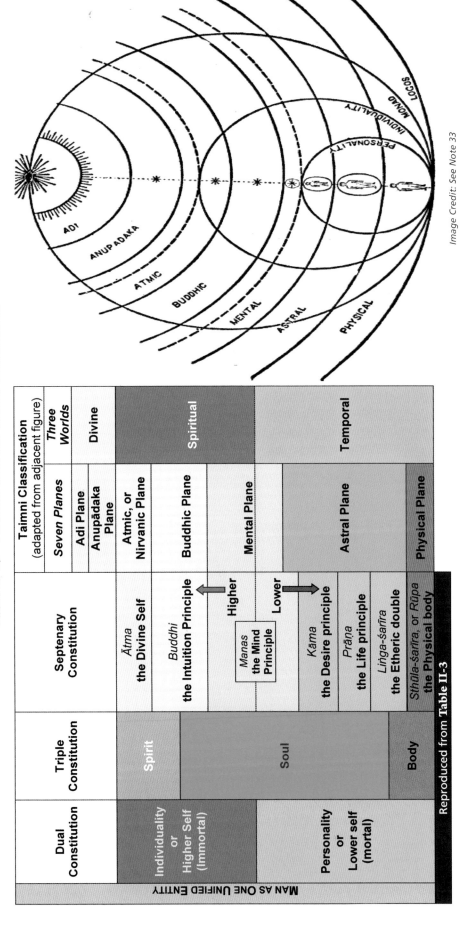

Image Credit: See Note 33

Dual Constitution	Triple Constitution	Septenary Constitution		Taimni Classification (adapted from adjacent figure)		
				Seven Planes		**Three Worlds**
MAN AS ONE UNIFIED ENTITY						
Individuality or Higher Self (Immortal)	**Spirit**	*Ātma* the Divine Self		Adi Plane	**Divine**	**Spiritual**
				Anupādaka Plane		
				Atmic, or Nirvanic Plane		
	Soul	*Buddhi* the Intuition Principle		Buddhic Plane		
		Higher		Mental Plane		
		Manas the Mind Principle				
		Lower				
Personality or Lower self (mortal)		*Kāma* the Desire principle		Astral Plane		**Temporal**
		Prāṇa the Life principle				
	Body	*Liṅga-śarīra*, the Etheric double				
		Sthūla-śarīra, or *Rūpa* the Physical body		Physical Plane		

Reproduced from **Table II-3**

fecundated later generations of occult writers and advocates of spiritual healing and complementary medicine.

Max Heindel, born Carl Louis von Grasshoff (1865–1919), was a Danish–American occultist, astrologer, and mystic. He was a contemporary of Blavatsky, whom he admired greatly and in whom he recognized his own physical and financial struggles of the pioneer life. The thought ever uppermost in his mind was to find some means by which he could help to lift the heavy karmic burdens of humanity. This light began to dawn when he contacted the teachings which had been given out by Blavatsky, especially regarding the Western occult tradition, the Rosicrucian philosophy, and mystic Christianity to which he was particularly drawn.[35]

Heindel recognized three subtle bodies. Adopting the exact terms, including capitaliza-tions from Heindel's book referenced above, they are: the Vital Body made of Ether, the instrument for specializing the vital energy of the sun, and seen by clairvoyant vision to extend about an inch and a half outside the Physical body; the Desire Body related to the Desire World, being the emotional nature, which pervades both the Vital and Dense bodies, seen clairvoyantly to extend about sixteen inches outside the visible body; and the Ego Mind (Mental Body), which functions like a mirror, reflecting the outer world and enabling the Ego, or Inner man, to transmit its commands as thoughts, words, and actions. The human being is seen as a threefold Spirit, possessing a Mind by which he governs the threefold Body that he transmutes into a threefold Soul. The Human Spirit aspect has emanated from itself the Desire Body to be transmuted into the Emotional Soul; the Life Spirit aspect has emanated from itself the Vital Body to be transmuted into the Intellectual Soul; and the Divine Spirit aspect has emanated from itself the Dense (Physical) Body to be transmuted into the Conscious Soul.

Samael Aun Weor, born Víctor Manuel Gómez Rodríguez (1917–1977) was a Columbian author, lecturer, and founder of the Universal Christian Gnostic Movement. In his over sixty books and hundreds of lectures, Aun Weor described his own teaching of gnosis, being the basis of Gnosticism.[36] These teachings, which emphasized the existence of the perennial philosophy of all religions, in both their esoteric and exoteric aspects, have been called 'neo-Gnostic' by Arthur Versluis (b.1959), the American historian of esotericism,[37] and by the Swiss historian Jean-François Mayer (b.1957), 'a science of consciousness or knowledge that may be attained through certain techniques.'[38]

'The Doctrine of Synthesis' is the term Aun Weor used to describe his teachings because it purportedly elucidates, and coherently syncretizes, an extensive variety of teachings which study the human condition.[39] He emphasized that his doctrine is experiential, and must be put into practice for it to be of any value to the student. Throughout his works there are hundreds of techniques and exercises that are supposed to facilitate the development of psychic powers, for example, leaving the dense Physical body at will (astral projection) in order to be taught in the schools of the 'Higher Worlds'. The techniques are always combined with meditation and sexual transmutation, and the perfection of such powers may take more than one lifetime.[40] It is stated that a student who is successful in awakening consciousness will eventually experience a continuous state of vigilance not only during the day but also while the Physical body is sleeping and, most importantly, after death. This is significant, because Aun Weor states that those who have a sleeping consciousness are not aware of their post-mortem condition, just as they are not aware

Later teachings based on subtle bodies and generally more experiential when they are physically sleeping. The awakening of consciousness allows students to continue to work regardless of their physical state. This idea resonates with the 'Fourth Way' teaching described shortly.

Aun Weor wrote extensively on the subtle vehicles, organizing them in accordance with the Qabbalistic Tree of Life. The average person only 'contains' the lunar vehicles of emotion (Astral body), thought (Mental Body), and will (Causal Body), concentrations of the collective animalistic intelligence, and the evolution of the Essence through the mineral, plant, and animal kingdoms. Becoming fully consciously human entails acquiring a Soul, a Solar Astral body, Solar Mental Body, and Solar Causal Body.

Barbara Ann Brennan (b.1939) is an American author, physicist, spiritual healer, businesswoman, and teacher working in the field of energy healing. Her first book, *Hands of Light: A Guide to Healing Through the Human Energy Field*[41] is considered a classic in the field of spiritual healing, with reputedly over one million copies in print in twenty-two languages. Brennan claims to receive intuitive information about her clients during sessions, and to see repetitive patterns in their energy fields, indicating common roots underlying their difficulties. Her books contain drawings of auras and energy fields, and descriptions of how human energy fields interact with each other. She has popularized a seven-layer model of the energy field, each layer being structured of differing frequencies and kinds of energy and performing different functions. Brennan views the *cākras* as transformers that receive and process universal energy, as well as enabling expression and healthy functioning of the individual's own consciousness and psycho-physical make-up. She is best known for taking a methodical approach to energy healing—to be expected from a trained scientist.[42] This has particular application to a type of energy healing technique that she has created, which she calls 'full spectrum healing'. This enables healing to be carried out on the seven layers of the human energy field, or aura.

In her second book *Light Emerging*,[43] Brennan added the dimension of 'intentionality' called 'hara' to her model of human subtle energies. The hara is the foundation for the human energy field. Because of this relationship, healing the hara is considered especially powerful for healing the auric field and, thereby, the Physical body. Hara is said to hold the human body in material manifestation until the *life purpose* is fulfilled, for only when man begins to act, think, feel, and 'be' in accordance with the unchanging and unchangeable divine laws which pervade and regulate all things, in the visible as well as the invisible worlds, does his psyche permit spiritual energy to flow through from hidden depths. When the hara is healthy, the individual acts naturally and effortlessly to fulfil his or her life purpose.

Healing, energy fields, and subtle bodies

There are several examples of those who have attained their life purpose and therefore seem to have easy access to massive reserves of physical energy and endurance lasting until a ripe old age. Amongst musicians, two cases that immediately spring to mind are the Polish born pianist Artur Rubinstein (1887–1982) who actively performed until the age of ninety, and the Argentinian conductor–pianist and philanthropist Daniel Barenboim (b.1942) who, in his early seventies, conducted Wagner's *Der Ring des Nibelungen* (The Ring Cycle) of four operas, comprising over fifteen hours of music in less than a week at the Henry Wood Promenade Concerts in 2013. In the case of social reformers, glowing examples are Annie Besant and Mahatma Gandhi who worked tirelessly in arduous circumstances to alleviate the poverty and suffering amongst the poor in India.

In her books *Hands of Light* and *Light Emerging*, Brennan refers to the subtle bodies as 'layers' in the human energy field. Causality proceeds downwards: each of the layers has its own characteristics and can have its own expression of disease, requiring individual healing. As with the general Theosophical teachings, each body, or aura, also has its own complement of cākras, which interrelate to those in the other layers.

Finally, mention must be made of the English chiropractor David V. Tansley (1934–1988), also a lecturer and Vice President of the British Radionics Association. He was a colleague of the English radionics[vii] pioneer George de la Warr (1904–1969), who founded the De La Warr Laboratories in Oxford, and several other distinguished complementary therapists like the prominent British lay homœopath and teacher John DaMonte (1916–1976), Thomas Galen Hieronymus (1895–1988), known as the father of American psionics,[viii] who patented radionics devices based on sympathetic vibratory physics, and Ruth Drown (1891–1965), the American chiropractic and proponent of radionics.

Tansley spent many years researching Eastern wisdom and studying Alice Bailey. His book *Subtle Bodies*[44] is especially noteworthy regarding its excellent illustrations combined with a clear understanding of how the wisdom of the East can be brought to bear upon an understanding of the subtle bodies of the human being.

Commentary

There is considerable merit in later expositions generally in line with the Theosophical doctrines, especially in cases where the latter have focussed on aspects of esoteric healing and associated knowledge about the cākras and human aura. Whereas all the above mentioned authors, and several others besides, do acknowledge their debt to Blavatsky and the Theosophical Society, their teachings are, generally speaking, more experientially orientated, and also more personally tailored to the ideas of the individual exponents. This writer has no issue with that: but there is more than a hint from such teachers claiming that their version happens to be the best and most up to date account of the ancient wisdom tradition. Thus there is a certain element of humility lacking.

The need for humility

Blavatsky, on the other hand, opens Volume II of her monumental work, *The Secret Doctrine*, with the following words:

> Ἡ ἐμὴ διδαχὴ οὐκ ἔστιν ἐμὴ, ἀλλὰ τοῦ πέμψαντός με·
> [*Eh eme didache ouk estin eme, alla tou pemphantos me*]
> 'My doctrine is not mine, but his that sent me.'
> — *John*, vii, 16, King James Bible

It would be hard to find a more sincere and open confession of debt and gratitude. Clearly, Blavatsky recognised that what she bequeathed to the world was not her invention but what she had been taught by her Adept instructors of immensely superior spiritual status and occult standing than herself.

---

vii Radionics is a branch of complementary medicine that diagnoses and heals by applying appropriate frequencies to balance the discordant energy frequencies of sickness. Unsurprisingly, it is discounted by orthodox medicine.

viii Psionics is a branch of complementary medicine whereby the trained practitioner is able to establish, by dowsing a blood or hair sample, which miasms (infectious or noxious influences) affect the patient and which compound homœopathic remedy will exactly neutralize them. Like radionics, it is not given any credence by orthodox medicine.

It would be good, therefore, to see these later exponents of Theosophy—as indeed all who write and teach the *philosophia perennis*—openly acknowledging that they too were 'standing on the shoulders of giants'.[ix]

Parallels with the Eastern Doctrines

This section compares and corroborates the core occult doctrine on man's constitution and nature with the systems representing the foremost occult schools of the East. The latter can be categorized broadly into two groups: (*a*) the Buddhist and Vedantic systems of India; and (*b*) the Egyptian and Zarathuśtrian (Zoroastrian) systems, which are also presented for comparative purposes alongside the Indian systems considered in general terms.

Indian Systems – Buddhist, Vedānta, and Tāraka Rāja-Yoga

This section provides more details on the Mystery Teachings of the Indians on man's composition, summarized earlier in Volume I, Chapter 9. The different Indian teachings comprise: (*a*) the classification in the book *Esoteric Buddhism*; and (*b*) the Vedantic classification, which includes the Tāraka Rāja-Yoga classification, being one of the Brahmanical Yoga systems for the development of purely spiritual powers and knowledge which lead to Nirvāna (the state of absolute consciousness as well as absolute existence, entered into by one who has attained the highest degree of holiness and perfection). The comparative Table II-20 on page 169 shows the classifications from these three esoteric schools alongside the core occult doctrine on the constitution of man disseminated through the instrumentality of modern Theosophy (reproduced from Table II-3 on page 21).

The Esoteric Buddhist Classification

The term 'Esoteric Buddhism' is liable to cause much confusion because this term is used in two different contexts. In explanation: first, the term happens to be the title of the book by A. P. Sinnett;[45] however, in the Preface to the Annotated Edition of the said book (pp. v–vi) it is stated that 'the name of "Esoteric Buddhism" was given to Mr. Sinnett's latest publication, not because the doctrine propounded therein is meant to be specifically identified with any particular form of faith, but because *Buddhism* means the doctrine of the *Buddhas*, the wise, i.e. the Wisdom Religion.' What this means is that the Esoteric Buddhism classification presented in Table II-20 pertains to the teachings of 'the wise' of any faith, including, of course Buddhism. It is important to note that Budha (spelt with only one *d*) signifies a wise man, a sage (belonging to any faith); whereas Buddha (spelt with two *d*'s) designates the status of the awakened and the illumined one, like Gautama. (The associated term 'Buddhi', derived from *budh* 'to awaken', 'to perceive', was defined in Chapter 2.)

The meaning of 'Esoteric Buddhism'

———

ix This famous expression is credited to Newton's letter to Hooke in 1676: 'If I have seen further, it is by standing on the shoulders of giants'. See 'Letter from Sir Isaac Newton to Robert Hooke', *Historical Society of Pennsylvania*, Simon Gratz collection [0250A], Box/Case: 12/11, Folder: 37. Newton's 'giants' were Pythagoras, Plato and indeed the initiates and adepts of the *prisca sapientia* tradition.

The classification of *Esoteric Buddhism*, shown in the fifth column of Table II-20, has been taken (in reverse order of enumeration for consistency with this Chapter) from *Esoteric Writings*[46] by the learned Vedantin scholar T. Subba Row (mentioned earlier in Chapter 1). Owing to its seminal value it is shown in Blavatsky's *The Secret Doctrine*[47] reprinted from *The Theosophist* of Madras,[48] and also included in *Five Years of Theosophy*[49] by G. R. S. Mead (1863–1933), an English historian, writer, and an influential member of the Theosophical Society, as well as the founder of the Quest Society. It is certainly representative of 'the "time-honoured" classification of the trans-Himālayan "Arhat Esoteric School"'.[50]

A venerable classification

The Vedantic and Brahmanical Classifications

The Vedantic and Tāraka Rāja-Yoga classifications are shown in the sixth and last column of Table II-20, respectively.

There is little merit in expounding each of the three Indian classifications in turn—rather, we treat these systems as a whole, and deal with points of general importance primarily in order to show their overall agreement with the core occult doctrines described in Chapters 2 and 3. The following exposition is based on a digest of the four sources as referenced.[51, 52, 53, 54]

In general, the *Esoteric Buddhism* and Tāraka Rāja-Yoga classifications deal with principles (the active agents), whereas the Vedantic classification is from the standpoint of planes (the passive forms as the vehicles for the action and expression of the active principles)— refer to the definitions and associated explanations given in Chapter 1, page 5 of the difference between principles and planes.

From Table II-20, it will be seen that the Vedantic classification enumerates only five principles, in addition to *Ātma*. This is because the Vedantins regard man essentially as that compound of spiritual aggregates consisting of various mental aspects, the Physical body being, in their view, merely an illusion. The fifth principle (counting from Ātma) in the *Esoteric Buddhism* classification (Vehicle of Prāṇa) is not separately mentioned in the Vedantic classification (which deals with the forms, or 'subtle bodies' of the active principles), hence classifies *Prāṇamaya-kośa* as the 'Sheath of Life', which includes *Prāṇa* and the Vehicle of Prāṇa in the *Esoteric Buddhism* classification (see the lower braced principles under the Vedantic classification). The fourth *kośa* of the Vedantins (*Manomaya-kośa*) includes the fourth principle of the *Esoteric Buddhism* classification (*Kāma-rūpa*) as this principle is the vehicle of will power, which is but an energy of the mind. As seen again by the upper braced principles under the Vedantic classification in Table II-20, the Manomaya-kośa also includes the 'lower part' (concerning volitions and feelings, etc.) of the third principle of the *Esoteric Buddhism* classification (Mind), clearly showing that this kośa is the the Lower mind, Desire-driven thought, or *Kāma-manas*.

Vedānta and Esoteric Buddhism systems

Notice also that in the Vedantic system, *Vijñānamaya-kośa* (the 'Sheath of Intelligence', or the Higher Mind) is considered to be distinct from the Manomaya-kośa (the 'Sheath of the Lower mind', or the Lower mind), as a division is made after death between the 'lower part' of the Mind (i.e., the Lower mind) which has a closer affinity with Kāma-rūpa, the desire nature (the fourth *Esoteric Buddhism* principle) than its 'higher part' (i.e., the Higher Mind) which attaches itself to the Spiritual Soul (the second *Esoteric Buddhism* principle)

Table II-20   Parallels with the Indian Teachings

Dual Constitution	Triple Constitution	Septenary Constitution	Classification in *Esoteric Buddhism*	Vedānta Classification*	Tāraka Rāja-Yoga Classification
Individuality or Higher Self (Immortal)	Spirit	*Ātma* the **Divine Self**	*Ātma*	*Ātma*	*Ātma*
	Soul	*Buddhi* the **Intuition Principle** — Higher	Spiritual Soul	*Ānandamaya-kośa* the 'Sheath of Bliss'	*Kāraṇopādhi* the 'Causal Body'
		Manas the **Mind Principle** — Lower	Mind (a) *Vijñāna* / (b) Volitions and feelings, etc.	*Vijñānamaya-kośa* the 'Sheath of Intelligence' / *Manomaya-kośa* the 'Sheath of the Lower mind'	*Sūkṣmopādhi* the 'Subtile Vehicle'
Personality or Lower self (mortal)		*Kāma* the **Desire principle**	*Kāma-rūpa*		
		Prāṇa the **Life principle**	The Vehicle of *Prāṇa* (Astral body, or *Liṅga-śarīra*)	*Prāṇamaya-kośa* the 'Sheath of Life'	
		Liṅga-śarīra the **Etheric double**	*Prāṇa*		
	Body	*Sthūla-śarīra*, or *Rūpa* the **Physical body**	*Sthūla-śarīra*	*Annamaya-kośa* the 'Sheath built of food'	*Sthūlopādhi* the 'Physical Vehicle'

MAN AS ONE UNIFIED ENTITY

Reproduced from **Table II-3**

*Note that in the Vedānta classification, the infix *maya* means 'made of' and is not the same as *māyā* (illusion).

which constitutes the basis for the Individuality, or Higher Self of man. This is also Plato's teaching as Emerson realized—see Volume I, Chapter 9 and the Recapitulation. What does Plato actually say?

He explains that the Soul, *psyche*, has two choices: either to aspire to *Nous* (divine spirit or substance), whereupon everything is done rightly and joyously; or else to get entangled with, and face, the unhappy consequences of such attachment with *Anoia*, the irrational, Animal soul.[55] We have merely to substitute *Nous* for the Spiritual Soul and *Anoia* for Kāma-rūpa to see that the Greek and Indian systems are fully in agreement about the dual nature of Mind—again reinforcing our recurrent theme about the self-consistency of the Wisdom Religion, the *philosophia perennis*, whether from the Occident or the Orient, either ancient or modern. Readers are asked to refer back to the more detailed occult exposition given in Chapter 3 about the double nature of the Mind Principle.

Plato's teaching in consonance with Eastern doctrines

The classification mentioned in the last column of Table II-20, page 169 is, for all practical purposes, the best and simplest classification connected with Raja Yoga. In addition to *Ātma*, this system enumerates three principles. However, their *Sthūlopadhi*, or the Physical vehicle (body) in its state of waking consciousness, their *Sūkṣmopadhi*, or Subtle vehicle, being the same body in *Svapna*, or the dreaming state, and their *Kāraṇopādhi*, or Causal Body, are all *dual* in aspect, and thus make six. Add to this Ātma, the impersonal divine principle, or the immortal element in man, undistinguished from the Universal Spirit, and seven principles are obtained. Hence, as previously explained in Chapter 3 regarding the *Upādhis*, 'though there are seven principles in man, there are but three distinct Upādhis [bases] in each of which his *Ātman* may work independently of the rest.'[56] Thus in the Tāraka Rāja-Yoga classification, the Sūkṣmopadhi (Subtle Vehicle) is equivalent to the Vedantic Vijñānamaya-kośa and Manomaya-kośa (shown by the middle braced kośas in the Tāraka Rāja-Yoga classification); in other words, the higher intellectual (*Vijñāna*) and the desire-seeking Lower mind are classified into one upādhi; while the Sthūlopadhi (the Physical Vehicle) includes the Vedantic Prāṇamaya-kośa and *Annamaya-kośa* (see the lower braced kośas in the Tāraka Rāja-Yoga classification). The latter term is derived from *anna*, meaning food, because this is the body which is sustained by food in the form of breakfast, lunch, and dinner; whereas the Manomaya-kośa (Lower Mental Body) is sustained by 'food' in the form of desires, emotions, and concrete thoughts.

Tāraka Rāja-Yoga system

To reiterate what was stated in Chapter 4 regarding the 'Causal Body', or that which subsists from one incarnation to another, 'this "body", which is [in fact] no body either objective or subjective, but *Buddhi*, the Spiritual Soul. It is called *Kāraṇopādhi*, "the basis of the Cause", by the Tāraka Rāja Yogis; and in the Vedānta system it corresponds to both the *Vijñānamaya-kośa* and *Ānandamaya-kośa* [see the upper braced kośas in the Tāraka Rāja-Yoga classification], the latter coming next to Ātma, and therefore being the vehicle of the universal Spirit. Buddhi alone could not be called a "Causal Body", but becomes so in conjunction with Manas, the incarnating Entity or Ego [Higher Ego].'[57]

We can now appreciate that there is a major overlap and no intrinsic difference between the three Upādhis of the Tāraka Rāja-Yoga system and its Ātma, and the core occult system with its three Upādhis, plus Ātma and additional three divisions. 'Thus, it matters very little whether one speaks of the *three Upādhis with their three aspects* and Ātman, the eternal and immortal synthesis, or calls them the "seven principles".'[58] We are informed that

Table II-21 Parallels with the Vedantic and Tāraka Rāja-Yoga Systems

Twofold Division	Quintuple Division	Septenary Classification	Vedantic Classification	Tāraka Rāja-Yoga Classification
		Functioning Principles		
The Spiritual Man	The Divine	*Ātma(n)*	*Ātma*	*Ātma*
		Hiraṇyagarbha		
	The Spiritual	*Ātma-Buddhi* the Monad		
		Buddhi-Manas	*Ānandamaya-kośa* the 'Sheath of Bliss'	*Kāraṇopādhi* the 'Causal Body'
	The Intellectual, or Mental	*Manas-Manas*	*Vijñānamaya-kośa* the 'Sheath of Intelligence'	*Sūkṣmopadhi*
The Animal Man		*Manas-kāma* or *Kāma-manas*	*Manomaya-kośa* the 'Sheath of the Lower mind'	the 'Subtile Vehicle'
	The Astral	*Prāṇa–Liṅga-śarīra*	*Prāṇamaya-kośa* the 'Sheath of Life'	*Sthūlopadhi*
		Kāma–Prāṇa–Sthūla-śarīra		
	The Physical	*Prāṇa–Liṅga-śarīra– Sthūla-śarīra*	*Annamaya-kośa* the 'Sheath built of food'	the 'Physical Vehicle'

(Side label, vertical: MAN AS A UNIFIED ENERGY-ENTITY, OR BEING)

Reproduced from Table II-5 on page 40

'these three Upādhis can be separated by an Adept without killing himself. [But] he cannot separate the seven principles from each other without destroying his constitution.'[59]

For completeness, a comparison of the septenary classification of man's nature (how he functions) taken from Table II-5 on page 40 is set against the Vedantic and Tāraka Rāja-Yoga classifications in Table II-21 above. The congruence between the various systems is again clear. Especially noteworthy is that Vijñāna signifies intellection, intelligence, understanding; and in some Vedantic schools of thought it is regarded as distinct from *jñāna*, 'true knowledge'. All the same, a distinction may readily be made, as explained earlier in Chapter 3, Table II-5, and plainly seen in Table II-21 by dividing 'knowledge' into the three categories of:

1. 'enlightened knowledge': Buddhi-Manas, Ānandamaya-kośa;

2. 'book knowledge', or intellection: Manas-Manas, Vijñānamaya-kośa;

3. 'knowledge driven by desire' (or 'desire disciplined by knowledge'): Kāma-manas (or Manas-kāma), Manomaya-kośa, Lower manas. It is Lower manas (the Lower mind) in conjunction with the Astral and the Physical (see the braced principles in Table II-20) that fashions the Personality—the individual who lives on Earth. This fact is considerably elaborated in the Coda by way of a simile with daily existence. Meanwhile, readers should also consult Table II-6, page 42 in Chapter 3 for more details about the three divisions of knowledge summarized above.

Three ways of knowing

Zarathuśtrian and Egyptian Teachings and their Corroboration with the Indian Teachings

A comparison of the teachings of the Egyptians[60] and Zarathuśtrians (Zoroastrians)[61] of the ancient Persian Empire and their overlap with the Indians[62] is shown in Table II-22 on the next page. The parallels between these systems and their corroboration with the core occult doctrine disseminated through the instrumentality of modern Theosophy shown in the first four columns of the table is striking, given that they stem from three different cultures widely spread across two continents—Africa and Asia.

The congruence between the Egyptian and Indian systems is highlighted by the common function associated with each equivalent term in the septenary classification. This is shown in Table II-22 by the horizontal inward pointing arrows to their respective common functions (shown in the seventh column), from the Egyptian system (in the sixth column) and the Indian system (in the eighth column). Thus, in view of the sophistication of the Egyptian and Indian systems, and considering the similarity of their doctrines on the post-mortem states, it is not surprising to see the subdivision of the Desire principle, Kāma, into the 'astral soul' and the post-mortem shade (shell) for the Egyptians corresponding to *Jiv-aṇu* and Kāma-rūpa for the Indians. The relative insignificance ascribed to the Physical body by the Egyptians and Indians is due to the form of gross matter not being regarded as a principle as such, but a cadaver, or container, of the higher principles.

The Zarathuśtrian classification is taken from the sacred liturgical texts of the *Zend-Avesta* (Zoroastrian scriptures), in particular, Yasna, Chapter 26, para 6 and Yasna, Chapter 54, para 1. The similarities of the Egyptian and Indian systems with the Zarathuśtrian occult doctrine speak for themselves, reinforcing our central theme about the unity of the *philosophia perennis*. But attention is drawn to *Daena*, the link between the personality and the Individuality. In so forming the connection between the lower and the higher triad, and after the death of the personality appears to it as an objectivized form of its own experiences, Daena corresponds to *Antaḥkaraṇa*, the Sanskrit term in Indian occultism for the bridge between the animal and spiritual aspects of man (see the last column of Table II-5 in Chapter 3). Readers are also referred to Chapter 5 on its function regarding post-mortem transitional states of consciousness. Furthermore, the fivefold classification of Yasna, given in Chapter 26, is also to be found in the Vedānta (see Table II-20 and Table II-21 earlier), and the *Tao-te-King* by Lao-Tze, who omits Ātma (presumably taking it for granted) and, like the Vedantins, regards the Physical body as what he calls 'the cadaver'.[63]

The Zarathuśtrian classification shown in Table II-22 is noteworthy, chiefly because the occult doctrines of this once magnificent religion which seeded Christianity, but which is now a minority sect, are entirely in harmony with those of other great religions. The following is an amplification of the section on 'Persian Teachings – Mithraism and Zarathuśtrianism' from Chapter 9, page 267 of Volume I.[64]

The Zarathuśtrian religion is regarded by many as essentially dualistic. This is simply not so. In the Zend tradition, the so-called opposites, *Ahura-Mazda* (later *Ormuzd*), the Supreme Being and *Angra-Mainyush* (later *Ahriman*), the hostile, or evil spirit, are *not* two fundamentally opposing beings. From Ahura-Mazda, in turn, arises the two primeval spirits—the duality of *Spento-Mainyush* and *Angra-Manyush*: the former is the 'Good Twin' and thus stands for 'Good Thought', or 'Expansive Thought' (from the Avestan

Table II-22 Parallels with the Egyptian, Indian, and Zarathuśtrian Classification

Dual Constitution	Triple Constitution	Septenary Constitution	Egyptian Hieroglyphic Names	Egyptian Version	→ function	Indian Version (generic)	Zarathuśtrian (Zoroastrian) Sevenfold (Yasna 54)	Fivefold (Yasna Ch. 26)
Individuality or Higher Self (Immortal)	Spirit	Ātma the Divine Self	Chu the Divine Spirit	Atmu	a divine or eternal Intelligence	Ātma(n)		Frawashem, or Farohar — Spirit, or guiding energy, completely independent of worldly objects. The spark of divinity in every being
		Buddhi the Intuition Principle	Cheybi the Spiritual Soul	Putah	the principle of Reason	Buddhi		Urwanem — Human Soul, which gets its 'reward' or 'punishment' after death
				Seb	the ancestral Identity	S(h)abda the 'Word' or 'Vehicle' of Divine Intent		
	Soul	Manas the Mind Principle (Higher / Lower)	Bai the Rational Soul	Akh(u)	the (dualistic) perceiving Intelligence	Manas the (personal) reincarnating 'Ego'	Baodhas — Body of physical consciousness, perception by the senses or the Animal soul	Daena – the link between the Lower Quaternary (personality) and the Higher Triad (Individuality)
Personality or Lower self (mortal)		Kāma the Desire principle	Abhati the Animal soul, or feeling principle	Kha-Ba	the (post-mortem) shade	Kāma-rūpa	Tevishis — Will, or where sentient consciousness is formed, also foreknowledge	Ahu — the personality in incarnation, the Lower self with its quaternary principles
		Prāṇa the Life principle	Ankh Vitality, the Life principle, Prāṇa	Ba	the 'astral' soul	Jiv-aṇu	Keherpas (see Note) — Aerial form, the airy mould	
		Liṅga-śarīra the Etheric double	Ka the Protean 'double'	Kha	the 'presence', or 'breath'	Jiva	Ushtanas (see Note) — Vital heat (or force)	
				Ka	the (Etheric) 'double'	Kaya/Liṅga-śarīra		
	Body	Sthūla-śarīra, or Rūpa the Physical body	Chat the Dense Physical body form				Tanwas — Body that consists of bones – grossest form of matter	

Man as One Unified Entity

Reproduced from Table II-3

Note: The classification of *Ushtanas* and *Keherpa*, as stated in Yasna Chapter 54, would appear on first sight to be a reversal of the ordering of the Life-force (*Prāṇa*) and the Etheric double (*Liṅga-śarīra*) in the occult (Theosophical) classification shown in the fourth column. However there is no real inconsistency between the two systems and hair-splitting taxonomy would be quite inappropriate regarding two such closely coupled principles. In fact, according to the Avestan scriptures, the ordering of *Keherpas* and *Ushtanas* corresponds exactly with the early Theosophical literature—see the classification of the Mahatma Letters and *Esoteric Buddhism* in Table II-14, page 152, sixth column.

span 'increase', or 'prosper' and *man* 'mind', 'thought'); and the latter is the 'Evil Twin' and so stands for 'Evil Thought', or 'Constrictive Thought' (from *ang* 'decrease', or 'destroy' + *man*). Regarding man, this is the great truth concerning the dual, or twin-nature of Mind. These twins govern the nature of the one human mind and move a man to good or to evil in thought, word, and deed. The double nature of the Mind Principle, i.e., *Buddhi-Manas* and *Kāma-manas*, is a cardinal tenet of the occult doctrine (see Chapters 2 and 3) and is explicitly taught in the Zarathuśtrian religion in its esoteric import. Naturally, therefore, we see clear parallels with the occult teaching of other world systems (such as the Greeks) as shown in the several tables in this Chapter.

Spento-Mainyush and Angra-Mainyush are thus impersonal, universal, and omnipotent forces—centripetal and centrifugal. In man, they characterize the good and the evil in the mind and psyche, as just said. But in a universal sense, they are the equivalent of *Puruśa* (Consciousness) and *Prakṛiti* (Matter) of Indian Sāṁkhya philosophy. Out of the twin, *born of the One*, emanate the seven hierarchies of spiritual intelligence and the seven material kingdoms of nature. Just as 'Light and darkness are the world's eternal ways' (*Bhagavad Gītā*, VII), so do Spento-Mainyush and Angra-Mainyush commence, sustain, and renovate the cycle of necessity, Ahura-Mazda Himself being the primal expression thereof. These two, the centripetal and centrifugal forces, respectively, are the basis of the universe. They cause manifestation and dissolution. As with Satan, the Devil of the orthodox Christians, Ahriman has been anthropomorphized into a living, personified, evil entity by some superstitious Parsis[x] and those who take metaphysical truths in a literal sense.

Then there are those who are so preoccupied with the mundane affairs and practicalities of life as to be quite disinterested in such matters without clear proof—in their terms. The philosopher and sage Phiroz Mehta has this witty piece of advice for 'those who say, "Show me God and the Devil in flesh and blood and I'll believe in them."' Quoted in Volume I, Chapter 9, it is worth repeating: 'Quite easily done. Look at yourself in a mirror. If you have clear-seeing eyes and a sound brain to interpret what you see, you will see both God and the Devil—and remember: Truth is not facetious!'[65] Esoterically, then, and in truth, Ahriman is but a force within each man—his own lower nature, i.e., Kāma, or personal and material desires. What differs between a good person and an offender is the proportion in him of 'God' to 'Devil', but not the fact of each. Only in the Perfected Holy Ones, known as prophets and saints, sages and rishis (Zarathuśtra, Buddha, the Christ, Ramana Maharshi, for example), has the 'Devil' been totally expunged, or rather, completely absorbed into the spiritual nature.

Parallels with the Western Doctrines

Throughout this work it has been emphasized that wisdom and occult knowledge are man's universal birthright and not just the prerogative of the East, which is still a common misperception. Accordingly, the major Western schools of esotericism represented in this section are:

---

x 'Parsis', whose name means 'Persians', are the followers of the Zoroastrian religion. They are a community descended from the Persian Zoroastrians who emigrated to India to avoid religious persecution in the wake of the Islamic invasion of Iran in the tenth century.

❖ The philosophy of the Greeks
❖ The Fourth Way School of Gurdjieff and Ouspensky
❖ The Anthroposophical doctrines of Rudolf Steiner
❖ The modern transpersonal psychology of Ken Wilber.

Corroboration with the Greek and Pauline Traditions

Table II-23 on page 179 displays a comparison of the core occult doctrine alongside the teachings of the Greeks, of Saint Paul, and the bearing of astrology on the human condition according to Plutarch. It represents a follow-on to the Mystery Teachings of the Greeks and Early Christians on man's composition, summarized in Volume I, Chapter 9, page 262.

Greek Teachings

The first column of Table II-23 shows the core occult doctrine (taken from Table II-3, page 21) as the benchmark for a comparison with the Greek teachings shown in the next six columns. The second column shows the Greek system in general, and it is evident that it is fully compatible with the occult doctrine on the sevenfold constitution of man. Such harmony between the two systems is hardly surprising since, as repeatedly stressed, the occult system as disclosed through the instrumentality of modern Theosophy represents the distillation of esoteric and initiatic teachings (of what could lawfully be divulged) of all religions, philosophies, and sciences of all nations since time immemorial, *based on eternal verities*. Note that in this general classification, the term *Psyche*, or Soul, is used in *a collective and general* sense. In this wise it corresponds to the Spiritual Soul, i.e., Buddhi of the occult system—see Chapter 3, Table II-7 on page 44.

Establishing the basis for comparison

The third column of Table II-23 shows the famous Platonic division of the Principles of Man, a scheme to which Socrates also subscribed. Plato 'regarded man as constituted of two parts—one eternal, formed of the same essence as Absoluteness, the other mortal and corruptible, deriving its constituent parts from the *minor* "created" Gods.' These 'two parts' were composed of three elements, namely: '(1) a mortal body, (2) an immortal principle [*Nous*], and (3) a "separate mortal kind of Soul" [*psyche*].'[66]

Plato and Socrates

This equates perfectly with the occult teaching shown in the first column of Table II-23. Plato's 'two parts'[xi] are found in the Upper Triad, and the Lower Quaternary. Moreover, his 'three elements' correspond to the occult division of: (*a*) Physical man (body); (*b*) the Spiritual Soul (Spirit); and (*c*) the Animal soul (see again Table II-7, page 44). Furthermore, *Agathon*, or Plato's Supreme Deity, fully accords with Ātma. It becomes apparent that Plato, and indeed Pythagoras, while speaking of three such 'principles', gives them seven separate functions. In other words, we find the seven
in the various combinations of Soul and Spirit, reminding ourselves of Plato's seminal teaching: 'when the Soul, *psyche*, "allies herself to the *Nous* (divine spirit or substance), she does everything aright and felicitously"; but the case is otherwise when

---

xi The inverted commas used here to make the point that the soul cannot be divided into discrete parts. The 'two parts' are of course two *functioning aspects* corresponding to *Nous* and *Anoia*, the Higher Mind and the Lower mind (see Table II-6 in Chapter 3, page 42).

Plato and the
occult teaching
on the Human
Soul as dweller in
the midst

she attaches herself to *Anoia* (folly, or the irrational animal Soul).'[67] Nous and Anoia
are clearly the equivalent of Spento-Mainyush and Angra-Mainyush in the Zarathuśtrian
teaching—see page 174.

So here we have the supreme occult teaching on the dual nature of Manas, or the Human
Soul in general: where on the one hand, Manas can rise to ally itself with Ātma-Buddhi
(Nous) to merge into the immortal, imperishable Ego (whereupon its spiritual consciousness of the personal existence that *was*, becomes immortal); or else Manas can descend
and become identified with Kāma (Anoia), the desire-driven Animal soul, and run
towards entire annihilation (as far as the Personal ego is concerned, as clearly shown in
Table II-23). The fact that Manas, which means, literally, 'Mind', is referred to as the
'Human Soul', should not cause any confusion. The section entitled 'Soul – A Conveyor',
referred to early in Chapter 3, explains that when a principle functions as a vehicle, it is
referred to as 'a soul', which is a generic term. In this case the Mind Principle functions as
the vehicle for the Monad; hence it is termed the Human Soul; additionally, because Mind
is involved, it is the Human Ego (see Table II-8 on page 46).

As an aside, writing in *The Spectator* (15 January 1977), the English Nobel physiologist
and biologist Sir Peter Medawar (1915–1987) glowingly approves of how Richard
Dawkins summarizes his position in the Preface to his famous book *The Selfish Gene*
(Oxford University Press, 1st edition, 1976). Dawkins posits that we humans are nothing
more, or other, than animals, essentially disposable survival machines, existing in order
to preserve the genes that made us. It becomes obvious in which direction the Simonyi
Professor for the Public Understanding of Science at Oxford University (1995–2008)[xii]
and his advocate are heading, and also our own fate, should we choose to subscribe to
their sterile conjectures.

But to continue, Pythagoras described the Soul as a self-moving Unit (monad)
composed of three elements: *Nous*; *Phren*; and *Thumos*, as shown in the fourth column
of Table II-23. This is basically the same as Plato's ideas just stated. Recalling again
Table II-7 on page 44, these three elements correspond to the occult teaching on:
(*a*) *Ātma-Buddhi* (Ātma with its vehicle, the Spiritual Soul); (*b*) *Manas*, the Human *thinking*
Soul, or Human Ego; and (*c*) *Kāma*, the Animal soul, in conjunction with the *lower* reflection
of Manas (the kamic principle acting through the vehicle of the subjective form created by
the mental and physical desires, known as the *Māyāvi-rūpa* during life, from which is formed
the *Kāma-rūpa* after physical death—see Table II-5 on page 40). Like Plato, Pythagoras also
allocated the soul into two parts: rational and irrational (see the quote above).

Turning to Anaxagoras, his essential teaching (quoted in part at the opening of Chapter 1)
is encapsulated in the fifth column of Table II-23. Summarized by Blavatsky: 'The Egyptians
revered the "One-Only-One," as *Nout*; and it is from this word that Anaxagoras got his
denomination *Nous* or, as he calls it, *Nous autokrates*, "the Mind or Spirit Self-potent," the
archetes kinedeos, the leading motor, or *primum-mobile* of all. With him the *Nous* was God,
and the *logos* was man, his emanation. The *Nous* is the spirit (whether in Kosmos or in

---

xii The Simonyi Professorship for the Public Understanding of Science is a chair at the University of Oxford.
The chair was established in 1995 for Richard Dawkins by an endowment from the Hungarian-born
American software executive and space tourist Charles Simonyi (*b*.1948). The aim of the Professorship is 'to
communicate science to the public without, in doing so, losing those elements of scholarship which constitute
the essence of true understanding.'

man), and the *logos*, whether Universe or [the human] astral body, the emanation of the former, the physical body being merely the animal [aspect of man]. Our external powers perceive *phenomena*; our *Nous* alone is able to recognise their *noumena*. It is the logos alone, or the *noumenon*, that survives, because it is immortal in its very nature and essence, and the *logos* in man is the Eternal Ego, that which reincarnates and lasts for ever [see Chapter 3, Table II-8 on page 46].'[68]

Anaxagoras on *Nous*

Our Higher Self alone can discern the underlying causes which our lower faculties feel as the effects.

Anaxagoras thus gave out an instruction of seminal importance: that our *Nous* alone is capable of recognizing the underlying and hidden causes (*noumena*) of what our external senses can perceive but the effects (phenomena).

Empedocles and Aristotle on souls

Empedocles firmly believed that all men and animals possessed two souls. So also did Aristotle refer to two souls: one, the reasoning soul, *nous*; and the other, the Animal soul, *psuche*,[xiii] which men shared with the brutes—see the sixth column of Table II-23. According to these philosophers, the reasoning soul comes from *within* the universal soul, and the other from *without*.

Finally we turn to Plutarch's teaching shown in the seventh column of Table II-23. Like Plato and Pythagoras, he regarded man—an emanation of the Supreme Deity—as constituted of the three elements and his soul made up of two parts: (*a*) the rational, or Spiritual Soul (noetic); (*b*) the instinctual, or irrational soul (*Agnoia*); and (*c*) the body composed of the breath, astral shadow, and physical frame.

In *Moralia, Volume XII: Concerning the Face Which Appears in the Orb of the Moon* Plutarch succinctly encapsulates his teaching on the incorruptible (immortal) and corruptible (mortal) aspects of man thus:

> Man is compound; and they are *mistaken who think him to be compounded of two parts only*. For they imagine that the understanding (brain intellect) is a part of the soul (the upper Triad), but they err in this no less than those who make the soul to be a part of the body, *i.e.*, those who make of the *Triad* part of the corruptible mortal *quaternary*. For the understanding (nous) so far exceeds the soul as the soul is better and diviner than the body. Now this composition of the soul (ψυχή) [*psuche*] with the understanding (νοῦς) [*nous*] makes reason; and with the body (or thumos, the animal soul) passion; of which the one is the beginning or principle of pleasure and pain, and the other of virtue and vice. Of these three parts conjoined and compacted together, the earth has given the body, the moon the soul, and the sun the understanding to the generation of man.[69]

Plutarch on man compounded of three parts

Plutarch clearly points out the common error (prevalent even to this day amongst those who are not ultra-materialists) of regarding man as 'compounded of two parts only', namely, spirit and body, and neglecting soul. Note carefully, however, that it is entirely legitimate, from a different standpoint, to divide man into the 'two parts' of the Individuality (i.e., the upper triad displaying his spiritual qualities) and the personality (i.e., the lower quaternary exhibiting his animal and physical propensities).

Accordingly, Plutarch affirms:

---

xiii *Psuche* (not to be confused with *psyche*) is the vital force which animates the body and shows itself in breathing. It is akin to prāṇa.

Plato and Pythagoras distribute the soul into two parts, the rational (noetic) and the irrational (agnoia); that that part of the soul of man which is rational is eternal; *for though it
be not God, yet it is the product of an eternal deity*, but that part of the soul which is divested
of reason (agnoia) dies [emphasis added].[70]

However, these 'two parts' are *compounded* of at least three parts, which may be further
subdivided according to a sevenfold classification as shown in Table II-23 opposite.

Teaching of Saint Paul

The penultimate column of Table II-23 shows that Saint Paul also adopted the same
division as Plato described above. As mentioned earlier, Paul taught the familiar threefold division of the constitution of man into Spirit (Spiritual Soul), Soul (Animal soul,
or Astral body), and body (Physical, or Animal body). He maintained that 'there is a
psychical body which is sown in the corruptible (astral soul or body), and a *spiritual*
body that is raised in incorruptible substance. Even *James* (iii, 15) corroborates the same
by saying that the "wisdom" (of our lower soul) descendeth not from the above, but is
terrestrial ("psychical", "demoniacal", *vide* Greek text); while the other is heavenly
wisdom.'[71]

Man mirrors the
macrocosm

Astrological Correspondences

Having just referred to Plutarch's teaching, what does he further have to say about the
correspondences between celestial influences and the human constitution? According to
Plutarch 'the earth has given the body, the moon the soul, and the sun the understanding
to the generation of man.'[72] (See the quotation above and the seventh and the last column
of Table II-23). Thus he considers the body 'a compound of physical frame, astral shadow,
and breath, or the triple lower part, which "from earth was taken and to earth returns"; of
the middle principle and the instinctual soul, the second part, derived *from* and *through*
and ever influenced by the moon; and only of the higher part or the *Spiritual Soul*, with
the Atmic and Manasic elements in it does he make a direct emanation of the Sun, who
stands here for *Agathon* the Supreme Deity.'[73]

In view of the above, the writer hopes that readers will have little difficulty in deciding
whether man is the child of solar and planetary influences and forces, plus terrestrial
(including genetic) material, or whether: 'Our genes [exclusively] made us [but we are
not informed by whom or why]. We animals exist [merely] for their preservation and are
nothing more than their throwaway survival machines.'[74]

Corroboration with the Fourth Way School of Gurdjieff and Ouspensky

The Armenian born George Gurdjieff (*circa* 1872–1949) was an influential early
twentieth-century mystic, philosopher, spiritual teacher, and composer. He taught
that the average person does not possess a unified mind-body consciousness and thus
lives out his existence in a state of 'sleep walking', or 'waking sleep'. However, it is
possible to transcend to a higher state of consciousness and achieve full human
potential according to his principles and instructions for awakening consciousness that
unite the methods of the fakir, monk or yogi; hence his method is referred to as the

Table II-23 Parallels with the Greek and Pauline Teachings

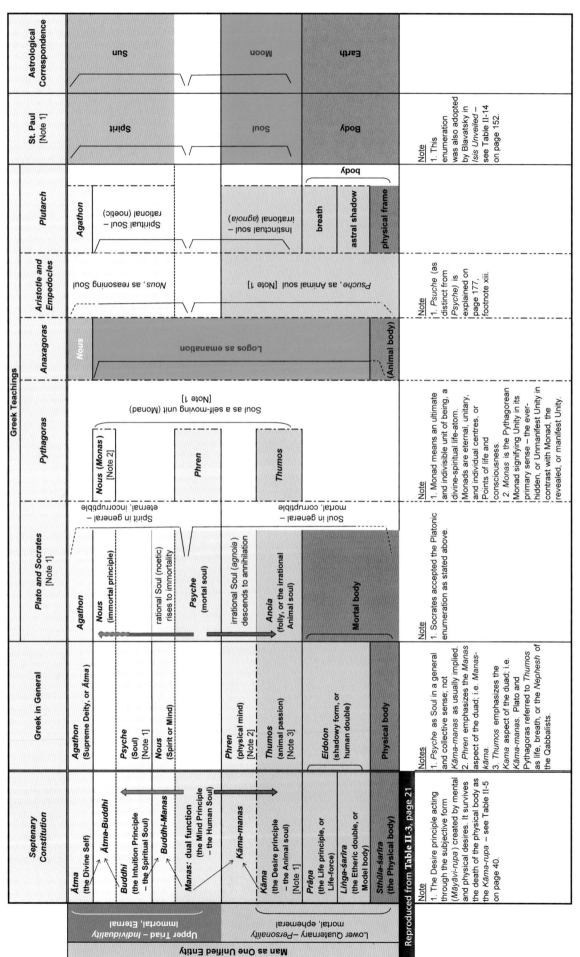

Table II-24 The Fourth Way Teaching on Centres

Centres		
Lower Centres	*Higher Centres*	*Subtle Bodies*
Intellectual or thinking centre – *Faculty*: reasoning and logic *Location*: head	Higher intellectual – *Faculty*: sustained states of profound thought and objective consciousness *Vehicle*: Mental (Intellectual body)	Causal Body
Emotional or feeling centre – *Faculty*: feeling emotions *Location*: as a brain comprising the nerves and 'nerve nodes' distributed throughout the body, the largest concentration of which lies in the solar plexus	Higher emotional – *Faculty*: sustained states of self-awareness and deep feelings. Note that as this is a separate centre, it is a substitute for, or 'raised' version of, the lower emotional centre *Vehicle*: Astral body	Intellectual (Mental) Body– A prerequisite to attaining the state of objective consciousness, which is the fourth possible state of man
Moving or physical centre – *Faculty*: physical actions that have been divided by some, but not all, Fourth Way schools into three distinct sub-centres: – Sexual: controlling sexual functions – Instinctive: controlling involuntary faculties like breathing and the heartbeat, but not reflexive or impulsive reaction. – Motor: controlling motor functions such as walking, the physical aspects of speech, and also functions that are considered as being 'knee-jerk' *Location*: as a brain located in the spinal column		Astral (Emotional) body – A prerequisite to attaining the state of self-consciousness
		Material – Physical body (obviously not a subtle body) considered the seat of the lower five centres: intellectual, emotional, sexual, instinctual, and motor

'Fourth Way'.[75] According to Gurdjieff, there are three main centres, or brains, in the human body: (*a*) the upper intellectual; (*b*) middle emotional; and (*c*) lower moving. The moving centre was further divided into three separate functions: sexual, instinctive, and motor.

Gurdjieff's system was studied under his supervision by his chief disciple, the Russian mathematician and esotericist P. D. Ouspensky (1878–1947) who had some contact with the Theosophical Society before the outbreak of the Great War.[76] In his book *The Fourth Way*, Ouspensky refers to Gurdjieff's three centres as the 'centre of gravity' from which people primarily operate (for example, sportsmen, artists, and intellectuals would operate primarily from the moving, emotional, and intellectual centre, respectively).[77] An outline of Ouspensky's teaching now follows.

Gurdjieff and Ouspensky on three centres of operation

Like his teacher, Ouspensky also divides the centres into three: Lower centres, Higher centres, and Subtle bodies. Table II-24 on the previous page shows a summary of their meaning and function. The essence of Fourth Way teaching is seen to be the development of human capacity and function through operational centres (brains) using the faculties of various bodies. The stress is laid on the passive, form-building, or material side, rather than the active, life-giving side using principles.

Table II-25 overleaf shows an attempted comparison of the Fourth Way teaching with the facet of occult teaching that similarly places the emphasis on form. As before, the first four columns of this Table, reproduced from Table II-3, provide the yardstick for comparison. The fifth column shows the Vedānta classification (using English terms as presented in Table II-15 on page 57), which aligns to some degree with the Fourth Way classification shown in the final column, because both systems are based on the form-side, i.e., bodies as the materials and vehicles of expression of their associated active principles. That said, any comparison between the two systems must be treated with caution because the esotericism of Blavatsky, and occultists of her school, is from a different stream from that of Gurdjieff and Ouspensky, despite the brief contact of the latter with the Theosophical Society in Adyar. With that rider, a few arbitrary comments of a general nature can be made about the correlation between the occult and Fourth Way classification, which again serves to underscore our thesis about the common thread running through the perennial wisdom tradition, however diversely the latter may be expressed.

The Fourth Way and occult teachings would seemingly appear to be in accord, at least in terms of the latter, as expressed through the Vedānta tradition. In both systems, the subtle bodies act as centres of consciousness, with the Physical body as the seat of the higher bodies. Interestingly, in the Fourth Way classification the seat of the lower emotional centre is concentrated in the solar plexus and not in the cranium as seen in the middle of the first column of Table II-24 on the previous page. This strongly alludes to this centre as a *cākra* (chakra) and indeed it could be equated with the solar plexus (*maṇipūra cākra*). (Refer to Chapter 9 of Volume III for a brief exposition on the cākras, their location in the human body, and their consciousness-function.) Furthermore, the physical motor function is governed by the brain located in the spinal column and not by the brain in the head.

Fourth Way in harmony with Vedānta

The use of the term 'brain' by the Fourth Way teaching to refer to a centre governing its sphere of influence is both significant and true. *It is high time that neuroscience recognized*

Table II-25   The Fourth Way Classification and its Comparison with Vedānta

	Dual Constitution	Triple Constitution	Septenary Constitution		Vedantic Classification	Fourth Way Classification
MAN AS ONE UNIFIED ENTITY	Individuality or Higher Self (Immortal)	Spirit	*Ātma* the Divine Self		Buddhic Body	Causal Body
			Buddhi the Intuition Principle		Causal Body	
		Soul	*Manas* the Mind Principle	Higher	Mental Body	Intellectual (Mental) Body
				Lower		
	Personality or Lower self (mortal)		*Kāma* the Desire principle		Astral body	Astral (Emotional) body
			Prāṇa the Life principle		Physical body	Material (Physical) body
		Body	*Liṅga-śarīra* the Etheric double			
			Sthūla-śarīra, or *Rūpa* the Physical body			

Reproduced from **Table II-3**

and understood this wider meaning of the brain instead of its current obsession with confining it to just the fleshly contents of the skull.

Corroboration with the Anthroposophy of Rudolf Steiner

Influences on Steiner's philosophy

The Austrian philosopher, social reformer, architect, and esotericist Rudolf Steiner (1861–1925) first gained recognition at the end of the nineteenth century as a literary critic and an author of philosophical works, notably, *The Philosophy of Freedom*.[78] At the beginning of the twentieth century, he founded an esoteric-spiritual movement called *Anthroposophy*, with roots in German idealist philosophy and theosophy. He was also influenced by Goethean science and Rosicrucianism. In his philosophical work Steiner attempted to find a synthesis between science and spirituality, which he termed 'spiritual science', seeking to apply the clarity of thinking characteristic of Western science and philosophy to spiritual questions, and differentiating this approach from what he considered to be the more nebulous approaches of mysticism. Around 1907, Steiner worked collaboratively in a variety of artistic media, including drama, the movement arts (developing a new artistic form of movement called Eurythmy), and architecture, culminating in the building of the Goetheanum in Dornach, Switzerland, a cultural centre to house all the arts and a world centre for the anthroposophical movement. After World War I, Steiner worked to establish various practical endeavours, including Waldorf education, biodynamic agriculture, and anthroposophical medicine.

Steiner wrote and lectured extensively about his spiritual experiences and described how he was able to make use of his scientific training in such a way that his spiritual investigations could become a science in their own right.

Albeit underplayed by many Anthroposophists, Steiner's early contact with, and influence from, the Theosophical Society is significant. He spoke regularly to the members of the Society, becoming the head of its newly constituted German section in 1902 (without ever, apparently, formally joining the Society). By 1904, Steiner was appointed by Annie Besant to be the leader of the Theosophical Esoteric Society for Germany and Austria. But in contrast to mainstream Theosophy, Steiner sought to forge a Western approach to spirituality based on the philosophical and mystical traditions of European culture. He maintained his own, individual approach, basing his spiritual research and teachings almost entirely upon the Western esoteric and philosophical tradition, chiefly the Rosicrucian, Hermetic, and Gnostic orders, and decided to replace Blavatsky's terminology with his own. This, and other irreconcilable differences, led to a formal split in 1912/13, when Steiner and the majority of members of the German section of the Theosophical Society broke off to form a new group, the Anthroposophical Society. Steiner took the name 'Anthroposophy' from the title of the work by the Austrian philosopher Robert von Zimmermann (1824–1898), published in Vienna in 1856,[79] but not the limitations on knowledge which Zimmermann proposed.[80] Moreover, despite his formal departure from the Theosophical Society, Steiner maintained his interest in Theosophy throughout his life, as evinced by the books in his own library.[81]

Steiner's Theosophical influence and early contact with the Theosophical Society

Like Blavatsky and others, Steiner depicted the human composition in different ways depending upon the context of enquiry; these various descriptions being, as ever, combinations of the primary elements of spirit, soul, and body, which in Steiner's teaching were:

1. Spirit: the human spirit as eternal yet becoming progressively more individualized and consciously experienced. Steiner maintained that humans pass between stages of existence, incarnating into an earthly body, living a life, leaving the body behind, and entering into the spiritual worlds before returning to be born again into a new life on Earth. In earthly life, the Individuality, or Ego, awakens to self-consciousness through the experience of its reflection in the deeds and sufferings of the Physical body. This is, of course, none other than the cycle of reincarnation summarized in Chapter 5.

2. Soul: the framework of consciousness that includes our set feelings, concepts, and intentions. As each human soul evolves through its experiences the Earth itself, and civilization as a whole, also evolves; thus, new types of experience are available at each successive incarnation.

3. Body: the term Steiner uses to describe the three aspects of human existence that endure for a single lifetime –

   ❖ the physical body, which is the most obvious of these;
   ❖ the 'life', or 'etheric body', being the forces of life, growth, and metamorphosis that permeate our physical existence and maintain and develop the physical

body—also an aspect of a lifetime that falls away after death;

❖ the 'body of consciousness' or 'sentient body', being that which receives sensory impressions.[82]

Steiner also applied the following fourfold articulation of the human body with subtle nuances of meaning, especially in the context of medicine and education:[83, 84, 85]

1. The physical body as physical-material structure held in common with the mineral world and comprising –

   ❖ the nerve/sense system, primarily centred in the nervous system, supporting thinking and perception;
   ❖ the rhythmic system, including the breathing and the circulatory system, supporting feeling;
   ❖ the motor-metabolic system.

2. The life, or etheric body, the source of life and growth, held in common with the plant world.

   All that lives has, in addition to a physical body, a permeating life organization. (Refer to the sections on vitalism, morphogenesis, and organizing fields in Volume I, Chapter 4, page 69 et seq.) Steiner cites as proof of this the physical identity of a dead and living organism; what is lacking in the former is the element of life itself. Plant life is the embodiment of this life element.

3. The consciousness, or astral body, held in common with the animal world.

   Animal life adds an element of sentience to the living world of plants. Steiner points to sleep life, when the physical body and life organization are identical with waking life, yet sentience is withdrawn, as proof that sentience is not purely a function of the physical and life bodies. Our instincts (and prejudices), emotions, and will impulses reside here; these are relatively fixed, in contrast with our more fluid and active soul life.

4. The ego, or 'I' of the human being, the faculty of self-awareness unique to humanity.

   Human existence includes an element distinct from other animate life—the ego. This awakens to self-awareness through its experience of the physical body. Steiner points to the lack of a true biography, more particularly of autobiography in animal existence, as an indication that the ego is particular to humans and each human has its own distinct 'concept'. The capacity for self-direction and full responsibility are connected to the ego, which anthroposophical researchers describe as only becoming independent around twenty-one years after conception.

It appears that in his mature work, Steiner identified twelve senses: balance, or equilibrioception; movement, or proprioception; pain/well-being, or nociception, also called life sense; touch, or tactition; taste, or gustation; smell, or olfaction; warmth, or thermoception; sight, or vision; hearing, or audition; word/speech; thought/concept; ego/self.[86]

Steiner's complete sevenfold enumeration of man's constitution is shown in Table II-26 on the next page, taken from his two books on theosophy.[87, 88] By any count, then, what-

Table II-26 Parallels with Rudolf Steiner's Anthroposophy

Dual Constitution	Triple Constitution	Septenary Constitution	Steiner Classification		
			Theosophy (1994)		*Theosophy,* (2011)
			page 58	page 61	page 34
Individuality or Higher Self (Immortal)	Spirit	*Ātma* the Divine Self	The spirit body	Spirit body as transformed physical body	Spirit Man
		Buddhi the Intuition Principle ↑	The life spirit	Life spirit as transformed life body	Life Spirit
	Soul	*Manas* the Mind Principle — Higher / Lower	The spirit-filled consciousness soul	Spirit self as transformed astral body	Spirit-filled consciousness soul
Personality or Lower self (Mortal)		*Kāma* the Desire principle ↓	The mind soul	The 'I' as the soul's central core	Intellectual soul
		Prāṇa the Life-force	The sentient soul body	Astral body	Sentient soul-body
	Body	*Liṅga-Śarīra* the Etheric double	The ether or life body	Life body	Etheric or life-body
		Sthūla-śarīra, or *Rūpa* the Physical body	The material, physical body	Physical body	Physical body

MAN AS ONE UNIFIED ENTITY

Reproduced from **Table II-3**

ever the differences in detail may be, his classification of man's constitution aligns with the core occult classification (disseminated through classical Theosophy) on the constitution of man, as seen in the first four columns of the Table reproduced from Table II-3 on page 21. The reasons why Steiner saw fit to alter Blavatsky's terms (which included a judicious use of Sanskrit when no satisfactory word existed in English) are too complex to enter into here; nor are they particularly relevant to the theme of this Chapter. An enquirer can readily consult the references cited above, and many others, on the website of the Anthroposophical Society, http://www.anthroposophy.org.uk/.

The Steiner enumeration shows that it is not possible to provide once-and-for-all definitive terms for a subject as abstruse and subtle as man's occult constitution. In the same way that Blavatsky modified her terms (see Table II-14 on page 152), Steiner has perforce done the same to suit best the subject context and perspective. However, the dual aspect of *Manas*, the Mind Principle, which is a central plank of occult science, as expounded by Blavatsky and succeeding generations of Theosophists, is not explicitly taught by Steiner. Nonetheless, uniquely, he highlights the polarities between principles, for example, the Spirit body is the transformed physical body, being the upper pole of which the latter is the lower pole—see the penultimate column of Table II-26.

Corroboration with Modern Transpersonal Psychology of Ken Wilber, et al.

The American philosopher and writer on transpersonal psychology Ken Wilber II (*b.*1949) devised a novel articulation of integral psychology—a psychology that is inclusive and holistic, rather than exclusive and reductive. It values and integrates multiple explanations and methodologies.[89] The basic model of Wilber's *Integral Psychology*[90] is a four-quadrant grid that seeks to synthesise all human knowledge and experience, suggesting that the latter can be placed along the axes of 'interior–exterior' and 'individual–collective'.[91] The perspectives in the four quadrants are: 'I' and 'We'; 'It' and 'They'.

Wilber maintains that the four perspectives are complementary, rather than contradictory, and all are necessary for a complete account of human existence. Each perspective, by itself, offers only a partial view of reality, as for example, modern Western society (driven by the predominantly materialistic scientific paradigm) with its focus on the exterior and objective perspective. Such obsessive perspectives, that value only what can be externally measured and tested in a laboratory, deny and marginalize individual experience, feelings, values, and personal gnosis—in short, the realm of subjectivity—as being scientifically unproven, hence having no intrinsic meaning. Wilber identifies this partial perspective as a fundamental cause of the malaise in contemporary Western society. (Iain McGilchrist has elucidated this malaise from the standpoint of mental functions and brain processes in impressive detail in *The Master and his Emissary*, with the apt subtitle, *The Divided Brain and the Making of the Western World*—see Chapter 7 on page 122.)

In line with several theories of developmental psychology, Wilber discerns progressive structural stages in the development of the human being.[92] These structures are complementary rather than mutually exclusive and can be grouped into three main stages: (*a*) pre-personal (subconscious motivations); (*b*) personal (conscious mental processes); and (*c*) transpersonal (integrative and mystical structures). The transpersonal would correlate with, for example, the Vedic Ātma and Aurobindo's Overmind in the East; and in the West, with Emerson's Oversoul, Plato's Forms, and Plotinus's *Nous*. Wilber's three stages could, arguably, be seen as corresponding broadly to the long-standing grouping of the human being into body, soul, and spirit, each of these terms being, of course, generalizations.

Developmental psychology complements spirtual and occult teachings

Table II-27 opposite shows Wilber's enumeration of the human being alongside that of three other influential contemporary thinkers and philosophers on human consciousness: Śrī Aurobindo (1872–1950) the Indian nationalist, philosopher, yogi, poet, and prominent spiritual reformer; Jean Piaget (1896–1980), the Swiss clinical psychologist known for his pioneering work in child development and theories of cognitive development and associated epistemological views; and the German philosopher, linguist, and poet, Jean Gebser (1905–1973) who described the structures of human consciousness. Regarding Aurobindo, note the differentiation between levels of being and developmental stages.

In order to effect a comparison with the occult teaching disseminated through the instrumentality of the modern Theosophical Society, the first four columns of Table II-27 are reproduced from Table II-3 on page 21. However, except in broad terms, such a comparison is of limited value, because with the exception of Aurobindo, the trajectory of Wilber and others of the school of transpersonal or developmental psychology has not originated, as such, directly from esoteric or spiritual traditions. With that proviso, a few arbitrary

Table II-27 Parallels with Modern Psychology

Wilber		Aurobindo — Levels of Being				Aurobindo — Development	Piaget	Gebser
		Overall	Outer	Inner	Psychic			
Transpersonal	Nondual	Supermind			Supermind	Supramentalisation		Integral
	Causal	Mind		Overmind	Overmind	Psychisation & Spiritualisation	Formal-operational	
	Subtle				Intuition			
	Psychic				Illuminated Mind			Rational
Personal	Centaur (Vision-logic)		Mind proper		Higher Mind			Mythic-rational
	Formal-reflexive					Normal Development	Concrete operational	
	Rule/role mind						Pre-operational	Mythic
	Rep(tilian)-mind							
Pre-personal	Phantasmic-emotional	Vital	Vital			Normal Development	Sensoric-motorical	Magical
	Sensori-physical	Physical	Physical			Normal Development		
	Undifferentiated or primary matrix	Unconscient				Unconscient		Archaic

Dual Constitution	Triple Constitution	Septenary Constitution
Individuality or Higher Self (immortal)	Spirit	the Divine Self
		the Intuition Principle ←
	Soul	Higher / Lower — *Manas* the Mind Principle →
Personality or Lower self (mortal)		the Desire principle
		the Life principle
	Body	the Etheric double
		the Physical body

MAN AS ONE UNIFIED ENTITY

English names reproduced from **Table II-3**

comments of a general nature can be made about the correlation between the occult classification and that of Wilber, et al., which again underscores our thesis about the self-consistency of the perennial wisdom tradition, however diversely it may be expressed.

Unsurprisingly, the highest principle, Divine Self, is alike for Wilber and Aurobindo, only given different names (Nondual, Supermind and Supramentalisation, respectively). The same similarity also exists at the opposite pole and lowest principle, the Physical body, which is given a variety of names. Taken together, Wilber's Formal-reflexive and Rule/role mind arguably equate to Kāma-manas (the desire-driven mind) in the occult terminology, the Concrete operational of Piaget, and the Rational and Mythic-rational of Gebser. Significantly, Aurobindo's Intuition and Illuminated Mind parallel with Buddhi-Manas (the Higher Mind illumined by Buddhi, the Spiritual Soul) of the occult system. In Wilber's system they parallel, respectively, the Subtle and Psychic of the Transpersonal category.

Summation

This Chapter has supplied ample evidence in support of a central thesis of this work, namely: that on the question of the composition of man, at all levels of his being, the perennial philosophy across widely differing cultures and epochs speaks 'with one voice, but in different tongues'. There is no need to labour this point further. But let us now delve further into the reasons why this must be so.

In the Proem (see Volume I, page xl f.), the justification for our claim about the unity and self-consistency of the perennial philosophy was on the grounds that (*a*) the diverse streams of esoteric learning have emanated from a central source; and (*b*) for that reason this universal wisdom is, in a sense, a thread stringing together and uniting all diverse esoteric systems.

The disease of sectarianism

This reconciling and uniting (not unifying) feature of the perennial philosophy was clearly perceived by the legendary polymath Gottfried Leibniz and encapsulated in the epigraph to this Chapter. Written in 1698, they are of seminal importance and bear repeating:

> The commonest failing is the sectarian spirit in which people diminish themselves by rejecting others.[93]

Or, as put more succinctly in his letter of 1714 to the Frenchman Nicolas Rémond (1638–1725), First Councillor of the Duke of Orléans with special interests in mathematics and philosophy:

> Most philosophical schools are largely right in what they assert, but not so much in what they deny.[94]

Therefore, since each side had part of the truth and was wrong in failing to recognize what was true in the opposing position, truth was best served, *not by accumulating facts or arguments to one side or another* like adding more pieces of a jigsaw puzzle, but by finding a *framework* to maximize the compatibility of the various points of view—a reconciling system of harmony, in his own words, 'a harmony of philosophers'—a system which would incorporate what he believed to be true in different, conflicting philosophical systems, while rejecting what was false. The philosophers here also include alchemists and this is a frequent theme in Leibniz's writings and letters where he is seeking to harmonise different philosophical schools. This means the coming together of different viewpoints (not discord) and not just one point of view, as for example in music, where harmony is the concurrence of both consonance and dissonance, not just the former.

It is suggested that the perennial philosophy, or *philosophia perennis*, to use Leibniz's own term is precisely that which provides this framework, or reconciling system of harmony. This point is fancifully illustrated in Figure II-8 overleaf, using an analogy with concave and convex lenses. As the concave lens diverges a light beam from a single source into multiple coloured rays that are then converged by the convex lens to a single focus of white light, so also the one universal source of wisdom, the *philosophia perennis*, diffused through the various teachings and esoteric philosophies are brought together by virtue of a reconciling framework that shows their common origin—universal wisdom. Just as the various colours are not the same or similar, but are all compatible and complementary, so, to continue the simile, the diverse, heterogeneous wisdom-streams the world over on the composition of man (of which this Chapter has provided a representative cross section) are not all the same, but in harmony, and can be mutually corroborated.

Analogy to illustrate 'a harmony of philosophers'

Had Leibniz lived in our age, we might well have referred to him as a 'networker'. Apropos, the writer suggests that these days, a fine example of a framework, or reconciling system of harmony, is provided by the Scientific and Medical Network, a leading international forum, which brings together diverse streams of learning from scientists, philosophers, medical practitioners, psychologists, and other professions, on to a common platform to engage in open dialogue and discussion with a plurality of viewpoints and no preconceived bias.

Leibniz was a networker

In the same mentality of open dialogue and networking, the declared Second Object of the Theosophical Society is 'to encourage the comparative study of religion, philosophy, and science'. And it is precisely in this spirit that the writer has produced the comparative tables showing the harmony, not uniformity or similarity, between the core occult doctrines disseminated through classical Theosophy, later expositions of Theosophy and, indeed, several other esoteric systems not directly connected with Theosophy. It is there-fore imperative that the Theosophical Society invokes the Second Object more strongly as the ideal framework and reconciling system of harmony to heal the rifts that have resulted from strongly polarized viewpoints about the supposed superiority and authen-ticity of one teaching over another that have dogged the Society ever since its inception.

Truth served by freedom of enquiry and plurality of approaches

This does not mean that any and every exposition is legitimate and permissible under the pretext of harmony. But it does mean that when differences are perceived in teachings coming from high sources (such as Blavatsky and Besant), the intelligent student will desist from arbitrarily taking sides, and instead look to the underlying premises, appreciating that no one single exposition can do full justice to the infinite subtleties and complexities of subjects like the composition of man. It becomes evident, therefore, that several ways of 'cross sectioning' the latter, depending on the nature of the enquiry, need to be evoked. Absolute freedom of thought and liberty to pursue one's individual path and teaching without imposed dogma, or the crutch of authority figures, are the hallmarks of the wisdom–seeker. This theme was stressed in the last section of the Introductory in Volume I in connection with the role of teachers and organizations in disseminating wisdom and truth (see pages lxxxi–lxxxiv). It is further developed in

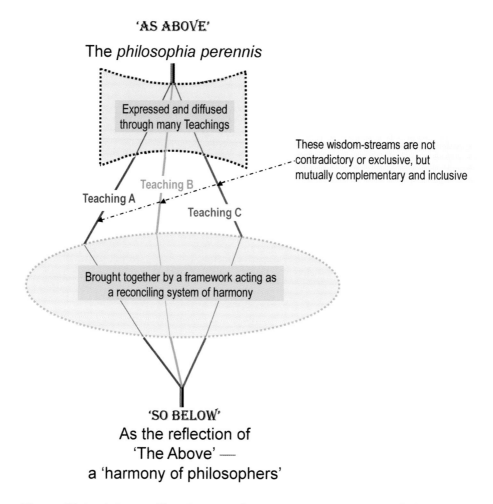

Figure II-8   A Reconciling System of Harmony – A Harmony of Philosophers

Appendix II-C specifically regarding the Theosophical Society, being particularly germane to this Chapter, although the general principles obviously apply to all societies that promulgate spirituality and the *philosophia perennis*.

In essence, therefore, the spiritual quest demands a plurality of approaches that are complementary and mutually inclusive: the *philosophia perennis* is larger than any one of its manifold expressions. But for those who treasure only dichotomies and therefore delight in widening fissures (actual or, more often, imagined) into chasms, nothing more need be said.[95]

This Chapter has demonstrated the harmony that exists between the widespread expositions of the *philosophia perennis* on *all* levels of man's being. The core precepts of the complex constitution and nature of man are drawn together in the following Coda to Volume II. However, it is again necessary to emphasize the importance of adopting a universal outlook free from factional attitudes and dogma for these are the mortal enemies of spiritual enquiry. The closing quotes to this Chapter leaves us in no doubt of this.

No membership of any church, temple, or ashram will save you if it becomes a cause of narrowing down ideas, relationships, mind—of sectarianism.

PAUL BRUNTON[96]

The 'Wisdom religion' is the inheritance of all the nations, the world over.

H. P. BLAVATSKY[97]

As the white ray of` light is decomposed by the prism into the various colours of the solar spectrum, so the beam of divine truth, in passing through the three-sided prism of man's nature, has been broken up into vari-coloured fragments called RELIGIONS. *And, as the rays of the spectrum, by imperceptible shadings, merge into each other, so the great theologies that have appeared at different degrees of divergence from the original source, have been connected by minor schisms, schools, and off-shoots from the one side or the other. Combined, their aggregate represents one eternal truth; separate, they are but shades of human error and the signs of imperfection . . . .*

H. P. BLAVATSKY[98]

NOTES

1   C. I. Gerhardt (ed.), *Die Philosophischen Schriften von Gottfried Wilhelm Leibniz* [The Philosophical Writings of Gottfried Wilhelm Leibniz], 7 vols (Berlin: Weidmann, 1875–90; repr. Hildesheim, Germany: Olms, 1965), iv, 523–4.

2   *NPB-12, Part 1: The Religious Urge*, 'Problems of Organized Religion – Sectarianism', ¶ 87, 108.

3   Adapted and amplified from Adam Warcup, 'An Inquiry into the Nature of Mind', the Blavatsky Lecture 1981 (London: The Theosophical Society), 32.

4   A. P. Sinnett, *Esoteric Buddhism* (8th edn, rev. and enl., London, US, India: Theosophical Publishing Society, 1898).

5   *CW-X*, 'Dialogue Between the Two Editors', 219.

6   *TSGLOSS*, 74.

7   *CW-XII*, 'Instruction No. 1', Diagram I facing p. 524.

8   *loc. cit.*

9   *loc. cit.*

10 Annie Besant, 'Among the Adepts: Madame Blavatsky on The "Secret Doctrine"', *The Pall Mall Gazette* (London, 25 April 1889), 3; repr. *The Theosophist* (Adyar, Madras, August 1889), 696–8.

11 Edi Bilimoria, 'Annie Besant: A Diamond Soul', in Ana-Maria Pascal (ed.), *Multiculturalism and the Convergence of Faith and Practical Wisdom in Modern Society* (Hershey, Pennsylvania: IGI Global, 2017), 28.

12 Susan Dobra, 'Annie Wood Besant: Orator, activist, mystic, rhetorician', dissertation, California State University, n.d. <http://www.csuchico.edu/phil/sdobra_mat/besantpaper.html> accessed 11 October 2017. Quoted also in Yogendra Yadav, 'Messages of Mahatma Gandhi; Part-14' (India: Gandhi Research Foundation, 2012).

13 Annie Besant, *The Seven Principles of Man* (rev. and corrected edn, London: Theosophical Publishing Society, 1909).

14 Annie Besant, *The Ancient Wisdom* (Adyar, Madras: Theosophical Publishing House, 1911), 194.

15 See for example the numerous references to *prāṇa* in: *H. P. Blavatsky Collected Writings*, compiled Boris de Zirkoff, 15 vols (Wheaton, Illinois: Theosophical Publishing House, 1966–1991); *The Inner Group Teachings of H. P. Blavatsky: to her personal pupils (1890–91)*, compiled and annotated Henk J. Spierenburg (2nd, rev. and enl. edn: San Diego, California: Point Loma Publications).

16 Annie Besant, *The Ancient Wisdom*, 194–5.

17 Letter from Blavatsky to Besant written from St. Helier, Jersey, 1889, reproduced in the Introductory to H. P. Blavatsky, *The Voice of the Silence* (Wheaton, Illinois: Theosophical Publishing House, 1992), 29a.

18 *The Theosophist* (April 1932), 20–1. Quoted also in *The Inner Group Teachings of H. P. Blavatsky*, 216.

19 *art. cit.*, 19–20. Quoted also in *The Inner Group Teachings of H. P. Blavatsky*, 218.

20 Letter of H. P. B. to W. Q. J., London, 27 March 1891, quoted in Constance Wachtmeister [The Countess], 'H. P. B. and the Present Crisis in the Theosophical Society [1895]', *Theosophy In Australasia* (5 July 1895), 6.

21 *ibid.* Quoted also in: *The Inner Group Teachings of H. P. Blavatsky*, xxxvi; *Theosophy* (Journal of the United Lodge of Theosophists) (February 1929), 151; *The O. E. Library Critic* (Washington, August–September 1935), no page number.

22 Pedro Oliveira (compiled), *CWL Speaks: C. W. Leadbeater's correspondence concerning the 1906 crisis in the Theosophical Society*, foreword by Robert Ellwood (NSW, Australia: Woy Woy, 2018).

23 Krishnamurti, as is well known, never minced his words, nor had any difficulty in calling a 'spade a spade'. And it was none other than Krishnamurti who (among others in his close circle) testified to Leadbeater's purity. Given a lifetime of companionship with Leadbeater, Krishnamurti was uniquely qualified to make this assertion—see Mary Lutyens, *Krishnamurti: The years of awakening* (UK: Rider, 1984), 143, 146, and other passages scattered throughout this authentic biography.

24 Arthur Ellison, 'Science, Consciousness and the Paranormal', the Blavatsky Lecture 1998 (London: The Theosophical Society), 7, 20 <http://resources.theosophical.org/pdf/Series/Blavatsky%20Lectures/BL_1998_Ellison_Science_Consciousness_and_the_Paranormal.pdf> accessed 20 May 2020.

25 C. W. Leadbeater, *The Inner Life* (Adyar, Madras: Theosophical Publishing Society, 1910).

26 C. W. Leadbeater, *A Textbook of Theosophy* (Adyar, Madras: The Theosophist Office, 1912), 61.

27 *op. cit.*, 61.

28 C. Jinarâjadâsa , *First Principles of Theosophy* (5th edn, rev., Adyar, Madras: Theosophical Publishing House, 1938).

29 *op. cit.*, 64.

30 P. Pavri, *Theosophy Explained in Questions and Answers* (5th edn, rev. and enl., Chennai, India: Theosophical Publishing House, 1999).

31 *op. cit.*, 73.

32 I. K. Taimni, *Man, God and the Universe* (Adyar, Madras, 1969; Wheaton, Illinois: Theosophical Publishing House, 1974).

33 ——*op. cit.*, 111.

34 Annie Besant, *A Study in Consciousness: A contribution to the science of psychology* (6th edn, Adyar, Madras: Theosophical Publishing House, 1972).

35 Max Heindel, *The Rosicrucian Cosmo Conception* (US: Pacific Publishing Studio, 2011), ix, x, 25–47 *passim.*

36 Samael Aun Weor, *The Perfect Matrimony* (n.p., Glorian Publishing, 2013).

37 Arthur Versluis, *Magic and Mysticism: An introduction to Western esotericism* (US: Rowman & Littlefield, 2007), 139.

38 Jean-François Mayer, *Les Nouvelles Voies Spirituelles: Enquête sur la religiosité parallèle en Suisse* [The New Spiritual Ways Research on Parallel Religiosity in Switzerland] (Lausanne: L'Age D'Homme, 1993).

39 Antoine Faivre, *Access to Western Esotericism* (New York: State University of New York Press, 1994), 104.

40 Samael Aun Weor, *The Mystery of the Golden Blossom: The marriage of spirituality, sexuality, and love* (n.p., Glorian Publishing, 2010).

41 Barbara Ann Brennan, *Hands Of Light: Guide to healing through the human energy field* (US: Bantam Books, 1990).

42 See for example, Diane Goldner, *How People Heal: Exploring the scientific basis of subtle energy in healing* (Newburyport, Massachusetts: Hampton Roads, 2003).

43 Barbara Ann Brennan, *Light Emerging: The journey of personal healing* (US: Bantam Books, 1993).

44 David V. Tansley, *Subtle Bodies: Essence and shadow* (UK: Thames and Hudson, 1977).

45 A. P. Sinnett, *Esoteric Buddhism.*

46 T. Subba Row, *Esoteric Writings* (2nd edn, rev. and enl., Adyar, Madras: Theosophical Publishing House, 1931; repr. 1980), 58.

47 *SD*-I, 'Theosophical Misconceptions', 157.

48 *The Theosophist*, 5/9 (Madras, June 1884), 225 <http://theosnet.net/dzyan/theosophist/ theosophist_v5_n9_june_1884.pdf> accessed 22 February 2020.

49 G. R. S. Mead, *Five Years of Theosophy* (1894) (US: Kessinger Publishing, 2003), 185–6.

50 *SD*-I, 'Theosophical Misconceptions', 157.

51 *SD*-I, 'Theosophical Misconceptions', 157–8.

52 *KT*, 'On the Various Principles in Man', 117–22.

53 T. Subba Row, *Esoteric Writings*, 57–9.

54 Geoffrey Barborka, *The Divine Plan* (2nd edn, rev. and enl., Adyar, Madras: Theosophical Publishing House, 1964; repr. 1980), 194–6.

55 Plato, *Timaeus*, xxxi, 69 c.

56 *SD*-I, 'Theosophical Misconceptions', 158.

57 *TSGLOSS*, 74.

58 *SD*-I, 'Theosophical Misconceptions', 158.

59 *ibid*. See also T. Subba Row, *Esoteric Writings*, 59.

60 J. S. Gordon, *Land of the Fallen Star Gods: The celestial origins of Ancient Egypt* (Bear & Company, 2004), 218.

61 *Yasna*, Chapters 26 and 54. Yasna is the name of the primary liturgical collection of Avesta texts, recited during the *yasna* ceremony.

62 *ibid*.

63 Lao-Tze, *Tao Te Ching*, trans. Stephen Addiss and Stanley Lombardo (Boston, Massachusetts: Shambhala Publications, 2007).

64 A compilation based on a digest of: H. P. Blavatsky, 'Zoroastrianism in the Light of Occult Philosophy', *The Theosophist*, 4/9 (June 1883), 224–6; H. P. Blavatsky, 'The Devil's Own: Thoughts on Ormuzd and Ahriman', *Sunrise* (Theosophical University Press, May 1971) <https://www.theosophy-nw.org/theosnw/world/mideast/mi-hpb.htm> accessed 8 March 2020; B. P. Wadia, *The Zoroastrian Philosophy and Way of Life* (Bombay, India: Theosophy Company, 1964); 'Esoteric Insights into Zoroastrianism', being a compilation from 'Zoroastrianism in the Light of Occult Philosophy' and 'The Devil's Own: Thoughts on Ormuzd and Ahriman' with excerpts from *Zoroastrian Philosophy and Way of Life* <https://www.theosophy-ult.org.uk/wp-content/ uploads/2016/07/zoroastrianism.pdf> accessed 8 March 2020.

65 Phiroz Mehta, *Holistic Consciousness: Reflections on the destiny of humanity*, ed. John Snelling (UK: Element Books, 1989), 119.

66 *KT*, 'The Septenary Nature of Man', 90–1.

67 Plato, *Timaeus*, xxxi, 69 c, quoted also in *KT*, 'The Septenary Nature of Man', 92–3.

68 See *KT*, 'The Distinction Between Soul and Spirit', 94–5.

69 *KT*, 'The Greek Teachings', 97. See also *Plutarch on the Face which Appears on the Orb of the Moon*, trans. with notes and appendix by A. O. Prickard (Winchester: Warren and Son; London: Simpkin and Co.), 1911, §28 <https://archive.org/details/plutarchonfacewh00plut/page/2/mode/2up> accessed 9 March 2020.

70 Plutarch, *De placitio philosophorum*, Bk. IV, iv, vii, cited in *KT*, 'The Distinction Between Soul and Spirit', 95. The modern term Agnostic comes from the cognate word, Agnosis.

71 *KT*, 'The Septenary Nature of Man', 91.

72 *KT*, 'The Greek Teachings', 97.

73 *op cit.*, 98.

74 Richard Dawkins, *The Selfish Gene* (1st edn 1977; 2nd rev. edn, Oxford and New York: Oxford University Press, 1989), 19–20.

75 See: 'Fourth Way', Wikipedia (last modified 10 January 2020) <https://en.wikipedia.org/wiki/Fourth_Way> accessed 29 February 2020; Gurdjieff International Review <https://www.gurdjieff.org/G.8-1.htm> accessed 29 February 2020; The Gurdjieff Foundation <http://www.gurdjieff-foundation.org/Home> accessed 29 February 2020.

76 P. D. Ouspensky, *In Search of the Miraculous: Fragments of an unknown teaching* (Library of Alexandria, 1957).

77 P. D. Ouspensky, *The Fourth Way* (Library of Alexandria, 1957).

78 Rudolf Steiner, *The Philosophy of Freedom (The Philosophy of Spiritual Activity): The basis for a modern world conception*, trans. Rudold Steiner Press (1894: 8th English edn, Forest Row, UK: Rudolf Steiner Press, 2011).

79 Robert von Zimmermann: *Anthroposophie im Umriss-Entwurf eines Systems idealer Weltansicht auf realistischer Grundlage* [Anthroposophy in the outline design of a system of ideal world-view on a realistic basis] (Vienna: Wilhelm Braumüller, K. K. Hof-Und Universitätsbuchhändler, 1882); *Geschichte der Aesthetik als philosophische Wissenschaft* [History of aesthetics as a philosophical science] (Vienna: Wilhelm Braumüller, K. K. Hofbuchhändler, 1858).

80 Rudolf Steiner, 'The Unveiling of Spiritual Truths', The Anthroposophic Movement: Lecture Two, 11 June 1923 (Dornach, Switzerland).

81 John Paull, 'The Library of Rudolf Steiner: The books in English', *Journal of Social and Development Sciences*, 9/3 (2018), 21–46.

82 'Anthroposophical view of the human being', in <http://dictionary.sensagent.com/anthroposophical%20view%20of%20the%20human%20being/en-en> accessed 26 February 2020; see also Wikipedia (last modified 24 February 2020) <https://en.wikipedia.org/wiki/Anthroposophy> accessed 26 February 2020.

83 Johannes Hemleben, *Rudolf Steiner: A documentary biography*, trans. L. Twyman (German edn, Rowohlt Taschenbuch Verlag; UK: Henry Goulden Books, 1976).

84 Carlo Willmann, *Waldorfpädogogik: Theologische und religionspädagogische Befunde* [Waldorf Education: Theological and religious education findings] (Cologne, Weimar, and Vienna: Böhlau Verlag, 2001).

85 Lía Tummer, *Rudolf Steiner and Anthroposophy for Beginners*, trans. Horacio Lato (New York: Writers and Readers Publishing, 2000).

86 Carrie Y. Nordlund, 'Art Experiences in Waldorf Education', PhD dissertation, Columbia: University of Missouri, 2006, 54 f.

87 Rudolf Steiner, *Theosophy: An introduction to the supersensible knowledge of the world and the destination of man*, trans. M. Cotterell and A. P. Shepherd (28th edn, Forest Row, UK: Rudolf Steiner Press, 2011).

88 Rudolf Steiner, *Theosophy: An introduction to the spiritual processes in human life and in the cosmos*, trans. Catherine E. Creeger (New York: Anthroposophic Press, 1994).

89 Mark D. Forman, *A Guide to Integral Psychotherapy: Complexity, integration, and spirituality in practice* (New York: State University of New York Press, 2010).

90 Ken Wilber, *Integral Psychology: Consciousness, spirit, psychology, therapy* (Boston, Massachusetts: Shambhala, 2000).

91 Matt Rentschler, 'AQAL Glossary', reviewed Ken Wilber, *Journal of Integral Theory and Practice*, 1/3 (AQAL, Fall 2006) <https://integralwithoutborders.net/sites/default/files/resources/AQAL_Glossary_01-27-07.pdf> accessed 3 March 2020.

92 For example, Piaget's theory of cognitive development, Kohlberg's stages of moral development, Erikson's stages of psychosocial development, and Jane Loevinger's stages of ego development, in 'Integral Theory (Ken Wilber)', Wikipedia, Note 1 (last modified 24 January 2020) <https://en.wikipedia.org/wiki/Integral_theory_(Ken_Wilber)#cite_note-sst-18> accessed 3 March 2020.

93 G. W. Leibniz, 'Clarification of the Difficulties Which Mr. Bayle Has Found in the New System of the Union of Soul and Body', in L. E. Loemker (ed.), *Philosophical Papers and Letters: The New Synthese Historical Library*, ii (Springer, Dordrecht, 1989). Also cited in C. I. Gerhardt (ed.), *Die Philosophischen Schriften von Gottfried Wilhelm Leibniz*, iv, 523–4.

94 C. I. Gerhardt (ed.), *op, cit.*, iii, 607. Quoted also in G. MacDonald Ross, *Leibniz* (Oxford and New York: Oxford University Press, 1984), 75.

95 Edi D. Bilimoria, 'Harmony of Teachers, Teachings and Interpreters: A sane and reverential attitude towards unified spiritual dissemination', *The Theosophist*, 124/9 (June 2003), 327–336; *cont.* 124/10 (July 2003), 375–84.

96 *NPB*-12, Part 1: *The Religious Urge*, 'Problems of Organized Religion – Sectarianism', ¶ 89, 108.

97 *SD*-I, 'Introductory', xviii.

98 *CW*-IX, 'Reply to the Mistaken Conceptions', 235.

Coda:
How to Construct and Energize a Human Being – a Temple of the Divine

Fear not; although we do 'cling superstitiously to the relics of the Past' our knowledge will not pass away from the sight of man. It is the 'gift of the gods' and the most precious relic of all. The keepers of the sacred Light did not safely cross so many ages but to find themselves wrecked on the rocks of modern scepticism. Our pilots are too experienced sailors to allow us [to] [sic] fear any such disaster.

AN EASTERN ADEPT[1]

SYNOPSIS

The Coda to Volume II draws together the core precepts of the occult teaching on the complex and multifaceted features of man's complete makeup. The insights of three celebrated scientists are shown to lend support to the edifice of occult science on the composition of man and the nature of mind: from the English Nobel laureate in neurophysiology and President of the Royal Society Sir Charles Sherrington OM; the Nobel physicist Erwin Schrödinger; and the British philosopher, author, and educator C. E. M. Joad who openly declared his admiration for Blavatsky's trailblazing ideas of her time. We show how the conjoined function of desire and mind acts as the pivot linking the immortal and mortal parts of man.

The construction of a temple comprising the foundation, apex, and internal storeys is used as a simile for the physical, spiritual, and soul components of the constitution of man. The transmission of electricity from a power station to domestic houses via transformers is used as a simile to describe how the Divine Self energizes the physical body via the three soul components. This makes the case that the man of flesh becomes man *in toto* only when Soul and Spirit are conjoined in the same way. To draw a parallel, a building of bricks and mortar in vacant possession becomes a temple when it is occupied and energized by a living human being.

KEY WORDS: consciousness, monad, noetic, individuality, personality, mind-desire pivot, body, constructing, energizing, Charles Sherrington, Ervin László, Erwin Schrödinger, C. E. M. Joad

Man is a highly complex entity in his constitution and most complicated in his nature. So any attempt to describe his traits, in depth, must inevitably be an intricate task. A recapitulation of the salient features of the preceding multifaceted and detailed expositions would therefore be useful. Accordingly, the core precepts of the occult teaching on the composition of man will be outlined, followed by some 'instructions' on how to 'construct' and 'energize' man on the basis of his occult anatomy and physiology as described in this Volume, especially in Chapters 2 and 3, respectively.

Cardinal Precepts

Man, spiritual in his innermost self, expresses himself through the intermediate vesture of his soul and externally through a physical body. So it is a grave mistake to conclude, on the one hand, as do the majority of scientists, that man is therefore nothing more than a higher form of animal or, even worse, that he is just a bio-physical machine operated by a 'wet computer'; or on the other hand, as gullible mystics do, that man is just a spiritual being, thus ignoring the basis of his earthly existence. Man is unitary; however his constitution displays immortal and mortal aspects: the former invisible and eternal, and the latter tangible and temporal. The temporary (false) personality—the lower nature of man—comprises a complex mortal, but non-physical component, the (animal) soul, housed in a mortal physical body of flesh. The Individuality—the upper and permanent nature of man—comprises the triad of Divine Self, Spiritual Soul, and Human Soul; and this is the consciousness-state of man after rebirth in *Devachan* following the 'second death', namely, the disintegration of the psychic vesture, or *Kāma-rūpa*.

Terrestrial man is neither just an animal nor a purely spiritual being

The Principles of Man

As microcosm of the universe, man mirrors in his compound nature all elements, forces, and powers of the universe, the macrocosm. The Principles of Man are the various aspects of the one real human entity: as per the quotation (on page 205) at the end of the Afterword, 'Man is essentially a permanent and immortal principle.' The ever-present danger of confusing 'the map with the territory' must be guarded against, namely, dividing up that which is essentially whole, isolating the various components, ascribing unique labels to them, and then mistaking the many labels—the descriptions, for the reality they represent—the described. Man is therefore not a compound, or aggregate of two, three, five or seven entities, but rather these represent the various *modes of consciousness* in which man can operate. In whatever way we may divide or categorize the Principles of Man, whether as a dual, triple, quintuple or a septenary being, the basic premise of any such esoteric taxonomy is the triplicity of Spirit and Body joined by the bridge of Mind (Soul in generic terms). How the immortal and the mortal parts of man are so conjoined has been explained in Chapters 2 and 3 and will become quite apparent in the human 'construction project' to follow shortly.

Man is a unitary enity, an organic being

As depicted in the occult doctrines, the septenary composition of man is derived from the various *combinations* of Spirit, Soul, and Body. Putting it in another way, man's composition (constitution and nature) has seven aspects, is composed of seven principles, and hence may be studied from seven different points of view. This classification is not at all arbitrary, and Chapter 2 explained the metaphysical rationale and mathematical basis behind the septenary classification evolved out of a single entity. Accordingly, the clearest way to think of man is to regard him as One—*Ātma*, the Divine Self, the True Self. Thus Man belongs to the highest region of the universe, and is universal, the same for all; and man, a ray of the Absolute, a spark from the Divine Fire, reflecting the Divine Perfection, a Son that grows into the likeness of his Father. For this purpose, Spirit is clothed in garment after garment, each garment belonging to a definite region of the universe and 'woven' from the substance thereof, thus enabling the Self to come into contact with that region, gain knowledge of it, and work in it. It thus gains experience, and all its latent potentialities are gradually drawn out into active powers. These garments, sheaths, or subtle bodies (but obviously not in a literal sense like onion skins as explained on page 10 of Chapter 1) are

The physical and subtle bodies are man's vehicles of expression

distinguishable from each other both theoretically and practically. They are separable, each from each, either during physical life or at death, according to the nature of any particular sheath. Whatever words may be used, the fact remains the same—that man, in his complete terrestrial composition is essentially sevenfold, an evolving being, part of whose nature has already been manifested, part remaining latent at present, so far as the vast majority of humankind is concerned. Man's consciousness is able to function through as many of these principles as have been already evolved in him into activity. Whereas every faculty must have a vehicle through which it can be expressed, *we can know of any principle only to the extent that we have evolved it so far through consciously directed self-effort.*

Consciousness and Mind

Based on the above, man's consciousness can be said to be fractionated, or refracted, into spiritual, mental, and material aspects, corresponding to the divine, psychic, and physical planes of nature.

Sir Charles Sherrington (1857–1952), the English President of the Royal Society and Nobel laureate in neurophysiology, who lived during the zenith of the Theosophical Society distinguishes brain from mind. In his Gifford Lectures, 1937–38, he fervently declared that even if the brain, the recording instrument on the physical plane, were paralysed the quintessential Self still Is. Why is this? He explains:

> Mind […] invisible, intangible […] it is not a "thing". It remains without sensual confirmation and remains without it forever. Stripped to nakedness there remains to it but itself. What, then does that amount to? All that counts in life. Desire, zest, truth, love, knowledge […]. Naked mind.[2]

Sir Charles Sherrington distinguishes mind from brain

Continuing in similar vein, in his book *Science and the Akashic Field*, Ervin László, the distinguished Hungarian philosopher of science and systems theorist,[i] gives robust evidence for consciousness beyond the brain, reincarnation, and immortality in line with the latest theories about an in-formation field, or Akashic field ('A-field'), whose intrinsic characteristic is holographic. Referring of course to science, he admits that:

> There is much that we do not yet understand about the farthermost reaches of human consciousness, but one thing stands out: consciousness does not vanish when the functions of the brain and body cease. It persists, can be recalled and, for a time at least, can also be communicated with. […] The perennial intuition of an immortal soul is no longer inconsistent with what we are now *beginning to comprehend* through science about the true nature of reality [emphasis added].[3]

Ervin László's scientific rationale for the immortality of the soul

Thus we may say that science is now legitimately, and on its own terms, widening its scope to embrace the *philosophia perennis* as foretold well over a century ago in the oft quoted maxim: 'Modern science is our best ally.' Even so, the next sentence of this famous quotation, barely ever mentioned, but of equal import states, 'Yet it is generally that same science which is made the weapon to break our heads with.'[4]

Additional modern examples in support of the above contentions are contained in *Network Review* (renamed *Paradigm Explorer*): *The Journal of the Scientific and Medical Network* (www.scimednet.org), which is replete with excellent papers by leading scientists,

---

i Ervin László, originally a classical pianist, is also an advocate of the theory of quantum consciousness.

medical practitioners, psychologists, psychiatrists, and philosophers on subjects such as out-of-body experiences, near-death experiences, transpersonal psychology, altered states of consciousness, and the multidimensional nature of existence. Taken as a whole, they all point to the primacy of consciousness.

Two of the finest scientific allies of the *philosophia perennis* come from Schrödinger and the British philosopher, author, and educator C. E. M. Joad (1891–1953). They bear careful scrutiny.

In the Epilogue to his lectures, entitled 'Determinism and Free Will', delivered under the auspices of the Dublin Institute for Advanced Studies at Trinity College, Dublin, in February 1943, Schrödinger muses thus:

> Let us see whether we can draw the correct, non-contradictory conclusion from the following two premises:
>
> (i)   My body functions as a pure mechanism according to the Laws of Nature.
>
> (ii) Yet I know, by incontrovertible direct experience, that I am directing its motions, of which I foresee the effects, that may be fateful and all-important, in which case I feel and take full responsibility for them.
>
> The only possible inference from these two facts is, I think, that I – I in the widest meaning of the word, that is to say, every conscious mind that has ever said or felt 'I' – am the person, if any, who controls the 'motion of the atoms' according to the Laws of Nature.[5]

What is this 'I – I'? Let Schrödinger continue:

> If you analyse it closely you will, I think, find that it is just a little bit more than a collection of single data (experiences and memories), namely the canvas *upon which* they are collected. And you will, on close introspection, find that what you really mean by 'I' is that ground-stuff upon which they are collected.[6]
>
> From the early great Upanishads the recognition ATHMAN = BRAHMAN (the personal self equals [is one with] the omnipresent, all-comprehending eternal self) was in Indian thought considered, far from being blasphemous, to represent the quintessence of deepest insight into the happenings of the world.
>
> Again, the mystics of many centuries, *independently, yet in perfect harmony with each other* [emphasis added] (somewhat like the particles in an ideal gas) have described, each of them, the unique experience of his or her life in terms that can be condensed in the phrase: DEUS FACTUS SUM (I have become God).[7]

Particularly noteworthy is Schrödinger's insight into the primacy of consciousness, described as the 'canvas *upon which*' and 'ground-stuff upon which' our experiences and memories are collected. Then the mystical experience is described as, 'I have become God', and *not* 'I am God'. In other words, the mystical state is one of an elevation of consciousness to the supreme heights of union with the All—the God-*like* state.

Turning to Joad, the term 'noetic' is significant. It is an adjective of *nous*, best defined by Blavatsky as 'divine consciousness or mind in man' and as 'a Platonic term for the Higher Mind or Soul […] It means Spirit as distinct from animal Soul—psyche.'[8] In the 1930s, much of the material in Blavatsky's seminal booklet *Psychic and Noetic Action*[9] was discussed in Joad's article entitled 'What is the Soul?' in which he wrote:

Madame Blavatsky […] postulates two souls or selves which are broadly defined as follows. The first is body-dependent, that is to say, the events in it are determined by prior events taking place in the body; it is known as the 'Lower Self,' or as 'psychic activity'. 'It manifests itself, through our organic system' and 'from its lowest to its highest manifestations it is nothing but motion.'

The second self, known as the 'Higher Self,' is self-conscious, active and freely willing. Instead of being a mere bundle of psychological events, like the first self, it is a unity, or rather, it is a unifying principle. It has no special organ as its counterpart in the body—for how can there be a specific organ to determine the motions of that which unifies all organs?—nor can it be correlated with any bodily movements. *It is not, therefore, located in the brain, and it has no counterparts in brain movements* [emphasis added]. Its activity, described as 'Noetic' as opposed to the 'psychic' activity of the first self, derives from the 'Universal Mind'. Finally, the Higher Self is identical and continuing in and through different lives. It is the permanent element which runs like a thread through the different existences which are strung like beads along its length [thus echoing the quotation on page 205 at the end of the Afterword]. [By contrast,] the Lower Self, being a reflection of the body which determines the events that occur in it, is different from life to life, as the body is different from life to life.

C. E. M. Joad upholds Blavatsky that Higher Self has no bodily organ

It is impossible not to feel the greatest respect for Madame Blavatsky's writings on this subject; of respect and, if the word be permitted, of admiration. Writing when she did, she anticipated many ideas which, familiar today [i.e., in the 1930s], were in the highest degree novel fifty years ago.[10]

Note, with every care, the words 'It [the Higher Self] has no special organ as its counterpart in the body. Its activity […] derives from the "Universal Mind" '; and most significantly, 'It is not, therefore, located in the brain, and it has no counterparts in brain movements.' Coming from a twentieth century professor of philosophy and psychology at Birkbeck College, University of London, they display an extraordinary understanding of esotericism. The corollary to be drawn with every force is the following complete inversion, suggested by the writer, of Francis Crick's crass manifesto (quoted in Volume I, Chapter 2, page 8):

> **'You', your joys and your sorrows, your memories and your ambitions, your sense of personal identity and free will, and the fountainhead of your creativity or genius, in any field of human endeavour, is primarily the action of the Higher Self and only secondarily the activity of the organ as its emissary on the physical plane, the physical brain with its vast assembly of nerve cells, glial cells and their associated molecules, etc.**

The writer can do no better than end this section by recasting Blavatsky's essential message on this subject perfectly endorsed by Joad. *Until science fully appreciates, and takes on board, the deep import of this core teaching of esotericism, its attempts to discover the stratospheres of consciousness—Universal Mind, the 'habitat' of the Higher Self—will be doomed to a squirrel-like progress around a wheel of cognitive science and brain research by whatever manner and means, like experimenting on hapless animals or with psychedelic drugs, all getting nowhere. The Higher Self is not an objective entity; it is not a 'thing' and so, as Joad puts it, 'it is not, therefore, located in the brain'. It would be easier to find a needle in a haystack than to locate the Noetic activity of Universal Mind and Higher Self in regions where they simply do not exist—in the brain.*[11]

So can science ever discover a physical basis and mechanism for consciousness?

In this wise, it is the writer's judgement that science has, in one sense, taken a major retro-grade step (see the examples given in Volume III, Epilogue) from its enlightened stance during the 1930s, when the novel ideas that Blavatsky had anticipated several decades earlier became somewhat familiar currency amongst enlightened psychologists and philosophers of that period, as exampled above.

Be that as it may, we now close Volume II by constructing man in such a way that the Noetic can be 'joined' to, and expressed through, the psychic and the physical; so that the immortal may dwell temporarily in the mortal.

Constructing and Energizing a Man for Terrestrial Existence

In any system, the component parts must first be constructed before the system as a whole can be energized. The human system is no different in principle. How, then, is man constructed and energized for life on Earth? The following two sections explain the 'occult engineering processes' by way of two familiar similes.

Constructing a Man for Life on Earth

In proceeding to construct a man of flesh and blood for life on Earth, it is not that far-fetched to draw upon the simile of constructing a three-storey temple on the grounds of extending the metaphor of the body as the temple of the spirit to encompass man as the temple of the Divine Self. In both cases, there are just two rules that must be obeyed.

Referring to Figure II-9 opposite:

> Rule No. 1: The (vertical) external boundaries of a temple are defined by the foundation and the roof apex above, as seen in Figure II-9 in the picture to the left. In man, they correspond to the Physical body and 'higher up' to *Ātma*, shown in the central tabulation of man's Principles.

> Rule No. 2: The internal spaces of the temple are demarcated by three floors or platforms, seen in the picture to the right. In man they correspond to the three *upādhis* that define the realm of the three souls acting as transformers and vehicles to 'step down' Consciousness to the physical level, that is, from Divine Self to the Physical body.

The Pivot-Point – The 'Cement' of Desire and Mind

But how are the immortal and the mortal parts of man so 'joined'? The following quotation speaks volumes. It highlights the absolute necessity of the 'cement' of the Desire principle and Mind Principle as a pivot to join the Individuality to the personality, needed *for a terrestrial existence*:

> The two higher principles [Ātma and Buddhi] *can have no individuality on Earth*, cannot be *man*, unless there is (*a*) the Mind, the *Manas-Ego*, to cognize itself, and (*b*) the terrestrial *false* personality, or the body of egotistical desires and personal Will, to cement the whole, as if round a pivot (which it is, truly), to the physical form of man. It is the *Third* and the *Fourth* principles [counting from *Ātma*]—*Manas* and *Kāma-rūpa*— that contain the dual personality: the real immortal Ego (*if it assimilates itself to the two*

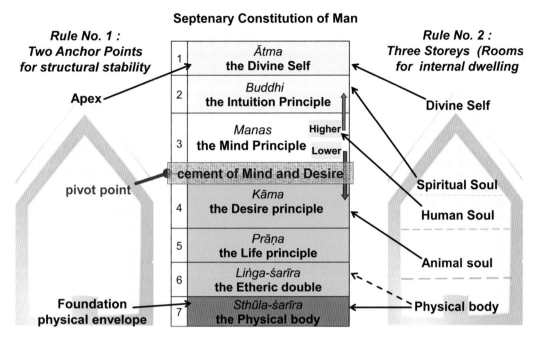

Figure II-9   Constructing a Man – A Temple of the Divine
(refer to Chapter 2, Table II-3, page 21 and Table II-4, page 31 for details)

higher) and the false and transitory personality, the *māyāvi* or astral body, so called, or the *animal-human* Soul—the two having to be closely blended for purposes of a *full* terrestrial existence. Incarnate the Spiritual Monad [Ātma-Buddhi] of a Newton grafted on that of the greatest saint on earth—in a physical body the most perfect you can think of—*i.e.*, in a two or even a three-principled body composed of its *sthūla-śarīra, prāṇa* (life principle), and *liṅga-śarīra*—and, if it lacks its middle and third principles, you will have created *an idiot*—at best a beautiful, soulless, empty and unconscious appearance. "*Cogito—ergo sum*"—can find no room in the brain of such a creature, not on this plane, at any rate.

H. P. Blavatsky[12]

Owing to the importance of the above quote, it is worth recasting it in simpler terms. The fundamental point being made is this: notwithstanding that man is immortal in himself—see the higher triad in the central classification of Figure II-9, yet, for the immortal Self to function temporarily through a mortal personality, there needs to be something that glues, or cements, the two parts together.

> Mind and Desire 'join' the immortal and mortal parts of man

Let us take a sidestep and ask: 'how do adhesives work?' The familiar two-part epoxy adhesive, Araldite, works by the chemical interaction of a resin with a hardener; cement hardens by virtue of being mixed with water as a chemical component in a curing process. In both these cases (and many more that could be exampled) two components are needed for the bonding agent.

Accordingly, that which bonds immortal man to his mortal self is the two-part 'cement' of mind and desire. Both components are needed. As the above quote elucidates, because the higher principles can have no individuality on Earth, they cannot be *physical* man, unless there is (*a*) the Mind and (*b*) the terrestrial personality, 'the body of egotistical desires and personal Will', to cement the whole, as if round a pivot to the physical form of man. It is the Mind Principle and Desire principle that have to be blended for the purposes of a full terrestrial existence. The purest Spiritual Soul grafted on to a most perfect body would result in a complete imbecile, on Earth, if the cement of mind and desire be lacking.

In passing, it is a common experience that the memory of an event lasts in proportion to the degree that it has evoked thought and desire, i.e., emotionally charged thought. 'Memory glue' is truly thought blended with emotion or desire!

Energizing a Man for Life on Earth

Having shown how to construct a man according to the perennial rules of 'occult structural engineering', how is he then energized? A particularly apt simile, shown in Figure II-10 opposite, is the transmission of electricity from a power station to domestic houses to energize lighting and electrical appliances. But domestic appliances would be completely destroyed if operated on the high power generated at source, which power must, therefore, be stepped down by transformer substations—say, three in number, as seen in the upper half of Figure II-10—to a level that consumer units can safely handle. Just so, the 'Divine Power' of Ātma must be progressively stepped down using 'transformers' to a lower value that the Physical body can safely handle. These transformers, depicted in the lower half of Figure II-10, are: (*a*) the Spiritual Soul; (*b*) the Human Soul; and (*c*) and the Animal soul (refer back to Chapter 3, page 37 explaining the generic meaning of Soul as carrier and transformer).

Interestingly, this goes a long way towards explaining why enlightened persons, or geniuses, in any field are invariably afflicted with protracted bouts of ill health. In his classic book *Autobiography of a Yogi* the Indian yogi and guru Paramahansa Yogananda (1893–1952) tells us that: 'the body of the average man is like a fifty-watt lamp, which cannot accommodate the billion watts of power roused by an excessive practice of *Kriya*,' as in the body of individuals who are attaining to enlightenment.[13] Kriya (Yoga) is a meditation technique of controlling through *prāṇāyāma* (methods of breath regulation and control) and meditation practices, which accelerates the spiritual progress of the aspirant. It is by no means the only such technique for arousing the latent powers in man—there are several others in the spiritual traditions of both the East and the West (see Chapter 9 in Volume III). The point being made is that the interior state of heightened psycho-spiritual intensity of the genius is similar to that of the Yogi attaining to enlightenment, and in both cases the body must prepared to withstand the brunt of the powerful 'spiritual currents' so aroused. Herein lies the indispensable benefit of physical culture, such as Yoga or T'ai Chi Ch'uan, which has nothing what-soever to do with cultivating physical prowess for its own sake, and all to do with developing the stability and strength of the body—the physical foundation—in order to sustain and harness the powers playing upon it from higher realms as the aspirant advances on the spiritual path.

'Billions of watts' is of course an electrical metaphor for the immeasurable power normally latent but which can be aroused under appropriate circumstances. But the dangers are commensurate with the benefits conferred. In similar vein, Blavatsky counsels

Divine Self 'powers' body via the soul

Enlightenment is a state of immense inner power

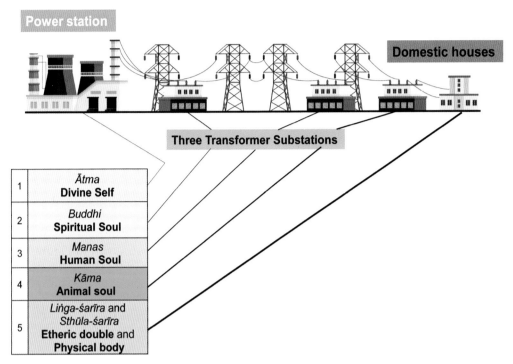

Figure II-10   Energizing a Man – 'Divine Electricity' Transformed for Terrestrial Life

Image Credit: https://www.freepik.com/vectors/mountain, artwork by Artefact Design

that good and evil are relative, and are intensified, or lessened, according to the conditions by which man is surrounded. One who belongs to what we might call the lay majority is, in many cases, relatively irresponsible. Crimes committed in *avidyā* (ignorance) involve physical, but not moral, responsibilities, or Karma; for example, as in the case of the mass of unthinking humanity who know no better, or those born with congenital defects, or children. But for individuals consciously seeking enlightenment— *those who are pledged to the Higher Self*—it is quite another matter. Such a pledge can never be revoked and once made, *no man can invoke this Divine Witness with impunity*, for once a man has consciously put himself under its tutelage, he has asked the Radiant Light to shine into, and search through, all the dark corners of his being; consciously, he has invoked the Divine Justice of Karma to take note of his motives, to scrutinize his actions, and to enter up all in his account. Furthermore, if we acknowledge that Karma relentlessly records in the Aspirant's account, bad deeds—that in the ignorant would be overlooked—by the same token the Aspirant's good deeds will also be assiduously recorded. Moreover, it is equally true that each of his good deeds is, *by reason of his association with the Higher Self*, a hundredfold intensified as a potency for good.[14] For this reason the aspirant who consciously sets out on the spiritual path is tested, sometimes to the extreme, thus providing greater opportunity to transform not only himself but conditions around him.[15]

Karmic consequences entirely dependent on degree of conscious awareness

When we look rather more closely at Blavatsky's terms: 'the Radiant Light' and 'association with the Higher Self, a hundredfold intensified', and compare them to Yogananda's term, 'billions of watts', we realize that they are conveying precisely the same message, the former in sterner tones.

Afterword

Volume II of this work makes our case cogently that occult science comprising, as it does, the wisdom of all ages, is unavoidably an enormous subject. In order to address the depth and complexity of the composition of man, this is necessarily the case. Thus, it demands a *holistic* approach based on universality of enquiry, which clearly cannot be constrained to a single exposition, however erudite that may be. Hence, a one-track purist approach is neither sensible nor true to the spirit of the esoteric and occult tradition. Whereas the Theosophical teaching has constituted the backbone of our exposition, we have clearly stressed the importance of teachings from the worldwide perennial wisdom tradition. It is hoped that by showing their nuanced differences, readers may not only see their meeting and merging points, but come closer to the spirit of *philosophia perennis* which is as one River fecundating innumerable individual streams.

As to the composition of man—the main thrust of this Volume—it is this: man can be constructed, and then energized, in any number of ways depending on the questions being addressed, provided that the 'two rules' are obeyed—namely, that the foundation and apex of the system, and the three 'internal platforms' are maintained. So, to maintain a doctrinaire attitude towards any one system of classifying man is wholly obtuse. Let us constantly remember that we are dealing with Forces and States of Consciousness, and not with water-tight compartments. Sadly, within the Theosophical Society much time and energy has been wasted on tedious squabbling over which occult system is the authentic one. Of course, as an organisation, it is by no means unique in this respect. Such feuds are born of a literal-minded, bookish attitude, instead of understanding the context and reasons for the different ways of classifying man's Principles and subtle bodies. This attitude has no place for the aspirant whose only concern should be with Truth wherever it may lead and from whatever source.

There are entirely reasonable grounds for expounding the composition of man in different ways from the classical expositions as carried out by the later generations of Theosophists; and also according to other occult doctrines of the East or the West. This was demonstrated in Chapter 8, the main purpose of which was to reveal the common thread running through the Mystery Teachings on the composition of man, uniting (not unifying) these diverse doctrines into an organic body of truth. And this makes it abundantly clear that the remarkable consistency found in the diverse ways of enumerating man's composition is no fortuitous concurrence amongst diverse authors or epochs, but is the universal wisdom of all ages—the *philosophia perennis*— as expressed by the uninterrupted record of thousands of generations of Seers from the Orient as well as the Occident.

Whereas the focus in Volume II has been inwards upon man, by contrast in Volume III we look outwards on man's role in the overall scheme of the universe and nature. We explain how and why the wisdom and powers that sustain the whole universe have gone into the making of man, including the human body. The core of this narrative is a detailed account of the derivation of the human senses: emanational emergence from the spiritual to the material—the handiwork of Divine Forces such that physical sensation can result in an internal experience. But to accomplish this, there has got to be a new way of knowing, understanding, and experiencing the subtle vistas of man and the universe.

Holistic approach demands a plurality of viewpoints

There is no one 'best' way to classify the Principles of Man

Outline of Volume III

These perceptive faculties, normally hidden from ordinary sight, but which must be engaged, are described at some length in Volume III. They are part and parcel of the language of the Mysteries and the keys to wisdom regarding which symbolism and the Hermetic Axiom are indispensable to an understanding of the unity of the universe and man. Furthermore, no exposition on the unfolding of consciousness would be complete without exploring evolution from the spiritual perspective which considerably extends the scientific viewpoint into matters of destiny and purpose.

Drawing to a close, a summary of the entire work is provided on the principal theme of consciousness and its unfoldment, as seen first by science and the *philosophia perennis*. Thereafter, an epilogue reviews the status of science and spirituality in our present civilization and then explains the onus on each individual to choose between which one of two paths will predominate in life in order to address the question uppermost in the mind of every human being—immortality, and how it may be attained.

In the meantime, we close Volume II with a quote first introduced at the end of the Proem in Volume I. What may have seemed perplexing at first sight should now be much clearer. Besides encapsulating the essential teaching on man's composition given in this Volume, it also situates man in the wider context of the macrocosm as Volume III will make evident.

*Man is a little world—a microcosm inside the great universe. Like a foetus, he is suspended, by all his **three** spirits, in the matrix of the macrocosmos; and while his terrestrial body is in constant sympathy with its parent earth, his astral soul lives in unison with the sidereal anima mundi. He is in it, as it is in him, for the world-pervading element fills all space, and **is** space itself, only shoreless and infinite. As to his third spirit, the divine, what is it but an infinitesimal ray, one of the countless radiations proceeding directly from the Highest Cause—the Spiritual Light of the World. This is the trinity of organic and inorganic nature—the spiritual and the physical, which are three in one, and of which Proclus says that 'the first monad is the Eternal God; the second, eternity; the third, the paradigm, or pattern of the universe'; the three constituting the Intelligible Triad.*

H. P. Blavatsky[16]

NOTES

1   *ML*, Letter No. 11.
2   Sir Charles Sherrington, *Man on His Nature* (Cambridge: Cambridge University Press, 1940), xxi.
3   Ervin László, *Science and the Akashic Field: An integral theory of everything* (2004; 2nd edn, Rochester, Vermont: Inner Traditions, 2007), 128.
4   *ML*, Letter No. 65.
5   Erwin Schrödinger, 'On Determinism and Free Will' from lectures delivered at Trinity College, Dublin, 1943, in *What is Life?* with *Mind and Matter* and *Autobiographical Sketches*, foreword by Roger Penrose (Cambridge: Cambridge University Press, 1993), 86–7.
6   ——*op. cit.*, 89.
7   ——*op. cit.*, 87.
8   *TSGLOSS*, 234.
9   H. P. Blavatsky, *Psychic and Noetic Action* (US: Kessinger Publishing), 2010; also in *CW*-XII, 350–374.
10 C. E. M. Joad, 'What is the Soul?' *The Aryan Path* (Bombay, India: Theosophy Company, May 1937), viii, no. 5, 201–3.

11 *CW*-XII, 'Kosmic Mind', 135.

12 *SD*-II, 'Stanza X: The History of the Fourth Race', 241–2.

13 'The Science of *Kriya Yoga*', in Paramahansa Yogananda, *Autobiography of a Yogi*, preface by W. Y. Evans-Wentz MA, DLitt, DSc (1946; rev. 1951; Bombay, India: Jaico Publishing House with Self-Realization Fellowship Los Angeles, California, US, 1972), 252.

14 Marginally reworded from *CW*-XII, 'Instruction No. III', 640.

15 *CW*-XII, 'Instruction No I: A Warning Addressed to All Esotericists', 515–16.

16 *IU*-I, 'The Elements, Elementals, and Elementaries', 212.

Appendix II-A:
Light, Ether, and the Theory of Relativity – an Extended Example of 'Knowledge Filtration' in Science

I t was stated in Chapter 3 that the ether is of major significance from the standpoint of occult science, as notable scientists like Sir William Crookes realized. Accordingly, the twofold purpose of this Appendix is: (*a*) to summarize the results of numerous, rigorous experiments that have cast serious doubts on the supposedly null verdict of the Michelson-Morley experiment and the associated theoretical edifice that has been built upon the assumption of the non-existence of the ether; and (*b*) to provide an extended example of the suppression of such unfavoured evidence by the process of 'knowledge filtration' described in Volume I, Chapter 4 on page 115, to supplement the several cases cited in that Chapter.

In the late nineteenth century, physics postulated the luminiferous (light-bearing) ether for the wave theory of light. It was the medium required for the theoretical explanation of the propagation of light waves through space, which was not considered possible in a spatial vacuum. The Scottish mathematical physicist, James Clerk Maxwell FRS, FRSE (1831–1879) wrote in *Encyclopædia Britannica*:

William Crookes and James Clark Maxwell on the significance of the ether

> Æthers were invented for the planets to swim in, to constitute electric atmospheres and magnetic effluvia […] and so on, until all space had been filled three or four times over with æthers […]. The only æther which has survived is that which was invented by Huygens to explain the propagation of light.[1]

A pivotal turning point occurred in 1887 when the famous Michelson-Morley experiment, widely cited in virtually all physics textbooks, claimed to have discovered 'null', or 'negative' results, thus having 'proved that the ether did not exist'.[2] Thereafter the postulate of 'empty space' was enthusiastically adopted along with the related concepts which demanded constancy in the speed of light—a central plank of Einstein's relativity theory.

Michelson-Morley experiment discovers no ether

What is less well known, but far more significant, is the work of other physicists, cited in numerous academic journals, that has identified variations in the speed of light and a positive 'ether drift' (i.e., Earth moving through a cosmological medium). The ensuing narrative on ether-drift is condensed from the paper, and associated numerous academic citations, by Dr James DeMeo (*b.*1949),[3] plus additional sources, as referenced in this Appendix. DeMeo is an American research scientist, formerly on the Faculty of Geography (Earth and Atmospheric Science) at Illinois State University and the University of Miami and currently Director of Research at the high-altitude Orgone Biophysical Research Laboratory near Ashland, Oregon, US.

Chief among such dissenting physicists was the American physicist, astronomer, and acoustician Dayton Miller (1866–1941), a graduate from Princeton University who became President of the American Physical Society and Acoustical Society of America,

Dayton Miller's
experimental
discovery of ether
drift

Chairman of the Division of Physical Sciences of the National Research Council, Chairman of the Physics Department of the Case School of Applied Science (today Case Western Reserve University), and Member of the National Academy of Sciences. Miller's 1933 paper in *Reviews of Modern Physics* details the positive results from over twenty years of experimental research into the question of ether-drift,[4] and remains, arguably, the definitive body of work on the subject of light-beam interferometry.[i] Miller's work, which ran from 1906 through the mid-1930s, strongly supports the idea of an ether-drift, with calculations made of the actual direction and magnitude of drift. He produced a series of papers presenting robust data on the existence of a measurable ether-drift, and he successfully defended his findings to a considerable number of critics, including Einstein himself.

Einstein's anxiety
concerning
validity of
relativity theory

There were undoubted tensions between Miller and Einstein, as seen in this extract from Einstein's letter to the American experimental Nobel physicist, Robert Millikan (1868–1953), in June 1921: 'I believe that I have really found the relationship between gravitation and electricity, assuming that the Miller experiments are based on a fundamental error. Otherwise, the whole relativity theory collapses like a house of cards.'[5] The 'fundamental error' Einstein was assuming (and hoping for) that could be demonstrated was thermal artefacts (temperature fluctuations) that would skew the results—an anomaly that Miller went to extreme lengths to exclude and was able to defend during his lifetime.

Systematic
suppression of
Miller's results

But after Miller's death in 1941, his work was quietly put to rest. This was due to the postmortem on his work organized by Miller's former student, the American physicist Robert Shankland (1908–1982), Chairman of the Physics Department at Case Western Reserve University. Capitalizing on Einstein's meteoric rise to fame, Shankland and his team pronounced Miller's work—a major impediment to Einstein's theory of relativity—to be of little worth, whilst declaring the Michelson-Morley experiment to be the most solid piece of evidence to settle, for all time, the question about null ether drift, and at the same time, reinterpreting all the positive ether-drift results of Miller, and other researchers, as spurious owing to 'experimenter bias'[ii] or 'observational inaccuracy'. As Shankland's analysis is fully accepted by mainstream physicists, the abandonment of the concept of the ether is nearly universal. What Shankland failed to point out was that the Michelson-Morley experiment ran for six hours over four days (8th, 9th, 11th, and 12th July 1887) with a total of thirty-six turns of their interferometer, whereas Miller's interferometry work was undertaken for over twenty-five years (1902 to 1928) involving over 200,000 individual readings, at different months of the year, from over 12,000 individual turns of the interferometer, using an apparatus (from 1902 to 1906) three times as sensitive as the original interferometer used by Michelson-Morley in 1887, and with additional refinementsts for sensitivity in his interferometer.

This theme about the incorrectness of the conclusions drawn from the Michelson-Morley experiment is concisely explained in an important paper by the contemporary Australian physics professor Reginald T. Cahill.[6] He points out that absolute motion (motion that does not depend on anything external to the moving object for its existence, that is, motion

---

i An interferometer is an optical instrument that separates a beam of light into two ray beams, usually by means of reflection, and brings the rays together to produce interference. It is used to measure such properties as wavelength and refractive index.

ii Also known as the 'observer-expectancy effect', or 'experimenter-expectancy effect', it refers to errors in a research study due to the predisposed notions, or beliefs, of the *experimenter*.

relative to space itself) was actually detected by Michelson and Morley in their 1887 experiment. However, they rejected the rotation-induced fringe shifts—the signature of absolute motion—on the basis of incorrect assumptions and therefore declared their famous null result. Cahill's paper explains that by this time, Einstein's influence was so great (as noted above) that the 1887 data were never re-analysed after 1905 using a proper relativistic-effects based theory for the interferometer. For that reason, modern-day vacuum Michelson interferometer experiments are badly conceived, *and their null results continue* to cause much confusion: only a Michelson interferometer in gas-mode can detect absolute motion.[7] What went unnoticed until 2002 was that the gas in the interferometer was a key component of this instrument when used as an 'absolute motion detector', and over time physicists were in fact using instruments with less and less sensitivity. Cahill cites robust evidence from the Miller experiments and explains why Einstein's postulate regarding the invariant speed of light has been in disagreement with experiment from the beginning (see below).

Einstein's influence biased impartial evaluation of results

However, the intention here is not to delve into the complex controversies about the analysis of Miller's results or to prolong the debate as to whether or not the ether exists and the implications regarding relativity theory. The reasons for mentioning all this are, as stressed in the opening to this Appendix, to furnish another significant example to those already cited in Chapter 4 of Volume I demonstrating that science is not so wedded to an impartial and objective discovery of nature free from personal bias as many scientists would like to claim. Moreover, the peer review system—only as good as the peer reviewer(s)—occasionally resorts to political measures to uphold and protect favoured theories by celebrity scientists with the emphasis on respectability rather than scientific discovery. Readers are again invited to revisit the section in Chapter 4 of Volume I describing how the scientific establishment deals with anomalous evidence by way of knowledge filtration. *Ground breaking theories (like relativity theory), especially when conceived by powerful, international scientists, soon develop into belief systems, which demand the automatic suppression of any new discoveries and evidence that could undermine established theories, hence dent the status of the politically dominant group of academics about the popular wisdom they wish to uphold and publicize.*

Political influences on peer review system

But there are some important facts to note. First, the fundamental physical constants of nature fluctuate, which includes the speed of light: they are not invariant over any period of time. Measurements of the speed of light in different laboratories, in different parts of the world, by different investigators, using different methods, show maximum variations of 0.01% from 1927 to 1972 and 0.3% from 1874 to 1972.[8] Other researchers have claimed that the speed of light may have more than one value depending on the direction in which light travels in space.[9]

Speed of light is not constant

Next, the ether is a material agent (albeit extremely tenuous)—hence it can only be detected by highly sensitive apparatus, as postulated above. Being a 'materialization' of the Divine Substance, it corresponds to (but is not the same as) a variety of other terms that are distinctly spiritual (hence, non-physical) agents central to the esoteric and occult sciences: for example, æther (the Divine luminiferous substance which pervades the whole universe, the 'garment' of the Supreme Deity), *ākāśa* (the subtle, supersensuous spiritual essence which pervades all space), *daivīprakṛiti* (primordial, homogeneous light-substance), and *anima mundi* (the Divine essence which permeates, animates, and informs all from the smallest particles of matter, to man, and the gods). These terms have distinctions of meaning, but they all signify an all-pervading, light-bearing substance. Newton referred to it in the General Scholium of *Principia* thus:

Newton's
reference to a
'subtle spirit' in
Principia

> And now we might add something concerning a certain most subtle spirit [*anima mundi*?] which pervades and lies hid in all gross bodies; by the force and action of which spirit the particles of bodies mutually attract one another at near distances, and cohere, if contiguous; and electric bodies operate to greater distances, as well repelling as attracting the neighbouring corpuscles; and light is emitted, reflected, refracted, inflected, and heats bodies; and all sensation is excited, and the members of animal bodies move at the command of the will, namely, by the vibrations of this spirit, mutually propagated along the solid filaments of the nerves, from the outward organs of sense to the brain, and from the brain into the muscles. But these are things that cannot be explain'd in few words […].10

Indeed, such things cannot be explained (only explained away) 'in few words'!

Newton's letter to
Boyle on cosmic
ether of space

Also of considerable significance is a letter, written in 1679, by the thirty seven year old Isaac Newton to the Anglo-Irish natural philosopher and chemist Robert Boyle FRS (1627–1691) on the question of the cosmic ether of space, arguably, *ākāśa*. The original is in the 1938 volume by J. W. N. Sullivan entitled, *Isaac Newton: 1642–1727*, Macmillan, NY, pp. 118–124. However, a longer and more complete version of the letter, found in an 1846 publication, containing information not previously available, is in Rev. William Vernon Harcourt, FRS, &c., 'Letter to Henry Lord Brougham, FRS &c., Containing Remarks on Certain Statements in his lives of Black, Watt and Cavendish, With an Appendix Containing Newton's Letters on Air and Aether', London: Richard & John Edward Taylor, 1846, pp. 131–141.iii A reproduction from this letter can be found in http://www.orgonelab.org/newtonletter.htm. It shows that Newton had a firm belief and working grasp of the cosmic ether of space as a thing of substance and 'ponderability', something which participated in the movement and ordering of the planets and universe, and as an active, intelligence-bearing agent in optics, chemistry, and gravitation.11 This is significant because Newton's earlyiv embrace of a tangible and motile ether was heresy not just to the Vatican in his time, but also for the modern departments of physics in nearly every university promulgating the quasi-religious concepts of empty-space, devoid of any tangible qualities. As nothing could be permitted to challenge this concept, it is tantamount to a dogma, first in religion, and still in mainstream science.

As it happens, Einstein also argues towards the necessity of the cosmic ether of space, as seen in the extract shown below from his lecture on 'Ether and the Theory of Relativity'. This lecture was delivered by Einstein himself, in German, on 5 May 1920 at the University of Leiden. Most revealing are Einstein's closing words:

> Recapitulating, we may say that according to the general theory of relativity space is endowed with physical qualities; in this sense, therefore, there exists an ether. According to the general theory of relativity space without ether is unthinkable; for in such space there not only would be no propagation of light, but also no possibility of existence for standards of space and time […]. But this ether may not be thought of as endowed with the quality characteristic of ponderable media […].12

---

iii The English scientist Rev. William Venables-Vernon Harcourt FRS (1789–1871) was founder of the British Association for the Advancement of Science, canon residentiary of the York Cathedral, Dean of Chichester, and later rector of Bolton Percy.

iv In his later years, Newton moved towards more abstract concepts, such as the divine 'prime mover' or deified 'absolute space'. However deified absolute space cannot be empty space, as it contains the God-essence, Æther.

In stating 'this ether may not be thought of as endowed with the quality characteristic of ponderable media', Einstein is arguably referring to *daivīprakṛti*, strictly speaking.

Readers who wish to pursue this topic and make their own independent judgement are invited to peruse the following references in addition to those cited in the narrative of this Appendix.

Source Reference Book

William R. Corliss (Compiler), *Mysterious Universe: A Handbook of Astronomical Anomalies*, The Sourcebook Project, Glen Arm, MD 21057, 1979. See 'Test of Relativity', pp. 659–672.

Academic Books and Papers

The following academic books and journals are an abridgement, in chronological order, from the large number of citations in James DeMeo's above referenced paper, 'Dayton Miller's Ether-Drift Experiments: A Fresh Look'. The formatting of all references is verbatim from the DeMeo paper.

1887: Albert A. Michelson, Edward W. Morley, 'On the Relative Motion of the Earth and the Luminiferous Ether', *American Journal of Science*, Third Series, Vol. XXXIV (203), Nov. 1887.

1913: M. G. Sagnac, 'L'Ether lumineux Démontre par l'effet du vent relatif d'aether dans interférometre en rotation uniforme', *Comptes Rendus*, 157:710, 1913, and 'Sur la preuve de la réalite de l'ether lumineux par l'expérience de l'interférographe tournant', *Comptes Rendus*, 157:1410–1413, 22 Dec. 1913. Also see John Chappell, 'Georges Sagnac and the Discovery of the Ether', *Arch. Internat. d'Histoire des Sciences*, 18:175–190, 1965.

1925: Michelson, A.A., H. Gale & F. Pearson: 'The Effect of the Earth's Rotation on the Velocity of Light' (Parts I and II), *Astrophysical Journal*, 61:137–145, April 1925. Also see: 'Letters to the Editor: The Effect of the Earth's Rotation on the Velocity of Light', *Nature*, 115:566, 18 April 1925.

1926: Albert Einstein, 'Meine Theorie und Millers Versuche', *Vossische Zeitung*, 19 January 1926, contained in: Klaus Hentschel, 'Einstein's Attitude Towards Experiments: Testing Relativity Theory 1907–1927', *Stud. Hist. Phil. Sci.*, Vol. 23, No. 4, pp. 593–624, 1992. Internet Posted: http://elib.uni-stuttgart.de/opus/volltexte/2010/5117/pdf/hen10.pdf.

1933: Dayton Miller, 'The Ether-Drift Experiment and the Determination of the Absolute Motion of the Earth', *Reviews of Modern Physics*, Vol.5(2), p. 203–242, July 1933. The complete text can be downloaded from http://www.orgonelab.org/EtherDrift/MillerRMP1933.pdf.

1934: Dayton Miller, 'The Ether-Drift Experiment and the Determination of the Absolute Motion of the Earth', *Nature*, Vol.133, p. 16–27, 3 February 1934.

1955: R.S. Shankland, S.W. McCuskey, F.C. Leone and G. Kuerti, 'New Analysis of the Interferometer Observations of Dayton C. Miller', *Reviews of Modern Physics*, 27(2):167–178, April 1955.

1963: Robert Shankland: 'Conversations with Albert Einstein', *Am. J. Physics*, 31:47–57, Jan. 1963.

1971: Ronald W. Clark: *Einstein: The Life and Times*, World Publishing Co., NY 1971.

1972: Loyd Swenson, *The Ethereal Aether: A History of the Michelson-Morley-Miller Aether-Drift Experiments, 1880–1930*, University of Texas Press, Austin, 1972.

1973a: Robert Shankland: 'Michelson's Role in the Development of Relativity', Applied Optics, 12(10):2280–2287, October 1973.

1973: Robert Shankland: 'Conversations with Albert Einstein. II', *Am. J. Physics*, 41:895–901, July 1973.

1996: James DeMeo, 'Independent Discovery of a Dynamic Bio-Cosmic Energy in Space and Atmosphere', & 'Dayton Miller's Discovery of the Dynamic Ether Drift', Proceedings, SW & Rocky Mountain Division, *American Association for the Advancement of Science*, 72nd Annual Meeting, Northern Arizona Univ., Flagstaff, Arizona, 2 6 June 1996. *Program and Abstracts*, pp. 41–42, 1996.

1997: Maurice Allais, *L'Anisotropie de L'Espace:La nécessaire révision de certains postulats des théories contemporaines*, Clément Juglar, Paris, 1997.

1998: Maurice Allais: 'Experiments of Dayton C. Miller (1925–1926) and the Theory of Relativity', *21st. Century Science and Technology*, Spring 1998, p. 26–34; also in *Pulse of the Planet #5*, pp. 132–137 2002.

1999: Maurice Allais: 'Des régularités très significatives dans les observations interférométriques de Dayton C. Miller 1925–1926', *Comptes Rendus de L'Académie des Sciences*, Paris, t. 327, Série II b, pp. 1405–1410.

1999: Maurice Allais: 'Nouvelles régularités très significatives dans les observations interférométriques de Dayton C. Miller 1925–1926', *Comptes Rendus de L'Académie des Sciences*, Paris, t. 327, Série II b, p. 1411–1419.

2000: Maurice Allais: 'L'origine des régularités constatées dans les observations interférométriques de Dayton C. Miller 1925–1926: variations de température ou anisotropie de l'espace', *Comptes Rendus de L'Académie des Sciences*, Paris, t. 1, Série IV, p. 1205–1210.

2000: James DeMeo: 'Critical Review of the Shankland, *et al.*, Analysis of Dayton Miller's Ether-Drift Experiments', Presented to the *Natural Philosophy Alliance*, Berkeley, Caif. May 2000.

2002: Maurice Allais, 'The Experiments of Dayton C. Miller (1925–1926) and the Theory of Relativity', *Pulse of the Planet*, 5: 131–136.

2002: Yu.M.Galaev, "The Measuring of Ether-Drift Velocity and Kinematic Ether Viscosity Within Optical Waves Band", (in English) Spacetime and Substance, Vol.3, No.5 (15), 2002, p. 207–224. Posted to: http://www.spacetime.narod.ru/0015-pdf.zip.

2005: Reginald T. Cahill, 'The Michelson and Morley 1887 Experiment and the Discovery of Absolute Motion', *Progress in Physics*, Volume 3, October 2005, pp. 25–29.

A separate webpage http://www.orgonelab.org/energyinspace.htm includes a long list of citations on the ether-drift experiments, and the larger question of dynamic energy in space. Where possible, download links are provided to the original items. Many, or most, of these are experimental papers showing positive results for the ether and ether-drift.

Closing Note

James DeMeo's note about the publication of his article 'Dayton Miller's Ether-Drift Experiments: A Fresh Look' (referenced above) is telling. He writes:

> In June of 2000, I contacted the editors of *Reviews of Modern Physics*—the same journal that published the original Miller 1933 paper and the Shankland, *et al.* paper of 1955 – informing them I wanted to submit my paper for publication consideration, giving them the title and some basic details. The editor replied quite negatively, but with a Freudian slip. After claiming that his journal did not go into such historical materials, he concluded by saying 'Thus, I *do* think [*sic*] it would be suitable for our review format.' Upon my follow-up inquiry, he corrected himself, saying he meant to say 'I *do not* think it would be suitable.' The bottom line is, the editors of *Reviews of Modern Physics* refused to even look at the paper, indicating how far the 'peer review' system has sunk into use of political measures to protect favored theories. The article was subsequently accepted for several non-mainstream publications which are not threatened by the idea of an ether or ether-drift.

Peer review skewed by knowledge filtration and politics

In substantiation of the 'knowledge filtration' of theories and evidence adverse to the dictates of establishment science, as summarized at the close of Volume I, Chapter 4, this Appendix has shown that the official scientific verdict on the non-existence of the ether is far from settled. In Volume I, Chapter 5, we quoted a seminal passage from a letter that Einstein wrote to his old mathematician friend Maurice Solovine. We close this Appendix with this same passage about how Einstein rated his own achievements of a lifetime:

> *You imagine that I look back on my life's work with calm satisfaction. But from nearby it looks quite different. There is not a single concept of which I am convinced that it will stand firm, and I feel uncertain whether I am in general on the right track.*
> ALBERT EINSTEIN ON HIS SEVENTIETH BIRTHDAY[13]

NOTES

1. James Clerk Maxwell, 'Ether', in T. S. Baynes (ed.), *Encyclopædia Britannica* (9th edn, New York: Charles Scribner's Sons, 1878), viii, 568–72.
2. Albert A. Michelson and Edward W. Morley, 'On the Relative Motion of the Earth and the Luminiferous Ether', *American Journal of Science*, Third Series, XXXVI/203 (November 1887) <https://history.aip.org/exhibits/gap/PDF/michelson.pdf> accessed 3 March 2020.
3. James DeMeo, 'Dayton Miller's Ether-Drift Experiments: A fresh look', *Pulse of the Planet* #5 (2002; postscript, 2003) <http://www.orgonelab.org/miller.htm> accessed 4 March 2020.
4. Dayton Miller, 'The Ether-Drift Experiment and the Determination of the Absolute Motion of the Earth', *Reviews of Modern Physics*, 5/2 (July 1933), 203–242. The complete text can be downloaded from <http://www.orgonelab.org/EtherDrift/MillerRMP1933.pdf> accessed 4 March 2020.
5. Ronald W. Clark, *Einstein: The life and times* (New York: World Publishing Co., 1971), 328.

6   Reginald T. Cahill, 'The Michelson and Morley 1887 Experiment and the Discovery of Absolute
    Motion', *Progress in Physics*, 3 (October 2005), 25–9. Cited also in <http://www.ptep-online.com/
    2005/PP-03-04.PDF> accessed 4 March 2020.

7   See for example Holger Müller, Sven Herrmann, Claus Braxmaier, Stephan Schiller, and Achim
    Peters, 'Modern Michelson-Morley Experiment Using Cryogenic Optical Resonators', *Physical
    Review Letters*, 91/2 (July 2003), 020401–4.

8   Rupert Sheldrake, *Seven Experiments that Could Change the World* (London: Fourth Estate, 1994),
    164–90. A summary is shown in Edi D. Bilimoria, *The Snake and the Rope: Problems in Western science
    resolved by occult science* (Adyar, Madras: Theosophical Publishing House, 2006), 229–30.

9   Borge Nodland and John Ralston, 'Indication of Anisotropy in Electromagnetic Propagation over
    Cosmological Distances', *Physical Review Letters*, 78/16 (21 April 1997), 3043–6.

10 Isaac Newton, *Philosophiæ Naturalis Principia Mathematica* [Mathematical Principles of Natural
    Philosophy], trans. Andrew Motte, rev. Florian Cajori, 2 vols (Berkeley, Los Angeles: University of
    California Press, 1962), ii, 'The System of the World – General Scholium', 547.

11 See here, David Castillejo, *The Expanding Force in Newton's Cosmos* (Madrid: Ediciones De Arte Y
    Bibliofilia, 1981).

12 'Ether and the Theory of Relativity', English trans. (London: Methuen & Co. Ltd, 1922)
    <http://www-history.mcs.st-andrews.ac.uk/Extras/Einstein_ether.html> accessed 20 May 2020.

13 Albert Einstein, 'Letter to Maurice Solovine', 28 March 1949, in Banesh Hoffmann in collaboration
    with Einstein's secretary, Helen Dukas, *Albert Einstein: Creator and Rebel* (1st edn, US: Viking Press,
    1 September 1972), 328. See also Claes Johnson, *Many–Minds Relativity* (2011), 89 [online]
    <http://citeseerx.ist.psu.edu/viewdoc/download?doi=10.1.1.441.6979&rep=rep1&type=pdf>
    accessed 9 July 2020.

Appendix II-B:
Antaḥkaraṇa – its Purpose and Function

This Appendix provides further amplification about the vehicle of consciousness known as *Antaḥkaraṇa*, and the part played by *karma*. The following extended extracts by Blavatsky describe, by way of a familiar simile, the purpose, function, and formation of Antaḥkaraṇa (Antaskaraṇa). A lamp represents the Divine Ego (see Table II-8, page 46 in Chapter 3), the light it throws out represents Lower manas, and the wall upon which the light falls represents man in his Physical body. In this simile, *Antaskaraṇa* is the 'atmosphere' that transmits the light ray from the lamp to the wall. That atmosphere can be anything in the range from clear to cloudy.

Antaskaraṇa is the name of that imaginary bridge, the *path* which lies between the divine and the human *Egos*, for they are Egos, during human life, to re-become *one* Ego in Devachan or Nirvāṇa. This may seem difficult to understand, but in reality, with the help of a familiar though fanciful illustration, it becomes quite simple. Let us figure to ourselves a bright lamp in the middle of a room, casting its light upon the solid plaster wall. Let the lamp represent the divine Ego, and the light thrown on the wall the lower Manas [Lower manas], and let the wall stand for the body. The atmosphere which transmits the ray from the lamp to the wall, will then in our simile represent the Antaskaraṇa. We must further suppose that the light thus transmitted is endowed with reason and intelligence, and possesses, morever, the faculty of dissipating all the evil shadows which pass across the wall, and of attracting brightness to itself, receiving their indelible impressions. Now, it is in the power of the human Ego to chase away the shadows (sins) and multiply the brightness (good deeds) which make these impressions, and thus, through Antaskaraṇa, ensure its own permanent connection, and its final reunion with the divine Ego. Remember that the latter cannot take place while there remains a single taint of the terrestrial, or of matter, in the purity of that light. On the other hand, the connection can never be ruptured, and final reunion prevented, so long as there remains one spiritual deed, or potentiality, to serve as a thread of union; but the moment this last spark is extinguished, and the last potentiality exhausted, then comes the severence. In an Eastern parable the divine Ego is likened to the Master who sends out his laborers to till the ground and to gather in the harvest, and who is content to keep the field so long as it can yield even the smallest return. But when the ground becomes actually sterile, not only is it abandoned, but the laborer also (the lower Manas) perishes.

Antaskaraṇa the means to gather a spiritual harvest

On the other hand, however, still using our simile, when the light thrown on the wall, or the rational human Ego, reaches the point of actual spiritual exhaustion, the Antaskaraṇa disappears, the light is no longer transmitted, and the lamp becomes non-existent to it. The light which has been absorbed gradually disappears and 'soul-eclipse' occurs; the being lives on earth and then passes into Kāma-Loka as a mere surviving congeries of material qualities; it can never pass outwards towards Devachan, but is reborn immediately, a human animal and scourge. Let 'Jack the Ripper' stand as a type [and the contemporary examples cited in Chapter 5].[1]

The above passage shows both the importance of the connection between the Human and Divine Ego, and the necessity and capability of the Human Ego to maintain and strengthen the link. In simplistic terms, man is a god in an animal body. When the indwelling god abdicates, man becomes 'a human animal and scourge'.

But why is Antaskaraṇa our only redemption; and what is the fate of an incarnation when that connection is sundered?

> The Antaskaraṇa is therefore that portion of the Lower Manas [Lower manas] which is one with the Higher, the essence, that which retains its purity; on it are impressed all good and noble aspirations, and in it are the upward energies of the Lower Manas, the energies and tendencies which become its Devachanic experiences. The whole fate of an incarnation depends on whether this pure essence, Antaskaraṇa, can restrain the Kāma-Manas or not. It is the only salvation. Break this and you become an animal [refer again to the contemporary examples cited in Chapter 5 if further proof be needed].[2]

Bearing of
Antaskaraṇa on
Karma

The next extract forcefully pronounces on what the fate of an incarnation depends on and the manner in which the personality awaits its karma in a new incarnation.

> The Higher Ego is, as it were, a globe of pure divine light, a Unit from a higher plane, on which is no differentiation. Descending to a plane of differentiation it emanates a Ray, which it can only manifest through the personality which is already differentiated. A portion of this Ray, the Lower Manas, during life, may so crystallise itself and become one with Kâma that it will remain assimilated with Matter. That portion which retains its purity forms Antahkarana [Antaskaraṇa]. The whole fate of an incarnation depends on whether Antahkarana will be able to restrain the Kama-Manas [the animal nature] or not. After death the higher light (Antahkarana) which bears the impressions and memory of all the good and noble aspirations, assimilates itself with the Higher Ego, the bad is dissociated in space, and comes back as bad Karma awaiting the [new] personality.[3]

The following extract emphasizes the importance of subordinating the lower, personal self to the absolute control of the higher, impersonal Self, before Antaskaraṇa be destroyed or severed.

> Seeing that the faculty and function of Antaskaraṇa is as necessary as the medium of the ear for hearing, or that of the eye for seeing, so long as the feeling of Ahamkāra (of the personal 'I' or selfishness) is not entirely crushed out in a man, and the lower mind not entirely merged into and become one with the Higher (Buddhi-Manas), it stands to reason that to destroy Antaskaraṇa is like destroying a bridge over an impassable chasm: *the traveller can never reach the goal on the other shore.* […] Therefore we are told that if we destroy Antaskaraṇa before the personal is absolutely under the control of the imper-sonal Ego, we risk to lose the latter and be severed forever from it, unless indeed we hasten to reëstablish [re-establish] the communication by a supreme and final effort.[4]

Circumstances
when
Antaskaraṇa is
no longer needed

So when is the proper time to destroy Antaskaraṇa ?[i]

> It is only when we are indissolubly linked with the essence of the divine Mind, that we have to destroy Antaskaraṇa.[5]

---

i In his novel *Strange Case of Dr. Jekyll and Mr. Hyde* Robert Louis Stevenson had a glimpse of a true vision regarding the dreadful catastrophe that ensues from the premature destruction of the Antaskaraṇa—when the psycho-animal Lower self detaches from its divine Parent source.

Or in terms of an occult axiom which beautifully expresses the involutionary descent of Spirit into Matter, and the evolutionary ascent from Matter back into Spirit:

> 'The unit becomes three, and three generate four. It is for the latter (the quaternary) to rebecome three, and for the divine three to expand into the Absolute One.'[6]

NOTES

1   *CW*-XII, 'Instruction No. III: The Philosophical Rationale of the Tenet', 631–2.
2   *CW*-XII, 'Instruction No. V: Lower Manas, or Kāma-Manas', 710.
3   'Some Notes on Oral Teachings – Self-Hood', in H. P. Blavatsky, *The Secret Doctrine*, 6 vols (London: Theosophical Publishing House, 4th (Adyar) edn, 1938; repr. London 1950), v, 553. Quoted also in Adam Warcup, 'An Inquiry into the Nature of Mind', the Blavatsky Lecture 1981 (London: The Theosophical Society), 28.
4   *CW*-XII, 'Instruction No. III', 634.
5   *ibid*.
6   *ibid*.

Appendix II-C:
The Traditionalist Stance and Mindset – Truth from just One Authority?

Problems arising from one-track idealism and undue devotion

The purpose of this rather extended Appendix is to explain, in some detail, the mind process and associated trends in organizations and societies when the message or teaching given out by its founders—ever-living and fresh at its inception—progressively loses its vitality in the charge of their followers, becoming congealed by degrees into a dogmatic theology; whereupon literal, dead-letter interpretation of words predominates over their inner content and essential meaning. Although this account applies essentially to the Theosophical Society, not in any way whatsoever to indict personalities of wrongdoing or indiscretion (in fact their motives were invariably genuine, if rather misguided), the general principles would apply to all organizations with similar visions and objectives. After nearly fifty years of intense work and involvement with the Theosophical Society, plus frequent, in-depth contact with other organizations of similar esoteric and spiritual ilk, the writer feels that his observations might be of some value.

Firstly then, no one denies that we are all drawn to teachings that resonate with our nature and meet the needs of our personal spiritual quest. This is the natural human condition. However, it is unfortunate, but it has to be admitted and recognized, as stated earlier, that societies dedicated to spiritual, religious, or even esoteric, study attract a small core of people of a fundamentalist mindset who cannot get away from thinking in terms of opposites and contradictions. Such over-zealous types invest their chosen teacher and books with omniscience, regarding them as the ultimate source of all knowldege and wisdom, every other source of learning being secondary or not worthwhile. Such closed mind-sets have great difficulty in sensing the underlying unity behind all diversities and opine that their chosen, self-appointed guru, master or book possesses the sole and ultimate authority on all matters. When this happens, the quest for fresh knowledge and insights is vitiated and the society in question consequently implodes upon itself. This problem is especially prevalent in spiritual societies founded by such powerful personalities as Rudolf Steiner and H. P. Blavatsky.

Such exclusivism is, of course, clearly evident in religion and science. As arbitrary examples, we may cite the debates on the nature of the underlying substance and the monotheist tension between heresy and orthodoxy in the former; and in the latter, the entrenched views of those who maintain that qualia, or phenomenal experiences, can be explained entirely in physical terms (the so-called 'soft problem of consciousness') and those who counter argue that mechanistic theories are not enough to explain how sensations acquire characteristic experiences, such as colours and sounds (the 'hard problem'). The important point, however, is that neither science nor religion in their official corpus and their protocols makes any explicit mention of a comparative study of different systems, cultures and traditions, as does the Theosophical Society, uniquely.

In the Theosophical Society then, despite the unequivocal message of universality of enquiry, detachment from authority figures, personal research, and experiential testing so clearly stated by the founders of the movement and enshrined in the Second Object, some factions, within the international body, have adopted a closed mind-set, maintaining that Blavatsky and her Adept Teachers must possess the final monopoly on all matters spiritual and occult, because their expositions on consciousness and the Principles of Man are (so-called) 'Master-inspired' literature. Others are fixated upon another founder member, William Quan Judge, and several more pin all authenticity to the Second International President, Annie Besant. As a result of this entrenched attitude by various factions, the vital teachings, especially Blavatsky's, have been fossilized and the consequent decline of the Theosophical Society from a magnificent player on the world stage of esotericism and spirituality to its now partisan status is apparent.

Eclectic outlook endorsed but not practised in the Theosophical Society

We find a similar attitude in the Anthroposophical Society, whose members claim that Rudolf Steiner expounded the ultimate dictum in all matters philosophical and occult. However, in fairness, it must be stated that the Anthroposophical Society is dedicated to the works and teaching of Steiner and not to the comparative study of other teachers. However, the Theosophical Society is emphatically not devoted to studying Blavatsky, or anyone else exclusively, so there is absolutely no justification for a purist–fundamentalist approach. The all-important Second Object of this Society is committed 'to encourage the comparative study of religion, philosophy, and science'. What further proof do we need about the need to guard against guru-, teacher- or book-worship than the Principal Founder's own words quoted in Volume I, Introductory, but which bear repeating: 'In its capacity of an abstract body, the Society does not believe in anything, does not accept anything and does not teach anything.'[1] No more can Blavatsky (or, for that matter, anyone else) be regarded as an ultimate spiritual authority than, for example, Mozart can be so regarded in music, or Newton in science. If we truncate all music post-Mozart we would not be listening to Beethoven; cut out all science after Newton in the eighteenth century and we would dispense with Einstein two centuries later. Similarly, the Perennial Wisdom, by whatever name, admits of no artificial cut-off point and great harm has been done to modern esoteric scholarship by the attempts of those few well meaning, but misguided, yet influential people in spiritual societies to downgrade and denigrate all teachings that do not accord with their chosen one. But this is a failing of individuals, common amongst those with a devotional bent, as such societies necessarily attract. It is not a failing of Theosophy (or Anthroposophy for that matter). The practice and the occasional over-zealous practitioner should always be carefully distinguished and not conflated.

Anthroposophical and Theosophical Societies differ in outlook

The Theosophical Society has no singular belief or teaching

Just as musicians and scientists revere and subsume their past luminaries in an ever-onwards evolutionary movement that embraces the creative output of contemporaries in their respective fields, so also the *philosophia perennis* must adopt a similar approach towards its advocates. Needless, therefore, to stress that when warning against the fetish of idolizing just one book or one author, we do not in any way mean that such a book or author should be discarded. For example in science, Einstein advanced upon the Laws of Motion established by Newton. But no modern astronomer, however much he may be drawn to General Relativity, would dream of discarding Newton's theories. Similarly we affirm that the *philosophia perennis* has been updated, enriched and cast into a modern idiom by such as Paul Brunton, I. K. Taimni, Manly P. Hall, and the English scholar and esotericist John Gordon (1946–2013). But that does not mean that we ignore the classical writings of Blavatsky and her proponents like the Americans Geoffrey Barborka (1897–1982) and Gottfried de Purucker or the English lecturer and writer Geoffrey Farthing (1909–2004), all of them deep students of H.P. Blavatsky's life, work, and teachings. So, a disciple of Blavatsky or Steiner (or any other spiritual teacher or sage for that matter) would certainly qualify for the appellation of a 'wisdom seeker' or a 'lover of truth'; but a puritanical devotee of Blavatsky would not so qualify because of an attitude veering towards that fundamentalism which is so inimical to the ethos and objects of the spiritual quest. Moreover, we are entitled to, in fact we must, share our enthusiasm with others concerning those who have inspired us on our journey. But we may not impose upon, or try to convert, others to our mode of thinking, or cause schisms when others disagree with us. There is no overriding spiritual authority in the Theosophical Society or, for that matter, in literally any other spiritual society, notwithstanding the claims to the contrary from the garrulous evangelists of such organizations. Anyone who sets up another as the ultimate authority and clones himself on such a person is merely projecting his own ego onto the authority figure.

It is obvious, then, that transcendent wisdom being, by its very nature, beyond words, no sage can have the final say-so, or capture its essence in a cage of words. (In fact, the deepest truths were invariably communicated orally and never written down.) Each proponent provides a necessarily incomplete cross section on a subject that is far too vast and sublime to be encapsulated fully by any one writer or one mode of expression. Furthermore, each teacher must formulate his teaching using a language appropriate to the mentality, religious climate, and intellectual development of his time, taking due cognizance of the level of scientific understanding prevailing. And science, especially physics, has advanced by quantum leaps since Blavatsky's day. Hence, to look for a 'gold standard' of authority for all time is nonsensical and it is sad that weak, hero-worshipping mentalities are driven by such a futile stance. A student of philosophy in search of truth cannot do that. His approach must be a balanced one and take in a plurality of ideas. But what does matter a great deal is the intellectual and spiritual pre-eminence of a teacher. Is he merely regurgitating the thoughts and ideas of others like so many parrots? Or is he able to speak from the standpoint of direct contact with, and experience of, the Higher Self, in which case he is worthy of our closest attention and reverence. Such were the likes of Blavatsky, Besant, Krishnamurti, Steiner, Ramana Maharshi, Manly Hall, Paul Brunton, and Phiroz Mehta, to mention a small and necessarily arbitrary selection of luminaries from the panoply of modern sages who have added immeasurably to our store of understanding the fundamentals of the *philosophia perennis* (arguably, in varying and unequal degrees except for Ramana Maharshi, the Saint of Arunachala who, by every count, was permanently centred in the Higher Self).

In view of all this, our scope in this work, particularly in Chapter 8 on the underlying harmony of diverse world teachings, encompasses a representative spectrum of teachings on the Principles of Man. The expositions of classical Theosophy, propounded by Blavatsky and her instructors, are explained in considerable detail, especially in this Volume. But this is done in order to provide backbone and structure to this work and also because her writings were arguably the most extensive, and changed considerably over the course of her life. There is no doubt that her teachings were being developed in a form best suited to science and the Western world; but not in any way to promulgate these teachings as the last word on man's Principles, against which all other teachings can be judged and evaluated. Even if such an ultimate teaching existed (which is to be doubted), the writer is in no way qualified to advocate it, his avowed purpose being to lay down the rich vein of teachings from diverse sources, ancient and modern, Eastern and Western, and to leave readers free to make up their own minds as to which systems and teachings best resonate with their own needs and aspirations.

On a different note, there is a lot of talk these days about 'good science' as opposed to 'bad science', or in other words, 'sound' science and 'pseudoscience'. It may now be apposite to introduce the terms 'good Theosophy' and 'bad Theosophy'. The proponents of good science and Theosophy will both, in their different ways, heed the advice of the British writer and lay theologian C. S. Lewis (1898–1963) in a letter to his former pupil, the British-born Benedictine monk and yogi Bede Griffiths (1906–1993): always to argue towards the truth and not assume that the truth is known to start with, and then seek to justify it. This underscores the difference between a closed mind of conclusions compared to an attitude of ever questing for 'truth wherever it leads' (the mission statement of the Scientific and Medical Network), which, in essence, is the same as 'There is no religion higher than Truth' (the motto of the Theosophical Society). Conversely, bad science and bad Theosophy seem to adopt an 'I-know-it-all' stance of omniscience and castigate the other side willy-nilly, with little qualifications in, or understanding of, the subject of their criticisms. (For example, it makes sense for scientists to know something about the *philosophia perennis* before rubbishing it; and for Theosophists to be qualified in science before criticizing it.) Bad science invariably takes the form of an invincible materialism whereby anything that cannot be explained mechanistically, like telepathy and spirituality, is nonsensical in principle, all hard data and evidence to the contrary being flawed by definition; therefore, selectively filtered out and trashed. In bad Theosophy we find an attitude exists whereby in any perceived disagreement between science and Theosophy, science loses out automatically by default; or in the case of any differences between Blavatsky and later writers, such as Besant and Steiner, Blavatsky wins outright in both cases because her monumental work *The Secret Doctrine* is arbitrarily taken as the ultimate benchmark, hence there is no need for recourse to other scientific or spiritual sources.

Quality and thoroughness apply as much to spirituality as to science

In relation to science and mysticism, Charles Tart (*b*.1937), the American psychologist, parapsychologist, and a founder of the field of transpersonal psychology, astutely pointed out that, 'the conflict is between second-rate science and second-rate mysticism, between dogmatic people'. However his remark could equally apply to conflicts that arise from second-rate players within science, religion, and Theosophy, either within, or across these disciplines; because 'when people become psychologically attached to their beliefs, they become defensive, and feel the need to attack other people's beliefs.'[2] Tart's primary goal is to build bridges between the scientific and spiritual communities, and to facilitate the integration of Western and Eastern approaches for knowing the world and for personal and social growth. He highlights the need for both scientists and mystics to smooth the split that separates the two by fostering humility, which opens the door to dialogue and counteracts arrogance, which keeps the door shut. We would take this further and argue that, in addition to open dialogue between Theosophists and scientists, Theosophists must also dissolve polarized opinions and build bridges between the various discordant factions within the Theosophical Society itself, such as those who zealously uphold the teachings of Blavatsky, Judge or Besant, and decry other avenues of wisdom.

Rapprochement obstructed by mediocrity and dogma

The writer attended several talks by the sage Krishnamurti, who once used a wonderful metaphor to illustrate the folly of investing ultimate authority in any one teacher or teaching:

Truth best served by a plurality of approaches

> The bee makes its honey from many flowers.

This clearly makes the point that honey is not a mixture or combination of nectar from several blossoms, but their essence. Equally, wisdom is neither syncretic, nor the jurisdiction of any one teaching, however erudite; it is the integrated essence drawn from numerous, sources of wisdom.

Entrenched Attitudes – Two Main Contributory Factors

At the risk of labouring the point, we bring together the above issues by highlighting two chief strands that have gradually brought about this entrenched tendency observed in some sections of the Theosophical Society:

1. That *The Secret Doctrine* is used as an infallible oracle in the same way as the Creationists do with the Bible, or for that matter, as neo-Darwinists do with Darwin's theories, which is another matter, but note that extremism is a character-istic of human nature equally in religion as in science. To take this view simply flies in the face of the spirit of constant questioning and freedom of enquiry that the founders and pioneering leaders of the Theosophical movement strove so mightily to inculcate. That Theosophists (by no means all, but enough of them) have adopted entrenched concepts, equating the whole of *theosophia* (the Divine wisdom) solely with Blavatsky's writings, so largely deceiving themselves and others by treating her books as the absolute authority, only serves to show that 'Theosophy is for those who can think, or for those who can drive themselves to think, not mental sluggards', to use Blavatsky's own words. 'Dumskulls' used to be her name for the middling student[3]. One shudders to think what language Blavatsky might have used for the average Theosophist or 'New Ager' of today! There is of course a great deal that scientific materialism can be taken to task for, so constructive speculation and lateral thinking based on solid esoteric principles is much to be encouraged since many of the concepts and principles in *The Secret Doctrine* were given in a general and incomplete manner, so were not, and could not be, properly understood at the time. As I. K. Taimni also points out, Blavatsky and her teachers both made it clear that the wisdom given out was partial and of a fragmentary nature; and that it had to be elaborated and deepened as it was meant to serve as a nucleus (never the last word) for further research and development, drawing espe-cially upon the findings of modern science. All to the good. But some Theosophists (and for that matter some of the New Age fraternity) with little, or no, scientific training will resort to conjectures on what they confidently think are the 'occult principles' behind just about every physical phenomenon.

The Secret Doctrine is not the ultimate authority – it needs progressing and updating

However, in fairness, it must be stated that the converse also applies. A few of the high-ranking scientists within the Theosophical Society have sought to comment adversely on some of the deepest aspects of occultism—for example, the profound doctrine of 'Rounds and Races' about the evolution of our solar system, prehistoric continents, the early races of man, and the evolution of mankind. Notwithstanding their unswerving dedication to the Theosophical Society, their criticisms are based purely on the grounds of scientific theories without evincing any understanding of the occult doctrines. But let us not forget that the Theosophical Society has attracted some of the very finest scientists such as: the American inventor Thomas Edison (1847–1931), Sir William Crookes (1832–1919) President of the Royal Society of London, and Sir Oliver Lodge FRS (1851–1940); more recently, E. Lester Smith, appointed as Fellow of the Royal Society for his discovery of Vitamin B12, Arthur Ellison, Peter Leggett, Rupert Sheldrake, and Stephen Phillips—the last four also strongly connected with the Scientific and Medical Network (https://scientificandmedical.net/).

Outstanding scientists have been drawn to the Theosophical Society and its teachings

2. Reading Blavatsky (or any other writer) without paying attention to the state of science and religion then prevailing. Taimni has given the example of the use of the term 'Fohat'. It was the only term available to Blavatsky in her day to denote the force she called 'Cosmic Electricity'. Compared to now, when Blavatsky wrote *The Secret Doctrine*, physics and chemistry were rudimentary subjects. Blavatsky was therefore handicapped by this lack of scientific knowledge, so had to explain the nature of Fohat in vague and sometimes confusing terms. But given the stupendous advances in the electrical and nuclear sciences since her time, now to regard what she said about Fohat as the last word, ignoring the scientific discoveries about atomic and nuclear structures, is against the spirit of never-ending enquiry into truth which her great book, her teachings, and the ethos of the Theosophical movement represent.

Immense advances in science after The Secret Doctrine

The Underlying Lesson

In summary then, there is a long overdue need for all spiritual seekers and Theosophists to put some steel into the backbone, meaning: always to question and enquire, not to assume a self-appointed stance of omniscience, to examine their own concepts and beliefs, and to acquire humility in order to live up to the magnificent motto of the Theosophical Society, which bears repeating: *There is No Religion Higher than Truth*. Thus, the essence of our critique is an absolutely high-time clarion 'wake-up' warning against traditionalism, stated courteously, or fundamentalism, put candidly. As an example of research work undertaken according to the exploratory spirit and freedom of thought, the work of the Theosophical Research Centre deserves glowing credit.

Work of the Theosophical Research Centre

This Centre was formed in the 1920s and worked actively for over sixty years. It comprised a group of eminent scientists who were also senior members of the Theosophical Society. They met and performed experiments in order to forge links between science and Theosophy and investigate whether some of the occult doctrines in Theosophical literature could be supported by modern science. Their declared attitude purported to be in the same investigatory spirit as that advocated by the founders of the modern Theosophical movement towards the teachings they promulgated, namely, that the latter should not be taken as authority, but rather investigated with openness, impartiality and without dogma. Topics covered by the Research Centre included occult chemistry, the etheric plane, clairvoyance, psychical research, cosmology, geology, medicine, and the nature of consciousness—the latter achieving its acme in *Intelligence Came First*, a book of composite authorship by eminent scientists with E. Lester Smith as the editor, for which he was awarded the Subba Row Medal by the Theosophical Society.[4]

Subsequently eminent scientists within the Theosophical Society, while maintaining their allegiance to the latter, gravitated towards the Scientific and Medical Network. For example, Arthur Ellison who was also, twice, President of the Society for Psychical Research and Chairman of the Science Group and Editorial Committee of the Theosophical Research Centre. In fact, the writer (who also participated in the latter-day Science Group meetings of the Centre and published in its journal) regards the Scientific and Medical Network (to which he is now strongly affiliated) very much in the nature of a modern incarnation of the former Science Group of the Theosophical Research Centre.

Do Theosophists then want to adopt an ethos of 'back to Blavatsky'?[5] If so, they must rest content with future generations of Theosophists merely tinkering with her words. We would then have a museum of esoteric fossils—guarded by a cult of fossilised esotericists. But moving forwards with Blavatsky, and other seers, would generate that practical, Truth-based, regenerating brotherhood for which the Principal Founder devoted her whole life and every ounce of her energies.[6] *An unquenchable, but selfless passion for Truth at all costs, and from all sources, is therefore obligatory. To restore a feeling for divinity in nature and man in an orthodox science still largely blighted by a materialistic and atheistic world-view, would be their noblest achievement.*

Truth cannot be fossilised

On a final note, the writer cannot stress too forcefully his lifelong love and study of Blavatsky's writings and doctrines, as this work should amply bear witness;[7] but he is not a fetishist worshipper of Blavatsky, or anyone else for that matter in the vast esoteric and occult pantheon, and this is the difference, he maintains, between an ardent student and a purist (let alone a fundamentalist). As we have been at pains to point out throughout, no one person or body has a monopoly on the Truth. The genuine teacher would never encourage sycophancy in the student. In fact, such a teacher would be the first to recognize that freedom of enquiry and independent thinking are two sides of one coin. They demand that the seeker walks the razor edge path between believing and disbelieving, agreeing and disagreeing—purely observing and questioning free from personal bias.

Freedom of enquiry, independent thought, humility, and doubt are the four humble servants of Truth

So to round off this Appendix, we remark that if, at the end of his long life, Newton likened his achievements to that of a 'boy playing on the sea shore, and diverting myself in now and then finding a smoother pebble or a prettier shell than ordinary, whilst the great Ocean of Truth lay all undiscovered before me';[8] if Einstein could say 'all these fifty years of conscious brooding have brought me no nearer to the answer to the question, "What are light quanta?"'[9] (quoted further in Volume I, Chapter 5); and if modern scientific heavyweights like the American Nobel physicist Richard Feynman ForMemRS (1918–1988) and the British-born American mathematical physicist and Templeton prizewinner Freeman Dyson FRS (1923–2020) would declare that they knew next to nothing about such things as the nature of force, then is not a deep humility—equally from scientists and Theosophists alike—the surest means of opening the portal to reach towards the Truth?

We close with extracts from what the writer considers to be the finest statement about freedom of thought and freedom of the Society. It was issued by the international General

Council of the Theosophical Society,[10] but its essential import could apply in full measure to other esoteric and spiritual organizations, or scientific societies, whose declared aim is to bridge science and spirituality.

FREEDOM OF THOUGHT

As the Theosophical Society has spread far and wide over the world, and as members of all religions have become members of it without surrendering the special dogmas, teachings and beliefs of their respective faiths, it is thought desirable to emphasize the fact that there is no doctrine, no opinion, by whomsoever taught or held, that is in any way binding on any member of the Society, none which any member is not free to accept or reject. Approval of its three Objects is the sole condition of membership. No teacher, or writer, from H.P. Blavatsky onwards, has any authority to impose his or her teachings or opinions on members. Every member has an equal right to follow any school of thought, but has no right to force the choice on any other. Neither a candidate for any office nor any voter can be rendered ineligible to stand or to vote, because of any opinion held, or because of membership in any school of thought. Opinions or beliefs neither bestow privileges nor inflict penalties. The Members of the General Council earnestly request every member of the Theosophical Society to maintain, defend and act upon these fundamental principles of the Society, and also fearlessly to exercise the right of liberty of thought and of expression thereof, within the limits of courtesy and consideration for others.

Resolution passed by the General Council of the Theosophical Society (1924)

The Theosophical Society: its fundamental ethos on freedom

FREEDOM OF THE SOCIETY

The Theosophical Society, while cooperating with all other bodies whose aims and activities make such cooperation possible, is and must remain an organization entirely independent of them, not committed to any objects save its own, and intent on developing its own work on the broadest and most inclusive lines, so as to move towards its own goal as indicated in and by the pursuit of those objects and that Divine Wisdom which in the abstract is implicit in the title 'The Theosophical Society'. Since Universal Brotherhood and the Wisdom are undefined and unlimited, and since there is complete freedom for each and every member of the Society in thought and action, the Society seeks ever to maintain its own distinctive and unique character by remaining free of affiliation or identification with any other organization.

Resolution passed by the General Council of the Theosophical Society (1949)

However men approach Me, even so do I welcome them, for the path men take from every side is Mine, O Partha.

BHAGAVAD GĪTĀ.[11]

NOTES

1   *CW-XI*, 'The New Cycle', 124.

2   Quoted in Stephanie Sorrell, *Depression as a Spiritual Journey* (UK: O Books, 2009), 116.

3   'Appendix A: *The Secret Doctrine* and its study – Notes recorded by Commander Robert Bowen in 1891', in *Foundations of Esoteric Philosophy from the writings of H. P. Blavatsky*, foreword and notes by Ianthe H. Hoskins (London: Theosophical Publishing House, 1990), 65.

4   E. Lester Smith (ed.), *Intelligence Came First*. rev. Patrick Milburn (1975; 2nd rev. edn, Wheaton, Illinois: Theosophical Publishing House, 1990).

5   For an in-depth discussion of this problem see Edi D. Bilimoria, 'Back to Blavatsky will Fossilize Theosophy – Forwards with Blavatsky will Vitalize Theosophy', *The Theosophist*, 131/1 (October 2009), 43–50.

6   Dara Tatray, 'The Theosophical Society for a New Generation of Enquirers', *The Theosophist*, 131/1 (October 2009), 38–42.

7   Edi Bilimoria, 'H. P. Blavatsky – A Spiritual Floodlight', *The Blavatsky Trust* <http://www.blavatskytrust.org.uk/html/articles/hpb%20spiritual%20floodlight.htm> accessed 26 April 2020.

8   Anecdote attributed by Joseph Spence to Andrew Michael Ramsay, in Joseph Spence, *Anecdotes, Observations, and Characters, of Books and Men*, ed. Samuel S. Singer (2nd edn, London: J. R. Smith, 1858; quotation from 1st edn, 1820), 368. Quoted also in Richard S. Westfall, *Never at Rest: A biography of Isaac Newton* (Cambridge: Cambridge University Press, 1995), 863.

9   Letter from Albert Einstein to his friend Michele Besso, quoted in Arthur Zajonc, 'Light Reconsidered', *Optics & Photonic News* (October 2003).

10 'Mission, Objects and Freedom', The Theosophical Society <http://www.ts-adyar.org/content/objects-and-freedom> accessed 5 March 2020.

11 Fourth Discourse, 'The Yoga of Wisdom', in *The Bhagavad Gita*, trans. Annie Besant (Adyar, Madras: Theosophical Publishing House, 1973), 65.

Endnotes to Volume II

Endnote II-1 Difficulty of finding English words for Sanskrit terms

'Higher Self' is a good example of the difficulty of finding a suitable word in English to convey the precise meaning of a Sanskrit term. On page 121 of *The Key to Theosophy*, Theosophical Publishing House, 1968, Blavatsky states that 'Atman is the Universal ALL, and becomes the HIGHER-SELF of man only in conjunction with *Buddhi*, its vehicle […].' Then on page 174 in discussing an essay on the 'Higher Self' by A. P. Sinnett, Blavatsky remarks that Sinnett uses the term to apply to '*Buddhi* (of course in conjunction with *Manas* […].' But there are also those, she goes on to say on page 175, 'who limit the term "Higher Self" to the Universal Divine Principle […] "Atma".' Hence in order to avoid further misapprehension, she proposes that the Higher Self should be translated as 'Atma, the inseparable ray of the Universal and ONE SELF. It is the God *above*, more than within, us.'

So, all in all, Blavatsky affirms the problems posed by the variable meanings attaching to metaphysical terms. She aptly remarks in a footnote to page 175 of *The Key to Theosophy* that:

> 'Shifting of *Metaphysical terms*' applies here only to the shifting of their translated equivalents from the Eastern expressions; for to this day there never existed any such terms in English, every Theosophist having to coin his own terms to render his thought. It is high time, then, to settle on some definite nomenclature.

> Problems of English terminology for precise Sanskrit terms

Despite the laudable injunction to ascribe precise meanings to metaphysical terms and apply definite words for definite things, this has not yet happened (and probably never can), mainly for the reasons given in Chapter 1, page 3 et seq. All we can hope for is as much clarity that is reasonably practicable in using an English word in place of an Eastern one. However, it should be noted that such ambiguity of meaning would be minimized, if not entirely eliminated, by resorting to a proper use of the technical Eastern (mainly Sanskrit) terms.

Henceforth in this work, for consistency (other than when used otherwise in quotations) and in order to avoid confusion, we shall adopt the term 'Divine Self' to refer to *Ātma*; and 'Higher Self', or 'Individuality' to refer to the union of *Ātma* with *Buddhi* (also known as the Monad) in conjunction with (*Higher*) *Manas*—see Table II-3 on page 21.

Endnote II-2 Contradictory meanings of terms

A good example of unavoidable contradictory use of terms is cited by the French–British Vedic scholar and author Jeanine Miller (1930–2013). She states in the Foreword to *Self-Consistent Kosmos* that in *The Key to Theosophy* Blavatsky enumerated the Physical body as the seventh principle; but in the Papers published as part of Volume Five (the Adyar edition of) *The Secret Doctrine*, it is admitted that the Physical body is not even a principle; that the 'Augoeides' stated as a principle, was not mentioned in the original enumeration. Again in *The Key to Theosophy*, the *Liṅga-śarīra* is translated as 'astral body' and numbered as the third principle (counting upwards), but in Volume Four of (the Adyar edition of) *The Secret Doctrine* it is given the same translation, but defined as the fifth principle. Furthermore, Blavatsky used the term 'adept' to cover a variety of meanings; and the word 'astral' to include both astral and etheric—a fact which subsequently caused much confusion in the study of the Principles of Man.[1]

Many other variants and inconsistent appellations could be cited. However, readers should always bear in mind the constraints and restraints under which Blavatsky laboured, as explained in Chapter 1.

Endnote II-3 Illustrating the two basic ways of using man's nature

Consider, as a simplistic example, man's fingers, say just his index finger. It is constituted of three phalanxes and associated tendons, and this is invariant with all men. However, its nature, i.e., how it will function is open to a whole variety of uses. For example, it can be used (along with other fingers) to play an instrument or to write an uplifting poem; alternatively, to pull the trigger of a gun to kill someone or to write a vitriolic letter. Of the countless ways in which an index finger can be used, we can readily classify such uses into two groups: what harms, and what benefits others.

Similarly, man can use his whole being like an instrument either to benefit or to harm others, and himself. So we can divide his nature into an enduring upper part which aspires towards its spiritual source, and a lower part which eventually passes away.

Endnote II-4 Brahman – 'to breathe out'

The term *Brahman* is derived from the Sanskrit root *brih* meaning 'to breathe forth', 'to expand'. Brahman could not manifest the universe without breathing out, so to say. In no way is this meant to be a facetious remark; rather, it illustrates the principle of 'as above, so below'. Physical cosmology has discovered this principle in terms of the 'Big Bang'. Just as the physical universe expands resulting in a change of state, so humans also expand and grow which results in a change of condition.

Brahman must be distinguished from *Brahmā* (derived from the same Sanskrit root), the so-called Creator and first member of the Trinity.

Endnote II-5 Reference books on post-mortem consciousness and reincarnation

In addition to the writer's own insights, Chapter 5 comprises a distillation of relevant material on the post-mortem states of consciousness and the process of reincarnation taken from the following sources:

❖ *The Mahatma Letters to A. P. Sinnett*, transcribed and compiled by A. T. Barker, Theosophical Publishing House, 1972.

❖ H. P. Blavatsky, *The Secret Doctrine*, Theosophical Publishing House, 1950.
—— *Theosophical Glossary*, Theosophical Publishing Society, 1892.
—— *Studies in Occultism: Practical Occultism* – a Collection of Articles from Lucifer, H. P. Blavatsky's magazine, between 1887–1891, Literary Licensing, 2014.
—— *The Key to Theosophy*, Theosophical Publishing House, 1968.

❖ G. de Purucker, *Occult Glossary*, Theosophical University Press, 1972.

❖ Geoffrey A. Farthing, *Deity, Cosmos and Man – An Outline of Esoteric Science*, Point Loma Publications, 1993.

❖ Manly P. Hall, *The Secret Teachings of All Ages*, The Philosophical Research Society, 1988.

❖ Volume I: Chapter 4, Endnote I-4, and Endnote I-5.

Endnote II-6 Erwin Schrödinger's observations on science

Sir Francis Walshe's insights into the limits and limitations of science are strongly echoed by Erwin Schrödinger thus:

> I am very astonished that the scientific picture of the real world around me is very deficient. It gives us a lot of factual information, puts all of our experience in a magnificently consistent order, but it is ghastly silent about all and sundry that is really near to our heart that really matters to us. It cannot tell us a word about red and blue, bitter and sweet, physical pain and physical delight; it knows nothing of beautiful and ugly, good or bad, God and eternity. Science sometimes pretends to answer questions in these domains but the answers are very often so silly that we are not inclined to take them seriously.

> Science cannot tell us a word about why music delights us, of why and how an old song can move us to tears? Science can, in principle, describe in full detail all that happens in our sensorium and 'motorium' from the moment the waves of compression and dilation reach our ear to the moment when certain glands secrete a salty fluid that emerges from our eyes. But the feelings of delight and sorrow that accompany the process, science is completely ignorant—and therefore reticent. And science is reticent too when it is a question of the great Unity the most popular name for which is God. We know, whenever God is experienced, it is an experience exactly as real as a direct sense perception, as real as one's own personality.

> For the purpose of constructing the picture of the external world, we have used the greatly simplifying device of cutting our own personality out, removing it; hence, it is gone, it has evaporated, it is ostensibly not needed. [...] In particular, and most importantly, this is the reason that the scientific world-view contains of itself no ethical values, no aesthetical values, not a word about our own ultimate scope or destination, and no God, if you please. [Therefore] we do not belong to this material word that science constructs for us. Consciousness cannot be accounted for in physical terms. For consciousness is absolutely fundamental. It cannot be accounted for in terms of anything else. The observing mind is not a physical system, it cannot interact [directly] with any physical system. And it might be better to reserve the term 'subject' for the observing mind [...]. For the subject, if anything, is the thing that senses and thinks. Sensations and thoughts do not belong to the [physical] 'world of energy'.

Science is, very usually, branded as atheistic. After what we said, this is not astonishing. If its world picture does not even contain blue, yellow, bitter, sweet—beauty, delight and sorrow—, if personality is cut out of it by agreement, how should it contain the most sublime idea that presents itself to the human mind? […] Whence come I and whither go I? That is the great unfathomable question, the same for every one of us. Science cannot tell us a word about this.[2]

Endnote II-7 Helen Keller letter

93 Seminole Avenue,
Forest Hills, L. I.,
February 2, 1924.

The New York Symphony Orchestra,
New York City.

Dear Friends:

I have the joy of being able to tell you that, though deaf and blind, I spent a glorious hour last night listening over the radio to Beethoven's 'Ninth Symphony'. I do not mean to say that I 'heard' the music in the sense that other people heard it; and I do not know whether I can make you understand how it was possible for me to derive pleasure from the symphony. It was a great surprise to myself. I had been reading in my magazine for the blind of the happiness that the radio was bringing to the sightless everywhere. I was delighted to know that the blind had gained a new source of enjoyment; but I did not dream that I could have any part in their joy. Last night, when the family was listening to your wonderful rendering of the immortal symphony someone suggested that I put my hand on the receiver and see if I could get any of the vibrations. He unscrewed the cap, and I lightly touched the sensitive diaphragm. What was my amazement to discover that I could feel, not only the vibrations, but also the impassioned rhythm, the throb and the urge of the music! The intertwined and intermingling vibrations from different instruments enchanted me. I could actually distinguish the cornets, the roll of the drums, deep-toned violas and violins singing in exquisite unison. How the lovely speech of the violins flowed and flowed over the deepest tones of the other instruments! When the human voice leaped up trilling from the surge of harmony, I recognized them instantly as voices. I felt the chorus grow more exultant, more ecstatic, upcurving swift and flame-like, until my heart almost stood still. The women's voices seemed an embodiment of all the angelic voices rushing in a harmonious flood of beautiful and inspiring sound. The great chorus throbbed against my fingers with poignant pause and flow. Then all the instruments and voices together burst forth—an ocean of heavenly vibration—and died away like winds when the atom is spent, ending in a delicate shower of sweet notes.

Of course, this was not 'hearing' but I do know that the tones and harmonies conveyed to me moods of great beauty and majesty. I also sensed, or thought I did, the tender sounds of nature that sing into my hand—swaying reeds and winds and the murmur of streams. I have never been so enraptured before by a multitude of tone-vibrations.

As I listened, with darkness and melody, shadow and sound filling all the room, I could not help remembering that the great composer who poured forth such a flood of sweetness into the world was deaf like myself. I marvelled at the power of his quenchless spirit by which out of his pain he wrought such joy for others—and there I sat, feeling with my hand the magnificent symphony which broke like a sea upon the silent shores of his soul and mine.

Let me thank you warmly for all the delight which your beautiful music has brought to my household and to me. I want also to thank Station WEAF for the joy they are broadcasting in the world.

With kindest regards and best wishes, I am,

Sincerely yours,

(Signed)

HELEN KELLER

Endnote II-8 Reference books on the human aura

The following books provide a fairly comprehensive and copiously illustrated account of the human aura:

- ❖ Walter J. Kilner, *Human Aura*, original 1920, Kessinger Publishing, 2003.
- ❖ Annie Besant and C. W. Leadbeater, *Thought-Forms*, Theosophical Publishing House, 1925.
- ❖ C. W. Leadbeater, *The Chakras*, Theosophical Publishing House, 1927.
- ❖ C. W. Leadbeater, *Man Visible and Invisible: Examples of different types of men as seen by means of trained clairvoyance*, Theosophical Publishing House, 1974.
- ❖ Barbara Ann Brennan, *Hands of Light: Guide to healing through the human energy field*, Bantam Books, 1990.
- ❖ Barbara Ann Brennan, *Light Emerging: The journey of personal healing*, Bantam Books, 1993.
- ❖ David V. Tansley, *Subtle Bodies: Essence and shadow*, Thames and Hudson, 1977.

Endnote II-9 Life-principles of plants, animals, and human beings

Blavatsky advises that 'the reader who would obtain a clear idea of the commutation of forces and the resemblance between the life-principles of plants, animals, and human beings, may profitably consult a paper on the correlation of nervous and mental forces by [the Scottish philosopher] Professor Alexander Bain [1818–1903] of the University of Aberdeen. This mandragora [a plant whose root has the human form] seems to occupy upon earth the point where the vegetable and animal kingdoms touch, as the zoöphites and polypi do in the sea; the boundary being in each case so indistinct as to make it almost imperceptible where the one ceases and the other begins. It may seem improbable that there should be *homunculi* [representations of small humans], but will any naturalist, in view of the recent expansion of science, dare say it is impossible? "Who," says Bain, "is to limit the possibilities of existence?" '3

Interface between kingdoms of nature

NOTES

1   J. S. Gordon, *Self-Consistent Kosmos* (UK: Orpheus Publishing House, 1995), ii–iii passim.
2   The above sections have been extracted from Erwin Schrödinger: *My View of the World*, trans. Cecily Hastings (New York: Cambridge University Press, 1964); *What is Life?* with *Mind and Matter* and *Autobiographical Sketches*, foreword by Roger Penrose (Cambridge: Cambridge University Press, 1993); *Nature and the Greeks* and *Science and Humanism*, foreword by Roger Penrose (Cambridge: Cambridge University Press, 1961); *The Observer*, 11 January 1931; 'General Scientific and Popular Papers', in *Collected Papers*, iv (Vienna: Austrian Academy of Sciences. Friedr. Vieweg & Sohn, Braunschweig/Wiesbaden, 1984), 334.
3   *IU*-I, 'Realities and Illusion', 466.